ADO *Programming* FOR DUMMIES®

by Rob Krumm

IDG BOOKS WORLDWIDE

IDG Books Worldwide, Inc.
An International Data Group Company

Foster City, CA ◆ Chicago, IL ◆ Indianapolis, IN ◆ New York, NY

ADO Programming For Dummies®

Published by
IDG Books Worldwide, Inc.
An International Data Group Company
919 E. Hillsdale Blvd.
Suite 400
Foster City, CA 94404
www.idgbooks.com (IDG Books Worldwide Web Site)
www.dummies.com (Dummies Press Web Site)

Library of Congress Control Number: 00-103652

ISBN: 0 7645 0747 8

Printed in the United States of America

10 9 8 7 6 5 4 3 2 1

1O/RY/RQ/QQ/IN

Distributed in the United States by IDG Books Worldwide, Inc.

Distributed by CDG Books Canada Inc. for Canada; by Transworld Publishers Limited in the United Kingdom; by IDG Norge Books for Norway; by IDG Sweden Books for Sweden; by IDG Books Australia Publishing Corporation Pty. Ltd. for Australia and New Zealand; by TransQuest Publishers Pte Ltd. for Singapore, Malaysia, Thailand, Indonesia, and Hong Kong; by Gotop Information Inc. for Taiwan; by ICG Muse, Inc. for Japan; by Intersoft for South Africa; by Eyrolles for France; by International Thomson Publishing for Germany, Austria and Switzerland; by Distribuidora Cuspide for Argentina; by LR International for Brazil; by Galileo Libros for Chile; by Ediciones ZETA S.C.R. Ltda. for Peru; by WS Computer Publishing Corporation, Inc., for the Philippines; by Contemporanea de Ediciones for Venezuela; by Express Computer Distributors for the Caribbean and West Indies; by Micronesia Media Distributor, Inc. for Micronesia; by Chips Computadoras S.A. de C.V. for Mexico; by Editorial Norma de Panama S.A. for Panama; by American Bookshops for Finland.

For general information on IDG Books Worldwide's books in the U.S., please call our Consumer Customer Service department at 800-762-2974. For reseller information, including discounts and premium sales, please call our Reseller Customer Service department at 800-434-3422.

For information on where to purchase IDG Books Worldwide's books outside the U.S., please contact our International Sales department at 317-572-3993 or fax 317-572-4002.

For consumer information on foreign language translations, please contact our Customer Service department at 1-800-434-3422, fax 317-572-4002, or e-mail rights@idgbooks.com.

For information on licensing foreign or domestic rights, please phone 650-653-7098.

For sales inquiries and special prices for bulk quantities, please contact our Order Services department at 800-434-3422 or write to the address above.

For information on using IDG Books Worldwide's books in the classroom or for ordering examination copies, please contact our Educational Sales department at 800-434-2086 or fax 317-572-4005.

For press review copies, author interviews, or other publicity information, please contact our Public Relations department at 650-653-7000 or fax 650-653-7500.

For authorization to photocopy items for corporate, personal, or educational use, please contact Copyright Clearance Center, 222 Rosewood Drive, Danvers, MA 01923, or fax 978-750-4470.

is a registered trademark under exclusive
license to IDG Books Worldwide, Inc.
from International Data Group, Inc.

About the Author

Rob Krumm has been using personal computers since 1979, when he was working as a teacher in Philadelphia. In 1981, he founded his own school in Walnut Creek, California, designed to teach people how to use personal computers. In 1983, he published *Understanding and Using dBase II,* the first of 50 books he has written on computers and software. In 1997, Rob worked with the OSCE in Bosnia building databases for the municipal elections. He's the owner of Enotech software, which produces Winebase II software for California wineries and other e-commerce clients. Rob teaches MCSE courses at Diablo Valley Community College in Concord, CA.

Rob can be reached at robkrumm@pacbell.net or through the Web site www.wbase2.com.

Dedication

For Terry and Diane, and Tom and Leah, for 20 years of friendship.

ABOUT IDG BOOKS WORLDWIDE

Welcome to the world of IDG Books Worldwide.

IDG Books Worldwide, Inc., is a subsidiary of International Data Group, the world's largest publisher of computer-related information and the leading global provider of information services on information technology. IDG was founded more than 30 years ago by Patrick J. McGovern and now employs more than 9,000 people worldwide. IDG publishes more than 290 computer publications in over 75 countries. More than 90 million people read one or more IDG publications each month.

Launched in 1990, IDG Books Worldwide is today the #1 publisher of best-selling computer books in the United States. We are proud to have received eight awards from the Computer Press Association in recognition of editorial excellence and three from Computer Currents' First Annual Readers' Choice Awards. Our best-selling ...*For Dummies*® series has more than 50 million copies in print with translations in 31 languages. IDG Books Worldwide, through a joint venture with IDG's Hi-Tech Beijing, became the first U.S. publisher to publish a computer book in the People's Republic of China. In record time, IDG Books Worldwide has become the first choice for millions of readers around the world who want to learn how to better manage their businesses.

Our mission is simple: Every one of our books is designed to bring extra value and skill-building instructions to the reader. Our books are written by experts who understand and care about our readers. The knowledge base of our editorial staff comes from years of experience in publishing, education, and journalism — experience we use to produce books to carry us into the new millennium. In short, we care about books, so we attract the best people. We devote special attention to details such as audience, interior design, use of icons, and illustrations. And because we use an efficient process of authoring, editing, and desktop publishing our books electronically, we can spend more time ensuring superior content and less time on the technicalities of making books.

You can count on our commitment to deliver high-quality books at competitive prices on topics you want to read about. At IDG Books Worldwide, we continue in the IDG tradition of delivering quality for more than 30 years. You'll find no better book on a subject than one from IDG Books Worldwide.

John Kilcullen
Chairman and CEO
IDG Books Worldwide, Inc.

*Eighth Annual
Computer Press
Awards ≥1992*

*Ninth Annual
Computer Press
Awards ≥1993*

*Tenth Annual
Computer Press
Awards ≥1994*

*Eleventh Annual
Computer Press
Awards ≥1995*

1/26/00

Contents at a Glance

Publisher's Acknowledgments

We're proud of this book; please register your comments through our IDG Books Worldwide Online Registration Form located at `http://my2cents.dummies.com`.

Some of the people who helped bring this book to market include the following:

Acquisitions, Editorial, and Media Development

Senior Project Editor: Pat O'Brien

Acquisitions Editor: Sherri Morningstar

Copy Editor: Christine Berman, Donna S. Frederick, Nicole A. Laux, Rebekah Mancilla, Amy Pettinella, Pam Wilson-Wykes, Jeremy Zucker

Proof Editor: Teresa Artman

Technical Editor: Michael A. Gibson

Permissions Editor: Carmen Krikorian

Media Development Specialist: Jamie Hastings-Smith

Media DevelopmentCoordinator: Marisa E. Pearman

Editorial Manager: Mary C. Corder

Media Development Manager: Laura Carpenter

Media Development Supervisor: Richard Graves

Editorial Assistant: Candace Nicholson

Production

Project Coordinator: Maridee Ennis

Layout and Graphics: Brian Drumm, Jacque Schneider, Brian Torwelle, Heather Pope, Julie Trippetti

Proofreaders: Laura Albert, Corey Bowen, Susan Moritz, Marianne Santy, Charles Spencer, York Production Services, Inc.

Indexer: York Production Services, Inc.

Special Help
Kyle Looper, Sheri Replin, Nicole Haims, Jeanne S. Criswell

General and Administrative

IDG Books Worldwide, Inc.: John Kilcullen, CEO; Bill Barry, President and COO; John Ball, Executive VP, Operations & Administration; John Harris, CFO

IDG Books Technology Publishing Group: Richard Swadley, Senior Vice President and Publisher; Mary Bednarek, Vice President and Publisher; Walter R. Bruce III, Vice President and Publisher; Joseph Wikert, Vice President and Publisher; Mary C. Corder, Editorial Director; Andy Cummings, Publishing Director, General User Group; Barry Pruett, Publishing Director

IDG Books Manufacturing: Ivor Parker, Vice President, Manufacturing

IDG Books Marketing: John Helmus, Assistant Vice President, Director of Marketing

IDG Books Online Management: Brenda McLaughlin, Executive Vice President, Chief Internet Officer; Gary Millrood, Executive Vice President of Business Development, Sales and Marketing

IDG Books Packaging: Marc J. Mikulich, Vice President, Brand Strategy and Research

IDG Books Production for Branded Press: Debbie Stailey, Production Director

IDG Books Sales: Roland Elgey, Senior Vice President, Sales and Marketing; Michael Violano, Vice President, International Sales and Sub Rights

◆

The publisher would like to give special thanks to Patrick J. McGovern, without whom this book would not have been possible.

◆

Cartoons at a Glance

By Rich Tennant

page 213

page 59

page 9

page 435

page 373

page 135

Fax: 978-546-7747
E-mail: richtennant@the5thwave.com
World Wide Web: www.the5thwave.com

Table of Contents

Introduction

"*E*verything is a database!" This is the remark that I make on the first evening of each course that I teach. I have always believed that if you want to understand anything about computers — from spreadsheets to the Internet — then you must look for the database within, and there you will find the key to the technology. And, if you want to control and customize the technology, the key is to understand how to use your own database programs.

Sounds pretty intimidating. And it can be. Databases have many different types — all of which have their own approach to storing and retrieving information. Some run on the desktop, like Access, and some run on networks like SQL Server or even over the Internet. Into this confusion comes ADO, or *Active Data Objects*. The purpose of ADO is to make order out of database chaos. With ADO, you need to learn only a single approach to accessing and creating data, whether you are writing a macro in Excel, an application in Visual Basic, or creating a Web site database.

ADO provides a simple, yet powerful set of tools that can be used to power database applications using a wide range of data sources, programming tools, and network platforms.

Who Needs This Book

The most common reason for writing a computer program is to store and retrieve information. These applications need to interact with some sort of database source. ADO gives you the tools that you need to perform a wide variety of database-related tasks using a single set of objects, properties, and methods. If you want to be able to use the data stored in an SQL Server, an Access database, an Oracle server, or another type of data source, then ADO is the wave of the future. Best of all, it's simple to learn and easy to use.

You can use ADO code in Web pages and Access databases, with Microsoft Office applications such as Outlook or Excel, in Visual Basic 6.0, or even in your own custom-designed ActiveX objects. ADO code is so uniform that you can even copy and paste the code from one type of application to another with little or no editing.

If you are new to database programming, you will find that ADO opens up a whole new world of possibilities with a simple, flexible, and powerful way to integrate data into an application.

If you have written applications using ODBC or Data Access Objects (DAO is found in Access 97), you can quickly get up to speed on the newest, most advanced database technology from Microsoft.

About This Book

This book is designed to open up the world of ADO programming to both new and experienced programmers. I concentrate on the practical applications of ADO technology so that you can quickly learn how to get ADO working for you. Although I do include some theoretical discussion of data access technology, the vast majority of the book consists of "how to" lessons that cover a wide variety of programming issues and techniques.

One concern I had in writing this book is that many readers do not have access to technologies such as SQL Servers or Web servers, which are needed to test some of the examples. In order to solve this problem, I provide resources on the Web for all readers. Many of the examples connect to an SQL Server located on a Web site that was set up just for the readers of this book. All of the Web examples for which code is provided in this book can be accessed live, on the Web. The details of the access to these resources appear throughout the book. For access to any of the Web examples, go to www.wbase2.com and select the *ADO For Dummies* image.

How This Book is Organized

This book is organized into seven parts. Feel free to begin at Chapter 1 and then progress sequentially through the chapters, or just skip around and look for the juiciest tidbits. (Hey, it's *your* book.)

Part I: Universal Data Access through ADO

Part I of this book explains the basic concepts involved with ADO and related technologies, such as ODBC, DAO, and OLE DB. Chapter 1 covers terms and concepts. I show you how ADO fits into Microsoft's database and networking platforms. Chapter 2 takes a detailed look at how an application using ADO can connect to a wide variety of data sources, ranging from Access databases to Oracle servers.

Part II: The ADO Data Access Programming Model

The beauty and power of ADO lies in its ability to address a wide range of potential data sources with a simple but powerful set of objects, properties, and methods. Part II of this book illustrates how to use the relatively small set of ADO elements to perform all of the standard database tasks, such as displaying, adding, deleting, and updating data. In this section, I show you how to use the three basic elements in ADO: connections, recordsets, and command objects.

Part III: Programming with ADO

After you master the ADO model, the next task is to use your new knowledge to create applications. Part III is concerned with applying what you know about the ADO object model to the practical business of building data-enhanced forms, dialog boxes, and other types of user interfaces that expose data obtained with ADO.

Part IV: Using ADO to Access Data through the Web

Part IV looks in great detail at how ADO technology can be used across networks using Internet services and Web browser applications. This section covers a wide range of technologies that can use and interact with ADO, such as Active Server Pages, Dynamic HTML, XML, ActiveX, and COM. The topics in this section range from generic Web programming that works with all browsers, to more Microsoft-centric technologies such as Dynamic HTML in Internet Explorer.

Part V: Using ADO and Non-Relational Data Sources

Part V examines how you can use ADO to work with data sources that aren't the traditional relational databases, such as file and mail systems, that are organized into tree structures containing folders, files, and messages. In addition, I explore the use of ADO in and with Office applications such as Outlook, Excel, and Word.

Part VI: The Part of Tens

Part VI is a quick tour through my favorite programming tool and my favorite shortcuts, along with a list of useful ADO-related resources on the Web.

Conventions Used in This Book

In any technical book (and let's face it — computers are nothing if not technical), it is necessary to distinguish between different types of text, or to write about computer stuff, such as shortcut keys or menu commands. Here's what you need to know about those special items.

Programming code

This book is full of text that represents programs written in the Access Visual Basic language. Programmers refer to this text as *code*. This is the stuff that you actually type into Access in order to create programs. You find code examples in this book styled like the following:

```
For k = 1 To 10
    Debug.Print "Number = " & k
Next
```

Syntax examples

A *syntax example* is a special type of code example used to illustrate the general form of a statement, rather than a specific example. In the following code line, see the words *somenumber, start,* and *end.* I italicize these words in the text you read here to indicate the location in the code where you enter some number, a start value, and an end value. I don't ask you to type in these specific examples. They are included for reference purposes.

```
For somenumber = start To end
```

Sometimes I draw your attention to a particular segment of code by formatting the segment in boldface. This formatting has no purpose other than to grab your attention.

Literals

Programming languages allow you to insert words and phrases that don't mean anything to the program but are useful for humans who need to read the output of your programs. These phrases are called *literals*. Literals are always enclosed in punctuation marks called *delimiters*. In Access, text items can be enclosed in either double quotes (" @") or single quotes (' ') so long as you use the same punctuation at the beginning and at the end of the literal.

```
"Walter Lafish" or 'Walter Lafish'
```

Access also supports literal dates. Dates are delimited with # (pound sign) characters, as the following line of code illustrates.

```
#1/1/2000#
```

Upper- and lowercase letters

Access Visual Basic isn't case sensitive. Therefore, when you enter code, it doesn't matter which of the letters is in uppercase or lowercase. The following three lines have exactly the same meaning:

```
Orders.RecordCount
Orders.Recordcount
orders.recordcount
```

Having said that, the code in this book uses the uppercase and lowercase conventions that appear in the official Access Visual Basic language guide from Microsoft. The guide uses uppercase letters in the middle of some words to make their meaning more clear. For example, the term *RecordCount* is shown with an uppercase C to indicate that it has something to do with the number of records.

```
Orders.RecordCount
```

If you type code, you really don't have to bother with uppercase letters at all if you don't want to. Access automatically changes the text to uppercase letters for you.

Line continuation

When you enter programming code into Access, you can type lines that are much wider than the width of the text that is printed in this book. In order to write code that fits the pages of this book, I have inserted line-continuation characters. The following two lines actually represent one line of code because the end of the first line has a space followed by an underscore (_). This tells Access that the statement continues on the next line.

```
StandardListPrice = Cost * CustomerDiscount _
  * TaxRate
```

If you retype the code, you are free to skip the line-continuation characters and enter the statement on a single line. If you choose to enter the line-continuation characters, remember that you must include a space followed by an underscore. Don't forget the space!

Shortcut keys

When you need to enter a special key combination (such as pressing and holding down Ctrl and then pressing G), I write it as Ctrl+G.

Menu command

When you need to use a command on a menu, such as choosing the Open Database command from the File menu, I write it as File⇨Open Database.

Foolish Assumptions

Any book written in the *For Dummies* style should avoid assuming too much about the potential reader. However, it's not possible to cover everything about Access in a single book. I assume that anyone reading about programming Access is familiar with (but not a master of) the following concepts:

- ✔ How to use either Access 2000 or Visual Basic 6.0
- ✔ How to create a table and define fields in Access 2000, SQL Server 7.0, or Oracle 8.1
- ✔ How to create a Web page and write basic HTML tags
- ✔ How to create a simple SQL query

Your knowledge of VB, VBA, or VBScript should at least be at the beginner level.

On the CD

The CD attached to the back cover of this book includes all of the sample databases, plus all of the programming code shown in this book. In addition, it contains copies of the latest versions of Internet Explorer, NetScape, and the Microsoft Data Access Components.

In order to use the CD, however, your system must have the following basic requirements:

- ✔ **Computer.** A 486-based (or higher) computer system with CD-ROM drive
- ✔ **Operating system.** Windows 95 or Windows NT 3.51 (or higher)
- ✔ **Application.** Access 2000 or Visual Basic 6.0
- ✔ **Free hard drive space.** 40 megabytes
- ✔ **RAM.** 32 megabytes

Icons Used in This Book

This icon flags useful information or suggestions that, while perhaps not part of the current example, may come in handy later on.

I have made my share of mistakes writing programs. A word to the wise will hopefully keep you out of some of these programming potholes.

This data is included for those of you who wonder about why some odd-looking thing works or where some strange-sounding term got its name. You can program perfectly well without this information, but some people find it comforting.

This icon marks information that I may have given to you already, but I want to be sure that you remember (hence the name, right?).

This icon shows you where to find a table, query, form, report, or module on the CD. In general, each heading in this book contains one or more examples. The text tells you about the problem or task and the Access 2000 technique that you need to use. The explanation ends with the result followed by one of these icons, which tells you where on the CD you can find the example.

Where to Go from Here

Now that you've got all of this preliminary stuff out of the way, you're ready to get started. Remember to check out the CD attached to the back cover of this book because it contains the files that you need to duplicate the examples in the chapters.

Time to get started. Fire up Access and get started programming right now!

Part I
Universal Data Access through ADO

The 5th Wave   By Rich Tennant

"We're much better prepared for this upgrade than before. We're giving users additional training, better manuals, and a morphine drip."

In this part . . .

The world is full of all sorts of data sources, from simple text files to massive client server databases. Unfortunately, very few of these data sources are organized in the same way. This used to mean that you had to buy special software and learn a new set of programs for each data source that you wanted to use. No more! Enter ADO, or *Active Data Object*, technology. ADO allows you to read, write, add, and delete data from a wide range of data sources using a simple set of tools, regardless which data source you work with.

In Part I, I show you what ADO is, how it works, and how you can connect ADO to the myriad of available data sources.

Chapter 1

What ADO Does for Me

ADO — what the heck is that? Do I need it? How do I get it? And, once I have it, what can I do with it? All very good questions.

Unlike Microsoft Access or Windows 2000, ADO isn't a specific product, but rather a technology that weaves in and out of a large number of products and other technologies. Before I dig into the details of ADO programming, it's useful to take a moment and look at the big picture to get comfortable with the technologies you use throughout the remainder of the book.

Why Data Access Is Important

ADO stands for ActiveX Data Objects. The key word in the phase is *data*. Why?

I begin the answer to that question with another question. What is the most significant change brought about by the growth of the Internet? My answer may surprise you. The biggest change is the expectation of universal data access. Before the Internet, most people using a computer started with the assumption that the PC was primarily a tool for manipulating their own information. They created word-processed documents and built spreadsheets to their hearts' content. But if they wanted information they didn't have, they used other technology.

Suppose that you were working on your PC and you wanted to know the weather forecast for tomorrow was going to be. You would look for a newspaper. If you wanted to know the Dow Jones average, you called your broker. Today that's all changed. The Internet has placed data at the fingertips of anyone whose PC can access that network.

But the same cannot be said for all of the information that you need on a daily basis. It seems ironic that the one area of data access that lags behind is the same data that most businesses depend on daily. If you need to know whether there are any X55 widgets on order, it is still more than likely that you try to get the answer by making a phone call. If you need the phone extension of a new employee, chances are that you won't be able to use the PC to access that data.

Why is it so easy to find the score of a cricket match in Pakistan but so hard to get this week's sales figures? There are two reasons.

First, the PC was originally designed to be a personal tool, like a typewriter or a calculator, that supported the work of one individual. The addition of hardware and software that connected PCs into local area networks (LANs), integrated networks (internets with a small *i*), and wide area networks (WAN), put in place the potential for sharing and exchanging information in new ways. But potential is only potential. Despite these changes to the infrastructure, most people continued to use their computers in more or less the same way: as a device that handles personal information. Instead of calling Joe (or leaving a voice mail) to get the sales figures, you send him an e-mail and hope to get back an e-mail with a spreadsheet inside. While this activity does take advantage of the network technology, it still has the flavor of personal computing.

The second factor is a technical one. Traditionally, applications were developed to meet specific needs, such as accounting, sales, inventory, warehouse management, and budgeting. The makers of the software selected the data-storage mechanism that best fit their needs. They may have chosen to license the database technology from an existing vendor or to create their own proprietary data formats.

The result of different information formats for different business needs is often that the different parts of a business become fragmented into incompatible data structures and formats. Figure 1-1 illustrates a business that has its sales, marketing, and human resources data in three different data sources: Oracle, SQL Server, and FoxPro. To access each of the data sources, it is necessary to write or install software that is designed to interact with each data source. This type of software is called a *native* driver because it interacts with the API (application programmer interface) of the data source.

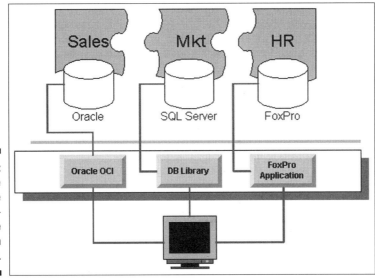

Figure 1-1:
Parts of the
data puzzle
don't com-
municate
with each
other.

The term *API* refers to an application programmer interface. When someone writes a Windows program, usually in the C++ language, the software writer can choose to expose some of the features so that they can be accessed from other programs. For example, Excel can calculate the internal rate of return (IRR) of a series of cash flow values. This calculation is not built into Access or Visual Basic. If you are writing a program in Access or VB to perform an IRR calculation, you have two choices. You can learn the math involved and write your own code to do the calculation, or you can choose to take advantage of the fact that all of the users in your company have Excel installed on their computers. Instead of writing code to calculate the IRR, you issue a *call* to the IRR calculation in Excel through the Excel API. A *call* is a request from another program to perform an operation and return the result to your program.

There are several problems that occur when data access is provided through native drivers that talk directly to the API of the data source:

✔ **Language/operating is system-specific.** Most professional APIs are written in C++ and stored in files with DLL extensions. To execute functions that reside in the API DLL files, you must use programming techniques that closely parallel the original language in which the API was written. In addition, languages such as C++ are tied very closely to the operating system under which they were designed to run. The API functions used for Windows 3.*x* (16-bit) and Windows 9*x* (32-bit) are different and incompatible.

✔ **Product-specific knowledge is required**. Even if you assume an understanding of C++ conventions, data types, and language, a programmer must also have specific knowledge about the procedures supported by the API. This knowledge is rather arcane and always specific to the product involved. Someone familiar with the SQL Server DB API would not be able to use that knowledge to access procedures in the Oracle OCI.

While you can use the native API of a data source to implement custom software, the process is complex, expensive, and time-consuming. Experience shows that most data consumers do not have the technical resources to efficiently and economically develop customized access to vendor-specific data sources. This was the state of computing in the early 1990's.

The universal database

It doesn't take a genius to see that a company is better off if its data can be available to all the users who need that data. One approach to solving this problem is called the *Universal Database*, depicted in Figure 1-2. In this approach, all the data resources utilized within a company are gathered into a single, centralized database. Every time a user has a data request of any kind, the universal database processes the request. In Figure 1-2, SQL Server is the universal database, and all the data is placed into a homogenous environment.

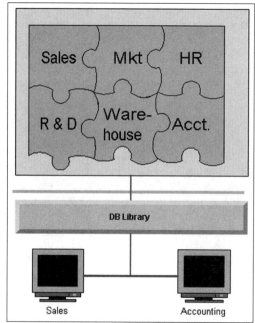

Figure 1-2:
The Universal database approach to data resources.

While this looks like a good solution in theory, it has several significant practical limitations:

- ✔ **Data in an enterprise is typically stored in various structures and formats.** To get all this data into a single database, the data must be converted and imported into the universal database.

- ✔ **Certain applications, many of which are mission-critical, are designed at the API level to interact with a specific data source.** These are replaced, if possible, with applications that work with the selected universal database.

- ✔ **Some data must stay in its original format and then be periodically exported to a common format that is loaded into the universal database.** This need is caused by specific business needs or incompatible IT architectures.

- ✔ **To accommodate a wide variety of applications, the universal database may require extensive modification and extensions to handle nontraditional data.** Examples of such nontraditional data include e-mail messages, calendar data, and spreadsheet models.

The universal database approach is difficult to implement because it requires that the data be altered to fit into the structure of the central database. Importing and exporting large blocks of data puts a considerable amount of stress on networks and servers. In addition, data updates can take a considerable amount of time to move through the conversion process into the central database.

Universal Data Access

In contrast to the Universal Database approach, the Universal Data Access (UDA) approach does not require the data itself to be transformed, copied, or moved from its original location. Instead, a new layer of software is added between the user and the data sources, as shown in Figure 1-3. In the UDA model, this new layer of software hides the specific structure of each data source from the data consumers. Requests for data are addressed to the UDA software, which then deals with the details of the specific data sources to return the desired information.

The goal of UDA is to provide a software developer with the ability to access data sources without having to interact with or know anything about the native API of the data source. Instead, the UDA layer provides a common set of commands that can be applied to accessing data from a wide variety of data sources.

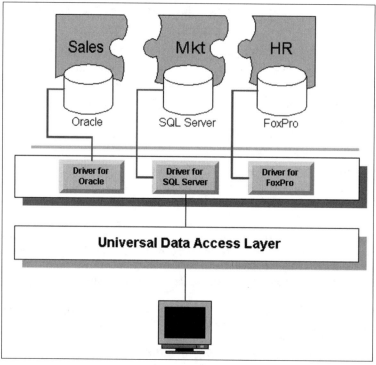

Figure 1-3:
The Universal Data Access model uses a middle layer of software to insulate users from varied data storage formats.

On the other side of the UDA layer is a set of drivers. Each driver connects the UDA layer to a specific data source. The drivers convert data requests from the applications to the specific instructions required by the data source. On the other hand, the UDA layer formats any data being returned by the data source to a standard format used by all applications that work with the UDA.

UDA has several key advantages that make application development less complex, more reliable, and more economical.

- **No conversion required:** Data does not need to moved or converted. It can be accessed in its original format and location. All that is needed is a driver that connects the data source to the UDA layer.

- **Vendor-independence:** Applications developed using the UDA are vendor-independent. A programmer can build the application based on the UDA standards without reference to vendor-specific details.

- **Heterogeneous sources:** The fact that all the data sources can be accessed from the UDA layer enables operations that involve multiple data sources and different data types. For example, an accounting user may need a list of vendor contact names and address for their 1099 forms. The 1099 data stored in an Oracle database can join a vendor table stored in a SQL Server to generate the required information.

✔ **Language/platform-independence:** To allow custom-designed database applications to be quickly and reliably produced, the UDA should provide a consistent programming interface that is independent of the conventions of any specific programming language or operating system platform.

Microsoft's first try: ODBC

Starting in 1992, Microsoft introduced a universal data access system called Open Database Connectivity, or *ODBC* for short. The system was designed to implement the concept of a UDA layer that operates with a wide variety of file-based and server-based databases running on networks. ODBC provided a standard API through which a variety of databases can be accessed.

ODBC is an important step toward the creation of a functional UDA system. It supports the use of SQL (Structured Query Language) as the standard key language component used for retrieving data from the various data sources. Because SQL was already the defacto standard on mainframe computers, ODBC helped spread this technology to PC databases.

ODBC consisted of two parts:

✔ **The ODBC manager:** This program, which runs in the Control Panel of all Windows operating systems, contains information needed for making a connection to data source. The manager creates *data source names*, DSNs, for each set of connection specifications.

✔ **ODBC drivers:** The driver software contained the data source-specific information needed to process.

Using ODBC, a programmer can create a database application without having to include any vendor-specific information. All the programmer needs is the name of the DSN (as defined in the ODBC manager) and the SQL statement that defines the data operations, as shown in Figure 1-4. This information passes to the ODBC driver by means of the DSN. When the data source retrieves the desired information, the information is returned through ODBC to the program.

ODBC requires that you install a driver for a data source to work with that data source. For example, if you want to connect to a SQL Server, you need the ODBC driver for SQL Server. Oracle, Sybase, or DataFlex require additional drivers.

However, once installed, you use the same programming approach to perform database operations on source databases. ODBC has been very successful since its introduction in 1992. Today, almost every significant database format can be accessed through an ODBC driver.

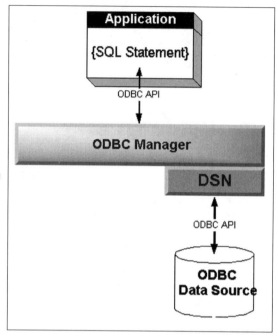

Figure 1-4:
The ODBC
manager
creates a
data source
name (DSN)
for each
database
connection.

ODBC was an important first step in creating a universal data access standard. It helped establish SQL as the standard method for accessing data in any ODBC-compliant data sources. However, its traditional API syntax was closely associated with C language programming. To process a single database query, the programmer was required to perform a series of API functions in the proper order.

For example, if a query returned one or more rows of information, the API required the programmer to write a structure that returned one column from each row. A loop was required to continue loading data until the API signaled that there were no more rows left to read. The ODBC API solved one part of the UDA puzzle, but the price was that the programming needed to create an application was still too difficult and complicated to satisfy the need for rapid application development.

DAO — Database Object Technology

The solution to the problem of creating an easy-to-use interface for ODBC databases came in the form of object technology. Microsoft's initial effort in this area was called *Data Access Objects* (DAO). It was introduced to complement the Jet Database Engine that was included in accompanied Microsoft

Access. The purpose of the Jet Engine was to provide support for Access MDB files as a standard data format for both Access and Visual Basic. In addition to support for Access MDB files, Jet can connect to ODBC data sources. Figure 1-5 shows how a SQL query starting in an Access or Visual Basic program uses DAO to get data stored in an ODBC data source.

The important part of this increasingly complex model is that, from a programmer's point of view, the instructions to process a query are the same, regardless of the data source. The combination of DAO and Jet is a standard approach for data access that avoids complex API programming and is still vendor-independent.

Problems with DAO/Jet

While in theory the combination of DAO and the Jet Engine provided an easy-to-use-and-understand programming structure for building data-related applications, its performance was uneven. If you were using Access MDB files as the data source, Jet worked well. But access to other ODBC sources, such as SQL Server or Oracle, suffered because ODBC moves through the Jet Engine, which is not primarily designed for client/server databases like SQL Server or Oracle.

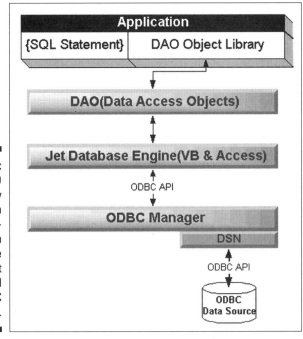

Figure 1-5:
DAO
technology
provided an
easy-to-
program
interface
that
connected
to ODBC
databases.

Microsoft's reaction was to upgrade various parts of the DAO system to improve client/server database operations. RDO (Remote Data Objects) was provided as an object technology oriented toward database services such as SQL Server. RDO was connected to the DAO programming model by means of an option inside DAO called ODBC Direct. Using ODBC Direct, a program can avoid the Jet Engine and use the RDO technology to go directly to the ODBC API to work with client/server databases.

You can see, just from reading the preceding paragraph, that the original idea (a simple, straightforward way to write data-oriented applications) was getting lost in a jumble of similar-sounding technologies. As a programmer using DAO, you had to remember to use one approach for MDB file access but a different set of options within DAO to connect a SQL Server.

At the same time, additional concerns emerged about data access:

- **Web access:** The dramatic growth of the Internet begged for a data access interface that could provide data to Web-based applications. Ideally, this would be an extension of a standard, universal data-access technology so that Web applications could leverage the knowledge that programmers had acquired from building more traditional network-based database applications.

- **Non-relational data sources:** Network services, such as online analytical processes, e-mail, and directory services, contained important information that was not stored in the traditional relational database structure. If applications were to mine these important data sources along with traditional relational databases, it was necessary to get beyond the strictly relational scope of DAO.

ADO to the rescue

The solution to all of the problems listed in this chapter before now is, oddly enough, the subject of this book — ADO (ActiveX Data Objects). As shown in Figure 1-6, the ADO object library provides a single, uniform programming tool that can access data stored in both traditional relational database and non-relational systems.

To provide compatibility with previous technologies, ADO contains support for both the Jet database engine and ODBC databases. In some cases, such as SQL Server, you can connect directly through ADO or indirectly by using ADO to connect to ODBC.

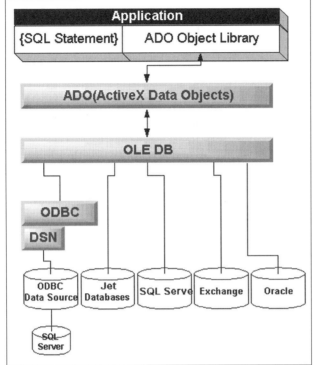

Figure 1-6:
ADO
provides
uniform
access to
relational
and non-
relational
data
sources.

In addition to simplifying the programming interface by having a single approach to all data source connections, ADO is fast. In general terms, I have found that ADO runs as much as 50 percent faster than the equivalent DAO code. This is true even when the network connection has a 28.8 kbps dial-up speed to the Internet.

But wait a minute! Right in the middle of the diagram, Figure 1-6, is OLE DB. What the heck is that?

In ODBC, a special piece of software — the ODBC Driver — actually connects the application to the specific data source. ADO technology also requires vendor-specific drivers. These new drivers are constructed under a new standard called Object Linking and Embedding Database (OLE DB). OLE DB works with ADO to form a universal data-access system, as follows:

> ✔ **OLE DB:** This is *system-level* software. The purpose of OLE DB is to provide a framework for the vendor-specific details required for each unique database format. In OLE DB, the vendor-specific elements are called *providers*. An OLE DB provider plays a similar role to an ODBC driver.

OLE DB moved beyond the direct database support in ODBC. OLE DB can also provide database services. Keep in mind that not all the databases that connect to the OLE DB system support the same set of features. An OLE DB service can compensate for important features that a given OLE DB data source may lack. Application developers don't need to know the details of OLE DB. All that they need to do is install it.

✔ **ADO:** ADO is *application-level* software. When you create applications that use database resources, you use ADO to communicate with the data source. Software that uses OLE DB data resources is called a *consumer*.

Figure 1-7 illustrates how OLE DB and ADO work together. You can use ADO to directly access data resources or you can use an OLE DB service to access the data source indirectly.

Figure 1-7:
OLE DB
organizes
data access
into three
parts:
consumers,
services,
and
providers.

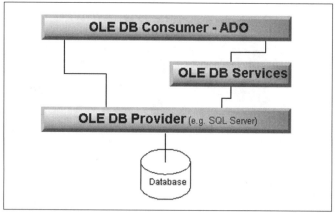

Chapter 2 looks closely at the details of using OLE DB providers and services.

Relational and non-relational data

One of the significant features of ADO/OLE DB is that it provides access to relational and non-relational sources of data. It is useful to take a look at exactly what these terms mean.

Relational databases

A relational database stores data in lists called *tables*. What is special about the tables in a relational database is that the table structure is designed to eliminate any duplicate information.

For example, suppose that you have a sales database in which you have a table of customers and a table of orders. In a relational database, all the name and address information is stored in the Customers table. You don't repeat the customer address in the Orders table. Instead, you enter a value, such as a Customer ID, into the Orders table. The value in the Orders table points at the record in the Customers table. These pointers are called *links*. Figure 1-8 shows part of the relational model of my Winebase software. Each of the tables contains an ID value that is linked to the data in another tables.

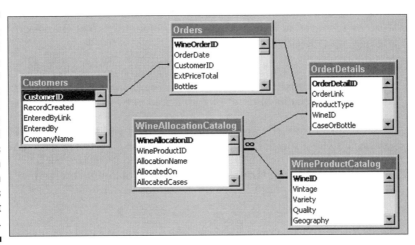

Figure 1-8: Relational data sources store data in tables and retrieve data based on links between common data values in different tables.

When I want to print an invoice, I must issue an instruction that tells the database which items from the linked tables to use to fill out my invoice report. The database uses the links to collect the required data and returns the assembled block of data to my program where it appears on the printed invoice.

When you work with relational databases, you may take for granted that this is the most logical way to work with data. However, relational databases do follow some rules that are not all that intuitive to non-database users.

- ✔ **All of the recordsets are temporary.** When a database returns the result of a linking operation, that set of data is temporary. It is discarded as soon as the operation is complete.

- ✔ **A relational database repeats all of the steps needed to create a recordset each time you request it.** Figure 1-8 shows that five tables are involved to print an invoice. If you print the same invoice three or four times, the relational database must repeat the entire linking process each time as if it had never compiled the data before.

When you think about it, this seems like a lot of work that isn't entirely necessary. After all, the data on an invoice ought to be the same each time that you print it.

Why does a relational database do all this work over and over again? The answer is that it needs to take into consideration the possibility that changes may have been made to the database that change the contents of the record-set. Relational databases allow multiple users to make additions, changes, and deletions to the database tables simultaneously and in real time. These systems are often referred to as *online transactional processing* (OLTP).

OLAP data marts

The relational database model provides the maximum amount of flexibility. Any user with sufficient permissions can alter data at any time. Recordsets can be retrieved at any time, and they reflect the latest changes to the under-lying data tables.

But there is a price to pay for all this flexibility. Because recordsets are con-stantly being constructed, discarded, and reconstructed, the relational data-base uses a sizeable amount of server and network resources.

If you look closely at many business activities and processes, you find that many activities require the flexibility provided by a full-powered, relational database. Many other activities, however, do not require such flexibility. For example, sales analysis, marketing research, planning, budgeting, and other analytical tasks do not require the instantaneous updates provided by an OLTP system.

Analytical activities typically look at blocks of data that are historical in nature and are only periodically updated, such as at the end of each month or quarter. Suppose that you want to summarize the dates for sales by fiscal year, financial quarter, and geographical region. Because the data is histori-cal, you can calculate all of the possible summary values and store them in a format similar to the diagram in Figure 1-9. This type of summarized data is often called a *cube* because it's a multi-dimensional arrangement of values. The process by which data is summarized and stored in cubes is called an *online analytical process* (OLAP).

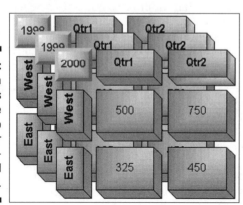

Figure 1-9:
OLAP data
marts
organize
data into
two- or
three-
dimensional
cubes.

OLAP cubes are an example of a data source that isn't based on the relation model discussed in the preceding section. Some of the differences between OLAP (non-relational) and OLTP (relational) are:

- ✔ **OLAP cubes are calculated in advance.** When data is retrieved from an OLAP source, it is already summarized so that no additional work is required.

- ✔ **OLAP data is only recalculated when an OLAP user or administrator decides that it is necessary.** The values in the cube do not automatically reflect changes to the tables from which the cube was calculated.

- ✔ **Because OLAP cubes do not store data in relational tables, you cannot use the SQL Language to request data.** Requests must be made using syntax and terminology understood by the OLAP processor.

OLAP cubes can greatly enhance data analysis. Their special data storage format and precalculated values ensure that analytical queries don't put undue stress on server and network resources.

If you use relational tables to support analytical operations, the relational database expends a large amount of resources recalculating the same summary values over and over again.

Tree-structured data sources

Another important form of non-relational data is systems that organize information into hierarchical tree-style structures. In fact, tree-structured data sources are even more common than relational databases. For example, the drive and folder system used by all Windows computers to organize the data stored on drives is an example of a non-relational, tree-structured system.

A common example is the way that Outlook and Exchange organize data into folders and items (see Figure 1-10). The tree-structured data source has the opposite characteristic of a relational data source. The tree represents a hierarchical type of organization along the lines of an outline. In Outlook/Exchange, the highest level in the tree is a mailbox. Within each mailbox are standard folders, such as inbox mail, outbox mail, contacts, and appointments. Outlook allows you to add folders to any part of the tree and to move or copy items from one folder to another.

I use the term Outlook/Exchange to refer to a network where Outlook and Exchange are running as client and server. Outlook and Exchange are separate, but related, products. The two programs work together to form a network e-mail system.

> ✓ **Exchange is an e-mail server program that resides on network servers.**
>
> ✓ **Outlook is an e-mail client program that is installed on user desktops.** However, Outlook can be used with other e-mail servers, including e-mail servers provided by Internet service providers.

Figure 1-10:
Tree-struc-
tured data
sources
organize
data in a
hierarchical
fashion.

In a tree structure, the relationship between the folders and the items contained in the folders is fixed. In a relational data source, the links between tables are fluid and change with each query.

When you access the information stored in a tree-structured data source, you work with the already existing relationships between folders to add, change, or remove items. Relationships in a tree structure are often expressed in terms of generations: that is, parents and children. For example, a recordset made on an Outlook mailbox defines the mailbox as the parent with the inbox and outbox folders as children.

ADO provides a means by which you can access the tree-structured data stored in the Windows 2000 Active Directory Service as well as the Outlook/Exchange mail system. This is a significant advantage for programmers because it opens up new and useful information sources that can be integrated into applications that also use data from traditional relational data sources.

Chapter 2

OLE DB Providers

*B*efore you can do any ADO programming, you must make a connection to one or more data sources. This means that the first step you have to take in every ADO program, from the simplest query to the most complex application, is to get connected. If you can't do that, nothing else is going to do you much good. This chapter focuses on making connections.

All the code shown in this chapter can be found in the file `chapter2.mdb`. Check out the Appendix at the back of this book for details on accessing the code.

Providers

In the world of Universal Data Access (UDA), the provider has the data for you, the consumer. You can classify OLE DB providers (which I introduce in Chapter 1) based on two fundamental qualities:

▶ **Network architecture:** ADO allows providers to be file-based or service-based. A file-based provider allows access to data stored in a specific file located somewhere on the network or on a local drive. When you use a file-based provider, you need to know the exact physical location of the data source file, such as `F:\finanace\budget01.mdb` or `\\jupiter\finanace\budget01.mdb`. A service-based provider is one that runs as a service on a network. To access a network service, you don't have to know the physical location of any specific file. Instead, you use a network name that identifies the service. When you attempt to connect to the service, the network uses various protocols to locate the computer that is running the named service.

One of the many advantages of service-based providers is that they avoid some of the confusion that can occur with drive and path names. For example, your application may use the file F:\finance\ budget01.mdb, where F is a shared drive on the network. However, some users have multiple hard drives, partitions, or a CD-ROM drive, and the letter F is already taken for a local drive. Server-based resources don't depend on drive mapping or path names. This makes them simpler to work with because you need to specify only the name of the service; the network is responsible for finding the actual location using network protocols.

✔ **Internal structure:** Unlike its predecessor DAO (Data Access Objects), ADO supports both relational data sources, such as Access and SQL Server, and nonrelational sources, such as Outlook folders, OLAP (online analytical processing) services, or Windows 2000 Active Directory Services. Although ADO provides a single programming approach to all data source access, it cannot completely improve the significant distinction between the way that relational and nonrelational data sources store and retrieve data. Most relational sources utilize SQL (structured query language) commands. Nonrelational sources don't typically conform to standard SQL instructions. As a developer, you need to understand the structure of the nonrelational sources that you want to access and the language and syntax that the provider understands. For example, Microsoft's OLAP Service uses a variation on the SQL language called *MDX* (*MultiDimensional eXpressions*) to retrieve data stored in OLAP cubes. To use the OLAP provider, you must know how to write commands in MDX.

Provider interactions

One of the differences between the old DAO technology and the new ADO technology is that ADO can function as both a client and a server technology. This makes it possible to create operations in which you use several different providers to connect to multiple data sources.

Imagine that you have data stored in both a SQL Server and an Access MDB file. In some cases, you find that some of the data your SQL Server query requires is actually stored the Access MDB file.

Under DAO technology, the client desktop has to establish separate links to each data source and then any required operations, such as joining the data from two tables, at the desktop. Figure 2-1 shows that in the DAO case, the desktop system performs most of the work because the data providers — SQL Server and Access — aren't aware of each other.

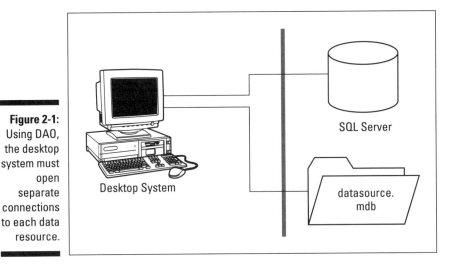

Figure 2-1:
Using DAO, the desktop system must open separate connections to each data resource.

OLE DB provides alternative strategies; Figure 2-2 shows one of them. The diagram in Figure 2-2 shows the SQL Server, instead of the desktop system, using the OLE DB provider for Access to link to the Access database. The outcome is that when the desktop system requests a data set that involves both SQL Server and Access data, the result is returned to the desktop through a single connection. Further, the server, rather than the desktop system, handles most of the work needed to do complex operations, such as joins between tables. Because servers typically are more powerful computers than desktop computers, the approach that I illustrate in Figure 2-2 makes better use of network resources.

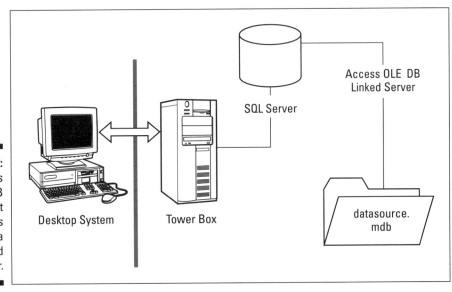

Figure 2-2:
SQL Servers use OLE DB to connect an Access MDB as a linked server.

ADO is also flexible. You can take a slightly different approach to the same problem, as shown in Figure 2-3. In this case, Access uses ADO to link to the SQL Server so that Access can query both local Access tables, as well as SQL Server tables based on the desktop user's request for data.

The approach that I illustrate in Figure 2-3 doesn't make as efficient use of network resources as the technique shown in Figure 2-2 because Access doesn't run as a network service. This means it cannot take full advantage of the server's computing power. But it does illustrate that the flexibility of OLE DB to run on both client and server platforms gives you many ways to get a job done. It's up to you to choose the best approach in any given circumstance.

The role of ADO

The preceding section illustrates how OLE DB provides the ability for both desktop and server computers to access data resources of different architectures and formats. If that's what OLE DB does, what's ADO for?

The answer to that question depends on whether you're building applications or just using existing applications. If you're using a program like Access or Excel, you can simply use the built-in menus and dialog boxes to access OLE DB. Figure 2-4 shows the Create New Data Source dialog box that appears in Excel 2000. This dialog box is used to connect an Excel Pivot table to a Microsoft OLAP data mart. Note the reference to the OLE DB provider for OLAP Services. This is an example of a desktop application directly interacting with OLE DB.

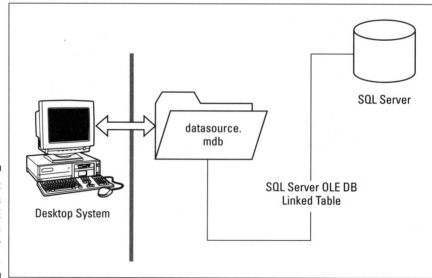

Figure 2-3:
Access uses OLE DB to link to SQL Server tables.

SQL Server

datasource.
mdb

SQL Server OLE DB
Linked Table

Desktop System

Figure 2-4:
Excel users
can make
use of OLE
DB provider
for OLAP
services
without
using ADO.

Another example of an application using OLE DB directly is Access 2000. In Access 2000, you can create Access projects. An Access 2000 project is a special form of Access database in which OLE DB providers are used to directly connect the project file with a SQL Server database. Figure 2-5 shows the dialog box that appears when you create an Access 2000 project from an existing SQL Server database.

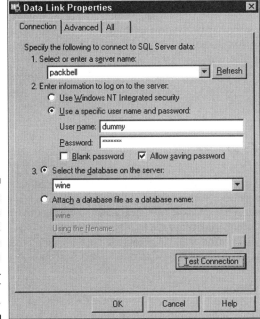

Figure 2-5:
Access
uses OLE
DB to create
an
Access/SQL
Server
project.

That still leaves this question: When do you use ADO? The answer: You use ADO when you want to write custom-designed programs or procedures. Why not use OLE DB? Although you can use OLE DB to do everything you can do with ADO, the big drawback to OLE DB is that it requires too much detailed knowledge of each specific data source. ADO shields you from those details and enables you to use the same set of commands with all data sources.

Making the connection

The gateway to all ADO programming is the connection object. Creating a connection object is a bit like making a phone call. To make a call, you have to know the information that identifies the person you want to call. Typically, this is an area code, phone number, and perhaps an extension number. When you dial those numbers, you open a direct line of communication to a phone in another location. All the information you get or give during that communication passes through that connection. When the connection ends, so does the ability to communicate.

An ADO connection works in roughly the same fashion. The most significant point of similarity is that you need to start with some basic information about the source that you want to connect to. Without that information, nothing can happen in an ADO program.

Unfortunately, unlike the telephone system, which has a simple standard for numeric phone numbers, communication with an OLE DB data source requires at least some provider-specific information. After you make a connection, your ADO programming works at a provider-independent level. To get there, you have to deal with provider-specific settings at the connection level.

The Connection Object

The goal of Universal Data Access (UDA) is an environment in which you can access data without reference to the specific structure in which it is stored, such as SQL Server or an Access MDB file. But wishing for some universal standard doesn't make incompatible data structures go away. The trick is to use OLE DB technology to connect to a variety of data services. After you connect, you can use ADO to build applications without addressing vendor-specific details.

In the ADO programming model, you use the connection object to open a channel of communication between an application and a data source. In ADO, that connection can be made simply with two statements, as shown in the following example:

✔ **The first statement defines a new connection object and assigns the connection object a variable name.**

```
Dim ConnectionName as New ADODB.Connection
```

Note: You use the ADO DB prefix to indicate that the connection object is an ADO connection. DAO, the system that ADO replaced, also included a connection object. Using the prefix avoids confusion in environments where DAO can also be used. For example, although Access 97 uses DAO by default, it is possible to use ADO as well if you include the ADO library in your Access 97 database. If you simply specify a connection object, then Access 97 assumes that you wanted a DAO — not an ADO — connection. Prefixes avoid this problem and allow you to mix DAO and ADO in the same program or procedure.

✔ **The second statement uses the open method of the connection object to actually connect to the data source. It's in the string that the details of the connection appear.**

```
ConnectionName.Open connectionstring
```

I cover connection strings in the "Connection strings" section later in this chapter.

The following example creates a connection to an Access database, Test.Mdb.

```
Dim Cnt as New ADODB.Connection
Cnt.Open "Data Source=C:\test.mdb;" & "Provider=Microsoft.Jet.OLEDB.4.0;"
```

After you create the connection object, you use it as the conduit to send requests and receive data from the connected data source. You can use a single connection to make one or more requests for data. You can also use the connection object to send instructions to the data source that perform operations that do not return data such as updates or deletions.

The New keyword

One confusing area of object programming in Visual Basic (VB) and Visual Basic for Applications (VBA) is the keyword New. Many of the statements in VB or VBA came into use at a time before the creation of object technology. The Dim statement was originally used to designate array variables. The following statement defines a variable X as a three-row, two-column matrix:

```
Dim X(3,2)
```

Although `Dim` can still be used to define arrays of empty memory cells, VB/VBA now supports more sophisticated structures called *objects*. Each object has a specific set of properties that are characteristic of the type of object it is. The following statement defines an *instance* of an ADO connection object:

```
Dim Cnt as New ADODB.Connection
```

What is an instance? When dealing with simple structures like arrays, it makes sense to say that you create them as part of your program. But the term *create* is a bit misleading when it comes to an object.

Instead, the preferred term is *instantiate,* which means to create an instance of something. The reason instantiate is a more accurate term is because objects aren't created from nothing. To create an object, such as an ADO connection, you must have already installed the computer code for ADO (in the form of EXE, DLL, and other supporting files) on your computer. When you execute a statement like the preceding one, you are using the ADO files as a template to create a temporary copy of an ADO object in memory.

Each instance of an object is a unique incarnation of the general object type. You can use your program to assign specific values to the object and have it return information to your program or instances of other related objects.

You can also instantiate an object using the `Set` statement. In the following example, the `Dim` statement doesn't specify if the `ADODB.Connection` is a new or an existing connection. The following `Set` statement uses the `New` keyword to complete the definition of the object.

```
Dim Cnt As ADODB.Connection
Set Cnt = New ADODB.Connection
```

Keep in mind that you don't use the `New` keyword if you're creating a reference to an existing instance. The following example is a commonly used technique in Access 2000. When you open an Access database, the program automatically creates an ADO connection to itself because any Access database can contain data tables as well as forms and reports.

```
Dim Cnt As ADODB.Connection
Set Cnt = CurrentProject.Connection
```

By default, Access 97 uses DAO as a data access system. The following code shows how to create a reference to the currently open database in Access 97. `CurrentProject.Connection` is roughly the ADO equivalent of `CurrentDB`.

```
Dim D as Database
Set D = CurrentDB
```

So now you can discard the concept of creating an object in favor of the more accurate term *instantiate*. Well, not entirely. When you use ADO with Active Server Pages, objects are created by using the `CreateObject( )` function. The following example shows a connection object is instantiated in a Web ASP. The statement instantiates a connection on the Web server.

```
<% Set Cnt = Server.CreateObject("ADODB.Connection") %>
```

You can see that the terminology related to objects isn't 100 percent consistent. In this book, I use the term *create* as a synonym for *instantiate* when talking about objects like connections.

Connection strings

The key item involved in creating a connection is the *connection string*. The term *string* is used in programming languages to refer to a series of text characters. An ADO connection string is a block of text that contains the names of the specific elements required to make a connection to a specific data source.

The type, number, and names of the elements needed to form a connection to the data source you want to work with are what determine the exact contents of a connection string. The remainder of this chapter gives specific examples of connection strings that you can use with many widely used data sources.

Despite the many differences between the connection information required by different data sources, connection strings have a general structure and most strings contain a few key elements.

The basic unit in a connection string is called a *parameter*. A parameter consists of a parameter name and the specific value that you want to assign to that parameter for the purpose of making a connection to a specific data source. Each parameter follows the general form shown below. Note the semicolon marks the end of each parameter. This allows you to have many parameters in one connection string.

```
Parameter=value;
```

For example, all ADO connections utilize an OLE DB provider. The `provider` parameter in a connection string specifies which OLE DB provider should be used to make the connection. The following example specifies the provider as the Microsoft OLE DB provider for Oracle.

```
"Provider=MSDAORA;"
```

The four most common parameters for connection strings are the following:

- ✔ **Provider:** This is the name of the OLE DB provider that you use for a connection such as Microsoft Jet, SQL Server, or Oracle. Each connection can have only one provider. The names of the providers are defined in the OLE DB provider software installed on the computer where the program you are writing is running. The provider name *MSDAORA* is always the name of the Microsoft provider for Oracle.

  `"Provider=MSDAORA;"`

- ✔ **Data source:** The value of this parameter is usually either the name of a network service or a file. If you are connecting to a network service data source such as SQL Server or Oracle, the data source is the name of the service (or server). If the data source is file-based like Access or dBase, then this parameter is a fully qualified path name.

  `"Data Source=O:\ADO Book\db\chp2\ds.mdb;"`

The fully qualified path name refers to the full, unique identifier that points to a specific file. `O:\ADO Book\db\chp2\ds.mdb` refers to the ds.mdb file on the O drive in the `ADO Book\db\chp2` folder. Keep in mind that when you use letters (such as *O*) to refer to drives located on a network, other users may not have the same drive mapping; O on a different computer may not refer to the same resource. To avoid confusion, you can replace the drive letter with the name of the computer, such as `\\RKPNTSR2`. This makes the fully qualified path `\\RKPNTSR2\ADO Book\db\chp2\ds.mdb`.

- ✔ **User ID:** This is the name of the user login or user name. Most network data source systems have some sort of security structure that establishes logins and passwords in order to control access to data resources. File-based data sources may omit internal security. For example, Access has a security feature that is inactive until you specifically activate security on a given Access file. However, even when security is inactive, the user name `Admin` is automatically created to serve as a default login name.

  `"User ID=Admin;"`

- ✔ **Password:** This parameter is the password that identifies the user and allows access to the data source. The following example shows a password supplied as a connection-string parameter.

  `"Password=qzx#12;"`

  The password parameter is often left empty if a password is not required for use by the User ID parameter.

  `"Password=;"`

The full connection string lists all of the required, along with any optional, parameters as one block of text. The following example connects to a SQL Server called `rkpntsr2`, using the login name `sa` with the password `dummy`. The semicolon after the last parameter is optional because it appears at the end of the connection string.

```
CntStr = "Provider=SQLOLEDB;UserID=sa;Password=dummy;Data Source=rkpntsr2;"
```

Note that you use a single pair of quotation marks to enclose the entire connection string because you must contain all of the parameters in one text block.

Connection strings aren't order sensitive. Because each parameter is named, you can write the items in any order. The following example accomplishes exactly the same function as the preceding example because the order of the parameters isn't significant.

```
CntStr = "Password=dummy;UserID=sa;Data Source=rkpntsr2; Provider=SQLOLEDB;"
```

By convention, the provider is typically the first parameter; however, it isn't a requirement.

Passwords

When you write a program in Excel, Access, or a client-side script in a Web page, the password value in the connection string can be viewed by the users if they inspect the code.

If you work with Access 97 or newer, you can protect your code from view by converting the MDB file to a MDE file using the Tools⇨Database Utilities⇨Make MDE File command. However, even then there is a potential area of exposure. Access allows you to store passwords when you link external tables. You can even view the connection string by opening the design mode of the linked table and selecting View⇨Properties in an MDE file. You can also display the connection string by entering the statement ? `CurrentDB("Tname")`. Connect in the immediate window (replace *Tname* with the actual name of the linked table).

There are two approaches to handling security when your code is open to users.

> ✔ **Rely on network security:** Networks such as Windows NT or Windows 2000 provide methods of limiting user access to the resources on the network. If you have an Access application that contains passwords, you can rely on network security to control access to the MDB file so that

only valid users with the correct permissions can access the folder in which your Access program is stored. In this way, only valid users can open the Access file and see the passwords. Of course, this approach assumes that network security is implemented properly. Even so, there always remains the possibility that someone can go to a workstation that is logged in but unattended and view information they should not see. On the other hand, you eliminate the need to reinvent the wheel by using the already established security environment on the network.

✔ **Require password entry::** Instead of placing the password in your code in any form, you simply insert a variable, such as PWD, in the connection string. You then require the user to enter the password and store the response in the variable. The following example uses the Inputbox( ) statement to insert the user's input into the string that connects to the SQL server PACKBELL.

```
Sub Password1()
    Dim Cnt As New ADODB.Connection
    Dim PWD
    PWD = InputBox("Enter Your Password")
    Cnt.Open _
        "Provider=SQLOLEDB;" & _
        "Data Source=packbell;" & _
        "user id=dummy;" & _
        "password=" & PWD
    MsgBox Cnt.State
End Sub
```

When you use a complied language like Visual Basic or when your write server-side Web scripts, you do not have to concern yourself with exposing passwords. Visual Basic is compiled, and the text of your source code changed to binary instructions, which cannot be read by people using your Visual Basic program. If you write server-side Web scripts, the code never leaves the server; users accessing the pages through the Web cannot see any password information. I cover server-side scripting in Part IV of this book.

Opening a connection

You can open a connection to an ADO-supported data source in two basic ways:

✔ **Setting the** ConnectionString **property:** Each connection object has a ConnectionString property. The following example sets the ConnectionString property and then executes the Open method of the connection object. The State property of the connection returns a value of one (1) if the connection is successfully opened or zero (0) if it fails.

```
Sub OpenConnection1()
    Dim Cnt As New ADODB.Connection
    Cnt.ConnectionString = _
    "data source=O:\ADO Book\db\chp2\ds.mdb;" &
    "Provider=Microsoft.Jet.OLEDB.4.0;"
    Cnt.Open
    MsgBox Cnt.State
End Sub
```

✔ **Setting the** `ConnectionString` **argument:** You can eliminate one statement by using the connection string text as an argument for the `Open`
method, as shown in the following code:

```
Sub OpenConnection2()
    Dim Cnt As New ADODB.Connection
    Cnt.Open ConnectionString:= _
    "data source=O:\ADO Book\db\chp2\ds.mdb;" & _
    "Provider=Microsoft.Jet.OLEDB.4.0;"
    MsgBox Cnt.State
End Sub
```

You can skip the argument name by making sure that the connection
string is the first argument.

```
    Cnt.Open "data source=O:\ADO Book\db\chp2\ds.mdb;" &
    "Provider=Microsoft.Jet.OLEDB.4.0;"
```

There is yet another valid variation on the object syntax. `Connection4` starts
by defining `Cnt` as a generic object. The `Set` statement then specifies the precise type of object (a new connection) that `Cnt` is going to be.

```
Sub OpenConnection4()
    Dim Cnt As Object
    Set Cnt = New ADODB.Connection
    Cnt.Open CntStr
    MsgBox Cnt.State
End Sub
```

In an application, you may always use the same connection string in many
different places. You can specify the connection text as a constant. If you
specify the constant in the declarations section of the module, you can use it
with any procedure in the module, as shown in the following code:

```
Const CntStr = _
"data source=O:\ADO Book\db\chp2\ds.mdb;" & _
"Provider=Microsoft.Jet.OLEDB.4.0;"

Sub OpenConnection3()
    Dim Cnt As New ADODB.Connection
    Cnt.Open CntStr
    MsgBox Cnt.State
End Sub
```

If you want to make the connection string available to any procedure in the application, declare it as a public constant, as shown in the following code:

```
Public Const Global_CntStr = _
"data source=O:\ADO Book\db\chp2\ds.mdb;" & _
"Provider=Microsoft.Jet.OLEDB.4.0;"
```

Connecting to Specific Providers

The remainder of the chapter looks at the type of connection strings you use to create ADO connections to specific data source providers. Although all connection objects provide the same set of features, connecting to specific data sources requires connection strings that match those providers.

ODBC data sources

The open database connectivity (ODBC) provides a structure for applications to connect to a wide variety of relational databases. Almost every significant database manufacturer supports ODBC.

The OLE DB provider for ODBC is called *MSDASQL (MicroSoft Data Access SQL)*. With this provider, ADO can connect to any ODBC data source.

Follow these rules:

 ✔ **If an OLE DB native provider is available, use it as the provider.**

 ✔ **If native OLE DB isn't available, use the MSDASQL.**

Defining a ODBC DSN

As originally conceived, the ODBC system depended on the use of data source names (DSNs), which are created by using the ODBC Manager. The ODBC Data Sources program is found in the Control Panel folder under Windows 9*x* and Windows NT. In Windows 2000, the Data Sources applet is located in the Administrative Tools folder of the control panel. Figure 2-6 shows the ODBC Data Source Administrator dialog box.

Three types of DSNs exist:

 ✔ **User DSN:** This type of DSN is stored in the file (ODBC.INI) located in the Windows System folder. The DSN is specific to the currently logged in user and isn't visible to other logins on the same computer.

 ✔ **System DSN:** This DSN is also stored in the Windows System folder but it is visible to all logins.

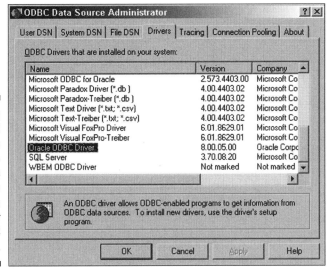

Figure 2-6:
The ODBC
Data Source
Adminis-
trator is
used to
create
DSNs for
ODBC
databases.

✔ **File DSN:** A File DSN differs from the User or System DSN in that its settings aren't stored in the `ODBC.INI`. Instead, the settings are stored in a
separate file with a DSN extension. You don't have to store this file in the
Windows System folder; you can store it on any available drive, including network shared drives. This makes it possible for a number of users
to share a single DSN that's stored on a network share. Another advantage of a File DSN is that if you make a change in the settings, all the
users that use the File DSN are automatically updated. To change a user
or system DSN, you need to repeat the change on each desktop. Keep in
mind that a File DSN only works if the users sharing the file have the
specified ODBC driver installed. Using a File DSN does not install the
ODBC driver on a client workstation.

Using a DSN

After a DSN is defined in the ODBC Manager, you can use the DSN as part of
the connection used to create an ADO connection. An ODBC connection
string has five parameters.

✔ **Provider = MSDASQL:** Because the default provider in ADO is the OLE
DB ODBC provider, it isn't required that you include this parameter in
the connection string. However, you may find that it helps clarify your
code if you explicitly state the name of the provider. Note that connections strings other than ODBC require the provider parameter.

✔ **DSN:** If you use a User or System DSN, this is the name of a DSN that has
already been created using the ODBC Manager applet. This is the only
required parameter for an ODBC connection string.

✔ **FileDSN:** This is the fully qualified path name of the DSN file that you want to use as the ODBC DSN. This file can reside on any local or network drive.

✔ **Database.** This parameter is optional because any ODBC drivers that support multiple databases, such as SQL Server, require that you specify which database within the server should be opened. If you omit this parameter, the default database automatically opens when the connection is made.

If you use SQL Server or a similar client/server database that supports a full-security model, you can link a login with a specific database so that every time someone uses the user login, the same database automatically opens. For example, to set the default database for a user in SQL Server 7.0, use the Enterprise Manager to open a registered server. Expand the tree to locate the Security folder. Under Security, select Logins. Double-click a login name to open the Properties box. In the Specify Default box, select the name of the default database for this login. Each time this login is used, the default database automatically opens.

✔ **UID/PWD:** The User ID and password allows you to login to secured data sources. By default, Access databases are assigned the UID Admin with no password.

The following example connects to the data source assigned to the DSN SampleData. In this case, the DSN represents a link to an Access database. But you can't really tell that by looking at the connection string. When you use ODBC DSNs, the driver information, which tells you the type of data source being used, is stored in the `ODBC.INI` file instead of appearing in the connection string.

```
Sub DSN()
    Dim Cnt As New ADODB.Connection
    Cnt.Open "DSN=SampleData;UID=admin"
    MsgBox Cnt.State
End Sub
```

Although an ODBC connection does require the provider to be specified, you have the option to include the provider name as part of the connecting string if you want your code to clearly indicate what type of connection is being made.

```
Cnt.Open "Provider=MSDASQL;DSN=SampleData;UID=admin"
```

This example uses a DSN to connect to a SQL Server. Note that because the driver information isn't present in the connection string, it is indistinguishable from a connection to an Access or other database.

```
Sub DSNToSQLServer()
    Dim Cnt As New ADODB.Connection
    Cnt.Open "DSN=DBTest;UID=sa;PWD=;"
    MsgBox Cnt.State
End Sub
```

When the data source can contain multiple databases, such as a SQL Server, you can use the DATABASE parameter to specify which database you are connecting with.

```
Sub DSNToSQLServerWithDatabase()
    Dim Cnt As New ADODB.Connection
    Cnt.Open "DSN=DBTest;UID=sa;PWD=;DATABASE=pubs;"
    MsgBox Cnt.State
End Sub
```

Using a File DSN

If you want to use a file DSN, you include the FileDSN parameter in the connection string. This parameter requires the fully qualified path name of the FileDSN file. In the following example, the file DSN is MASDS.DSN is located on a network drive — O — rather than in the local System folder.

```
Sub DSNFile()
    Dim Cnt As New ADODB.Connection
    Cnt.Open _"FileDSN=O:\ADO Book\db\chp2\MASDS.dsn;UID=Admin"
    MsgBox Cnt.State
End Sub
```

A file DSN is a simple text file. The minimum requirements for a DSN file that connects to an Access database follow. The file specifies the driver and the database file. If you create a file DSN using the ODBC Manager, it contains a number of optional settings. However, only the two following elements shown are required:

```
[ODBC]
DRIVER=Microsoft Access Driver (*.mdb)
DBQ=O:\ADO Book\DB\chp2\ds.mdb
```

Connecting to an ODBC source without a DSN

As you can see, ODBC DSNs are a simple way for users to create ODBC database connections using the Windows user interface. However, when programming, it can present some problems.

- ✔ The name of the driver isn't included in the connection string, making it unclear what sort of data source you are working with.

- ✔ Any application built around a DSN requires that the DSN be created on every desktop that uses the application or that each desktop has access to a File DSN on a network share.

You can eliminate these problems by creating an ODBC connection string that doesn't depend on a DSN. To eliminate the need for the DSN, you simply include the information that was previously stored in the DSN as part of the connection string. The DSNLess subroutine shows an ODBC connection string that contains a DRIVER and a database (DBQ) parameter. The connection string now contains all the information that was stored in the DSN so that a connection can be established without reference to any DSN.

```
Sub DSNLess()
    Dim Cnt As New ADODB.Connection
    Cnt.Open _
    "DRIVER=Microsoft Access Driver (*.mdb);" & _
    "DBQ=O:\ADO Book\DB\chp2\ds.mdb"
    MsgBox Cnt.State
End Sub
```

If you're sure of the exact name of an ODBC driver, ODBC can write all the information you need. Simply use the ODBC Manager to create a file DSN for the data source you want to use. Open the DSN file in Notepad, and copy and paste the parameters into your code.

While ADO includes an OLE DB provider specific to SQL Server, you may want to use the ODBC connector to SQL Server in applications that were originally constructed with DAO.

```
Sub DSNLessSQL()
    Dim Cnt As New ADODB.Connection
    Cnt.Open _
    "DRIVER={SQL Server};" & _
    "SERVER=rkpntsr2;UID=sa;PWD=;DATABASE=pubs"
    MsgBox Cnt.State
End Sub
```

DSN-less connections make it simpler to maintain and distribute applications that require connections to ODBC data sources because you can include all of the required information in the program code. This eliminates the need to set up DSNs on each desktop.

Writing a function that creates a DSN

Using a DSN-less connection eliminates the need to worry about whether or not a given desktop has the required DSN or not. However, if you have already written a significant amount of code that assumes the presence of a DSN, you may want to avoid changing the code. One solution is to use the RegisterDatabase method available in VB and VBA. You can place this code in the form or the procedure that starts your application.

The RegisterDatabase command adds an entry to the ODBC.INI file using a program statement in place of user entries into the ODBC Manager. CreateDSN adds a new DSN, NewDS.

`RegisterDatabase` has four parameters:

- ✔ The first parameter specifies the name of the DSN.
- ✔ The second parameter selects the ODBC Driver.
- ✔ The third parameter is set to `True` if you want to suppress any dialog boxes that ODBC may display if the registration information is insufficient.
- ✔ The last parameter is a text string that contains one or more items of information that define the ODBC connection.

For example, look at the `CreateDSN` subroutine:

```
Sub CreateDSN()
    DBEngine.RegisterDatabase DSN:="NewDS", _
    DRIVER:="Microsoft Access Driver (*.mdb)", _
    Silent:=True, _
    Attributes:="DBQ=O:\ADO Book\DB\chp2\ds.mdb"
End Sub
```

You can run a procedure like `UseNewDSN` to test to see if the preceding procedure actually created a valid DSN.

```
Sub UseNewDSN()
    Dim CntStr
    Dim Cnt As New ADODB.Connection
    Cnt.Open "DSN=NewDS;UID=admin;PWD=;"
    MsgBox Cnt.State
End Sub
```

If you want to pass a setup string that contains more than one value, separate each item with a carriage return character. For example, to create a DSN for a SQL Server, you need to include both a `Server` and a `Database` parameter. `CreateDSN2` uses a setup string that contains the VB constant `vbCr` (which is equivalent to the ASCII value 13, a carriage return) to separate the two parameters.

```
Sub CreateDSN2()
    Dim CntStr
    CntStr = "Server=rkpntsr2" & vbCr & "Database=Pubs"
    DBEngine.RegisterDatabase DSN:="NewDSSQOL", _
        DRIVER:="SQL Server", _
        Silent:=True, _
        Attributes:=CntStr
End Sub
```

If you use the `RegisterDatabase` method and the specified DSN already exists, the DSN data is updated with the data supplied with the `RegisterDatabase` method. This takes place without any warning so you need to take care that you aren't overwriting needed information.

DAO and ADO with ODBC

Before moving on to other types of connections, it may be useful for readers who have worked with ODBC prior to ADO to review some of the differences between the way that DAO and ADO connect to ODBC sources. This is particularly important if you have existing applications that you want to convert from DAO to ADO. If you used Access 97 to build an application, converting to Access 2000 changes the file format but it does not automatically alter the DAO code to now work with ADO.

DAO1 shows the use of the `OpenDatabase` method in DAO to connect to a SQL Server data source.

```
Sub DAO1()
    Dim RemDB As DAO.Database
    Set RemDB = OpenDatabase("", False, False, _
    "ODBC;DRIVER={SQL Server};" & _
    "SERVER=rkpntsr2;UID=sa;PWD=;DATABASE=pubs")
End Sub
```

Notice that the one significant difference between the DAO connection string and ADO is the ODBC identifier. In ADO you can simply omit that item. The string works because ADO assumes that the connection is ODBC unless you specify some other provider.

Microsoft Jet data sources

When Microsoft released Access 1.0 in 1992, the program consisted of two functions: a user interface that provided datasheets, forms, and reports; and a database engine that performed data storage and retrieval functions in a single product.

Microsoft soon came to the conclusion that the SQL-based data engine inside Access can be a useful tool for other applications, such as Excel and Visual Basic. Microsoft separated the engine, Jet, from Access so that Excel users can access data without installing Access on their desktops. It also provided Visual Basic programmers with an SQL-based data format, which made Visual Basic applications easier to create.

The Jet concept can be a bit confusing because it overlaps ODBC in certain areas. For example, if you install an ODBC driver for a specific database product, such as a DOS-based DataFlex database, you can use ODBC to connect directly (called ODBCDirect) or use Jet to connect indirectly to the ODBC data source.

The problem is that each connection method provides a different set of features. This means that your programming code has to be written differently for the approach that you choose to use. There are also performance and memory resource considerations.

This is exactly the type of problem ADO eliminates. In ADO, only a single method exists for connecting to any data source. The product-specific details occur within the connection string, and they are always applied to the same method, the Open method of the connection object.

In order to connect to the Jet Engine data sources, you specify the Jet Engine as your provider. The following example shows Jet Engine 4.0 as the provider used to connect to an Access database file:

```
Sub AccessViaJet()
    Dim Cnt As New ADODB.Connection
    Cnt.Open "Provider=Microsoft.Jet.OLEDB.4.0;Data Source=O:\ADO
             Book\db\chp2\ds.mdb;"
    MsgBox Cnt.State
End Sub
```

Another popular Jet Engine data source is Excel spreadsheets that contain database information. AccessViaJet1 shows how to make a connection to an Excel file, Customers.xls.

```
Sub AccessViaJet1()
    Dim Cnt As New ADODB.Connection
    Cnt.Open "Provider=Microsoft.Jet.OLEDB.4.0;" & _
    "Excel 5.0;" & _
    "DATABASE=O:\ADO Book\DB\chp2\Customers.xls;"
    MsgBox Cnt.State
End Sub
```

Because of the nature of Excel spreadsheets, you can include optional parameters that more specifically define the data inside the spreadsheet with which you want to connect. JetXLS specifies the Customers worksheet (TABLE=) and that the first row in the worksheet contains field names (HDR=YES).

```
Sub JetXLS()
    Dim Cnt As New ADODB.Connection
    Cnt.Open "Provider=Microsoft.Jet.OLEDB.4.0;" & _
        "Excel 8.0;DATABASE=O:\ADO Book\DB\chp2\Customers.xls;" & _
        "HDR=YES;TABLE=Customers$;"
    MsgBox Cnt.State
End Sub
```

AccessViaJetText shows the Jet Engine used to open a connection to a comma-delimited text file (CSV):

```
Sub AccessViaJetText()
    Dim Cnt As New ADODB.Connection
    Cnt.Provider = "Microsoft.Jet.OLEDB.4.0"
    Cnt.Open "Text;FMT=Delimited;HDR=NO;" _
    "DATABASE=O:\ADO Book\DB\chp2;TABLE=Customers.txt"
    MsgBox Cnt.State
End Sub
```

AccessViaJetDbase shows the Jet Engine applied to a dBase DBF data file:

```
Sub AccessViaJetDbase()
    Dim Cnt As New ADODB.Connection
    Cnt.Provider = "Microsoft.Jet.OLEDB.4.0"
    Cnt.Open "dBase 5.0;HDR=NO;DATABASE=O:\ADO Book\DB\chp2;TABLE=CUSTOMER.DBF"
    MsgBox Cnt.State
End Sub
```

The data sources used in JetXLS, AccessViaJetText, and AccessViaJetDbase are flat-file, non-relational sources in which each table is a separate file. In order to fit these into a relation model in which tables reside in a larger structure called a database, the folder in which the file is contained is specified as the database. This is a fiction that allows these flat-file data sources to fit into the ODBC model.

SQL Server

As I cover earlier in the chapter, ADO can use the ODBC drivers to connect to SQL Server databases. However, the preferred method is to directly connect to SQL Server using the OLE DB provider for SQL server.

The OLE DB provider for SQL Server is:

```
SQLOLEDB
```

SQLSrv shows the basic technique for connecting to a SQL Server database. The data source is the name of the SQL Server.

```
Sub SQLSrv()
    Dim Cnt As New ADODB.Connection
    Cnt.Provider = "SQLOLEDB"
    Cnt.Open "Data Source=rkpntsr2;" & _
    "user id=sa;password=dummy"
    MsgBox Cnt.State
End Sub
```

OLE DB is sensitive about the parameter names you use in the connection string. The OLE DB parameter names data source and user id must be written with a space. If you use userid, OLE DB ignores the parameter and tries to login into the SQL Server by using your NT login if it happens that NT Security is enabled on the SQL Server.

You have the option to use ODBC style parameter names with the ADO connection strings. SQLSrv1 uses SERVER in place of *Data Source*, UID for u*ser id*, and PWD for *password*.

```
Sub SQLSrv1()
    Dim Cnt As New ADODB.Connection
    Cnt.Provider = "SQLOLEDB"
    Cnt.Open "SERVER=rkpntsr2;UID=sa;PWD=dummy"
    MsgBox Cnt.State
End Sub
```

By including the Provider parameter, you can pass all of the required information in a single string as shown in SQLSrv2.

```
Sub SQLSrv2()
    Dim Cnt As New ADODB.Connection
    Cnt.Open "PROVIDER=SQLOLEDB;" & _
    "SERVER=rkpntsr2;UID=sa;PWD=dummy"
    MsgBox Cnt.State
End Sub
```

Conversely, the Open method allows you to pass the user and password as separate arguments outside the connection string. In SQLSrv3, the Provider and Connection strings are set with separate statements. Because the connection string does not contain any security information, that data is passed directly to the Open method using the named arguments UserID and Password.

```
Sub SQLSrv3()
    Dim Cnt As New ADODB.Connection
    Cnt.Provider = "SQLOLEDB"
    Cnt.ConnectionString = "Data Source=rkpntsr2;"
    Cnt.Open Userid:="sa", _
        Password:="dummy"
    MsgBox Cnt.State
End Sub
```

Oracle databases

Oracle databases are relational databases that work on a client/server model. From an ADO point of view, they are most similar to the SQL Server as a data source. The OLE DB provider for Oracle is:

```
MSDAORA
```

However, when connecting to an Oracle data source, there is one small quirk. When you connect to a SQL Server, you can include the security information (user name and password) directly inside the connection string as parameters. With an Oracle data source, however, the security information must be passed as separate arguments for the Open method.

Oracle1 shows how you can do this. The Provider property is set to MSDAORA, which is the name of the OLE DB provider for Oracle. The Open statement has three arguments: ConnectionString, Userid, and Password. Oracle requires that you assign specific parameters to the security information.

```
Sub Oracle1()
    Dim Cnt As New ADODB.Connection
    Cnt.Provider = "MSDAORA"
    Cnt.Open ConnectionString:="Data Source=ADODummyORC.world;", _
    Userid:="bruce", Password:="frisky"
    MsgBox Cnt.State
End Sub
```

Oracle2 is a minor variation in which the Provider and ConnectionString properties are assigned first, and then the security information items are the only arguments used in the Open method.

```
Sub Oracle2()
    Dim Cnt As New ADODB.Connection
    Cnt.Provider = "MSDAORA"
    Cnt.ConnectionString = "Data Source=ADODummyORC.world;"
    Cnt.Open Userid:="bruce", Password:="frisky"
    MsgBox Cnt.State
End Sub
```

OLAP services

OLAP stands for online analytical processing. SQL Server 7.0 included an OLAP service, which can be accessed through the OLE DB Provider for Multidimensional Databases included with Office 2000.

An OLAP database doesn't store data in list-style tables that are characteristic of relational databases. Instead, table information is summarized into grids of summary data. For example, you can take a table of orders from a relational database and create an OLAP grid in which each column represented a fiscal period (such as a quarter) and each row a sales region. I cover OLAP data sources in Part V.

OLAP1 shows how you use ADO to make a connection to an OLAP service running on the server RKPNTSR2. The code is identical to what you use to connect to a relational database. Only the provider name, MSOLAP, indicates that it's a non-relational source.

```
Sub OLAP1()
    Dim Cnt As New ADODB.Connection
    Cnt.Provider = "MSOLAP"
    Cnt.ConnectionString = "Data Source=rkpntsr2"
    Cnt.Open
    MsgBox Cnt.State
End Sub
```

Internet services

OLE DB also accesses Internet servers. The OLE DB provider for Internet publishing allows you to interact with the data stored by an Internet server. Note that this isn't the same as the Web service that an Internet server provides. The Internet publishing service allows you to manipulate the files stored by the Internet server. The files that you manipulate may be documents that don't appear through the Web service. Internet publishing is closer to the FTP (file transfer protocol) service that most Web servers use to upload and download files.

The Windows NT server always asks whether you want to install an Internet server as part of its installation. Most network administrators simply click Yes as a matter of habit. This usually means that there are any number of intranet Web servers running on a LAN that most people don't even know are there. For example, suppose you have an NT server call SNIDELY on your LAN. If you open the Internet Explorer and enter `http://snidely`, you may be surprised to see a Web page for Microsoft Internet Information Server.

IIS shows how you can use OLE DB to connect to a computer running an Internet service under the HTTP protocol:

```
Sub IIS()
    Dim Cnt As New ADODB.Connection
    Cnt.Open "Provider=MSDAIPP.DSO;Data Source=http://packbell"
    MsgBox Cnt.State
End Sub
```

You may have noticed that there isn't security information in the preceding example. This is because many Internet servers allow anonymous logins. If the service does not permit anonymous logins, a dialog box appears asking you for the login and password before the connection is made.

If you know the login and password, you can include them in the Open statement into to complete the connection without seeing the Internet server dialog box. IIS1 shows this type of login. In IIS1, an IP address is used in place of the name to identify the Internet server.

```
Sub IIS1()
    Dim Cnt As New ADODB.Connection
    Cnt.Open "Provider=MSDAIPP.DSO;Data Source=http://209.237.129.67" _
    ,"bruce", "#dummy@"
    MsgBox Cnt.State
End Sub
```

Other tasks related to making connections

Before you can build applications that make use of the OLE DB providers, there can be some additional issues to deal with that are related to how to communicate with remote computers and the items installed on the client computers where your application is going to run.

Setting up database clients for remote servers

When you make an ADO connection to an OLE DB provider, the data source is referenced by a name. There are two types of names:

- **File name:** If the data source is a file-based source, such as Access, then the path name of the file is the name of the data source. Any application based on a file data source must be able to reach the drive and folder. On a network, this means that the application user has access to the specified drives and folders with sufficient permissions to interact with the data source file. When connecting to files located on network drives, you may encounter problems if you use mapped drive letters because it is possible that different users have different drive mappings. One common way to standardize drive-letter mapping is to include Net USE statements in the NT Logon script to map standard drives to the same letters each time a user logs onto the network. Another approach is to use the server name, such as \\RKPNTSR2\netSharename, instead of a drive letter to avoid depending on drive mapping.

- **Service name:** Data sources, such as SQL Server or Oracle, also store data in files. SQL Server 7.0 stores data in MDF files. However, applications that work with SQL Sever data do not directly read and write to the database server files. Instead, they communicate with the data source through a network service. The application and the database exchange messages across a network using the name of the database service to locate the server providing the service.

What is a network service? A *network service* is based on the concept of exchanging messages between two computers. One of the computers — the client — sends a message that requests information. The message does not refer to a specific file but instead contains the name of a service. When the computer that is running the named service receives the message, it analyzes the request and returns to the client computer an answer to their request. This is exactly what happens when you send a SQL query to an SQL server. No files or file names are directly involved. Only messages and service names.

Note that I use the term *service* rather than *server.* I am trying to make a technical, but significant, distinction. A computer is considered a server if it supplies a service to other computers on the network. A *server* can run more than one *service.* For example, a Windows 2000 server can be both an Internet Information Server (IIS) and an SQL Server at the same time. It can provide OLAP services, Active Directory, and Exchange services. Of course, this distinction is one that usually isn't of much practical importance, so people use server and service interchangeably.

When you communicate with a machine that offers one or more of these services, you technically communicate with the specific service, not the server itself. On a LAN, the name of the service is usually the same as the name of the computer hosting the service. For example, if the server RKPNTSR2 provides the SQL Server 7.0 database service the name of the service is the same as the computer, RKPNTSR2. On NT networks, these are called the NETBIOS names and NT is responsible for making sure the messages get to the named computer.

However, with the growth of the Internet and the use of large corporate intranet networks, many applications need to connect to services that may not be available though the NT networking and NETBIOS names. To reach these services, you may need to identify the server computers with an IP address. An IP address is an address usually written as four numbers connected with periods, such as 208.222.107.6. On the global Internet, these address are unique; that is, each number identifies one specific computer and no others. If a computer with a unique IP address on the Internet is running a SQL Server or Oracle database service, you can use OLE DB to connect to these services (security permitting) just as you do with data sources on your LAN.

The only difference is that you need to configure a service client on your desktop that matches the IP address of the service that you can use in your connection string. For example, suppose that you want to connect to an SQL Server with an IP address of 208.222.107.6.

1. **Click the Start button and choose Run.**

2. **Type** cliconfg; **then click OK to load the SQL Server Client Network Utility program, as shown in Figure 2-7.**

3. **Click the Add button.**

4. **Type a Server Alias name.**

    This can be any name. It is the name of the service named on the current computer. If you intend to distribute an application, use the same name each time you set up the client on another computer.

5. **Click the TCP/IP button.**

6. **In the Computer Name box, type the IP address of the server.**

    For example: **208.222.107.6**.

    The port number for SQL Server is 1433 by default. You should change this only if the network administrator tells you that the service runs on a different port.

7. **Close the program by clicking OK twice.**

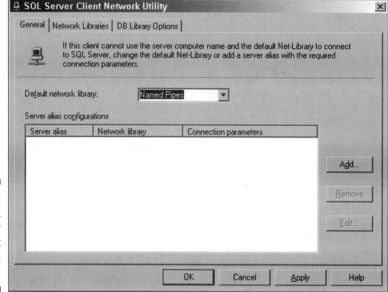

Creating an Oracle client

If you want to access an Oracle database across the Internet, you can follow a similar procedure to create an Oracle client for your desktop. The utility program required for Oracle is supplied with the Oracle for Windows CD, or you can download it from www.oracle.com. This program isn't installed as part of Office 2000 or Windows 2000.

In addition to the IP address of the Oracle server, you need to know the System Identifier (SID) of the Oracle Server.

There are two programs supplied with the Oracle 8 utilities that that you can use to define desktop clients:

- ✓ **Oracle Net8 Easy Configure.** This program begins with a client wizard-style interface that takes you step by step through the process of creating a client.

- ✓ **Oracle Net8 Assistant.** This program is similar to the SQL Server CLI-CONFG program in that it displays a list of existing client definition. You can choose to add, modify, or delete definitions.

I typically use the Net8 Assistant program when I create a new desktop client for an Oracle database. Here's how to use it:

1. **Start Oracle Net8 Easy Configure.**

   Click the Start button and then choose Programs⇨Oracle for Windows
   NT or 95⇨Oracle Net8 Easy Configure.

   The program displays the opening screen, as shown in Figure 2-8. Before
   this screen, you may see a dialog box that warns you about Comment
   Information on your system. If you see this box, click Yes.

2. **Select the Add New Service radio button in the Choose Action panel.**

3. **In the New Service Name box, type the name that you want to use for
   the service and then click Next.**

   For this example, type **ADODummyORC** and then click the Next button.
   Remember that this name only applies to applications running on the
   current desktop.

4. **Select TCP/IP (Internet Protocol); then click Next.**

5. **In the Host Name box, type the name of the computer providing the
   Oracle service and then click Next.**

   This can be a name on a LAN or an IP address. For this example, type
   208.222.107.6.

   The default port for the Oracle service is 1521. Don't change this unless
   the network administrator has instructed you.

6. **In the Database SID box, enter the Oracle System Identifier for the service, and then click Next.**

   For this example, type **ADOData**.

7. **Click Test Service.**

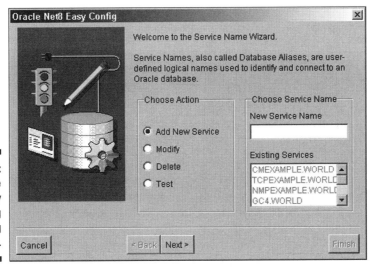

Figure 2-8:
The Oracle
Net8 Easy
Config
opening
screen.

8. **Enter your login and password.**

   For this example, enter **dummy** and **#1234@**, respectively.

   If the setting and the login are valid, you see `The connection test was successful` in the dialog box.

9. **Click Done; click Next; and then click Finish.**

By default, Oracle adds the suffix WORLD to the client name. In this example, the service created is referenced as `ADODUMMYORC.WORLD` in an OLE DB connection string.

References

One of the most advanced features of the Visual Basic languages is that they are extensible. The term *extensible* is one of the hot terms in computer. It refers to a system that is open-ended and can be extended to include new structures that were not part of the original implementation.

In Visual Basic, you have several ways to extend the features available for building applications. One way is installing and using object libraries. Object libraries provide a programming interface to a set of functions installed on a computer or network.

To include the functions supported by the OLE DB providers installed with Office 2000, you need to extend the Visual Basic environment by including the ADODB object library. If you want to perform OLAP operations within a Visual Basic program, you need to reference the objects in the ADOMD library.

There are two steps involved in extending Visual Basic to use additional libraries:

- **Install:** You must install the DLL files onto any desktop that runs an application that uses those objects. All the libraries referenced in this book are installed along with Office 2000.

- **Reference:** You must set a reference to a library before you can use it in the code for your program.

You can manually set which libraries are available to an application using the References dialog box, as shown in Figure 2-9. The dialog box lists all the currently selected object libraries (the checked items), as well as all of the available object libraries.

In Access 2000, you can access this dialog box by opening any code module and choosing Tools⇨References. In Visual Basic, choose Project⇨References.

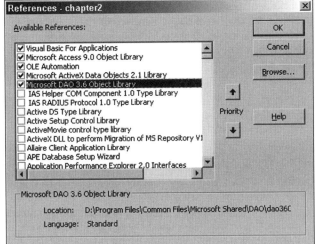

Figure 2-9:
The
References
dialog box in
Access
2000.

Adding a reference in code

Because references are typically set at the time you design your application, you can add or remove references using programming code. In VBA applications, such as Access, the References collection can be modified during program execution.

ListReferences uses a For . . . Each loop to display the name of each of the libraries currently included in the application. Note that the names produced by this code aren't the names you see in the dialog box, such as Visual Basic for Applications, but the short name, such as VBA.

```
Sub ListReferences()
    Dim R As Reference
    For Each R In References
        Debug.Print R.Name
    Next
End Sub
```

To add a reference, use the AddFromFile method of the References collection. The AddFromFile method adds a reference by locating the file (DLL, OCX, OLD, TLB, or EXE) that contains the object library. In this example, the DAO library (usually stored in the path shown below) is added to the module.

```
Sub References1()
    Const Pathname = "C:\Program Files\Common Files\Microsoft Shared\DAO\"
    Const Library = "dao360.dll"
    References.AddFromFile Pathname & Library
End Sub
```

References can be dropped from a module by using the `Remove` method, as shown in `DropReference`. Note that this does not remove the object library from the list or delete any files from the disk. It merely unselects that library from the current application. You can add it back at any time.

```
Sub DropReference()
    References.Remove References("DAO")
End Sub
```

Note: The `References` collection is available only in VBA and not in VB.

Problems with references

After you develop an application, you need to make sure that any references included with that program are also available on any other computers that run that application. If you are distributing an application with a package that you create by using the Access or Visual Basic installation wizard, the reference libraries required for your application are automatically added to the setup package.

However, when you share an application, such as an Access 2000 application, you may find that not all of the users have all the referenced libraries.

When this happens, users encounter problems running the application even if they aren't specifically using the parts of your application that require the library.

For example, suppose that you include in your application a reference to the library for DAO 3.6. However, some of the users that run your program are on desktops that have only DAO 3.5.

If this occurs, you notice the word *MISSING* placed in front of any reference that cannot be found on the local computer. In Access, if any library is missing, it is likely to prevent the application from using any of the libraries even though they are installed on the client computer. This is called a *broken* reference. You can locate any missing references in the references collection by checking the value of the `IsBroken` property.

```
Sub ListBrokenReferences()
    Dim R As Reference
    For Each R In References
        If R.IsBroken Then
            MsgBox R.Name
        End If
    Next
End Sub
```

In Access 2000, if your code contains an object that is part of a missing or unselected library, the quick fill-in lists don't appear in the module window until you resolve the reference.

Part II

The ADO
Data Access
Programming
Model

The 5th Wave — By Rich Tennant

WELL, OBVIOUSLY ONE OF THE CELLS IN THE NAVIGATIONAL SPREADSHEET IS CORRUPT!

In this part . . .

One of the most important aspects of ADO is that it simplifies the complex world of databases by providing a few simple but powerful tools that work with all the data sources to which ADO can connect.

In Part II, I show you what those tools are and how to use them to retrieve, create, update, and delete information stored in any ADO data source.

Chapter 3

Using ADO Recordsets

In This Chapter

▶ Creating recordsets using SQL statements

▶ Creating recordsets using data tables

▶ Editing and updating recordset data

*T*he *recordset* object is the essential structure in ADO database programming. Creating recordsets and using data in them is fundamental to ADO and applications that include interaction with various types of data sources. In this chapter, I show you how to create and use recordsets.

Getting Information with a Recordset

The basic goal of ADO programming is to retrieve recordsets from data sources when that data is needed by an application. A recordset is a table of information. Each column in the table represents a field. Each row in the table represents a record.

Remember, a recordset exists solely in the memory of the computer you're working on. Recordsets are

✔ **Temporary.** Often, they exist only as long as code in the procedure runs. You can keep ADO recordsets alive while an application runs, but when the application stops, recordsets are discarded. If you want a permanent record of the data set information, you must use a technique to save the data in a file or database.

✔ **Invisible.** Recordsets exist in memory only. To display the information in the recordset, you need to place it in a message box, assign its value to a control on a form, or bind the recordset to a data-aware control in a form or a Web page. Sometimes, work goes on behind the scenes (such as validating a zip code) without your having to expose the contents of the recordset in the user interface.

You may need to display some or all of the data to determine whether you're getting the information that you think you need. ADO's programming techniques get tangled with user interface programming techniques for displaying, editing, adding, and deleting data. In this chapter, I use ADO with only the most basic user interface elements and then progress to place ADO within the context of broader operations.

Counting customers

The best way to get a feel for ADO programming is to start with a simple task, such as finding out the exact number of customers that are stored in the *Customers* table in the WINE.MDB file included on the CD. In order to get that answer, you need to know how to use the following:

- ✔ **SQL:** Despite that fact that ADO isn't limited to SQL databases (as was ODBC), SQL remains the dominant tool for making data requests from data sources. Even nonrelational data sources, such as the Microsoft's OLAP cubes, use a variation of SQL syntax. To get a customer count, you must express your request as a SQL statement.

- ✔ **ADO connection:** The SQL statement must be sent to some type of data source, which returns the requested information. To send a SQL statement and receive an answer, you need to establish a connection between your application and the data source.

  Chapter 2 explains how ADO connects to data sources.

- ✔ **Get and use a recordset:** After the request for data (SQL statement) is sent to the data source (via the connection), your application receives a recordset object. This is the container for the information you requested. Displaying the information to the user or any other activity based on the data in the recordset requires manipulating this object.

Although these elements (SQL, connection, and recordset) must be present in the code that retrieves the number of customers, you see that ADO allows you to arrange these elements in different ways. Which approach you take is primarily a matter of preference because you get the same result. To look at it another way, ADO doesn't depend on writing code in a strict sequence. If you prefer, you can get the answer to the question, "How many customers?" with two statements.

Simple SQL

Discussing SQL fully is beyond the scope of this book, but I cover enough SQL to get you started programming data-oriented applications. The most basic set of SQL tools consists of statements that contain these keywords:

✔ SELECT: Specifies what information you want to retrieve. This can be

  - One field

  - Multiple fields

  - A summary calculation, such as SUM( ) or COUNT( )

✔ FROM: Specifies the table or tables from which the data is drawn.

✔ WHERE: Specifies criteria for selecting which table records are included. If you omit it, all records are included.

In this example, the SQL statement to count the number of customers is

```
SELECT Count(*) FROM Customers
```

 I follow a convention of writing SQL keywords in all uppercase characters. This generally isn't required by the data sources. Case-sensitivity may be a factor in some data sources. SQL Server and Oracle can be configured for case-sensitivity so that *Customers* and *customers* are seen as two different table names. The database administrator should know whether the databases are case-sensitive.

A SQL statement doesn't mean much to ADO — it's simply a block of text that ADO needs to transmit to a data provider. You can specify the SQL statement as literal text (enclosed in quotation marks), a text expression, or a variable that contains text. An advantage of treating SQL as text is that you can use all your programming techniques to compose the SQL text. For example, you can store user input in a variable or a control on a form and then use it to fill in parts of a SQL statement.

However, a disadvantage is that ADO doesn't check the SQL statement for errors. You won't know whether the statement is incorrect until the data provider receives and evaluates the request. You probably want to verify complicated SQL statements outside the context of your application to make sure you have the SQL correct.

Executing SQL with ADO

After you compose an SQL query to execute, you're ready to write the ADO code that uses your statement to obtain the number of customers.

You need two objects to obtain the desired data:

✔ **Connection object:** Specifies the data provider, opens a communication channel to the source, and performs an security logon that may be required.

✔ **Recordset object:** Requires at least two properties:

- **Source:** This property is text instruction that passes to the data source. If the data source is a relational database, the source is a SQL statement.

- **Connection:** You can fill in this property by referring to any existing connection object.

These two statements create a new `Connection` and `Recordset` object:

```
Dim Cnt As New ADODB.Connection
Dim Cust As New ADODB.Recordset
```

The next step is to use the connection object to connect to a data source: in this case, the `WINE.MDB` file supplied with this book. The `Open` method of the connection object creates the communication channel with the data source.

```
Cnt.Open "Provider=Microsoft.Jet.OLEDB.4.0;" & _
"data source=C:\ADO Book\db\chp3\wine.mdb;"
```

After the connection is established, the connection object can be used to pass a SQL statement to the provider for execution. The `Open` method of the recordset object contains the SQL statement. In this example, the statement is entered as literal text, enclosed in quotation marks:

```
Cust.Open "SELECT count(*) FROM Customers", Cnt
```

The recordset object, `Cust`, is now a collection of data containing information that the data provider retrieved based on the SQL statement. In this example, the collection consists of a single item. In other cases, the recordset may contain multiple columns and multiple rows of information.

How you deal with the retrieved data depends upon the amount of data returned by the SQL request. This example presents the simplest possible case, which is a SQL statement that returns a single value, meaning that there's only a single column of data. You can refer to a column of data contained in a recordset object four ways:

✔ **Ordinal:** A column's position number is its *ordinal* value. Ordinal is derived from *order* because the columns are assigned column numbers based on their order in the recordset. ADO recordsets use 0, not 1, as the first ordinal. The following statement displays the contents of the first column (column 0) in a message box.

```
MsgBox Cust(0)
```

✔ **Column Name as text:** You can refer to columns by name by using a text string in place of the ordinal number. The following line of code displays the data contained in the `LastName` column of the `Cust` recordset.

```
MsgBox Cust("LastName")
```

But what is the column name when the column is a calculation rather than an existing field in the data table? ADO automatically generates column names for any column that is the result of a calculation or string manipulation. The names begin Expr1000, followed by Expr1001, and so on. Using the current recordset as an example, you write the column name's type reference this way:

```
MsgBox Cust("expr1000")
```

If you aren't sure what name ADO assigned to a calculated column, ask it for the name by using the Name property. The following statement displays Expr1000 in the message box.

```
MsgBox Cust(0).Name
```

✔ **!:** ADO supports a style of column reference that is more compact than using text to specify the column name. You can simply attach the column name to the recordset name by using ! as the connector.

```
MsgBox Cust!expr1000
```

If the column name contains a space, you need to add [ ] if you want to use the ! operator.

```
MsgBox Cust![Last Name]
```

✔ **Fields collection:** This collection contains each of the columns in the retrieved recordset. However, because the Fields collection is the default collection for the recordset object, you never have to include it. However, if you want to use it, do it this way:

```
MsgBox Cust.Fields(0)
MsgBox Cust.Fields("expr1000")
```

The dot operator is one style that isn't supported by ADO. Most SQL databases, such as Access, SQL Server, and Oracle, allow you to use table names as prefixes in SQL statements. The following example shows the dot operator used correctly in a SQL statement.

```
Cust.Open "Select Orders.Count(*) FROM Customers" & _
cnt
```

The following statement isn't valid for an ADO recordset object.

```
Msgbox Cust.LastName
```

CountCustomers1 shows the complete procedure:

```
Sub CountCustomers1()
    Dim Cnt As New ADODB.Connection
    Dim Cust As New ADODB.Recordset
    Cnt.Open "Provider=Microsoft.Jet.OLEDB.4.0;" & _
    "data source=C:\ADO Book\db\chp3\wine.mdb;"
    Cust.Open "SELECT count(*) FROM Customers", Cnt
    MsgBox Cust(0)
End Sub
```

Defining column names in SQL

You can assign aliases to any column included in a SQL recordset by using the `As` operator in the selection list. An *alias* is a temporary name that's assigned to an existing field or a calculated field in a recordset. In the following example, I assign the name `CustCount` to the calculated customer total column.

```
SELECT count(*) As CustCount FROM Customers
```

`CountCustomers2` uses an `As` clause to assign the name `CustCount` to the recordset field. Using an alias eliminates the generic field names. An example is Expr1000, from the ADO recordset.

```
Sub CountCustomers2()
    Dim Cnt As New ADODB.Connection
    Dim Cust As New ADODB.Recordset
    Cnt.Open "Provider=Microsoft.Jet.OLEDB.4.0;" & _
    "data source=C:\ADO Book\db\chp3\wine.mdb;"
    Cust.Open _"SELECT count(*) As CustCount FROM Customers", Cnt
    MsgBox Cust!CustCount
End Sub
```

Different providers recognize additional or alternative methods of assigning a field alias:

✔ SQL Server, which supports the `As` operator, also allows you to use an assignment-style reference to assign a name to a column, like this:

```
SELECT CustCount=count(*) FROM Customers
```

✔ Oracle doesn't use `As` or `=`. Instead, the alias name follows the field name or calculation with a space separating the alias from the field. For example, if the provider is an Oracle database, the statement looks like this:

```
SELECT count(*) CustCount FROM Customers
```

Records without separate connections

The `CountCustomers1` procedure uses separate connection and recordset objects in order to extract the requested data from the data source. The advantage of this approach is that you can create multiple recordset objects from a single connection, something you use later in this chapter.

ADO is flexible. If you work with a single recordset, you can eliminate the separate connection object and create the recordset with a single statement that contains both the recordset and the connection information.

The format for opening a recordset with a single statement is shown below in which both the SQL statement text and the connection string text are included in a single statement.

```
Recordsetobject.Open SqlText,ConnectionText
```

`CountCustomers3` creates only a single object — a recordset named `Cust`. The connection string information is included as the `Connection` argument of the `Open` method.

```
Sub CountCustomers3()
    Dim Cust As New ADODB.Recordset
    Cust.Open "SELECT count(*) FROM Customers", _
    "Provider=Microsoft.Jet.OLEDB.4.0;" & _
    "data source=C:\ADO Book\db\chp3\wine.mdb;"
    MsgBox Cust(0)
End Sub
```

The result is identical to the `CountCustomers1` although the connection wasn't created prior to the opening of the recordset. The reasoning behind this feature is that ADO programming should be as free as possible from sequencing issues. You don't have to remember to create a connection before you open a recordset. ADO allows you to generate the required connection at the same time that you request a recordset.

If you intend to open two or more recordsets from the same source, you get better performance and better use of system resources by creating a separate connection object and having all the recordsets share that connection than by having each recordset create its own connection.

The point is that you have the option to use whatever method makes the most sense within the application that you're building. This provides ADO with more consistent object interfaces because operations are less dependent on your following specific steps.

Deciding not to use Option Explicit

In VBA and VB, you're not required to `Dim` each variable or object unless the statement `Option Explicit` appears at the beginning (the declarations section) of the module.

Not using `Option Explicit` enables you to create objects and variables implicitly at any point in the procedure. `CountCustomers4` shows the `New` keyword with the `Set` statement to create a recordset object, `Cust`, without using the `Dim` statement.

```
Sub CountCustomers4()
    Set Cust = New ADODB.Recordset
    Cust.Open "SELECT count(*) FROM Customers", _
    "Provider=Microsoft.Jet.OLEDB.4.0;" & _
    "data source=C:\ADO Book\db\chp3\wine.mdb;"
    MsgBox Cust(0)
End Sub
```

Using `Option Explicit` is usually a good idea. It avoids errors and name conflicts by forcing the programmer to `Dim` each user-defined variable or object name before the variable or object can be used in any program statements. If you spell an object name incorrectly (that is, differently from the Dim statement spelling), VB/VBA flags the error before the program runs or compiles.

VB and VBA support explicit naming. I use explicit naming in this book wherever it's supported. However, you may see examples in other books or articles that create objects by using the implicit syntax shown in CountCustomers4.

Using late binding to create recordsets

Late binding is another way to create ADO recordsets. This approach is called *late* binding in contrast to the methods shown already, which are referred to as *early* binding.

In the following line of code, early binding defines the object type so that VBA or VB knows at the time that the code is compiled what type of object it's going to be:

```
Dim Cust As New ADODB.Recordset
```

However, it's possible to use objects that are bound to the supporting ActiveX object types only when the program is executed. This is called late binding because the object and its ActiveX library come together only after the program is executed.

To create a late-binding object in VBA or VB, use the generic object type called (logically enough) Object. Then use the CreateObject( ) function to connect the generic object to a specific object type. CountCustomers5 provides an example of late binding. The Cust object is defined as a recordset.

```
Sub CountCustomers5()
    Dim Cust As Object
    Set Cust = CreateObject("ADODB.Recordset")
    Cust.Open "SELECT count(*) FROM Customers", _
    "Provider=Microsoft.Jet.OLEDB.4.0;" & _
    "data source=C:\ADO Book\db\chp3\wine.mdb;"
    MsgBox Cust(0)
End Sub
```

Note that the object type, "ADODB.Recordset", is simply a text string that contains a name. If the name matches the name of an object installed on the current computer, that object is bound to the object variable when the program executes.

In general, early binding is preferred and yields the best performance. On the other hand, when you use ADO code in a Web-based Active Server Page (ASP), early binding isn't available, so late binding is required. In VB or VBA, you have the option to use early or late binding. If you want to copy and paste code between VBA/VB and ASP, I suggest that you use late binding because it's the lowest common denominator.

Some tricks exist in using late binding that you can't perform when objects are bound early. In `CountCustomers6`, the actual object type isn't included anywhere in the code. Instead, an `InputBox( )` statement provides an opportunity for the user to enter the object type as a text entry in an input dialog box. If the user enters `adodb.recordset`, the program correctly binds to the ADO library and produces the customer count. An invalid entry causes an error when the program attempts to bind the object.

```
Sub CountCustomers6()
    Dim Cust As Object, ObjectName
    ObjectName = InputBox("Enter the Object Type:")
    Set Cust = CreateObject(ObjectName)
    Cust.Open "SELECT count(*) FROM Customers", _
    "Provider=Microsoft.Jet.OLEDB.4.0;" & _
    "data source=C:\ADO Book\db\chp3\wine.mdb;"
    MsgBox Cust(0)
End Sub
```

Using recordsets that contain more than one record

SQL queries can return recordsets that contain many records. When that happens, any application working with the data contained in a multiple-row recordset needs to navigate the complete set of data.

When you open an ADO recordset, the first record in the set is immediately available to the application. The available record is called the *current record*. To access any additional records, you need to employ two ADO features:

✔ **MoveNext:** This makes the next record (if any) in the recordset the current record.

✔ **Eof:** The Eof (End of file) provides a means of determining when you have reached end of the records.

  This property is false in all cases except:

  • If the recordset is empty, no records are returned, or

  • The application attempts to read a record after the last record in the recordset has been returned.

Use these features in a loop structure like the one below. In this structure, the first statement checks to see whether the recordset is at the end. The loop then moves to the next record in the set and repeats the action until all the records are processed.

```
Do Until recordset.EOF
   ' Do something with the records
   recordset.MoveNext
Loop
```

CountCustomersByState1 shows multiple rows processed by a loop:

```
Sub CountCustomersByState1()
    Dim Cust As New ADODB.Recordset
    Dim strConnect, strSQL
    strConnect = "Provider=Microsoft.Jet.OLEDB.4.0;" & _
    "data source=C:\ADO Book\db\chp3\wine.mdb;"
    strSQL = "SELECT BillState,Count(*) " & _
    "FROM Customers GROUP BY BillState"
    Cust.Open strSQL, strConnect
    Do Until Cust.EOF
        Debug.Print Cust(0), Cust(1)
        Cust.MoveNext
    Loop
End Sub
```

The data retrieved from the data source is displayed in the Immediate (debug) window using the Debug.Print method. In Access, you can display the Immediate window by pressing Ctrl+G; in Visual Basic, select View⇨Immediate. The output looks like this:

```
Null          175
AK            9
AL            6
AR            5
AZ            28
CA            2067 ...
```

Opening entire tables

In some situations, you want to create a recordset that contains the contents of an entire table without selecting any rows or columns. AllCustomers uses the SQL statement SELECT * FROM Customers to select all the fields and records from the Customer table. In SQL, the * is a wildcard that selects all fields. When you execute AllCustomers, a long list of names (more than 4,000) appears in the Immediate window. Press Ctrl+Break if you don't want to wait for all the names to scroll past.

```
Sub AllCustomers()
    Dim Cnt As New ADODB.Connection
    Dim Cust As New ADODB.Recordset
    Cnt.Open "Provider=Microsoft.Jet.OLEDB.4.0;" & _
    "data source=C:\ADO Book\db\chp3\wine.mdb;"
    Cust.Open "SELECT * FROM Customers", Cnt
    Do Until Cust.EOF
        Debug.Print Cust!LastName & "," & Cust!firstname
        Cust.MoveNext
    Loop
End Sub
```

ADO also lets you open a table by name. To do this, use adCmdTable as the option argument of the Open recordset method. CustomersTable is identical to AllCustomers with two exceptions. First, instead of using a SQL statement as the source argument of the Open recordset method, only the name of the table is used: for example, Customers. Second, an Options argument, adCmdTable, is added to the Open method indicating that the source isn't a SQL statement but a table name. CustomersTable produces the same result as AllCustomers.

```
Sub CustomersTable()
    Dim Cnt As New ADODB.Connection
    Dim Cust As New ADODB.Recordset
    Cnt.Open "Provider=Microsoft.Jet.OLEDB.4.0;" & _
    "data source=C:\ADO Book\db\chp3\wine.mdb;"
    Cust.Open "Customers", Cnt, Options:=adCmdTable
    Do Until Cust.EOF
        Debug.Print Cust!LastName & "," & Cust!firstname
        Cust.MoveNext
    Loop
End Sub
```

ADO automatically figures out that the source is a table name rather than a full SQL statement and executes the operation even if you didn't explicitly call for the adCmdTable option. Statements (1) through (4) in the following example produce the same result if you use them in the CustomersTable procedure.

```
(1)    Cust.Open "Customers", Cnt,,,adCmdTable
(2)    Cust.Open "Customers", Cnt, Options:=adCmdTable
(3)    Cust.Open "SELECT * FROM Customers", Cnt
(4)    Cust.Open "Customers", Cnt
```

Enumeration of constants and named arguments

You may easily overlook some programming issues. In the CustomersTable procedure, the Options argument is written as a named argument:

```
Options:=adCmdTable
```

That's because Options is the fifth argument of the Open method. The CursorType and LockType arguments precede the Options:

```
RecordsetObject.Open Source(1), Connection(2), CursorType(3), LockType(4),
            Options(5)
```

To include an Option without filling in the CursorType and LockType arguments, you can use either of the following statements:

```
(1)    Cust.Open "Customers", Cnt,,,adCmdTable
(2)    Cust.Open "Customers", Cnt, Options:=adCmdTable
```

Statement (1) in the preceding example looks awkward because of its string of commas. What happens if you make a mistake and use two commas instead of three?

```
Sub CustomersTable1()
    Statements...
    Cust.Open "Customers", Cnt, , adCmdTable
    Statements...
End Sub
```

What happens when you execute `CustomersTable1`? Surprise! No errors! Why not? It's by sheer dumb luck that the missing comma didn't create a problem.

To understand what's going on here, look carefully at what `adCmdTable` is and how it functions in ADO. Many methods supported by the ADO model use numeric values as arguments (see Table 3-1). These constants become available to VBA/VB when you include the object library (such as ADODB) in the current project.

You can look up information about ADO-supported objects, methods, properties, and constants or any other object library by using the Object Browser. In any VBA or VB code module, press F2. In the first combo box, select the library (such as ADODB) that you want to browse. In any library, the `<globals>` object lists all constants supported by that library.

Table 3-1	Open Method Options	
Constant	**Value**	**Description**
adCmdText	1	SQL text
adCmdTable	2	Table
adCmdStoredProc	4	Stored procedure
adCmdUnknown	8	Type not known

You may wonder why the constant values are 1, 2, 4, and 8 rather than 0, 1, 2, and 3. The numbers used are 1, 2, 3, and so on, except that the numbers are applied as exponents 2, such as $2^0 = 1$, $2^1 = 2$, $2^2 = 4$, and $2^3 = 8$. This allows an argument to include two or more values at the same time, such as `Options:=adCmdText(1) + adCmdtable (2)` for a total of 3. This may seem weird until you consider how these numbers look when they're translated to binary. When you add 0001(1) and 0010(2), you get 0011. Each constant that you add changes one of the 0s (zero) to a 1 (one). You can judge by the place value which set of options is specified; for example, 0101 means 4(adCmdStoredProc) + 1(adCmdText). If arguments shouldn't be added, they start at 0 and increment from 1, 2, 3, and so on.

Table 3-1 shows that `adCmdTable` is a constant with a real value is 2. You can replace `adCmdTable` with the numeral 2 and get the same result.

```
(1)   Cust.Open "Customers", Cnt,,,2
(2)   Cust.Open "Customers", Cnt, Options:=2
```

In fact, when you're programming ADO in an ASP, you need to use the actual numeric values because the constants aren't available.

What about the dumb luck? The luck is that if you omit a comma, as shown below, the constant value of 2 is assigned to a different argument: in this case, the `LockType` argument. As it turns out, a `LockType` value of 2 has no adverse effect within this particular procedure because `LockType` is meaningful only when a recordset is being changed.

```
Cust.Open "Customers", Cnt,,2
```

You can see that by using named arguments, especially when you aren't filling in all the arguments consecutively, you can avoid a lot of confusion. A mistake, such as dropping a comma, may end up having a negative effect on a procedure (one that included recordset changes) but may also be hard to locate because the statement looks at first glance as if the `LockType` argument hasn't been changed from the default. In fact, it's set at 2, `adLockPessimistic`. I cover `adLockPessimistic` later in this chapter.

```
Cust.Open "Customers", Cnt,,adCmdTable
```

Recordcounts and cursor types

When you open a recordset, you may find it useful to know the number of records it contains. ADO (like its predecessor DAO) includes a recordset property, `RecordCount`, which returns the number of records included in a recordset.

`RecCounter1` opens a recordset that includes all the records in the `Customers` table. The `RecordCount` property displays the total number of records in the recordset.

```
Sub RecCounter1()
    Dim Cust As New ADODB.Recordset
    Cust.Open _
        "SELECT * FROM Customers", _
        "Provider=Microsoft.Jet.OLEDB.4.0;" & _
        "data source=C:\ADO Book\db\chp3\wine.mdb;"
    Debug.Print Cust.RecordCount
End Sub
```

If you execute `RecCounter1`, you may be surprised to see the value returned by the `RecordCount` property is –1. In effect, –1 tells you that the recordset you opened doesn't actually support this property. Is there any way to get an accurate recordcount from a recordset?

The answer relates to another recordset property called `CursorType`. To understand cursor types, you have to step back and consider the role of cursors in databases. The word *cursor* is derived from the Latin word for movement. A SQL database responds to a `SELECT` statement by returning a set of rows, which meet the criteria in the `SELECT` statement. However, applications generally don't process the entire recordset at once. Instead, they work with the results one row at a time.

Cursors are the mechanisms that you use to manage the movement of an application through the rows of a recordset. Because different types of operations require different levels of computing resources, data sources can supply different types of cursors. ADO supports four different types of cursors: adOpenForwardOnly, adOpenKeyset, adOpenDynamic, and adOpenStatic. The default cursor type is adOpenForwardOnly. Because you haven't specified the cursor type in the previous examples, the recordsets have been adOpenForwardOnly cursor types.

Cursor types differ with regard to:

- **Navigation:** Movement within a recordset is limited to these two options:

    - adOpenForwardOnly: You can move forward one row at a time.

    - adOpenKeyset, adOpenDynamic, and adOpenStatic: You can move anywhere within the recordset.

- **Additions, changes, and deletions:** Three key characteristics relate to the following questions. First, can you make additions, changes, and deletions in the recordset? Second, are the additions, changes, or deletions that you make visible to other users? Third, are the additions, changes, or deletions that other users make visible to you?

    - adOpenForwardOnly and adOpenStatic: These cursor types don't allow changes, additions, or deletions. They represent a snapshot of the data when the recordset is created. Changes that other users make to the data source aren't reflected in these cursor types. A Static recordset is more flexible than a ForwardOnly because it allows movement in any direction.

    - adOpenKeyset: Keysets allow movement in all directions, and the recordset can be changed. A keyset recordset identifies the data source records that are included in your record set. This means that any updates you or others make become visible to everyone. If other users delete or add records, they're not available to the recordset.

    - adOpenDynamic: A dynamic recordset allows all movements; additions, changes, and deletions by others are visible in your recordset.

The adOpenKeyset cursor type requires that the recordset being created has a unique key value for every record in the recordset. In most SQL data sources, this means that the tables must contain a primary key. A *primary key* is a column or set of columns that always contains a unique value. When an adOpenKeyset recordset is built, it actually consists of the primary keys for the records included the in the recordset. Each record accessed in an adOpenKeyset shows the latest changes because the data isn't retrieved until you make the record the current record.

You can discover some practical characteristics by performing experiments. To identify the name that's linked to a particular argument, I include a function `CursorTypeName`, which is used in the following procedures. The function returns a text name for any numeric value.

```
Function CursorTypeName(v)
   Select Case v
      Case adOpenForwardOnly
         CursorTypeName = "adOpenForwardOnly"
      Case adOpenKeyset
         CursorTypeName = "adOpenKeyset"
      Case adOpenDynamic
         CursorTypeName = "adOpenDynamic"
      Case adOpenStatic
         CursorTypeName = "adOpenStatic"
   End Select
End Function
```

`CType1` uses a `For . . . Next` loop structure to repeat the process of opening a recordset and displaying the `RecordCount` property four times. Each time, the `CursorType` property is given a different value, and the results are printed to the Immediate window.

```
Sub CType1()
   Dim CType
   Dim Cnt As New ADODB.Connection
   Dim Cust As New ADODB.Recordset
   For CType = 0 To 3
      Cnt.Open "Provider=Microsoft.Jet.OLEDB.4.0;" & _
      "data source=C:\ADO Book\db\chp3\wine.mdb;"
      Cust.CursorType = CType
      Cust.Open _"SELECT * FROM Customers", Cnt
      Debug.Print CursorTypeName(Cust.CursorType), Cust.RecordCount
      Cust.Close
      Cnt.Close
   Next
End Sub
```

The following code shows the results. You can see that one of the differences between cursor types is that some return a valid recordcount while others don't.

```
adOpenForwardOnly  -1
adOpenKeyset       4143
adOpenStatic       -1
adOpenStatic       4143
```

When you ran `CType1`, some of the lines appeared faster than others. You can see how long it takes to perform each of the `Open` methods using a different cursor type:

1. **Use a variable to store the current time (the `Now( )` function) at the start of each operation.**

2. **Calculate the elapsed time (`StartTime - Now( )`).**

CType2 adds this timing mechanism to the procedure. CType1 (on the CD at the back of this book) executes the same procedure against my SQL Server.

```
Sub CType2()
    Dim ETime, CType
    Dim Cnt As New ADODB.Connection
    Dim Cust As New ADODB.Recordset
    For CType = 0 To 3
        ETime = Now
        Cnt.Open "Provider=Microsoft.Jet.OLEDB.4.0;" & _
        "data source=C:\ADO Book\db\chp3\wine.mdb;"
        Cust.CursorType = CType
        Cust.Open _
        "SELECT * FROM Customers", Cnt
        Debug.Print CursorTypeName(Cust.CursorType), Cust.RecordCount, Format(Now _
            - ETime, "ss")
        Cust.Close
        Cnt.Close
    Next
End Sub
```

Although your exact output may vary, the pattern should be similar to the code that follows. The adOpenForwardOnly and adOpenDynamic cursors are the fastest to open, but they don't provide an accurate recordcount. Conversely, the slowest cursor is the adOpenKeyset, preceded slightly by the adOpenStatic cursor. These slower opening recordsets do provide an accurate recordcount.

```
adOpenForwardOnly      -1        01
adOpenKeyset          4143       07
adOpenDynamic          -1        01
adOpenStatic          4143       06
```

You can see that to get an accurate recordcount, you have to wait a few seconds for the data source to analyze the data. If you want to get to the data as quickly as possible, you have to trade off some features.

Of course, there are lots of ways to skin a cat. If all you want is the recordcount, there are other ways to get it than changing the cursor type. Ctype3 uses the default cursor type, adOpenForwardOnly, to open two recordsets:

✔ A recordset that opens the Customers table

✔ A recordset that calculates the number of records in the table

The result is that you get the recordcount and the table without using a slower opening cursor type.

```
Sub Ctype3()
    Dim Cnt As New Connection
    Dim Cust As New Recordset
    Dim CustCounter As New ADODB.Recordset
    Cnt.Provider = "SQLOLEDB"
    ETime = Now
    Cnt.Open "Provider=Microsoft.Jet.OLEDB.4.0;" & _
    "data source=C:\ADO Book\db\chp3\wine.mdb;"
```

```
    Cust.Open _
    "SELECT * FROM Customers", Cnt
    CustCounter.Open _
    "SELECT count(*) FROM Customers", Cnt
    Debug.Print CursorTypeName(Cust.CursorType), CustCounter(0), Format(Now -
            ETime, "ss")
    Cust.Close
    Cnt.Close
End Sub
```

Cursor types affect more than the Recordcount property. They also control your ability to modify the data included in a recordset.

Modifying data using Lock Type

As you can see from the discussion of cursor types, ADO requires you to select certain options to obtain an editable recordset. If you want to edit, add, or delete records, you must select either an adOpenKeyset or an adOpenDynamic cursor type.

Selecting a cursor type isn't the only requirement. The Open method (of the Recordset object) also supports an argument called Lock Type. See Table 3-2 to find out the Lock Type options. By default, the lock type of a recordset is adLockReadOnly. Recordsets with this lock type can't be edited, regardless of the cursor type. If you want to edit a recordset, you must specify one of the three other supported Lock Types listed in Table 3-2.

Table 3-2	Lock Types	
Constant	*Value*	*Description*
adLockReadOnly	1	Read-only (default)
adLockPessimistic	2	Pessimistic locking
adLockOptimistic	3	Optimistic locking
adLockBatchOptimistic	4	Optimistic batch updates

What's locking, and which option should you choose? Locking techniques relate to the fact that databases, unlike most applications, allow multiple users to access the same information at the same time. When the access is restricted to read-only, multiple users aren't an issue.

On the other hand, if one or more users want to edit the data, you need a mechanism to control saving changes when multiple users can change the same record simultaneously. The database must follow rules to determine which changes end up as the permanent data entry for that record.

Locks temporarily restrict access to a record. When you apply a lock to a record, only one user has access to the data. Any other users who want access must wait until the lock is removed.

The terms pessimistic and optimistic describe the two basic types of locking strategy. An *optimistic* locking strategy minimizes the amount of time that a lock must be applied to a record. Optimistic locking doesn't take place when a user edits the contents of a record. Instead, multiple users can access and edit the data. A lock is placed on the record as soon as one of the users executes an update, which permanently stores the data in the data source.

Conversely, *pessimistic* locking places a lock on a record as soon as the first user opens the record for editing. The lock stays in place until the user who obtained the lock stops using the record. Although the pessimistic lock is in place, no other users can edit, or in the case of some providers, see the data, until the initial user finishes with the record. This can delay other users who may be editing recordsets that contain one or more records already locked by other users.

A third approach to locking reduces the amount of time required for record locking by performing multiple record updates as a batch. The `adLockBatchOptimistic` doesn't immediately write updated records to the data source. Rather, changes made to a set of records are held in the client computer until you either send all of the updates as a batch or cancel all of the changes as a batch.

Batch updates can be used only with `adOpenKeyset` cursor types.

The most common approach is to use optimistic locking for situations in which users are unlikely to contend for the same data. For example, if you perform service tasks, it's likely that each customer service user deals with a problem from a different customer rather than having multiple users working on the same customer. Optimistic locking works fine for customer service. But if you book seats on an airplane, customers contend for space on that flight. You want to use pessimistic locking to ensure that after you edit a record, no other users can edit that same record.

Simple updates

The most common way to modify the contents of a record is to open the recordset using these arguments:

- ✔ `CursorType = adOpenKeyset`
- ✔ `LockType = adLockOptimistic`

You can use these arguments to change the value of any field with an assignment statement. The general form of an assignment statement specifies the name of the field in the recordset you want to change and sets it equal to some expression.

```
Recordset(FieldName) = expression
```

In Edit1, the recordset contains the information for a customer named
Krumm. The Cust.Open statement specifies the cursortype and locktype that
permit modification of the recordset.

```
Sub Edit1()
    Dim Cnt As New Connection
    Dim Cust As New Recordset
    Cnt.Open "Provider=Microsoft.Jet.OLEDB.4.0;" & _
    "data source=C:\ADO Book\db\chp3\wine.mdb;"
    Cust.Open _
    "SELECT * FROM Customers WHERE LastName = 'Krumm'", _
    Cnt, adOpenKeyset, adLockOptimistic
    Debug.Print "Start:", Cust("LastName") & ", " & Cust("FirstName")
    Cust("FirstName") = "Rob" 'Changes First Name
    Debug.Print "End:", Cust("LastName") & ", " & Cust("FirstName")
End Sub
```

The Immediate window displays the change from Kent to Rob.

```
Start:          Krumm, Kent
End:            Krumm, Rob
```

Recordset updates

To make sure that the change was actually stored in the data source, you can
run the CheckEdit procedure to retrieve the current information for Krumm.

```
Sub CheckEdit()
    Dim Cnt As New Connection
    Dim Cust As New Recordset
    Cnt.Open "Provider=Microsoft.Jet.OLEDB.4.0;" & _
    "data source=C:\ADO Book\db\chp3\wine.mdb;"
    Cust.Open _
    "SELECT * FROM Customers WHERE LastName = 'Krumm'", _
    Cnt
    Debug.Print "Current:", Cust("LastName") & ", " & Cust("FirstName")
End Sub
```

The result indicates that the editing change made in Edit1 wasn't permanently saved in the data source.

```
Current:        Krumm, Kent
```

Both Edit1 and CheckEdit use the same statements to display the contents
of the FirstName field, yet they yield inconsistent results. Why? When you
edit data contained in a recordset, you change the copy of the data that ADO
retrieves from the data source. Any changes you make are temporary and
exist only within the memory of you computer. They're automatically discarded when you close the record of end the procedure.

If you want those changes to become a permanent part of the data source's database, you must have ADO perform an update. You can do this by using the recordset `Update` method. `Edit2` adds an additional statement, `Cust.Update`, that sends the edited data back to the data source for permanent storage.

```
Sub Edit2()
    Dim Cnt As New Connection
    Dim Cust As New Recordset
    Cnt.Open "Provider=Microsoft.Jet.OLEDB.4.0;" & _
    "data source=C:\ADO Book\db\chp3\wine.mdb;"
    Cust.Open _
    "SELECT * FROM Customers WHERE LastName = 'Krumm'", _
    Cnt, adOpenKeyset, adLockOptimistic
    Cust("FirstName") = "Rob" 'Changes First Name
    Cust.Update 'saves changes to data source
End Sub
```

If you run `CheckEdit` again, you find that the first name has been permanently changed to Rob.

Keep in mind that an update saves all the changes made to a record prior to the `Update` statement. `MultiEdit1` shows a series of changes to different fields of billing address information. All the changes made to the record are saved when the `Update` method is executed.

```
Sub MultiEdit1()
    Dim Cnt As New Connection
    Dim Cust As New Recordset
    Cnt.Open "Provider=Microsoft.Jet.OLEDB.4.0;" & _
    "data source=C:\ADO Book\db\chp3\wine.mdb;"
    Cust.Open _
    "SELECT * FROM Customers WHERE LastName = 'Krumm'", _
    Cnt, adOpenKeyset, adLockOptimistic
    Cust("BillAddress1") = "1234 Evergreen Terrace"
    Cust("Billaddress2") = Null
    Cust("BillCity") = "Springfield"
    Cust("BillState") = "CA"
    Cust.Update
End Sub
```

Direct updates

Using assignment statements to modify the contents of a field is the most common form of update, but it's not the only method of updating ADO supports. An alternative technique is to specify the change as arguments of the Update method. The following statement changes the `FirstName` to `Bruce` directly with the `Update` method.

```
Cust.Update "FirstName", "Bruce"
```

Update1 is similar to Edit1, except that no assignment statement is needed to change the value of FirstName because the change is specified directly in the Update method. In Update1, you don't need to remember to add a separate Update statement to save the changes.

```
Sub Update1()
    Dim Cnt As New Connection
    Dim Cust As New Recordset
    Cnt.Open "Provider=Microsoft.Jet.OLEDB.4.0;" & _
    "data source=C:\ADO Book\db\chp3\wine.mdb;"
    Cust.Open _
    "SELECT * FROM Customers WHERE LastName = 'Krumm'", _
    Cnt, adOpenKeyset, adLockOptimistic
    Cust.Update "FirstName", "Bruce"
End Sub
```

You can also use direct updating to modify more than one field by listing a series of updates — one for each change that you want to make. MultiUpdate1 contains a series of changes to the billing address information made with direct updates.

```
Sub MultiUpdate1()
    Dim Cnt As New Connection
    Dim Cust As New Recordset
    Cnt.Open "Provider=Microsoft.Jet.OLEDB.4.0;" & _
    "data source=C:\ADO Book\db\chp3\wine.mdb;"
    Cust.Open _
    "SELECT * FROM Customers WHERE LastName = 'Krumm'", _
    Cnt, adOpenKeyset, adLockOptimistic
    Cust.Update "BillAddress1", "4830 Milano Way"
    Cust.Update "Billaddress2", Null
    Cust.Update "BillCity", "Martinez"
    Cust.Update "BillState", "CA"
End Sub
```

Although the results of MultiEdit1 and MultiUpdate1 are the same (changes made to the billing address), you get the results in different ways. In MultiEdit1, you save changes by a single Update method. If an error halts the procedure before the Update was issued, none of the changes are saved.

In contrast, each of the fields changed in MultiUpdate1 is saved as the change is made. If an error halts execution of MultiUpdate1 before all the updates are made, those updates made before the error are permanent.

In using these various methods, you need to consider whether partial updates create a problem. Using a single Update to store all of the changes ensures that the edits are saved or discarded as a group. Direct updating treats each field change as a separate operation so that it's possible to have a record in which some fields have been correctly updated but others haven't.

Keep in mind that this discussion refers to updates of a single record. In Chapter 4, I talk about updates that are applied to recordsets containing two or more records.

Updates stored in arrays

You can use the `Update` method to perform multiple updates in another way, by using data stored in arrays as the basis for updating the recordset. You do this by creating two arrays of equal size. The first contains the names of the fields that you want to update. The second lists the values that you want to assign to the fields. You can then pass these arrays to the data source by using the `Update` method.

```
Cust.Update FieldNameArray, FieldValueArray
```

`MultiUpdate2` shows the array method of updating values. Two arrays, `Columns` and `Changes`, are defined and populated. They are then passed to the data source as arguments of the `Update` method. Notice that you need to insure that the sequence of values in one array matches the sequence of field names in the other array. Also, the value for column 2, `Billaddress2`, is missing in the `Changes` array. Because an empty row has a `Null` value, leaving the row out of the `Changes` array assigns a null value to the field.

```
Sub MultiUpdate2()
    Dim Cnt As New Connection
    Dim Cust As New Recordset
    Cnt.Open "Provider=Microsoft.Jet.OLEDB.4.0;" & _
    "data source=C:\ADO Book\db\chp3\wine.mdb;"
    Cust.Open _
    "SELECT * FROM Customers WHERE LastName = 'Krumm'", _
    Cnt, adOpenKeyset, adLockOptimistic
    Dim Columns(4)
    Dim Changes(4)
    Columns(1) = "BillAddress1"
    Columns(2) = "Billaddress2"
    Columns(3) = "BillCity"
    Columns(4) = "BillState"
    Changes(1) = "4830 Milano Way"
    Changes(3) = "Martinez"
    Changes(4) = "CA"
    Cust.Update Columns, Changes
End Sub
```

The array approach is useful in situations when you want to acquire information from a source, such as an Excel spreadsheet or a text file, in which the data isn't organized as a database record.

The array technique updates the record with all the changes in a single batch.

In `MultiUpdate2`, the arrays number their rows start at 1 rather than 0. Traditionally, arrays are zero-based in VB/VBA. This means that when you dimension an array, the first row is 0, such as `Columns(0)`. If you prefer that your arrays start at 1 rather than 0, add the statement `Option Base 1` to the declarations section of the module.

Using one recordset to update another

The purpose of the code shown in this chapter so far has been to illustrate as simply as possible the features of ADO. I end this chapter by putting the techniques together into a simple, but practical example.

You may notice that in the previous section that the zip code isn't included in the billing address information. Table ZIP_USA, which contains the zip codes, city, and state names, is included in the sample data in the wine.mdb database. Because you already know the city and state (for example, Martinez and CA), you can use an ADO recordset to obtain the zip code. Of course, this approach works only for those cities that have a single zip code. You need more data techniques when searching for a multiple zip code.

The following code defines a VB/VBA function that can provide the zip code (or the first of several zip codes) for any city and state you specify:

```
Function Zip(CityName, StateName)
    Dim ZipCodes As New Recordset
    ZipCodes.Open _
    "SELECT Zip FROM ZIP_USA WHERE PO_NAME = '" & _
    CityName & "' AND State ='" & StateName & "'", _
    "Provider=Microsoft.Jet.OLEDB.4.0;" & _
    "data source=C:\ADO Book\db\chp3\wine.mdb;"
    Zip = ZipCodes(0)
End Function
```

The function employs a technique that I call *composing* SQL statements. For example, the SQL statement that retrieves the zip code for Martinez, CA is

```
SELECT Zip FROM ZIP_USA
WHERE PO_NAME = "Martinez" AND State = "CA"
```

In ADO, the SQL statement that you send to the ADO data provider must be a text block. However, because the SQL statement contains quotation marks, you need to alter the statement by converting the quotation marks around Martinez and CA to apostrophes. The following statement shows how you send the above SQL statement to an ADO provider:

```
ZipCodes.Open _
"SELECT Zip FROM ZIP_USA " & _
"WHERE PO_NAME = 'Martinez' AND State = 'CA'"
```

However, in the Zip function, the actual name of the city and state changes each time that the function is used. You can modify the expression by substituting the variables CityName and StateName in place of Martinez and CA. The result is an expression that is dynamically composed each time the function is used. Note that the apostrophes are part of the literal text.

```
ZipCodes.Open _
"SELECT Zip FROM ZIP_USA WHERE PO_NAME = '" & _
CityName & "' AND State ='" & StateName & "'"
```

You can test the function by using the `TestZip` procedure:

```
Sub TestZip()
    Debug.Print Zip("martinez", "ca")
    Debug.Print Zip("langhorne", "pa")
    Debug.Print Zip("shrewsbury", "ma")
End Sub
```

Now that you have a function that uses ADO to obtain the zip code, you can incorporate that function into the procedure that updates the billing address for Krumm. `MultiEdit2` adds a statement, which updates the zip code along with the rest of the data. In this case, the value of the zip code is the result from the `Zip( )` function. Further, the arguments passed to the `Zip` function aren't literal either. The city and state values are extracted from the `Cust` recordset and passed to the `Zip` function.

```
Sub MultiEdit2()
    Dim Cnt As New Connection
    Dim Cust As New Recordset
    Cnt.Open "Provider=Microsoft.Jet.OLEDB.4.0;" & _
    "data source=C:\ADO Book\db\chp3\wine.mdb;"
    Cust.Open _
    "SELECT * FROM Customers WHERE LastName = 'Krumm'", _
    Cnt, adOpenKeyset, adLockOptimistic
    Cust("BillAddress1") = "4830 Milano Way"
    Cust("Billaddress2") = Null
    Cust("BillCity") = "Martinez"
    Cust("BillState") = "CA"
    Cust("BillZip") = Zip(Cust("BillCity"), Cust("BillState"))
    Cust.Update
End Sub
```

Composing SQL statements

The SQL composing technique used in the `Zip( )` function is a powerful tool for creating functions that that use ADO data sources. However, watch out for the following things when you use this technique:

- ✔ **No apostrophes for numeric values:** If you compose a statement that uses a numeric value, (such as a customer ID number) as the search criteria, you don't have to use the apostrophes because numeric values don't have to be delimited (enclosed in quotation marks) in SQL statements. The following `Open` statement, taken from the `CustomerName( )` function, doesn't use the apostrophes because `CustomerID` is a number:

```
C.Open _
"SELECT LastName, FirstName FROM Customers " & _
"WHERE CustomerID = " & C_ID
```

- ✔ **The Irish problem:** The apostrophe approach works well in most cases, except if the value being compared is a text string that contains an apostrophe, such as these items.

```
O'Brien
Joe's Bar & Grill
```

One solution is to use the `Chr( )` function instead of the apostrophe. The `Chr( )` function returns a character according to its ASCII code value. The expression `Chr(34)` returns the " character. The following example, used in the `CustomerID( )` function, uses `Chr(34)` to insert quotation marks wherever you need them in the expression. This code runs correctly even if the last name contains an apostrophe. (I cover other solutions in Chapter 4.)

```
C.Open _
    "SELECT CustomerID FROM Customers " & _
    "WHERE LastName = " & Chr(34) & _
    C_LastName & Chr(34)
```

✔ **Include spaces where required:** Take care when writing expressions that evaluate to SQL statements that you don't omit required spaces. Following are two expressions meant to evaluate as SQL statements. One contains a mistake that results in an error.

```
C.Open _
    "SELECT CustomerID FROM Customers" & _
    "WHERE LastName = " & Chr(34) & _
    C_LastName & Chr(34)
```

```
C.Open _
    "SELECT CustomerID FROM Customers " & _
    "WHERE LastName = " & Chr(34) & _
    C_LastName & Chr(34)
```

If you look carefully at the end of the lines that begin `SELECT CustomerID`, you notice that the first example doesn't contain a space before the closing quotation mark, whereas the second one does. Does this matter? Yes, it does. It may not be obvious from looking at the code, but when the parts of the expression assemble, `Customers` pushes up against `WHERE`. `CustomersWHERE` isn't recognized by the data provider as a valid part of a SQL statement, thus resulting in an error.

```
SELECT CustomerID FROM CustomersWHERE...
```

One way to check the validity of a SQL expression is to print it into the Immediate window, as shown in the following example, so that you can see if the text from the expression is a valid SQL statement.

```
Debug.Print _
    "SELECT CustomerID FROM Customers " & _
    "WHERE LastName = " & Chr(34) & _
    C_LastName & Chr(34)
```

Chapter 4

ADO Database Operations

• •

In This Chapter

▶ Updating batches of records

▶ Adding and deleting records

▶ Archiving old records

▶ Getting rid of duplicates

▶ Copying data from one table to another

▶ Normalizing database tables

• •

*O*ne of the most powerful features of databases is the ability to alter the contents of records by encapsulating the logic of the changes in SQL statements. ADO provides a number of ways in which a database updates additions and deletions applied to a data source.

Updating, Adding, and Deleting in Recordsets

The code examples in this chapter deal with two data sources:

ON THE CD

✔ **Local:** This is an Access 97 format MDB file called `WINE.MDB`, included on the CD at the back of this book. The connection string for this database is `FileDS`.

✔ **Internet:** This is a SQL Server database available though any Internet connection. You simply need to set up the ADODUM client on your system to access this database. The connection string for this database is `NetDS`.

The connection strings for these two providers are entered as constants in the declarations section of the `More Recordsets.MDB` files.

```
Const FileDS = "Provider=Microsoft.Jet.OLEDB.4.0;" & _
    "data source=C:\ADO Book\db\chp4\wine.mdb;"
Const NetDS = "Provider=SQLOLEDB;Data

Source=ADODUM;UID=ubad1d1;pwd=21@1n3z"
```

The procedures that modify data on the Internet data source are designed to be run in groups. Any changes that you make are reset to the original so that other readers can use the data source after you finish. As a courtesy to other readers, please take care to run reset procedures before you stop working.

Updating multiple records

Often, an operation requires updates to one or more records of a recordset that contains more than one record.

For example, the Customers table contains a Fullname field. You can fill in this field by combining the Lastname and Firstname fields to form a full name, such as Lafish, Walter.

The Update1 procedure fills in the Fullname field for all of the customers in zip code 94553. What's interesting about this procedure is that none of the statements contain any specific references to editing or updating. In contrast to DAO, the edit and update operations in ADO are implicit. The implicit nature of ADO is explained in the following list:

✔ **Implicit editing:** You don't need special statements to modify the contents of a recordset as long as the recordset cursor type and lock type support updates (see Chapter 3 for a discussion of cursor and lock types). Update1 changes the content of the Fullname field by assigning it a value: in this case, based on the contents of other fields in the same record.

✔ **Implicit updates:** ADO automatically updates the current record whenever you apply a method, such as MoveNext or MovePrevious, that moves to another record.

```
Sub Update1()
    Dim Names As New ADODB.Recordset
    Names.Open "SELECT Lastname,Firstname,Fullname " & _
    "FROM Customers WHERE Billzip = '94553'", _
    FileDS, adOpenKeyset, adLockOptimistic
    Do Until Names.EOF
        With Names
            !FullName = !lastname & ", " & !firstname
        End With
        Names.MoveNext
    Loop
End Sub
```

Because of the implicit edits and updates, the code required to update a batch of records is greatly simplified from the equivalent ADO code. `Update1DAO` shows how the same basic procedure has to be coded using DAO as the data access platform. You can see that the `.Edit` and `.Update` methods don't really add anything to the logic of the procedure. It's unlikely that you would assign a value to the `Fullname` field and not mean to edit and update the record. However, in DAO, if you forget the `.Update` method, your code runs without saving any changes.

```
Sub Update1DAO()
    Dim DB As DAO.Database
    Dim Names As DAO.Recordset
    Set DB = OpenDatabase( _
    "O:\ADO Book\db\chp4\wine.mdb")
    Set Names = DB.OpenRecordset( _
    "SELECT Lastname,Firstname,Fullname" & _
    " FROM Customers WHERE Billzip = '94553'")
    Do Until Names.EOF
        With Names
            .Edit
            !FullName = !firstname & " " & !Lastname
            .Update
            .MoveNext
        End With
    Loop
End Sub
```

One of ADO's goals is to eliminate some of the arcane requirements of earlier technologies and allow code with a structure more in keeping with the way databases are used. You can use `Update1Check` to check the results of `Update1` and `Update1DAO`.

```
Sub Update1Check()
    Dim Names As New ADODB.Recordset
    With Names
        .Open "SELECT Lastname,Firstname,Fullname " & _
        "FROM Customers WHERE Billzip = '94553'", _
        FileDS, adOpenKeyset, adLockOptimistic
        Do Until .EOF
            Debug.Print !FullName, !Lastname, !firstname
            .MoveNext
        Loop
    End With
End Sub
```

The procedures in this section use the `With . . . End With` statement to eliminate the need to repeat the name of the recordset object, `Names`. Because all the procedures perform most of their operations on the `Names` object, required typing is significantly reduced. In `Update1Check`, the `Names` object is explicitly written twice.

Batch updates

Some ADO providers support batch updating. When a recordset is opened in a batch update mode, updates to individual records aren't committed to the data source until an UpdateBatch method is executed. Then all the pending changes are written to the data source. If you close the recordset without executing an UpdateBatch, all the changes are discarded.

You also have the option to include an explicit CancelBatch statement that tells ADO to discard the changes.

After you execute a CancelBatch method, the changes can't be retrieved even if you subsequently execute UpdateBatch.

If you want to perform updates in a batch mode, you specify batch updating in the locktype argument of the Open method by using the constant adLockBatchOptimistic (numeric value 4). Batch updates are supported for Keyset and Static recordsets. Of course, if you want to make actual changes to the source data, you must use the Keyset cursor type. Following is the general form of the Open method you use to create a batch update recordset.

```
Recordset.Open source, _
    connection, _
    adOpenKeyset, _
    adLockBatchOptimistic
```

BatchUpdate1 performs essentially the same type update as Update1 in the preceding section. In fact, the only difference between the two procedures is the zip code (94111 instead of 94553) and the lock type (adLockBatchOptimistic instead of adLockOptimistic).

```
Sub BatchUpdate1()
    Dim Names As New ADODB.Recordset
    With Names
        .Open "SELECT Lastname,Firstname,Fullname " & _
        "FROM Customers WHERE Billzip = '94111'", _
        FileDS, adOpenKeyset, adLockBatchOptimistic
        Do Until .EOF
            !FullName = !firstname & " " & !Lastname
            .MoveNext
        Loop
    End With
End Sub
```

When you execute BatchUpdate1, the procedure generates the error shown in Figure 4-1. First, the error doesn't come from lack of support for the batch update feature, at least in theory.

Figure 4-1:
Access
batch
update
support is
limited to a
single
record.

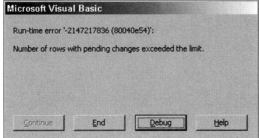

BatchUpdate1a uses the Supports property to determine whether the batch update feature is supported by the Names recordset. When you run this procedure, you find that the message box returns True, indicating that the feature is supported.

```
Sub BatchUpdate1a()
    Dim Names As New ADODB.Recordset
    Names.Open _
        "SELECT Lastname,Firstname,Fullname " & _
        "FROM Customers WHERE Billzip = '94111'", _
        FileDS, adOpenKeyset, adLockBatchOptimistic
    MsgBox Names.Supports(adUpdateBatch)
End Sub
```

In Figure 4-1, the error occurs when the batch update support provided by an Access MDB data source is limited to a single record. When the procedure attempts to place a second pending update into the batch, Access sends a message through to ADO that its resources have reached their limit. In theory, Access supports batch update. But in practice, it turns out that it can handle only one record at a time.

True batch updating works best on transaction based data sources, such as SQL Server or Oracle. These systems have robust facilities for isolating batches of changes made to parts of a database so that they can be committed or discarded as a batch. BatchUpdate2 is identical to BatchUpdate1 except that the connection string refers to a SQL Server data source. This code executes without error because the specific provider supports full implementation of the batch update feature.

```
Sub BatchUpdate2()
    Dim Names As New ADODB.Recordset
    With Names
        .Open "SELECT Lastname,Firstname,Fullname " & _
        "FROM Customers WHERE Billzip = '94111'", _
        NetDS, adOpenKeyset, adLockBatchOptimistic
        Do Until .EOF
            !FullName = !firstname & " " & !Lastname
            .MoveNext
        Loop
    End With
End Sub
```

You can use the procedure `BatchUpdateCheck` to display the results. You see that all the records list `Null` for `Fullname`. `BatchUpdate2` didn't change any data. Because `BatchUpdate2` is almost identical to `Update1`, you may have expected saved changes because of ADO's implicit update feature.

However, the difference between the procedures — the use of the Lock Type `adLockBatchOptimistic` — turns off the implicit update feature. Instead, all of the updates are registered as pending changes. If the procedure ends without the `UpdateBatch` method being applied to the recordset, ADO discards all the changes. `BatchUpdate3` adds the `UpdateBatch` method needed to commit the changes permanently to the data source. `BatchUpdateCheck` now shows the `Fullname` field populated with the `Firstname` and `Lastname` combined.

```
Sub BatchUpdate3()
    Dim Names As New ADODB.Recordset
    With Names
        .Open "SELECT Lastname,Firstname,Fullname " & _
        "FROM Customers WHERE Billzip = '94111'", _
        NetDS, adOpenKeyset, adLockBatchOptimistic
        Do Until .EOF
            !FullName = !firstname & " " & !Lastname
            .MoveNext
        Loop
        .UpdateBatch 'saves all pending changes
    End With
End Sub
```

One reason for using batch updating is to enable the user to approve or reject a group of up dates. `BatchUpdate4` uses a message box to enable the user to keep or reject the changes made to the recordset object.

```
Sub BatchUpdate4()
    Dim Names As New ADODB.Recordset
    Dim DoIt
    With Names
        .Open "SELECT Lastname,Firstname,Fullname " & _
        "FROM Customers WHERE Billzip = '94111'", _
        NetDS, adOpenKeyset, adLockBatchOptimistic
        Do Until .EOF
            !FullName = Null
            .MoveNext
        Loop
        DoIt = MsgBox("Changes have been made to " & _
            .RecordCount & " records. Save changes?", vbYesNo)
        If DoIt = vbYes Then
            .UpdateBatch
        Else
            .CancelBatch 'default action
        End If
    End With
End Sub
```

You don't have to execute the `CancelBatch` method explicitly because the changes are automatically discarded when the recordset is closed. On the other hand, it's usually a good idea to write code that clearly shows what you mean to do. In `BatchUpdate4`, the code achieves a balanced look when you specifically state that the batch cancels when the user clicks something other than Yes.

Run `BatchUpdate4` and click Yes when you finish this section to return the Internet database to its original state.

Adding records

Use the `AddNew` method of the recordset object to add new records to the database. `AddNew1` shows the typical way to add records to a recordset. First, apply the `AddNew` method to the recordset. The `AddNew` method places the recordset into an edit mode, allowing you to assign values to the fields in the new record. The new record is saved as part of the recordset when an `Update` method is executed.

```
Sub AddNew1()
    Dim Cust As New ADODB.Recordset
    Cust.Open "Customers", FileDS, adOpenKeyset, adLockOptimistic
    Cust.AddNew
    Cust!Firstname = "Morgan"
    Cust!Lastname = "Krumm"
    Cust.Update
End Sub
```

The `AddNew1Check` procedure confirms that `AddNew1` added a new record to the `Customers` table.

```
Sub AddNew1Check()
    Dim Cust As New ADODB.Recordset
    Cust.Open "SELECT Count(*) FROM Customers " & _
    "WHERE FirstName ='Morgan' AND Lastname ='Krumm'", _
    FileDS
    MsgBox Cust(0)
End Sub
```

Less common is an alternative method for adding a record based on the contents of two arrays. One array contains the names of the fields while the other contains the values to be assigned to the fields.

`AddDirect` uses this approach to add a record to the `Customers` table. The procedure creates two arrays, `FieldList` and `FieldValue`, into which the field names and values are placed. The relationship between the field name and the field value is based on the position of each item in their respective arrays: that is, field name 1 uses field value 1, and so on. The two arrays are then used as arguments for the `AddNew` method. This technique doesn't require an `Update` method to save the new record. It's immediately committed to the data source when the `AddNew` method is executed.

```
Sub AddDirect()
    Dim Cust As New ADODB.Recordset
    Dim FieldList(2), FieldValue(2)
    FieldList(1) = "Firstname"
    FieldList(2) = "Lastname"
    FieldValue(1) = "Rusty"
    FieldValue(2) = "Krumm"
    Cust.Open "Customers", FileDS, adOpenKeyset, adLockOptimistic
    Cust.AddNew FieldList(), FieldValue()
End Sub
```

In VB and VBA, arrays are zero based. This means that the first element in the array is X(0), not X(1). To avoid any confusion, you can force VB/VBA to start arrays with 1 (one) instead of 0 (zero) by adding the statement `Option Base 1` to the declarations section of the code module. This statement affects only the code in the module in which it's entered.

The `AddNoDulpicates` example shows how various ADO techniques can work together. This procedure eliminates the entry of duplicate names in the `Customers` table. The procedure stores the user entry for first and last names in variables. A recordset is then created that counts the number of records with the same name. If that count is greater than 0, the assumption is that the customer has already been entered and the `AddNew` method shouldn't apply. Otherwise, the `AddNew` method creates a new record.

When I ran `AddNoDuplicates` the first time, I entered the first name Rusty and the last name Krumm. Because this is a new name, it's added to the database. Repeat the execution of `AddNoDulpicates` and re-enter Rusty Krumm. This time, the procedure locates the duplicate name and skips the addition of a new record.

```
Sub AddNoDuplicates()
    Dim Fname, LName
    Dim Cnt As New ADODB.Connection
    Dim Cust As New ADODB.Recordset
    Fname = InputBox("Enter First name:")
    LName = InputBox("Enter Last name:")
    Cnt.Open FileDS
    Cust.Open "SELECT Count(*) FROM Customers " & _
        "WHERE Lastname ='" & LName & _
        "' AND Firstname = '" & Fname & "'", Cnt
    If Cust(0) > 0 Then
        MsgBox Fname & " " & LName & " already exists."
    Else
        With Cust
            .Close
            .Open "Customers", Cnt, adOpenKeyset, adLockOptimistic
            .AddNew
            !Firstname = Fname
            !Lastname = LName
            .Update
        End With
    End If
End Sub
```

Another interesting programming point is the way AddNoDuplicates is coded. In most of the procedures in this chapter, the connection string is used directly with the recordset Open method to connect to the record source. In AddNoDuplicates, a separate connection object is created. The reason for this change is that in the AddNoDuplicates procedure, it's possible that you need to create more than one recordset. Instead of creating a separate connection for each recordset, sharing a single connection is more efficient.

Deleting records

You can use the Delete method to delete records from a data source through a recordset object. As with changes and new records, a deletion is performed in two phases. The Delete method itself simply marks the record for deletion. When the record is actually removed from the data source depends on the Lock Type used to open the recordset.

- ✔ **Immediate (**adLockOptimistic**).** Records marked as deleted are removed immediately from the record source.

- ✔ **Batch (**adLockBatchOptimistic**).** Records marked as deleted aren't removed from the data source until you issue a BatchUpdate method against the recordset. If the recordset is closed without a BatchUpdate, the deletions are discarded. Cancel Batch also discards the deletions.

Use a subset of the data where the customer's billzip is 60060. (No hidden meaning here, I just picked it out of the air.) The CheckDelete counts the number of records in this subset. Use the function to keep track of the records that are deleted from the data source.

```
Function CheckDelete()
    Dim Check As New ADODB.Recordset
    Check.Open "SELECT Count(*) FROM Customers " & _
        "WHERE billzip ='60060'", FileDS
    CheckDelete = Check(0)
End Function
```

The simplest way to delete a record is to open the recordset in the Immediate (adLockOptimistic) mode and apply the Delete method to the record you want to delete. In DeleteOne, the Delete method is applied to the first record in the opened recordset. Because the recordset was opened in the immediate mode, adLockOptimistic, the deletion is immediately applied to the data source. When you run the procedure, the count of records is reduced from 6 to 5 as a result of the deletion.

```
Sub DeleteOne()
    MsgBox CheckDelete() 'shows 6
    Dim Cust As New ADODB.Recordset
    With Cust
        .Open "SELECT * FROM Customers " & _
            "WHERE billzip ='60060'", FileDS, _
            adOpenKeyset, adLockOptimistic
        .Delete
    End With
    MsgBox CheckDelete() 'shows 5
End Sub
```

Note that the record count provided by the CheckDelete function shows the actual number of records in the data source, not the number in the Cust recordset. CheckDelete doesn't count the records in Cust. Instead, it opens a completely independent recordset that reflects the actual contents of the source database. Other users working with the same data source see this.

You can delete multiple records by moving through the recordset and applying the Delete method to one or more records. DeleteSeveral applies the Delete method to any records in the specified recordset that have a RecordCreated date in 1999. Note that the CheckDelete function is called after every Delete method to show that each deleted record is removed from the data source immediately.

```
Sub DeleteSeveral()
    MsgBox CheckDelete() 'shows 5
    Dim Cust As New ADODB.Recordset
    Cust.Open "SELECT * FROM Customers " & _
        "WHERE billzip ='60060'", FileDS, _
        adOpenKeyset, adLockOptimistic
    Do Until Cust.EOF
        If Year(Cust!RecordCreated) = 1999 Then
            Cust.Delete
            MsgBox CheckDelete()
        End If
        Cust.MoveNext
    Loop
End Sub
```

In contrast, you can mark one or more records for deletion without immediately removing them from the data source if you open the recordset in batch mode (adLockBatchOptimistic). You can then commit or discard all of the changes to the recordset (deletions, edits, and addition) using the UpdateBatch method.

Keep in mind that you, the provider, must support batch operations to execute a procedure like DeleteGroup. Because the Access MDB won't support this function, the DeleteGroup procedure operates on the SQL Server data source. I have commented about using the UpdateBatch method to keep the changes from actually being made to the online database because ADO discards all changes contained in the batch unless UpdateBatch is specifically executed.

```
Sub DeleteGroup()
    MsgBox CheckDeleteNet()
    Dim Cust As New ADODB.Recordset, DoIt
    Cust.Open "SELECT * FROM Customers " & _
        "WHERE billzip ='60060'", NetDS, _
        adOpenKeyset, adLockBatchOptimistic
    Do Until Cust.EOF
        Cust.Delete
        Cust.MoveNext
    Loop
    MsgBox CheckDeleteNet()
    DoIt = MsgBox("Remove Deleted Records?", vbYesNo)
    If DoIt = vbYes Then
        'Cust.UpdateBatch
    Else
        Cust.CancelBatch
    End If
    MsgBox CheckDelete()
End Sub

Function CheckDeleteNet()
    Dim Check As New ADODB.Recordset
    Check.Open "SELECT Count(*) FROM Customers " & _
        "WHERE billzip ='60060'", NetDS
    CheckDeleteNet = Check(0)
End Function
```

Putting Additions and Deletions to Work

After you know the basics of adding and deleting records, you can explore how to use these operations to accomplish specific tasks:

- ✔ Archiving old records into another table
- ✔ Deleting duplicates from a table
- ✔ Adding new records that are based on existing records
- ✔ Deleting detail records that no longer match records in other tables

Although various applications or specific databases have features for dealing with these problems, you can use ADO to perform these operations on any ADO data source.

Archiving records

If you successfully create a database application, you find that over time, your initial tables may fill with outdated records. Having outdated records is common in databases that deal with day-to-day operations, such as order processing. You don't want to delete the old records, but you may want to move them to another table. Archiving the old records in another table keeps your tables at a reasonable size. If you need the older records, they're preserved in the archive table.

Moving the data involves two tasks:

✔ Adding a copy of each old record to the archive table

✔ Deleting the original record from the source table

The first task in archiving is to copy a record that exists in one table into another table. You assume that both the source recordset and the destination recordset have the same structure. If that's true, you can copy all the fields without having to specify the field names by looping through the contents of the fields collection. The following code shows a general routine that creates a duplicate record in the DestRS recordset based on the current record in the SourceRS recordset. Because the reference to the fields collection is dynamic, you can apply this code to any two tables that have the same structure.

```
DestRS.AddNew
For Each Fld In SourceRS.Fields
    DestRS(Fld.Name) = SourceRS(Fld.Name)
Next
DestRS.Update
```

Approach any task that involves deletions carefully because the last thing you want to do is destroy the data you worked so hard to accumulate. The Status property of the recordset object provides information about the state of the current record. The values returned by this property are listed in Table 4-1.

Table 4-1	Recordset Status Values	
Constant	*Value*	*Description*
AdRecOK	0	The record was successfully updated.
adRecNew	1	The record is new.
adRecModified	2	The record was modified.
adRecDeleted	4	The record was deleted.
adRecUnmodified	8	The record was not modified.

The Status property returns 18 different numeric codes. The full list is available at http://msdn.microsoft.com/library/psdk/dasdk/ mdaelru5.htm.

Use the Status property to make sure that an operation (such as saving a new record) is successful so that you can determine programmatically whether you should continue and delete the original record. The following block of code checks the status of current record in the DestDS recordset. If the property returns the value AdRecOK, that indicates that the copying process was successful. You can now apply the Delete method to the original record in the SourceRS recordset.

```
If DestRS.Status = adRecOK Then
    SourceRS.Delete
    SourceRS.Update
    MoveRecord = True
Else
```

The MoveRecord function creates a routine that you can use to archive any record given two recordset objects with the same structure. The specific recordsets used by the function aren't specified. Instead, the procedure calling this function passes the source and destination recordsets as arguments. The function returns a True value if the record is moved, or a False value if the status indicates lack of success.

```
Function MoveRecord(SourceRS As ADODB.Recordset, _
    DestRS As ADODB.Recordset) As Boolean
    Dim Fld As ADODB.Field
    DestRS.AddNew
    For Each Fld In SourceRS.Fields
        DestRS(Fld.Name) = SourceRS(Fld.Name)
    Next
    DestRS.Update
    If DestRS.Status = adRecOK Then
        SourceRS.Delete
        SourceRS.Update
        MoveRecord = True
    Else
        MsgBox "Record Copy Failed!"
        MoveRecord = False
    End If
End Function
```

After you have the MoveRecord function in place, you can archive records by using the approach shown in ArchiveRecords. This procedure creates two recordsets. Orders is the source of the records that need to be archived. In this example, all records before Feb. 1, 1999 comprise the recordset that needs to be archived. Both the source and destination recordsets should be updateable because one loses records while the other gains. When the procedure is complete, it moves a block of records from one table to another.

```
Sub ArchiveRecords()
    Dim Cnt As New ADODB.Connection
    Dim Orders As New ADODB.Recordset
    Dim OrdersBackup As New ADODB.Recordset
    Cnt.Open FileDS
    Orders.Open "SELECT * FROM Orders " & _
        "WHERE orderdate <= #2/1/1999#", Cnt, _
        adOpenKeyset, adLockOptimistic
    OrdersBackup.Open "OrdersArchive", Cnt, _
        adOpenKeyset, adLockOptimistic
    Do Until Orders.EOF
        If MoveRecord(Orders, OrdersBackup) Then
            Orders.MoveNext
        Else
            Exit Do
        End If
    Loop
End Sub
```

Eliminating duplicate records

To get rid of duplicate records, you must first decide what criteria you want
to use to determine that two records are duplicates.

For example, I use a table in the Wine database called Zips_With_Duplicates.
This table should be a list of all the zip codes in the U.S., including the cities
and states where the zip codes are located. If this table is correctly populated, each record should contain a unique combination of zip, city, and state.
If more than one record should contain the same values for zip, city, and
state, then that repetition constitutes a duplicate that needs to be removed.

To determine the existence and number of duplicates, use two SQL keywords:

✔ DISTINCT. When used with SELECT, DISTINCT limits the contents of a
   recordset to one row for each unique combination of field values listed
   in the SQL statement. The following example lists the unique combinations of first and last names only once, no matter how many records
   contained duplicates.

```
SELECT DISTINCT lastname,firstname FROM customers

Abbott        Heather
Abbott        Victor
Abbottwheeler     Gez
Abbottwheeler     John Jr.
Abbottwheeler     Kevin
```

✔ **GROUP BY.** GROUP BY, like DISTINCT, also limits the contents of a recordset to one record for each unique set of values. However, GROUP BY also allows you to have summary calculations based on the records that fall into each group. The following statement lists each unique last name and the number of records in each group.

```
SELECT lastname, count(*) FROM customers GROUP BY lastname


Abbott    2
Abbottwheeler    3
```

The HasDups procedure uses the DISTINCT keyword to determine whether the target table, Zips_With_Duplicates, contains duplicate records. The procedure first counts the total number of records in the table and then counts the number of distinct records. If the counts are different, you have duplicate records.

```
Sub HasDups()
    Dim Cnt As New ADODB.Connection
    Dim RS As New ADODB.Recordset
    Dim RawCount, UniqueCount
    Cnt.Open FileDS

    RS.Open _
    "SELECT Zip, City, State FROM Zips_With_Duplicates", _
    Cnt
    Do Until RS.EOF
        RawCount = RawCount + 1
        RS.MoveNext
    Loop
    RS.Close

    RS.Open _
    "SELECT DISTINCT Zip, City, State FROM Zips_With_Duplicates", _
    Cnt
    Do Until RS.EOF
        UniqueCount = UniqueCount + 1
        RS.MoveNext
    Loop
    RS.Close

    If RawCount = UniqueCount Then
        MsgBox "No Duplicates"
    Else
        MsgBox "Contains " & RawCount - UniqueCount & " Duplicates"
    End If
End Sub
```

If a table contains duplicates, you need to figure out which records are duplicated. Again, the solution relies on a SQL operation. Look at the following data. The number column represents the count of records within each lastname group. Abbott, Abbottwheeler and Adam have duplicates because their counts are greater than 1.

```
Abbott      2
Abbottwheeler      3
Abele      1
Achilles      1
Adam      3
```

The SQL keyword HAVING allows you to select records based on their group value. The following SQL statement picks out the groups that have duplicates.

```
SELECT lastname, count(*)
FROM customers
GROUP BY lastname
HAVING count(*) > 1

Abbott      2
Abbottwheeler      3
```

The ListDuplicates procedure applies this SQL technique to an ADO recordset object. When executed, the technique produces a list of the Zip, City, and State duplicates in the specified table.

```
Sub ListDuplicates()
    Dim Cnt As New ADODB.Connection
    Dim RS As New ADODB.Recordset
    Dim Col As ADODB.Field
    Cnt.Open FileDS
    RS.Open "SELECT " & _
        "Zip, City, State, Count(*)" & _
        "FROM Zips_With_Duplicates " & _
        "GROUP BY Zip, City, State " & _
        "HAVING count(*) > 1", Cnt
    Do Until RS.EOF
        Debug.Print RS(0), RS(1), RS(2)
        RS.MoveNext
    Loop
End Sub
```

After you know which items are duplicates, you need to get rid of them. Keep in mind that the recordsets returned by SQL GROUP BY operations don't contain deleteable records. These records represent a summary of the data in the table. They have no permanent existence.

However, you can use the list of duplicate data items to access the duplicate records that can be deleted. The DuplicateList procedure produces a list of duplicate records based on a common element — in this example, the zip code.

```
Sub DuplicateList(C As ADODB.Connection, ZipCode)
    Dim DList As New ADODB.Recordset
    DList.Open "SELECT * FROM Zips_With_Duplicates " & _
        "WHERE Zip = '" & ZipCode & "'", C
    Do Until DList.EOF
        Debug.Print DList(0), DList(1), DList(2)
        DList.MoveNext
    Loop
End Sub
```

The ShowDuplicates procedure begins with a grouped recordset that lists the zip codes that have duplicate entries. Each zip code is passed to the DuplicateList, which produces a list of the specific records in each group. ShowDuplicates produces a list of the deleteable records. You need this list to eliminate the duplicates.

```
Sub ShowDuplicates()
    Dim Cnt As New ADODB.Connection
    Dim RS As New ADODB.Recordset
    Dim Col As ADODB.Field
    Cnt.Open FileDS
    RS.Open "SELECT " & _
        "Zip, City, State, Count(*)" & _
        "FROM Zips_With_Duplicates " & _
        "GROUP BY Zip, City, State " & _
        "HAVING count(*) > 1", Cnt
    Do Until RS.EOF
        DuplicateList Cnt, RS("Zip")
        RS.MoveNext
    Loop
End Sub
```

Finally, convert the DuplicateList procedure, which lists the duplicates, to DeleteDuplicates, which eliminates them by adding the Delete method. However, take care not to delete *all* the records in the DList recordset. You need to retain one of the records and eliminate only the extra ones. You can do this by using the MoveNext method before you begin to delete. The MoveNext methods skips the first record in the set and applies the deletion to records two, three, and so on.

```
Sub DeleteDuplicates(C As ADODB.Connection, ZipCode)
    Dim DList As New ADODB.Recordset
    DList.Open "SELECT * FROM Zips_With_Duplicates " & _
        "WHERE Zip = '" & ZipCode & "'", C, adOpenKeyset, adLockOptimistic
    'skip the first records
    DList.MoveNext
    Do Until DList.EOF
        DList.Delete
        DList.MoveNext
    Loop
End Sub
```

The DropDuplicates procedure executes the DeleteDuplicates operation on each zip code that has one or more duplicates. When the procedure is done, the recordset is cleared of duplicate records while still retaining the first record of each group.

```
Sub DropDuplicates()
    Dim Cnt As New ADODB.Connection
    Dim RS As New ADODB.Recordset
    Dim Col As ADODB.Field
    Cnt.Open FileDS
    RS.Open "SELECT " & _
        "Zip, City, State, Count(*)" & _
        "FROM Zips_With_Duplicates " & _
        "GROUP BY Zip, City, State " & _
```

```
        "HAVING count(*) > 1", _
        Cnt
    Do Until RS.EOF
        DeleteDuplicates Cnt, RS("Zip")
        RS.MoveNext
    Loop
End Sub
```

Working with Data in Multiple Tables

In relational databases, relationships exist among tables. Additions to one table may require that additions be made to other tables in order to preserve the relationships. Conversely, relationships between tables may require that related records be deleted from certain tables whenever a record is delete from a related table. The following sections describe some ways that you can use ADO to add or delete in multiple tables.

Adding related records

If you build an application such as an order-processing system, you find that new records often are based on existing records. When you create a new order, you can obtain many of the values used in the Orders table (for example, shipping address or credit card information) automatically from the customer's record in the Customers table.

The Add Order function starts with a record from the Customers recordset, which is used to fill values in a new record being added to the Orders table. Note that one critical data transfer is the CustomerID, which is copied from the Customers record into the Order record. This value forms the logical link between the orders and the customers. The function returns the order number of the new order.

```
Function AddOrder(Customer As ADODB.Recordset)
    Dim NewOrder As New ADODB.Recordset
    With NewOrder
        .Open "Orders", Customer.ActiveConnection, _
            adOpenKeyset, adLockOptimistic
        .AddNew
        !CustomerID = Customer!CustomerID 'links records
        !Orderdate = Date
        !ShipFirst = Customer!ShipFirstName
        !shiplast = Customer!shiplastname
        !ShipAddress1 = Customer!ShipAddress1
        .Update
        AddOrder = !WineOrderID
    End With
End Function
```

One interesting twist in the AddOrder code is the use of the ActiveConnection property. In this example, the function passes the entire Customer recordset as an argument. Because that Recordset object already has a connection object associated with it, there's no need to open a new connection to create an Orders recordset. You can use the ActiveConnection property of the Customer record to supply a connection to any other recordset objects that access the same data source.

Use the CreateNewOrder procedure to start the order creation process. The user inputs the name of any customer. The procedure then locates the corresponding customer record, which is then passed to the AddOrder function. That function creates a new Order based on the customer information.

```
Sub CreateNewOrder()
    Dim Name
    Dim Cust As New ADODB.Recordset
    Name = InputBox("Add New Order for:", , "Clifford Morgan")
    Cust.Open "SELECT * FROM Customers " & _
        "WHERE firstname & ' ' & Lastname = '" & _
        Name & "'", FileDS
    If Not Cust.EOF Then
        MsgBox "Order #" & AddOrder(Cust) & " created."
    Else
        MsgBox "No Match"
    End If
End Sub
```

Note how the customer record is selected. You may recall that the Customers table uses separate Firstname and Lastname fields. In this case, the user is supposed to enter a full name in a single entry box. The trick here is to compare the user's entry to an expression, specifically one that combines the first and last names, to the user's full name entry. The expression is on the left side of the equation — not the right — but it's a perfectly valid formula.

```
"WHERE firstname & ' ' & Lastname = '" & Name & "'"
```

CreateNewOrder uses a default value, Clifford Morgan, to fill in the input box with a default value rather than showing an empty entry box.

Using field maps

The AddOrder function has one significant drawback. To copy the data stored in the customer record into a new order record, you have to write a series of assignment statements that specifies each item that you want to copy.

In `AddOrder`, the copying is hardwired into the code. A better approach is to use a map table. The data in a *map table* consists of the names of the fields in each table that need to be copied to another table. Following are the contents of the `Map_NewOrder` table. The `Source` column lists the fields in `Customers` that are to be copied to the `Destination` fields in `Orders`.

```
ID   Source           Destination
1    ShipFirstName    ShipFirst
2    ShipLastName     ShipLast
3    ShipAddress1     ShipAddress1
4    ShipAddress2     ShipAddress2
5    ShipCity         ShipCity
6    ShipState        ShipState
7    ShipZip          ShipZip
8    DayPhoneNumber   ShipPhone
9    CreditCardNumber CreditCardNumber
10   Expires          Expire
11   CustomerID       CustomerID
```

You can use this table as a map for copying by using a procedure designed like `AddOrderwithMap`. In this procedure, the field list is replaced with a `Do . . . Loop` that draws the name of the fields to be copied from the `Map_NewOrder` table. At the heart of the procedure is the following statement in which the names of the fields are supplied from the `Destination` and `Source` fields of the map table.

```
.Fields(Map!Destination.Value) = Customer(Map!Source.Value)

Function AddOrderwithMap(Customer As ADODB.Recordset)
    Dim NewOrder As New ADODB.Recordset
    Dim Map As New ADODB.Recordset
    Map.Open "Map_NewOrder", Customer.ActiveConnection, adOpenStatic, _
            adLockReadOnly
    With NewOrder
        .Open "Orders", Customer.ActiveConnection, _
            adOpenKeyset, adLockOptimistic
        .AddNew
        !Orderdate = Date
        Do Until Map.EOF
            Debug.Print Customer.Fields(Map!Source.Value)
            .Fields(Map!Destination.Value) = Customer(Map!Source.Value)
            Map.MoveNext
        Loop
        .Update
        AddOrderwithMap = !WineOrderID
    End With
End Function
```

The `CreateNewOrder_Map` procedure generates a new order by calling the `AddOrderwithMap` function.

```
Sub CreateNewOrder_Map()
    Dim Name
    Dim Cust As New ADODB.Recordset
    Name = InputBox("Add New Order for:", , "Clifford Morgan")
    Cust.Open "SELECT * FROM Customers " & _
        "WHERE firstname & ' ' & Lastname = '" & _
        Name & "'", FileDS
    If Not Cust.EOF Then
        MsgBox "Order #" & AddOrderwithMap(Cust) & " created."
    Else
        MsgBox "No Match"
    End If
End Sub
```

Map tables are useful because they enable you to add, remove, or change the flow of data between the two tables quickly. Such changes require only editing of the map table, thus eliminating the need to change the procedure's code just to change the data transfer details.

Obtaining sequence values

ADO's goal is to allow basically the same code to run against any ADO data source. However, when it comes to linking new records in multiple tables such as the Order and the OrderDetails tables, there's a subtle, but significant, difference between the behavior of Access and SQL Server (and other client server databases).

In the preceding section, you add a new order based in part on an existing customer record. The order and the customer are linked when the customer's CustomerID is copied to the Orders table CustomerID field. On the other hand, if you want to add an order detail that's linked to a new order, you don't have a pre-existing WineOrderID number to use as the link between Orders and OrderDetails.

To ensure that you have unique ID for new records, Access supports the Autonumber feature, which automatically generates a new value each time a record is added to the table. In Orders, the WineOrderID is an AutoNumber field. The SQL Server equivalent feature is called an Identity column, which also generates unique, sequential values.

But AutoNumber and Indentity differ in one respect — exactly when the new ID number for the new order record becomes available in the order-adding process. To see what's at stake here, you can run the Sequence1 procedure. This procedure opens two recordsets, both of which point to the Orders table in the Access MDB and the SQL Server database, respectively. A new record is added to each table and the value of the WineOrderID field is displayed in the Immediate window.

```
Sub Sequence1()
    Dim NewOrderSS As New ADODB.Recordset
    Dim NewOrderMDB As New ADODB.Recordset
    NewOrderMDB.Open "Orders", FileDS, _
        adOpenKeyset, adLockOptimistic
    NewOrderSS.Open "Orders", NetDS, _
        adOpenKeyset, adLockOptimistic
    NewOrderMDB.AddNew
    NewOrderSS.AddNew
    Debug.Print "MDB:", NewOrderMDB!wineorderid
    Debug.Print "SQL Server:", NewOrderSS!wineorderid
End Sub
```

When the procedure runs, the Immediate window shows an output like the one that follows. The Access-based recordset shows the new WineOrderID value but the SQL Server doesn't. The SQL Server WineOrderID is a Null, which means you can't link the details to the new order because you haven't obtained the WineOrderID number.

```
MDB:            24669
SQL Server:
```

The difference is in the details of the implementation. In Access, adding the new record immediately triggers the generation of an AutoNumber for the new record. SQL Server, a client/server database, doesn't add the new record until the client application executes an update. Only when the update is executed does SQL server become aware of the new record and execute its routine for generating a new identity number.

You can work around this difference by adding an Update method to the SQL Server recordset code.

```
Sub Sequence2()
    Dim NewOrderSS As New ADODB.Recordset
    Dim NewOrderMDB As New ADODB.Recordset
    NewOrderMDB.Open "Orders", FileDS, _
        adOpenKeyset, adLockOptimistic
    NewOrderSS.Open "Orders", NetDS, _
        adOpenKeyset, adLockOptimistic
    NewOrderMDB.AddNew
    NewOrderSS.AddNew
    NewOrderSS.Update
    Debug.Print "MDB:", NewOrderMDB!wineorderid
    Debug.Print "SQL Server:", NewOrderSS!wineorderid
End Sub
```

Sequence2 results in a display that indicates both recordsets have new, unique ID values with which to link the details to the main order.

```
MDB:            24672
SQL Server:     19779
```

If you add new records to a SQL Server table that contain Boolean fields (True/False in Access; Bit in SQL Server), you may encounter the message `the column x in table y may not be null`. The message appears because of a significant difference between an Access and SQL Server regarding Boolean fields. In Access, any Boolean fields in a new record are automatically assigned a false, or 0, value. But in SQL Server, the default value of a Boolean field is `Null`. Further, by definition, Boolean fields in SQL Server can't be saved as `Null` values. If you normally don't specifically assign values to these fields when you create a new record, you can avoid this error by adding a field default of 0 to the structure of the SQL Server table. Do this easily in the SQL Enterprise Manger by typing **0** in the Default column of the table design grid. This also works in SQL Server 6.5.

Locating orphans

ADO can solve problems related to deletion. In a database such as `Wine`, you expect that each record in the `OrderDetails` table is linked to an order in the `Orders` table. If that's true, the tables are normalized.

However, such links don't always exist. In a standard relational database, there's no automatic feature that prevents the deletion of records from one table, such as `Orders`, without deleting related records in other tables, such as `OrderDetails`. If deletions occur, you get results that don't correspond to any order. These records are called *orphans* because their order is missing.

You can locate orphan records by performing a SQL operation called an `OUTER JOIN`. In a standard `JOIN` between two or more tables, link relationships are defined between tables. The following SQL statement lists each order and all the detail information by linking the `OrderLink` field in `Details` to the `WineOrderID`. This statement results in a recordset that contains only records where the linked fields actually match. By definition, a standard `JOIN` ignores any orphan records.

```
SELECT Orders.*, OrderDetails.*
FROM OrderDetails
JOIN Orders ON OrderDetails.OrderLink = Orders.WineOrderID
```

It's not necessary that the common fields in related tables have the same name. In this example, `WineOrderID` is joined to `OrderLink`. I often use a `NameID` for the one side of a one-to-many relationship and a `NameLink` field on the many side.

If you want to find the orphan records, you need to force the recordset to include records in one table that don't have a match in the related table. Do this by adding the keyword `LEFT` to the `JOIN`. This forces the left side of the join, in this case the OrderDetails, to display all records, regardless of whether they match any records in the orders table. In fact, the WHERE clause turns the tables and limits the recordset to only those records that don't have a matching order. These are the orphan records:

```
SELECT Count(OrderDetailID)
FROM OrderDetails
LEFT JOIN Orders
ON OrderDetails.OrderLink = Orders.WineOrderID
WHERE WineOrderID Is Null
```

The CountOrhpanDetails lists each record in OrderDetails that doesn't correspond to a record in the Orders table:

```
Sub CountOrhpanDetails()
    Dim SQL
    SQL = "SELECT Count(OrderDetailID)" & _
        " FROM OrderDetails " & _
        " LEFT JOIN Orders ON " & _
        " OrderDetails.OrderLink = Orders.WineOrderID " & _
        " WHERE WineOrderID Is Null"
    Dim Orph As New ADODB.Recordset
    Orph.Open SQL, FileDS
    MsgBox Orph(0)
End Sub
```

To get the tables into a "normal" state, you need to delete the orphans. Deleting orphan records after they're gathered into a recordset seems straightforward. Orphans1 seeks to apply the Delete method to the orphan records:

```
Sub Orphans1()
    Dim SQL
    SQL = "SELECT Count(OrderDetailID)" & _
        " FROM OrderDetails " & _
        " LEFT JOIN Orders ON " & _
        " OrderDetails.OrderLink = Orders.WineOrderID " & _
        " WHERE WineOrderID Is Null"
    Dim Orph As New ADODB.Recordset
    Orph.Open SQL, FileDS
    Do Until Orph.EOF
        Orph.Delete
        Orph.MoveNext
    Loop
End Sub
```

However, when you attempt to execute Orphans1, you can't delete the records. The reason is that the contents of the Orph recordset represent the result of a relational operation inside the data source. While the data may appear to be a table, it's only a virtual table, assembled on-the-fly in response to the SQL statement. You can't delete records from this type of recordset, which is a result of a one-to-many join.

Deleting orphans records with Find

To delete orphan records from `OrderDetails`, you need a second recordset that allows for deletions. `DeleteOrphans` shows how the second recordset can actually remove the orphan details.

The `Find` method is a new feature in `DeleteOrphans`. `Find` allows you to search through a recordset for a record that matches some logical expression.

```
RecordsetObject.Find CiteriaString
```

In this case, the sought record is the one that matches the `OrderDetailID` of the current record in the `Orph` recordset. For each record in `Orph`, the `Find` method is used to search the `OrderDetails` table for the corresponding records. When located, the `Delete` method is applied to the records, eliminating then as orphan records.

```
Sub DeleteOrphans()
    Dim SQL
    SQL = "SELECT OrderDetailID" & _
        " FROM OrderDetails " & _
        " LEFT JOIN Orders ON " & _
        " OrderDetails.OrderLink = Orders.WineOrderID " & _
        " WHERE WineOrderId Is Null"
    Dim Orph As New ADODB.Recordset
    Dim Details As New ADODB.Recordset
    Orph.Open SQL, FileDS
    Details.Open "OrderDetails", FileDS, _
        adOpenKeyset, adLockOptimistic
    Do Until Orph.EOF
        Details.Find "orderdetailid = " & Orph(0)
        If Not Details.EOF Then
            Details.Delete
        End If
        Orph.MoveNext
    Loop
End Sub
```

Note that using the `Find` method to locate individual records inside a large recordset is a more efficient technique then trying to open a new recordset for each `Order`. `Find` allows you to use a single recordset object to delete as many records as necessary using a single recordset and a single connection object.

Deleting related records

Cleaning up orphan records within a database is a good idea, but preventing them is better. For example, each time that you delete an order from the Orders table, you should delete all the detail records in the OrderDetails tables. You can create an ADO procedure that performs this related set of deletes so that you don't allow orphan details creation.

The `DropOrder` procedure defines two recordsets, `Ord` and `Det`, by using the `OrderID` value in the `WHERE` clause of the data source statement. Note that in the details recordset, the `OrderID` value is used to select values in the `OrderLink` field because that's the field in the OrderDetails table that provides the link to the related order.

```
Sub DropOrder(OrderID)
    Dim Cnt As New ADODB.Connection
    Dim Ord As New ADODB.Recordset
    Dim Det As New ADODB.Recordset
    Cnt.Open FileDS
    Det.Open "SELECT * FROM OrderDetails " & _
        "WHERE OrderLink = " & OrderID, Cnt, _
        adOpenKeyset, adLockOptimistic
    Do Until Det.EOF
        Det.Delete
        Det.MoveNext
    Loop
    Ord.Open "SELECT * FROM Orders " & _
        " WHERE WineOrderID = " & OrderID, _
        Cnt, adOpenKeyset, adLockOptimistic
    If Not Ord.EOF Then
        Ord.Delete
    End If
End Sub
```

The `TestDeleteOrders` invokes the `DropOrder` procedure to delete order #22100 and any details linked to that order.

```
Sub TestDeleteOrders()
    DropOrder 22100
End Sub
```

The `DropOrder` function is typically used on a form where the `On_Click` event of a button control deletes a record. The button currently displayed on the form, `DeleteButton`, uses the following procedure to remove all records related to the order from the database:

```
Private Sub Delete_Button_Click()
    DropOrder Me.WineOrderID
End Sub
```

Chapter 5

The ADO Command Object

In This Chapter

▶ Using the ADO Command object

▶ Using parameters with commands

▶ Using multiple parameters

▶ Inserting and deleting with commands

▶ Performing mass updates

*T*he code examples in this chapter (and also in Chapter 4) deal with two data sources: a local MDB and an Internet-based SQL Server. The connection strings for these two providers are entered as constants in the Declarations section of the Commands.MDB files.

```
Const FileDS = "Provider=Microsoft.Jet.OLEDB.4.0;" & _
    "data source=C:\ADO Book\db\chp4\wine.mdb;"
Const NetDS = "Provider=SQLOLEDB;Data Source=ADODUM;UID=ubad1d1;pwd=21@1n3z"
```

You can connect to the Internet database server by using the IP address rather than the server name ADODUM, if you prefer. To use the IP address, you need to change the default protocol that's used by the OLE DB driver. You can do so by running the client configuration program (`cliconfg.exe`). The default setting is "Named Pipes." Change the default to "TCP/IP." You can use the following connection string to connect to the database server:

```
Provider=SQLOLEDB;Data Source=208.222.107.6;UID=ubad1d1;pwd=21@1n3z"
```

Commands versus Recordsets

A hallmark of ADO is that it consists of a rather limited number of objects, which has not always been characteristic of Microsoft technologies. If you've ever tried to write applications that use the object model for Excel (over 250 objects) or Outlook (I lost count), you're often overwhelmed by a host of objects that are related in a complicated, hierarchical web. For example, just to set the value of a single cell in an Excel worksheet in Visual Basic requires references to at least four different objects, as the following code line shows.

```
Application.Workbooks(0).Worksheets(0).Range("A1") =1
```

Data Access Objects (DAO) also suffered from a plethora of objects, such as Databases, TableDefs, QueryDefs, and Recordsets. ADO does a lot of stuff by using two objects: connections and recordsets. In fact, the flexible nature of ADO allows you to directly create a recordset and a connection in a single statement when you don't want to have a separate connection.

This chapter covers the Command object, which is a major element in ADO objects. What does the Command object do? In one sense, you can say it doesn't do anything. The purpose of the Command object is to pass instructions from your program to the specified data source and then to receive the results.

When you use a recordset object, you start with the assumption that you're going to be dealing with columns and rows of data. A Command object may also return a recordset, but it can also perform all sorts of tasks, many of which don't return recordsets or any data at all.

On the other hand, it's important to remember that because Command objects merely pass on instructions to the OLE DB provider, the type and structure of valid commands depend on the specific provider that you're working with. Although ADO doesn't care what type of instruction it assigns to a Command object, the provider that receives the instruction certainly does. Working with the Command object often requires specific, detailed knowledge of the features of the OLE DB provider.

The Command object has two functions:

- **Create recordsets:** You can create recordsets with Command objects. However, Command objects allow you to create records by using special options, such as query parameters. They also allow you to create recordsets based on data source structures, such as procedures (written in the native language of the data source), stored on the data source.

- **Execute operations:** You can pass an instruction to a data source by using a Command object. These operations may include standard tasks, such as insert, delete, and update with SQL, or special tasks, such as creating tables, indexes, and views that are supported by the specific provider.

Command object basics

The Command object is a bit more complicated to work with than the recordset object, which makes sense because the Command object supports a wider variety of operations. The four basic steps that are involved in using a Command object are

✔ **ActiveConnection property.** You can set the connection by using either an existing connection object or a valid connection string. If you don't want to create a separate connection object, use a connection string.

✔ **CommandText property.** This property defines the instruction that the Command object passes to the OLE DB provider. The text must be written to conform to the instruction set for your provider. Because Access, Oracle, and SQL Server have different instruction sets, you need to know the language and syntax of the specific provider referenceded in the `ActiveConnection` property.

✔ **Execute.** This operation actually submits the command to the provider.

✔ **Get the result.** The result of the command differs, depending on the task specified in the command. In some cases, you may not have a visible result at all. In other cases, the result may be a value or a complete recordset. Handling the result may involve the creation of other objects. For example, if the command creates a recordset, you need to create a recordset object based on the command in order to manipulate the data.

Creating a recordset with a command

To acquaint you with the use of the Command object, I take a look at how you can create a recordset by using a Command object.

The simplest way to use a Command object is with `SimpleCmd1`. Here's how:

1. **Assign a connection, in the form of a connection object or a connection string, to the command.**

2. **Assign an instruction to the** `CommandText` **property of the command.**

   In this case, the instruction is a simple SQL statement that counts the number of records in the Customers table. The `Execute` method is what causes the specified instruction to be sent to the provider.

```
Sub SimpleCmd1()
    Dim Cmd As New ADODB.Command
    Cmd.ActiveConnection = FileDS
    Cmd.CommandText = "SELECT Count(*) FROM Customers"
    Cmd.Execute
End Sub
```

You need to use an equal sign (=) with the ActiveConnection property because in Visual Basic object terms, you use this character when you assign a value to property. When you specify an argument for a method, you don't use an equal sign. For example, `Open` is a method, so you don't use an equal sign. On the other hand, ActiveConnection is a property of the Command object, so it requires one.

What happens when you execute `SimpleCmd1`? Nothing! Well, not really nothing. What I mean is that nothing visible happens. The provider does receive the instruction but because the result is a recordset, you need to create a recordset object to manipulate the data.

To create a recordset based on the result of a command, you use a statement that assigns the command to the `Source` property of the recordset, like this:

```
RecordsetObject.Open Source:=CommandObject
```

`SimpleCmd2` uses this approach to create a recordset, RS, which in turn is used to display the data (in this case the number of customer records) in a message box.

```
Sub SimpleCmd2()
    Dim Cmd As New ADODB.Command
    Dim Rs As New ADODB.Recordset
    Cmd.ActiveConnection = FileDS
    Cmd.CommandText = "SELECT Count(*) FROM Customers"
    Cmd.Execute
    Rs.Open Cmd
    MsgBox Rs(0)
End Sub
```

An important feature of a recordset that's created from a command is that you don't need to specify a connection for the recordset. The connection to the provider is already part of the Command object so that the recordset automatically inherits the connection. (`SimpleCmd2SS` performs the same task by using the Internet database as the source.)

Command objects can operate on the same type of data-source items as a recordset. In addition to a SQL statement, you have the option to use the name of a table or view as the data source. `SimpleCmd3` references `CustomerCount`, which is a query stored in the Access database. If you use a SQL or Oracle Server as the source, you can reference views as well as tables.

```
Sub SimpleCmd3()
    Dim Cmd As New ADODB.Command
    Dim Rs As New ADODB.Recordset
    Cmd.ActiveConnection = FileDS
    Cmd.CommandText = "CustomerCount"
    Cmd.Execute
    Rs.Open Cmd
    MsgBox Rs(0)
End Sub
```

Parameter queries

Of course, the preceding examples didn't do anything that you can't do by using a recordset object by itself, with a Command object. The advantage of the Command object is its ability to support the use of parameters.

`Param1` shows a procedure that executes a SQL statement that counts the number of customers in California (CA):

```
Sub Param1()
    Dim Cmd As New ADODB.Command
    Dim RS As New ADODB.Recordset
    Cmd.ActiveConnection = NetDS
    Cmd.CommandText = "SELECT count(*) From Customers " & _
        "WHERE BillState = 'CA'"
    Cmd.Execute
    RS.Open Cmd
    MsgBox RS(0)
End Sub
```

Suppose that now you want to count the customers in Colorado (CO) or Washington (WA). One way to do so is to alter the text of the SQL statement to reflect a different criterion. The alternative is to remove the specific value from the SQL statement and replace it with a placeholder. ADO allows you to insert a question mark (?) in place of a specific value within a SQL statement, as shown in the following example. This command creates a query that can be used to retrieve information about any state.

```
SELECT count(*) From Customers WHERE BillState = ?
```

You now have a new challenge. For the data provider to process the query, the question mark must be replaced with an actual value. The Command object supports a `Parameters collection`. Each parameter can hold a single value, such as a date, a number, or some text. When the `execute` statement sends the Command object to the provider, ADO sends both the `CommandText` and any values stored in the `Parameters collection`.

By default, the `Parameters collection` of a Command object is empty. To execute a parameter query in ADO, follow these steps:

1. **Insert one or more question mark (?) placeholders in the command text.**

2. **Create one Parameter object for each placeholder in the command text.**

   When you create the Parameter object, you define what type of data (such as text, number, and date) that the parameter holds.

3. **Add the Parameter objects to the** `Parameters collection` **of the Command object.**

4. **Assign a value to the parameter.**

Now you can execute the command and load the resulting data into a recordset.

Creating a parameter

The parameters used with a SQL command are treated as a collection of objects in the ADO model. A Parameter object has six properties:

- **Type (required).** This property determines the data type of the parameter, which is a value or a constant. Table 5-1 shows some commonly used data types. In many cases, this property is the only one required to create a parameter.

  The full list of DataType values can be found at
  `http://msdn.microsoft.com/library/psdk/dasdk/mdae8o19.htm`.

- **Size (required for some data types):** Some of the data types supported by ADO, such as `adVarChar`, require a size property. For example, in `adVarChar`. the size equates to the maximum number of characters that can be assigned to the parameter's value.

- **Name:** You can assign a descriptive name to the parameter so that you can refer to it by name rather than by its position number, such as `Parameter(0)`:

  ```
  CommandObject.Parameters("param name")
  ```

- **Direction:** Parameter values can be passed from the application to the provider (input) or from the provider to application (output). The default is an input.

- **Attribute:** Attributes refer to the type of data a parameter can handle. For example, in some cases, parameters cannot support null values.

- **Value:** This property is the value of the parameter. This `parameter` property is the only one that can be changed after it's been added to the `Parameters collection` of a Command object.

Table 5-1	Parameter DataType Values	
Constant	**Value**	**Description**
adInteger	3	4-byte integer
adVarChar	200	Variable length text (requires size property)
adCurrency	6	Currency numeric values
adDate	7	Date values

The CreateParameter method

The Command object supports a method called `CreateParameter`, which can be used to define a parameter, as follows:

```
Commandobj.CreateParameter (Name,Type,Direction,Size,Value)
```

Keep in mind that creating a `Parameter object` doesn't add the parameter to the Parameters collection of the Command object. Doing that requires a second step in which the `Append` method is used to add the parameter to the command's `parameters` collection, such as:

```
Commandobj.Parameters.Append parameterobj
```

If you create the parameter but don't append it, the command won't be able to retrieve the data. `Param2` shows how to use the `CreateParameter` method to create a query with a parameter. First, the `CreateParameter` method is used to define a `Parameter object` called `WhichState`. Note that this parameter is assigned the value `CA` when it's created. However, you can assign or change the value at any time. When you execute the command, the last value assigned to the parameter is the value passed to the provider.

Before the command is executed, `WhichState` is added to the `Parameters collection` of `Cmd` with the `Append` method. Note that the parameter is appended to the `Parameters collection` of the `Cmd` object, not directly to the `Cmd` object itself.

```
Sub Param2()
    Dim Cmd As New ADODB.Command
    Dim RS As New ADODB.Recordset
    Dim WhichState As ADODB.Parameter
    Cmd.ActiveConnection = NetDS
    Cmd.CommandText = "SELECT count(*) From Customers " & _
        "WHERE BillState = ?"
    Set WhichState = Cmd.CreateParameter( _
        "StateAbbr", adVarChar, adParamInput, 2, "CA")
    Cmd.Parameters.Append WhichState
    Cmd.Execute
    RS.Open Cmd
    MsgBox RS(0)
End Sub
```

You can get confused easily between the name of the `Parameter` object and the `Name` property of the parameter. In `Param2`, the parameter is called `WhichState`. When that parameter is appended to the Command object, it's assigned the name `StateAbbr`. When you refer to the parameter that's part of the Command object, you use the name `StateAbbr`, not `WhichState` — which is the name of the `Parameter` object.

Creating a parameter with CreateParameter

As with most operations in ADO, you can write the code that creates a parameter in more than one way. In `Param3`, the keyword `New` is used to create a `Parameter` object, which in this case is called `WhichState`.

The parameter is defined by using separate statements to set the `Type`, `Size`, and `Value` properties. Note that you must still append the Parameter object to the `Parameters collection` of the Command object to execute the query.

```
Sub Param3()
    Dim Cmd As New ADODB.Command
    Dim RS As New ADODB.Recordset
    Dim WhichState As New ADODB.Parameter
    Cmd.ActiveConnection = NetDS
    Cmd.CommandText = "SELECT count(*) From Customers " & _
        "WHERE BillState = ?"
    WhichState.Type = adVarChar
    WhichState.Size = 2
    WhichState.Value = "CA"
    Cmd.Parameters.Append WhichState
    Cmd.Execute
    RS.Open Cmd
    MsgBox RS(0)
End Sub
```

In Param3, the parameter isn't given a name. The name is optional because parameters can always be referenced by their position (ordinal) within the Parameters collection. In ADO, the Parameters collection is zero-based, meaning that the first parameter in the collection is referenced as Parameters(0).

Setting parameter values after appending

In the parameter examples shown so far, the value of the parameter is assigned before the parameter is appended to the Command object. However, you can alter the value of the parameter at any time before or after the parameter has been added to the Command object. Keep in mind that other parameter properties, such as Type or Size, are locked after the parameter is added to the Command object. Value is an exception to this rule. In Param4, the value of the parameter is assigned through the Parameters collection of the Command object.

```
Sub Param4()
    Dim Cmd As New ADODB.Command
    Dim RS As New ADODB.Recordset
    Dim WhichState As New ADODB.Parameter
    Cmd.ActiveConnection = NetDS
    Cmd.CommandText = "SELECT count(*) From Customers " & _
        "WHERE BillState = ?"
    WhichState.Type = adVarChar
    WhichState.Size = 2
    Cmd.Parameters.Append WhichState
    Cmd.Parameters(0) = "CA"
    Cmd.Execute
    RS.Open Cmd
    MsgBox RS(0)
End Sub
```

This small difference is significant because it indicates how you can use a single Command object to retrieve any number of recordsets by merely changing the value of the parameters and reexecuting the command. I cover this technique later in this chapter.

You may find that your code reads better if you use descriptive names rather than ordinals to reference parameters. Param5 is identical to Param4 with the exception that the parameter is assigned the name StateAbbr. The Name property makes it possible to use the StateAbbr name when you assign a value to the parameter within the Parameters collection of the Command object.

```
Sub Param5()
    ...same as Param4
    WhichState.Name = "StateAbbr"
    Cmd.Parameters.Append WhichState
    Cmd.Parameters("StateAbbr") = "CA"
    ...same as Param4
End Sub
```

Of course, the value assigned to a parameter needn't be hardwired into your code. The advantage of the parameter is that you can easily acquire its value from any source. In Param6 the value is obtained from the user through an input box. When this procedure is executed, the user can enter any state abbreviation and get the results of the customer count.

```
Sub Param6()
    Dim Cmd As New ADODB.Command
    Dim RS As New ADODB.Recordset
    Dim WhichState As New ADODB.Parameter
    Cmd.ActiveConnection = NetDS
    Cmd.CommandText = "SELECT count(*) From Customers " & _
        "WHERE BillState = ?"
    WhichState.Type = adVarChar
    WhichState.Size = 2
    WhichState.Name = "StateAbbr"
    Cmd.Parameters.Append WhichState
    Cmd.Parameters("StateAbbr") = InputBox("Count Customers in ?")
    Cmd.Execute
    RS.Open Cmd
    MsgBox RS(0)
End Sub
```

The value of parameterized queries

You may have realized that the results obtained with Param6 (refer to Chapters 3 and 4) can be achieved without using parameters at all. Param6a is functionally identical to Param6 without using any parameters, like this:

```
Sub Param6a()
    Dim Cmd As New ADODB.Command
    Dim RS As New ADODB.Recordset
    Cmd.ActiveConnection = NetDS
    Cmd.CommandText = "SELECT count(*) From Customers " & _
        "WHERE BillState = '" & _
        InputBox("Count Customers in ?") & "'"
    Cmd.Execute
    RS.Open Cmd
    MsgBox RS(0)
End Sub
```

What's the rationale for going through all the trouble of creating parameters to perform this type of query? Programming style, that's what. Although `Param6a` is substantially shorter than `Param6`, it isn't necessarily easier to understand because the final shape of the command is difficult to picture. You need to imagine how the input from the user combines with the rest of the command and how the apostrophes function as delimiters to complete the command.

On the other hand, starting out with a parameterized query indicates clearly the role that the parameter value plays in the command. You also don't have to be concerned with the tedious business of inserting embedded apostrophes or other delimiters. That function is taken care of when you set the data type of the parameter. Here's what a parameterized query looks like:

```
SELECT count(*) From Customers WHERE BillState = ?
```

The advantage of using parameters increases as the number of parameters that need to be inserted into the command text increases. For example, if you need to insert parameters for city, state, and zip code, it's much easier to use placeholders and parameters than to compose a string that concatenates all the text and delimiters correctly.

Assigning values to parameters indirectly

After you append a parameter to a command, it seems logical that any changes to the value of the parameter are addressed through the Parameters collection of the Command object.

However, you can assign a value to the `Parameter` object and have that value flow through to the Command object. `Param7` contains a subtle but interesting variation on the preceding examples. Note that the state abbreviation `CA` is assigned after the `Append` method has added the parameter to the Command object. What's different is that it's being assigned to `WhichState`, the `Parameter` object.

```
Sub Param7()
    ...same as Param4
    WhichState.Size = 2
    WhichState.Name = "StateAbbr"
    Cmd.Parameters.Append WhichState
    WhichState = "CA"
    ...same as Param4
End Sub
```

In this case, the net result is the same as if you'd assigned the value to the parameter within the Command object. Because both objects are still in existence, you have the option to do it either way. I personally find this code confusing, and I include it only because I've seen examples that use this approach. My own instinct is to discard the Parameter object after it's been appended and address value changes directly to the Command object.

Using multiple parameters

You are by no means limited to using a single parameter when executing a command. For example, suppose that you want to count the number of orders in the Orders table for a range of dates. You can use a query like this one in which the start and end dates are parameters:

```
SELECT count(*)
FROM Orders
WHERE OrderDate Between ? and ?"
```

In this case, you need to create a Command object with two parameters in its Parameters collection. You can approach this problem by creating two Parameter objects and appending each one to the Command object. In ParamDates1, two Parameter objects (P1 and P2) are defined as date-type parameters, which are appended to the Parameters collection of the Cmd Command object.

```
Function ParamDates1(Sdate, Edate)
    Dim Cmd As New ADODB.Command
    Dim RS As New ADODB.Recordset
    Dim P1 As New ADODB.Parameter
    Dim P2 As New ADODB.Parameter
    Cmd.ActiveConnection = NetDS
    Cmd.CommandText = "SELECT count(*) FROM Orders " & _
        "WHERE OrderDate Between ? and ?"
    P1.Type = adDate
    Cmd.Parameters.Append P1
    P2.Type = adDate
    Cmd.Parameters.Append P2
    Cmd.Parameters(0) = Sdate
    Cmd.Parameters(1) = Edate
    RS.Open Cmd
    ParamDates1 = RS(0) & " orders between " _
    & Sdate & " - " & Edate
End Function
```

Because a date-type parameter doesn't require a size property, the Parameter object can be defined with a single statement.

Note that ADO allows only a question mark (?) to serve as a placeholder in a parameterized query. ADO assigns values to the placeholders sequentially so that the first question mark is assigned parameter(0), the second parameter(1), and so on. Even if the parameters have names assigned to their name properties, you cannot insert those names as placeholders in the command text.

Although nothing's wrong with using one Parameter object for each parameter you want to append to the collection, creating all the required parameters with a single Parameter object seems more elegant. In fact, you can use a single parameter to add as many parameters to a Parameters collection as you like. But there's a trick. When you look at the following code, it appears to add two date parameters to the Parameters collection of the Cmd object. But this code results in an error on the last line that reads Object already in collection. Cannot append.

```
'Incorrect
Dim P As New ADODB.Parameter
P.Type = adDate
Cmd.Parameters.Append P
Cmd.Parameters.Append P
```

The reason for the error relates to a point made earlier in the section, "Assigning values to parameters indirectly." After the parameter is appended, ADO doesn't terminate the Parameter object. In fact, the Parameter object is linked to the parameter in the Command object. Remember that if you change the value of the Parameter object, you also change the value of the parameter in the Command object. ADO sees the object P as the same parameter that's already in its collection and rejects the attempt to add the same thing a second time.

What's the trick? Terminate P before you try to add a second instance to the collection. Terminating an object is accomplished by setting the object to the keyword Nothing, as shown in the following example:

```
P.Type = adDate
Cmd.Parameters.Append P
Set P = Nothing
```

ParamDates2 uses this technique to add two parameters to the Cmd Parameters collection by using a single Parameter object P. After you set the parameter to Nothing, the parameter returns to its initial state, which is an empty set of properties. You must define the parameter's Type property to the desired data type before you append it to the collection.

```
Function ParamDates2(Sdate, Edate)
    Dim Cmd As New ADODB.Command
    Dim RS As New ADODB.Recordset
    Dim P As New ADODB.Parameter
    Cmd.ActiveConnection = NetDS
    Cmd.CommandText = "SELECT count(*) FROM Orders " & _
        "WHERE OrderDate Between ? and ?"
    P.Type = adDate
    Cmd.Parameters.Append P
    Set P = Nothing
    P.Type = adDate
    Cmd.Parameters.Append P
    Set P = Nothing
    Cmd.Parameters(0) = Sdate
    Cmd.Parameters(1) = Edate
    RS.Open Cmd
    ParamDates2 = RS(0) & " orders between " & Sdate & " - " & Edate
End Function
```

The `TestParamDates` procedure runs both functions, which return the same information:

```
Sub TestParamDates()
    MsgBox ParamDates1(#4/1/1999#, #6/30/1999#)
    MsgBox ParamDates2(#4/1/1999#, #6/30/1999#)
End Sub
```

Reusing a Command object

One of the main reasons for creating a `Command` object that uses parameters is that you can use one `Command` object to retrieve any number of recordsets. For example, suppose you create a `Command` object that returns the `CustomerID` after you enter the name of the customer. The following `LocateCustomerids` procedure creates a Command object that requires two parameters that correspond to the criteria for `Firstname` and `Lastname` in the `Customers` table:

```
Sub LocateCustomerids()
    Dim Cmd As New ADODB.Command
    Dim parmFname As ADODB.Parameter
    Dim parmLName As ADODB.Parameter
    Cmd.ActiveConnection = NetDS
    Cmd.CommandText = "SELECT CustomerID FROM Customers " & _
        "WHERE Firstname = ? and Lastname = ?"
    Set parmFname = _
        Cmd.CreateParameter(Type:=adVarChar, _
        Size:=50)
    Set parmLName = _
        Cmd.CreateParameter(Type:=adVarChar, _
        Size:=50)
    Cmd.Parameters.Append parmFname
    Cmd.Parameters.Append parmLName
    GetCustID Cmd
End Sub
```

Although `LocateCustomerids` creates the `Command` object and its `Parameters` collection, it doesn't assign values to the parameters nor does it execute the command. Rather, it passes the `Command` object to another procedure, `GetCustID`, which appears in the example that follows.

The `GetCustID` procedure is designed to use a loop that uses the `Command` object over and over to retrieve as many customer IDs as you like. This retrieval is accomplished with a `Do. . .Loop`, which contains an `InputBox` statement. The loop repeats until the user enters an empty input box.

If the input isn't empty, the entry is broken into a first- and last-name portion that's then assigned to the two parameters in the `Command Objects` collection. The `Command` object is then used to retrieve a recordset based on the parameters.

```
Function GetCustID(Qry As ADODB.Command)
    Dim CustName, RS As New ADODB.Recordset, Result
    Do
        CustName = InputBox("Get ID for Customer:", Result)
        If CustName = Empty Then Exit Do
        Qry.Parameters(0) = Left(CustName, _
            InStr(CustName, Chr(32)) - 1)
        Qry.Parameters(1) = Mid(CustName,
            InStr(CustName, Chr(32)) + 1)
        Qry.Execute
        RS.Open Qry
        Result = CustName & " & #" & RS(0)
        RS.Close
    Loop
End Function
```

This code assumes that the user will enter a valid Customer ID. If the customer ID isn't found in the table, any reference to a field in the recordset, for example, RS(0), results in an error. The Eof property can be used to avoid this error. GetCustID1 adds codes that check the Eof property of the RS recordset. If Eof is true, the Customer ID was invalid. GetCustID1 displays a message box if the Customer ID cannot be found.

```
Function GetCustID1(Qry As ADODB.Command)
    Dim CustName, RS As New ADODB.Recordset, Result
    Do
        CustName = InputBox("Get ID for Customer:", Result)
        If CustName = Empty Then Exit Do
        Qry.Parameters(0) = Left(CustName, _
            InStr(CustName, Chr(32)) - 1)
        Qry.Parameters(1) = Mid(CustName,
            InStr(CustName, Chr(32)) + 1)
        Qry.Execute
        RS.Open Qry
        If Rs.Eof Then
            Msgbox "Invalid Customer ID"
        Else
            Result = CustName & " & #" & RS(0)
        End If
        RS.Close
    Loop
End Function
```

The procedure needs to break up the name entered into first and last name. There's an assumption that the first space, Chr(32), is located at the break between first and last names. The Instr( ) function locates the position of the first space. The Left( ) function takes all the characters up to that location as the first name, while the Mid( ) function takes all the characters after the space as the last name.

Run LocateCustomerids and enter names like Bob Otis, Ian Hill, Harry Smith, or Gina Turner. The procedure locates the ID numbers for these customers by assigning new values to the parameters and re-executing the command. The result of each search appears as the title of the input box.

Commands That Don't Return Records

Command objects can be used to execute operations that don't return recordsets. These operations include the standard task's data-altering insert, delete, and update, plus other provider-specific operations. In this chapter, I focus on standard data operations that are supported by most providers. I cover provider-specific operations in Chapter 7.

In this section, you add, delete, and update records. The NewCustomer function helps you monitor the results of various operations. The function returns the ID and the name of the last customer in the Customers table. The function accepts a connection string as an argument, which makes it possible to check either the file or the Internet data sources with the same function. To check the local database, you pass FileDS as the argument. To check the Internet table, you pass NetDS as the argument.

```
Function NewCustomer(CntString)
    Dim RS As New ADODB.Recordset
    RS.Open "SELECT CustomerID, RecordCreated, FirstName, LastName " & _
        "FROM Customers WHERE Customerid = " & _
        "(SELECT Max(CustomerID) FROM Customers)", CntString
    NewCustomer = RS(0) & " " & _
    RS(1) & " " & RS(2) & " " & RS(3)
End Function
```

An interesting aspect of this function is that it employs an SQL technique called a subquery. A *subquery* is SQL query that is nested inside a SQL query.

The premise of the query is that the new customer is the one with the largest customer ID number because the CustomerID field is set to generate sequential values for customer IDs. Of course, you don't know in advance what the exact value of the largest ID is, so you can't hardwire that number into the statement. Instead, at the location in the query where the CustomerID should go is another SQL query enclosed in parentheses ( ). This query returns the largest value in the CustomerID field. When this command is passed to the provider, that program first executes the subquery and then uses the result to complete the main query.

```
SELECT CustomerID, FirstName, LastName
FROM Customers WHERE Customerid =
(SELECT Max(CustomerID) FROM Customers)
```

Inserting records with commands

An alternative to using AddNew to add records to a recordset (refer to Chapter 4) is to use a Command object to execute the SQL INSERT command, assuming that the data source is a SQL-based database. INSERT requires two lists: The first list, which uses no keyword, includes the fields in the new record that you want to populate with date. The VALUES list contains the data that's to be inserted into the new record. INSERT connects field names with values based on the order in which the items appear in the two lists. The SQL INSERT command has the following general form:

```
INSERT INTO tablename
(field1,field2,...)
VALUES(value1,value2,...)
```

InsertRecord creates a new record in the Customers table and places data in three fields of the new record:

```
Sub InsertRecord()
    Dim Cmd As New ADODB.Command
    Cmd.ActiveConnection = FileDS
    Cmd.CommandText = "INSERT INTO Customers " & _
    "(RecordCreated,FirstName,LastName) VALUES (Date(),'Carolyn','Krumm')"
    Cmd.Execute
    Set Cmd = Nothing
    MsgBox NewCustomer(FileDS)
End Sub
```

Conversely, you can use a Command object to execute a SQL Delete statement to remove a record from a table. The DeleteRecord removes the new record that you just added with InsertRecord.

```
Sub DeleteRecord()
    Dim Cmd As New ADODB.Command
    Cmd.ActiveConnection = FileDS
    Cmd.CommandText = "DELETE FROM Customers " & _
    "WHERE FirstName='Carolyn' AND LastName='Krumm'"
    Cmd.Execute
    Set Cmd = Nothing
    MsgBox NewCustomer(FileDS)
End Sub
```

Caching and object termination

You may wonder why DeleteRecord contains the statement Set Cmd = Nothing. If this statement isn't included, the NewCustomer procedure doesn't retrieve the newest record. The problem isn't caused by an error in the NewCustomer procedure, but by the way that ADO and the provider manage resources. In this case, the provider is an Access MDB file. As shown in Figure 5-1, ADO doesn't actually commit the new record that's added in the procedure to the provider database until the Command object that's inserted into the new record is terminated — which happens automatically at the end of the procedure.

However, the procedure that checks for the new record, NewCustomer, executes before the end of the InsertRecord procedure. The result is that NewCustomer reaches the provider before the new record and consequently returns the wrong record.

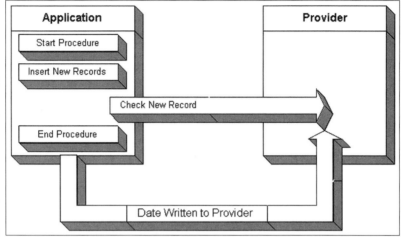

Figure 5-1:
Access
holds the
new record
in a cache
until the
Command
object is
terminated.

Figure 5-1 illustrates a technique called *caching*. Many systems use caching to delay physical implementation of logical instructions to better use system resources. In this case, ADO doesn't send the new record to the provider at the moment the Execute method is applied. Rather, it holds the new data in memory until the Command object is no longer needed. If you don't specifically terminate the Command object with a statement, such as Set Cmd = Nothing, then the new record remains in memory until the end of the procedure. By adding Set Cmd = Nothing before NewCustomer is executed, you resolve the problem by forcing ADO to commit the record before the end of the procedure, as shown in Figure 5-2. With this additional statement, the code runs as you expect.

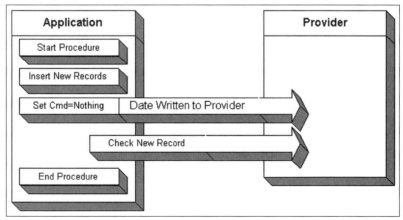

Figure 5-2:
Closing the
command
object
forces the
new data to
be written to
the provider
before the
end of the
procedure.

The previously described behavior does not apply to all ADO providers. The following procedures insert and then delete a new record, like InsertRecord and DeleteRecord. Despite the fact that these procedures don't include the Set Cmd = Nothing statement, they produce the desired results. In this case, because the provider is a SQL Server (a client/server database service), the INSERT operation is automatically committed to the provider database regardless of the state of the ADO Command object.

Because all readers of this book share the Internet database, please run both of these procedures if you run the first one so that you return the Internet database to its original state.

```
Sub InsertRecordSS()
    Dim Cmd As New ADODB.Command
    Cmd.ActiveConnection = NetDS
    Cmd.CommandText = "INSERT INTO Customers " & _
    "(RecordCreated,FirstName,LastName) VALUES (Getdate(),'Carolyn','Krumm')"
    Cmd.Execute
    MsgBox NewCustomer(NetDS)
End Sub
```

```
Sub DeleteRecordSS()
    Dim Cmd As New ADODB.Command
    Cmd.ActiveConnection = NetDS
    Cmd.CommandText = "DELETE FROM Customers " & _
    "WHERE FirstName='Carolyn' AND LastName='Krumm'"
    Cmd.Execute
    MsgBox NewCustomer(NetDS)
End Sub
```

If you don't live in the Eastern U.S. time zone, you may notice that the time portion of the RecordCreated value returned in InsertRecordSS appears to be wrong. That happens because the time isn't inserted by ADO running on your computer but by the provider database that's running on the database server. Because the server is located in the Eastern U.S., all new records are stamped with EST.

It's probably better programming form to terminate objects and close record-sets explicitly rather than simply depend on the application to perform these actions when procedures begin and end.

Note: In a majority of the cases, it won't make any practical difference whether you do or do not explicitly terminate or close the ADO objects you use. However, because in some cases the behavior of the application can be affected by automatic operations, such as caching, you should be aware that object terminate or the lack of it may be affect how the ADO work.

Terminating the object isn't the only matter at hand. In InsertRecord, the important factor is that the Set Cmd = Nothing statement precedes execution of NewCustomer. By placing Set Cmd = Nothing after calling NewCustomer, you won't solve the problem.

Using provider functions

If you look carefully at the two insert procedures, InsertRecord and InsertRecordSS, you notice that the SQL statements used to create the new records differ in one respect: namely, the function used to insert the current date. InsertRecord uses Date( ), while InsertRecordSS uses GetDate( ).

```
Cmd.CommandText = "INSERT INTO Customers " & _
"(RecordCreated,FirstName,LastName) VALUES (Date(),'Carolyn','Krumm')"
Cmd.CommandText = "INSERT INTO Customers " & _
"(RecordCreated,FirstName,LastName) VALUES (Getdate(),'Carolyn','Krumm')"
```

The functions represent the provider-specific functions that insert the current date. Because InsertRecordSS is executed by a SQL Server, you must use the SQL server date function, Getdate( ), rather than Date( ), which is used by Access.

When you send commands with the Command object, the syntax must match the syntax supported by the provider.

Inserting with parameters

You can avoid issues like the provider-specific date functions mentioned in the preceding section by using parameters with the Command object. InsertRecordParams creates three parameters; one for each field that's going to be inserted into the new record. The values are then assigned to each parameter individually.

```
Sub InsertRecordParams()
    Dim Cmd As New ADODB.Command
    Dim P As ADODB.Parameter
    Cmd.ActiveConnection = FileDS
    Cmd.CommandText = "INSERT INTO Customers " & _
    "(RecordCreated, FirstName,LastName) VALUES (?,?,?)"
    Set P = Cmd.CreateParameter(Type:=adDate)
    Cmd.Parameters.Append P
    Set P = Cmd.CreateParameter(Type:=adVarChar, Size:=50)
    Cmd.Parameters.Append P
    Set P = Cmd.CreateParameter(Type:=adVarChar, Size:=50)
    Cmd.Parameters.Append P
    Cmd.Parameters(0) = Date
    Cmd.Parameters(1) = "Ruth"
    Cmd.Parameters(2) = "Glass"
    Cmd.Execute
    Set Cmd = Nothing
    MsgBox NewCustomer(FileDS)
End Sub
```

This approach avoids problems with provider-specific operation because the date value is calculated in the application, in this example by using the Visual Basic function Date( ). The command passed to the provider already contains the current date as calculated by the application.

Another advantage of using parameters to insert data is that you can reuse the Command object simply by setting the parameters to new values and executing it again.

Updates

The SQL Update command can be used to modify the contents of one or more records. When you edit a recordset, you can only change one record at a time. To alter the values of multiple records, you must navigate through the recordset with a loop and repeatedly apply the change to each record.

In general, if you're updating a significant number of records, sending a SQL Update command is much more efficient than editing multiple records in a recordset. If the provider is a client/server database, such as SQL Server or Oracle, the benefits are even greater because the entire update process is handled at the server. None of the modified data needs to travel over the network. (See Chapter 7 for more information about client/server databases.)

UpdateFullname uses a Command object, Cmd, to perform an update query that fills the Fullname field with a combination of the first and last names and affects every record in the Customers table.

```
Sub UpdateFullname()
    Dim Cmd As New ADODB.Command
    Cmd.ActiveConnection = FileDS
    Cmd.CommandText = "UPDATE Customers " & _
        "SET FullName = FirstName & ' ' & LastName"
    Cmd.Execute
End Sub
```

UpdateCustTotalsSS performs an update query on a SQL Server database. The query calculates the total amount of sales recorded in the Orders table for each customer and writes that total into the TotalSales field in the Customer table.

```
Sub UpdateCustTotalsSS()
    Dim Cmd As New ADODB.Command
    Cmd.ActiveConnection = NetDS
    Cmd.CommandText = "UPDATE Customers " & _
        "SET TotalSales = " & _
        "(SELECT Sum(OrderTotal) FROM Orders " & _
        " WHERE Orders.Customerid = Customers.Customerid)"
    Cmd.Execute
End Sub
```

The SQL statement executed in UpdateCustTotalsSS uses a subquery to obtain the total of the orders from the Orders table for each customer. Although many providers are SQL based (which is worth remembering),

differences in implementation do exist. For example, the following query
cannot be executed against the Access MDB data source; SQL Server or
Oracle can execute this query. The query looks like this:

```
UPDATE Customers
SET TotalSales =
  (SELECT Sum(OrderTotal) FROM Orders
   WHERE Orders.Customerid = Customers.Customerid)
```

Executing directly with Command object

In ADO, you can execute a command without specifically creating a
Command object. Rather, the command text is used as an argument for the
Execute method of the connection (not the command) object.

```
ConnectionObj.Exexute commandtext
```

An example of a SQL operation that can be executed directly is an update
query like the one that follows. This query creates a new table,
SalesSummary, by inserting a summary of the number of bottles of each type
of wine sold. The INTO clause causes the output of the SELECT statement to
be directed toward a new table rather than a recordset object.

```
SELECT WineName,Sum(Bottles) As Units
INTO SalesSummary FROM OrderDetails
INNER JOIN WineProductCatalog
ON Orderdetails.WineID = WineProductCatalog.WineID
GROUP BY WineName
```

The ExecuteDirect procedure shows how an instruction, such as the preceding SQL statement, can be executed using only a connection object. Note
that the Execute method of the connection object can only be used after
the connection has been opened.

```
Sub ExecuteDirect()
  Dim Cnt As New ADODB.Connection
  Cnt.ConnectionString = FileDS
  Cnt.Open
  Cnt.Execute "SELECT WineName,Sum(Bottles) As Units" & _
  " INTO SalesSummary " & _
  "FROM OrderDetails " & _
  "INNER JOIN WineProductCatalog " & _
  "ON Orderdetails.WineID = WineProductCatalog.WineID " & _
  "GROUP BY WineName"
End Sub
```

ExecuteDirect is another example of how flexible the ADO model is. In this
case, a single object, Connection, is sufficient to execute a fairly complex
SQL statement on any SQL based OLE DB provider.

What you can't do with parameters

Parameter queries provide an organized structure for applying different criteria to a given command query. However, parameters are limited to substitution of the values within a query.

What you cannot do with a parameter is insert an element into the SQL statement. For example, suppose you want to create a procedure that counts the records in any table you specify. The idea is that the name of the table is a parameter in a SQL statement like this one:

```
SELECT count(*) From ?
```

Each time you execute the procedure, you can pass the name of the table you want to count as a parameter. Substitute1 shows how you can try to create such a procedure:

```
Sub Substitute1() 'does not work
    Dim Cmd As New ADODB.Command
    Dim RS As New ADODB.Recordset
    Dim P As New ADODB.Parameter
    Cmd.ActiveConnection = NetDS
    Cmd.CommandText = "SELECT count(*) From ? "
    P.Type = adVarChar
    P.Size = 40
    P.Name = "FieldName"
    Cmd.Parameters.Append P
    P.Value = InputBox("Table Name")
    Cmd.Execute
    RS.Open Cmd
    MsgBox RS(0)
End Sub
```

As you discover when you attempt to run Substitute1, parameters cannot be used this way. The only way to achieve this type of substitution for elements, such as table names or field names, is to compose SQL statements by combining literal text with text. Substitute2 composes a SQL statement that inserts the user input into the SQL statement at the position where the name of the source table should appear. This procedure allows you to select any table, that is, Orders or Customers, for counting.

```
Sub Substitute2()
    Dim Cmd As New ADODB.Command
    Dim RS As New ADODB.Recordset
    Dim P As New ADODB.Parameter
    Cmd.ActiveConnection = NetDS
    Cmd.CommandText = "SELECT count(*) From " & _
        InputBox("Table Name")
    Cmd.Execute
    RS.Open Cmd
    MsgBox RS(0)
End Sub
```

Part III
Programming with ADO

The 5th Wave   By Rich Tennant

©RICHTENNANT

"It's a ten step word processing program. It comes with a spell-checker, grammar-checker, cliche-checker, whine-checker, passive/aggressive-checker, politically correct-checker, hissy-fit-checker, pretentious pontificating-checker, boring anecdote-checker and a Freudian reference-checker."

In this part . . .

When you want to build an application that includes database access, ADO becomes a tool that can be used in a number of different ways. In Part III, I show you how ADO database operations can be integrated into the user interface elements that create a working application.

Chapter 6

Building Data-Enhanced User Interfaces with ADO

● ●

In This Chapter

▶ Using non-bound forms and controls

▶ Using a flex grid control to display a recordset

▶ Dynamically linking controls with ADO code

▶ Using the slider control to select names

▶ Linking multiple flex grid displays

● ●

*P*arts I and II of this book looked at the nuts and bolts structures of ADO. Now that you know how to use the basic ADO tool set, I now turn my attention to applying those tools to the part of the application that the users actually see: namely, the user interface that, in database applications, takes the form of data forms and dialog boxes.

Access and Visual Basic 6.0 have some very handy tools for automatically generating forms in which controls, typically text boxes, can be bound to data sources for editing the data stored in various data sources. In this book, I assume you're familiar with this type of form, which provides basic data entry in database applications. In Access 2000, these forms are bound to the tables that are in or attached to the current MDB. In Visual Basic 6.0, the forms are generated using the data form wizard, which can bind forms with either ADO or Data Access Objects (DAO).

My purpose in this chapter isn't to document this type of form creation, but to look at a different class of forms that provides interesting ways for users to navigate through large data sources. These forms combine ADO programming techniques with ActiveX controls, such as grids, sliders, and trees, to present data in interesting and intuitive displays. These forms represent and display the practical application of ActiveX data objects.

When you create a database application, locating specific records is your key to designing an intuitive user interface. ADO combined with ActiveX controls provides a wide range of visual options. This chapter shows you some useful code and hopefully stimulates your creativity when you design forms for your database applications.

Unbound Controls

In the following sections, you look at a number of ways in which the data in a relational database can be displayed for the purpose of navigating to specific records within the overall database. By its very nature, a relational database has no definite starting or entry point. In fact, throughout this book, I use a Wine-ordering database in which you can start with the Customers table, the Orders table, or the Product Catalog table as the entry point, depending on what type of task you have in mind.

Say you want to check on an order but you don't know the entry point into the database. You think it's the Orders table and perhaps it is, if you started out with an invoice number. More likely, you want to locate the most recent orders for a specific customer. The entry point is the customer name and that should let the system locate the orders related to that customer. However, finding the customer raises issues. What if you have 4,000 or 10,000 customer names in your table? And what if you're not sure of the exact spelling of the last name?

You need to create a screen interface that allows users to start with the type of data they usually know, such as the rough spelling of the last name (as obtained from a voice-mail message), and that quickly narrows their choices so they can locate the data they need.

This type of design is often as much art as it is science. I find that I get most of my ideas from watching people actually try to do their work with software (often my own). Then I go back to the drawing board and try to figure a better way to present the choices so that the application takes on a more intuitive feel.

The examples in this chapter are designed to show possible ways that you can make these presentations. In all cases, the controls aren't linked at design time to any specific data sources, which is what form generators do. Instead, the controls are all unbound. The data used to fill the controls is all acquired dynamically by using ADO code to generate commands and recordsets.

Inserting ActiveX Controls

The forms in this chapter move beyond the built-in controls that appear in the Standard tool box in Access 2000 and Visual Basic 6.0. These controls are typically installed with the Microsoft Office 2000 Developers edition or with Visual Basic 6.0.

ActiveX controls are typically supplied in the form of OXC or DLL files. If you use an ActiveX control as part of your application, that control must be installed on any other computers that are going to run that application. The best way to accomplish this is to use the Installation wizard that's included with either the Office 2000 Developers edition or with Visual Basic 6.0. Microsoft allows developers to install these controls free of charge so that your application can provide these features to your users.

Although all the controls and ADO techniques shown in this chapter run in either Access 2000 or Visual Basic 6.0, here are some of their differences:

- ✓ **Toolbar:** In Visual Basic 6.0, you add the ActiveX controls to the project so that the control becomes part of the project's tool box. You only need to do this once per project. When added to the tool box, you can add controls to any form by selecting the control's icon in the tool box and drawing the rectangle for the control at the location on the form where you want it placed. In Access 2000, you must open the Insert ActiveX Control dialog box each time that you want to add one of the controls to a form. Doing this is a bit less convenient than the Visual Basic 6.0 approach, but the result's identical.

- ✓ **Names:** In Visual Basic 6.0, the list of ActiveX controls lists the control OCX file. In Access, the individual controls are listed. This difference is important if the OXC file contains more than one ActiveX control. For example, the Slider control is actually one of nine controls included in the Microsoft Windows Common Control OCX file. In Access 2000, each control, such as Slider, Treeview, and Status Bar, is listed separately in the Insert ActiveX Control dialog box. In Visual Basic 6.0, you select Microsoft Windows Common Controls, and all nine individual controls are added to the tool box.

- ✓ **Library binding:** In VB/VBA, the type libraries for each object are automatically accessed to facilitate the auto-complete feature supported by the VB Editor. Each ActiveX control has a set of properties, methods, and collections that can be displayed in the auto-complete lists. However, the way that Access and Visual Basic 6.0 associate an ActiveX control with its corresponding object library is different. Visual Basic 6.0 automatically binds an ActiveX control to its corresponding library.

Access doesn't automatically link the library to the control because on an Access form, the ActiveX control is inserted in a special container called an ActiveX container. This extra layer means that the VB Editor in Access needs some additional help to figure out which object library matches an inserted ActiveX control. The help comes in the form of creating an object variable that's the same type as the ActiveX control, such as a slider. You then connect that control with the object variable by assigning the control's object property to the object variable like this:

```
Dim Sld As Slider
    Set Sld = Me.Slider1.Object
```

After you make this association, the auto-complete feature provides the correct list of properties and methods.

Library binding isn't required for the code to run properly. The following statement executes properly in either Visual Basic 6.0 or Access 2000. Library binding in Access 2000 is done only to make it more convenient to enter the code:

```
Slider1.Max = 26
```

ActiveX in Access 2000

You can insert any of the ActiveX controls installed on your system by opening a form and using the Insert ActiveX Control dialog box. Here's how:

1. **Choose Insert⇨Form from the menu bar.**

2. **In the New Form dialog box that appears, select Design View and click OK.**

3. **Click Insert and then click ActiveX Control.**

   Access 2000 displays a dialog box that shows all the ActiveX controls installed on the current system.

4. **Select the control you want to use, such as the Microsoft Hierarchical FlexGrid.**

   The control is inserted into the current form.

Access 2000 requires that each new ActiveX control be inserted by using the dialog box. You cannot copy and paste an existing control, and the control does not appear in the form design tool box.

ActiveX in Visual Basic 6.0

Visual Basic 6.0 can work with the same controls as Access 2000, but the implementation is a bit different. In Visual Basic 6.0, controls aren't added to forms but rather to the overall project. After they're added, the project's tool box includes icons that can be used to insert one or more instances of the specific control on any form in the project. To install ActiveX in Visual Basic 6.0, follow these steps:

1. **Choose Project⇨Components from the menu bar.**

   The Components dialog box appears.

2. **Use the scroll bar to locate the desired component and then click to put a check mark in the check box beside the component's name.**

   You can add as many components as you like while the dialog box is open.

The select ActiveX components are added to the project's toolbar. You then can add a control to a form by clicking the control icon in the toolbar and drawing the control rectangle on the form at the desired location.

Using the Hierarchical FlexGrid

The Hierarchical FlexGrid (HFG) control is a powerful tool for displaying data in a spreadsheet-style control. The hierarchical part refers to the ability of the grid to show one to many relationships by expanding rows to expose subsets of the primary. See Chapter 8 for more information about this feature. For now, the simple grid feature is of use.

The grid's key feature is that it provides a simple method for absorbing ADO and displaying it to the user. The `DataSource` property of the flex grid can be assigned a recordset object. After that's done, the grid automatically processes the record and displays each field in a column and each record in a row of the grid.

```
flexgridObj.Recordset = <adodb.recordset>
```

The `FillGrid` form utilizes the flex grid in about as simple a fashion as is possible. The code, entered in the `Form_Open` procedure, consists of three statements. The first statement creates a recordset, the second opens the recordset, and the third assigns the open recordset to the flex-grid control.

```
Private Sub Form_Open(Cancel As Integer)
    Dim RS As New ADODB.Recordset
    RS.Open "SELECT Customerid, Lastname ,FirstName " & _
        "FROM Customers", FileDS, adOpenStatic
    Set Me.NameList.DataSource = RS
End Sub
```

The result is a grid display that lists the Customers in the data provider.

Notice that the Form_Open event, not the Form_Load event, was used to exe-cute code that populated the grid. In Access 2000, two events occur after a form is opened. The Open event occurs as soon as the form opens but before any of the bound controls are populated with data. The Form_Load event occurs after the bound controls have been populated. In Visual Basic, you have only a Form_Load event. When there are no bound controls, there's no practical difference between the Open and the Load events.

Cursor type

The provider in this case is the FileDS, which is a copy of the WineMDB file. The same code runs with identical results. The form FillGridNet contains the following procedure, which is identical to the preceding example with the exception that the connection string is the NetDS rather than the FileDS.

```
Private Sub Form_Open(Cancel As Integer)
    Dim RS As New ADODB.Recordset
    RS.Open "SELECT Customerid, Lastname ,FirstName " & _
        "FROM Customers", NetDS, adOpenStatic
    Set Me.NameList.DataSource = RS
End Sub
```

These two examples mask one difference in implementation that you can encounter if you aren't careful to copy the examples exactly. The difference deals with the CursorType property, adOpenStatic, specified for the Open recordset method. If you think you won't be editing the data (note that no lock type is specified), why not simply use the default cursor type, adOpenForwardOnly(0)?

You get the same result when the provider is a SQL Server. But when the provider is the Jet engine, a cursor type of adOpenForwardOnly retrieves only the first record in the recordset. To force the Jet engine to load the com-plete recordset into the control, you must specify a cursor type other than the default.

Limiting the recordset

The preceding example shows how simple it is to populate a flex grid by using ADO. However, generating a list of 4,000 names is hardly a useful method for presenting the customer list effectively. In this form, you see two flex grids — one on the left that lists the letters A to Z and one on the right that lists the customers whose last names match the selected letter on the left.

The key to this form, `AlphaFill`, is the `Value` property of the flex grid. The value of the flex grid is the contents of the cell that's currently selected. Each time the user clicks a different letter, the value changes. The trick is to use the currently selected letter in the grid on the left, called `AlphaList`, to set the recordset of the grid on the right, called `NameList`.

The following procedure is attached to the `Click` event of the `AlphaList` control. This means that each time the user clicks a letter in the `AlphaList`, a new recordset is assigned to the `NameList` control. If you look carefully at the statement that opens the `RS` recordset, the expression `Me.AlphaList.Value` inserts the currently select letter (such as A, B, and C) into the text of the source query text. Note that the names of the fields in the recordset are the names that are displayed as the column heading on the grid.

```
Private Sub AlphaList_Click()
    RS.Open _
    "SELECT lastname & ', ' & Firstname as Customer," & _
    "shipaddress1 as Street, " & _
    "shipcity & ', ' & shipstate as Location, " & _
    "Dayphonenumber as Phone " & _
    "from customers where left(lastname,1) = '" & _
    Me.AlphaList.Value & "' Order By Lastname,FirstName", _
    Cnt
    Set Me.NameList.DataSource = RS
    RS.Close
End Sub
```

To simplify the coding, the Declarations section of the form contains the `Dim` statements that create the `Connection` and `Recordset` objects. All the ADO operations needed in the form can use the same objects. In the `Form_Open` procedure, the provider for the `Connection` is specified. Because all the data is drawn from the same connection, all the other procedures associated with this form can simply refer to the `Cnt` object.

```
Option Compare Database
Dim Cnt As New ADODB.Connection
Dim RS As New ADODB.Recordset
```

```
Private Sub Form_Open(Cancel As Integer)
    Cnt.Open FileDS
    ...
End Sub
```

Formatting the grid based on the recordset

One small but annoying item involves setting the width of the columns in the grid. Although the user can set the grid for manual adjustment by using the

`AllowUserResizing`, automatically adjusting the width of the columns based on the width of the data that needs to be displayed is useful.

```
FlexgridObj.AllowUserResizing = 1(Columns),2(Rows) or 3(both)
```

The `ColWidth` property is a zero-based collection of the individual column widths in the control. The following statement sets the column list of the `AlphaList` to ¼ inch.

```
Me.AlphaList.ColWidth(0)
```

The `BoxSettings` procedure takes a recordset `C` and adjusts the column width for each column based on the number of characters, `Len( )`, in each field.

```
Sub BoxSettings(C As Recordset)
    Dim Col
    Me.AlphaList.ColWidth(0) = 1440 * 0.25
    End With
    With Me.NameList
        For Col = 0 To C.Fields.Count - 1
            .ColWidth(Col) = (120 * Len(C(Col)))
        Next
    End With
End Sub
```

In the `AlphaList1` form, the `BoxSettings` procedure is executed each time a new set of records is loaded into the `NameList` control. The `AlphaList_Click` procedure executes each time a new letter is selected.

```
Private Sub AlphaList_Click()
    RS.Open _
    "SELECT lastname & ', ' & Firstname as Customer," & _
    "shipaddress1 as Street, " & _
    "shipcity & ', ' & shipstate as Location, " & _
    "Dayphonenumber as Phone " & _
    "from customers where left(lastname,1) = '" & _
    Me.AlphaList.Value & "' Order By Lastname,FirstName", Cnt
    Set Me.NameList.DataSource = RS
    Dim SetCol As ADODB.Recordset
    Set SetCol = RS
    BoxSettings SetCol
    RS.Close
End Sub
```

The result is that the column width of the grid adjusts as each different group of records is selected.

Recordsets and grids

If you look carefully at the code in the `AlphaList_Click` procedure shown in the previous section, you may notice that something looks redundant. The following code is the fragment of the procedure in which the odd coding occurs:

```
Set Me.NameList.DataSource = RS
   Dim SetCol As ADODB.Recordset
   Set SetCol = RS
   BoxSettings SetCol
```

You can see two separate recordset objects that represent exactly the same block of data. In fact, the recordset SetCol is an exact duplicate of RS.

Why bother? Why not just use the same recordset RS to populate the grid and to set the column width in the BoxSettings procedure? If you could use one recordset, you most certainly would. So why can't you?

You have every reason to think that you can, only it doesn't work. If you use a recordset object to fill a grid, it can't be used later in the same procedure to supply data for some other task. When the grid uses the recordset, it's done. Conversely, if you use the recordset for some purpose other than populating the grid before you assign it to the grid, that doesn't work either.

Therefore, if you need a recordset to fill the grid and one for calculating column widths, they must be separate-but-equal recordset objects. The statement Set SetCol = RS in the preceding code makes a duplicate of RS before RS is assigned to the grid. The duplicate recordset, SetCOL, is then passed the to the BoxSettings procedure.

Characters, pixels, and twips

In the following statement, the number of characters in the current column, Len ( ), are multiplied by 120:

```
.ColWidth(Col) = (120 * Len(C(Col)))
```

Why is that, and what are the units of measurement here? Why doesn't the column width fit the width of the text exactly? A couple of issues must be taken into account.

✔ **Characters versus text width.** An innovation of the Macintosh interface that's been replicated in Windows is the use of proportionally spaced text fonts on the screen display. If you've been around long enough to have worked with DOS and DOS applications, you know that in that operating system, the standard was what's now called *monospaced fonts* — every character took up exactly the same amount of horizontal space on the screen or on the printed page. In a case like that, the count of the characters, as obtained from the Len( ) function, tells you the exact horizontal length of the text because you can assume a constant character per inch (cpi) count, such as 12 cpi. But Windows fonts vary the horizontal space, depending on which characters are printed. For example, the word *ill* uses a lot less space than *wow,* even though both have the same Len( ) function value — 3. Because VB/VBS doesn't include a function that calculates the true physical length, you must approximate some number that is roughly equivalent to the length of a character and multiply it by the Len( ) values.

✔ **Twips and pixels.** To further complicate the situation, two incompatible units of measure are involved. In general, Windows measures distances in screen-image elements called *pixels*. A typical computer screen uses 92 pixels per inch, but that varies with display adapters, monitors, and the settings selected by the user. On the other hand, the ActiveX controls measure distance in *twips* — 1,440 twips are in an inch, and the number 1,440 has a large number of even divisors.

Well, you're probably not much closer to understanding my choice of 120 than you were before. All I actually did was to say that an inch has about 12 characters. Divide that into 1,440 twips per inch, and you get 120 * Len ( ) for the column width.

Sizing for the maximum

Of course, the approach used in AlphaList1 simply takes the first record in the recordset and uses the lengths of the items in that one particular record as the guide for setting the column width. You have no reason to assume that this entry is representative of all the data in that column. In fact, the entry may be significantly shorter than the average and certainly isn't the widest item in the column. Although this isn't a huge issue, you can employ ADO to create a more intelligent column-setting routine. For example, you may want to set the column based on the widest item that appears in the recordset. Because you have to create a separate recordset for the column-width calculation anyway, you're free to use whatever logic you want in returning data.

The following code fragment comes from the AlphaList_Click procedure in the AlphaList2 form. The code creates a recordset that uses the Max( ) and Len( ) functions to return the number of characters in the longest entry in each field:

```
Dim SetCol As New ADODB.Recordset
SetCol.Open "SELECT Max(len(lastname & ', ' & Firstname))," & _
"Max(Len(shipaddress1)), " & _
"Max(Len(shipcity & ', ' & shipstate)), " & _
"Max(Len(Dayphonenumber)) " & _
"from customers where left(lastname,1) = '" & _
Me.AlphaList.Value & "'", Cnt
```

The BoxSettings procedure is modified slightly to work with the data returned to the SetCol recordset, which now contains the maximum width for each field. The conversion factor is lowered to 92 because the column width is going to be adjusted to the widest item and you have less need to compensate for proportional spacing.

```
Sub BoxSettings(C As Recordset)
    Dim Col
    Me.AlphaList.ColWidth(0) = 1440 * 0.25
    End With
    With Me.NameList
        For Col = 0 To C.Fields.Count - 1
            .ColWidth(Col) = (92 * C(Col))
        Next
    End With
End Sub
```

Open the AlphaList2 form to see the columns adjust dynamically.

Provider-specific operations

For the most part, the ADO code that populates the forms for AlphaList works with any ADO provider. The one area in which the code must be modified to work with a SQL Server rather than a Jet database, such as Access, is within the embedded SQL code. The operators and functions that are provider-specific are used in the SQL statements. If you want to convert the AlphaList2 form to the AlphaList2Net form, you have to make the following changes.

- ✔ **Concatenation operator.** The & symbol isn't used to combine text and character fields; the + is used in SQL Server, like this.

  ```
  lastname & ', ' & Firstname ==> lastname + ', ' + Firstname
  ```

- ✔ **String functions.** The Left( ) function isn't available on a SQL Server. Use the SubString( ) function instead.

  ```
  Left(Lastname,1) ===> SubString(Lastname,1,1)
  ```

The form AlphaList2Net draws the data from the Internet database. If you have a DSL or faster connection, you may be surprised at how quickly the form responds to user selections.

Using the Slider

The slider control is typically used to select numeric values. The slider is designed to allow the user to drag the pointer back and forth across the bar. As the pointer is dragged, the value increments until the user releases the mouse button. At that point, the slider's value changes to the numeric value that corresponds to the pointer's location on the slider bar.

Although the slider control deals only with numeric values, it's possible to make it appear as if you're selecting a letter rather than a number. The trick is to exploit the fact that each text character corresponds directly to numeric value. You can use a slider to select the letters of the alphabet by assigning values from 1 to 26 to the ticks on the slider. Each tick then corresponds to a letter: A=1, B=2, and so on. For example, if the pointer is in the center of the slider, then the value of the control is 13. However, the control displays the letter M — the 13th letter. Although the idea may seem unusual, I find that scrolling through the alphabet with the slider has a more intuitive feel than clicking the letter in the AlphaList forms.

Compared with the flex grid control, the slider is a very simple control. The following code fragment, taken from the Form_Load procedure of the Slider form, sets the values for the slider to a range between 1 and 26. The SmallChange property sets the amount of change between each tick mark. The LargeChange sets the size increment for larger movements across the bar.

```
Dim Sld As Slider
Set Sld = Me.AlphaSlider.Object
Sld.Min = 1
Sld.Max = 26
Sld.LargeChange = 4
Sld.SmallChange = 1
Sld.Value = 1
Sld.Text = Chr(Sld.Value + 64)
```

In the last line of the procedure, an interesting trick occurs that sets the text value of the slider. The text that appears when you click or drag the pointer is controlled by the text property. In this case, the text is linked to the value of the pointer by using the Value property as part of the argument for the Chr( ). Chr( ) returns the character when you supply the ASCII character code. In the ASCII code, uppercase letters A to Z correspond to the number values 65 to 90. By adding 64 to the slider values 1 to 26, you arrive at the correct ASCII code value for the letters A to Z.

The slider control has a Scroll event that is triggered each time the pointer is dragged one tick in either direction. The following procedure updates the text property of the pointer so that it shows the corresponding letter for each tick mark on the slider. If the user drags the pointer across the slider, this event is triggered continuously until he stops.

```
Private Sub AlphaSlider_Scroll()
    Me.AlphaSlider.Text = Chr(Me.AlphaSlider.Value + 64)
End Sub
```

When the user finally stops dragging the pointer, the Change event takes place. That's the signal to execute code, which updates the names in the flex grid. In this case, the update is stored in a separate procedure called PopulateGrid.

```
Private Sub AlphaSlider_Change()
    PopulateGrid
End Sub
```

The `PopulateGrid` procedure also uses the `Chr (Me.AlphaSlider.Value + 64)` expression to act as the criteria for the recordset.

```
Sub PopulateGrid()
    RS.Open "SELECT lastname & ', ' & Firstname as Customer, " & _
    "shipaddress1 as Street, shipcity & ', ' & shipstate as Location," & _
    "Dayphonenumber as Phone from customers where left(lastname,1) = '" & _
    Chr(Me.AlphaSlider.Value + 64) & "'", Cnt, adOpenStatic
    Set Me.NameList.DataSource = RS
    RS.Close
End Sub
```

By converting the numerical value of the slider to a character, the slider value controls the criteria used for the recordset, which is displayed in the flex grid. Changes in the slider are dynamically reflected in the contexts of the grid.

Test Searches

The least intuitive type of name-search interface is one in which you are required to enter the last name of the customer to have the application locate the desired name. However, you can add a twist to that idea and create a text box that is dynamically linked to a flex grid. At the top of the form is a text box in which the user can type in characters. Typically, the application waits until the user enters a name and then presses return before searching for the corresponding records.

As the user enters additional characters, such as following k with ru , the records in the flex grid are narrowed to those that match the three characters, kru.

When you work with this type of interface, you discover that you can quickly narrow down your search by typing two or three characters to a list that allows you to easily pick out the name you're looking for.

The key to the programming that's used with the TextSearch form is the Text property of the text-box control. In most cases, when you have text boxes on a form, you're interested in the value of the text box. However, text-box controls distinguish between the value and the text properties.

✔ **Value:** This property is the last updated value of the control. The control's value is updated each time the control loses focus, such as when you tab to another control or select another control with the mouse.

✔ **Text:** This property refers to the characters currently being entered into the text box. Note that the text property reflects what you see in the box, regardless of whether the control has been updated.

In this case, the goal is to change the contents of the flex grid each time the text changes. You can accomplish this by linking the flex grid updates to the Change property of the text-box control. The change event is triggered each time a character is added or deleted from the text box. The Text property consists of the character currently visible in the text-box control.

In the TextSearch form, the connection and recordset objects are defined in the Declarations section along with a text constant called ColListLocal. This text constant contains the field list that's used to populate the grid. Using a constant makes sense because the list of fields isn't going to change during the execution of the application. You can store the value once, as a constant, and reference it in all the procedures in the form module. Constants use less memory and work faster than variables.

```
Option Compare Database
Dim Cnt As New ADODB.Connection
Dim RS As New ADODB.Recordset
Const ColListLocal = " Lastname & ', ' & FirstName As Customer, " & _
    "Shipcity & ', ' & ShipState & ' ' & shipzip As Location, " & _
    "DayPhoneNumber As Phone"
Private Sub Form_Open(Cancel As Integer)
    Cnt.Open FileDS
    BoxSettings
    Me.NameList.Visible = True
End Sub
```

The dynamic element of the form is created by the Change of the text-box control. The following procedure is triggered each time a character is added or deleted from the text box. The SQL statement uses the LIKE operator to specify the partial match, which compares the text value of the text-box control (Me.Text4.Text) to the Lastname field. This procedure is all that's needed to have the flex grid dynamically linked to the text box.

```
Private Sub Text4_Change()
    RS.Open "SELECT " & ColListLocal & " from customers " & _
        " where lastname LIKE '" _
        & Me.Text4.Text & "%' Order By Lastname, Firstname", _
        Cnt, adOpenStatic
    Set Me.NameList.DataSource = RS
    RS.Close
End Sub
```

Using the grid contents as criteria

The TextSearch form is useful in quickly narrowing a long list to a few qualified items. But what happens after you find the desired customer? Perhaps the purpose in locating the customer is to then locate that customer's orders.

The next step to the search takes you to the entry box, which controls the list of names that appears in the flex grid in the center of the form. In turn, when the user clicks on a name in the middle flex grid, that triggers the code that populates the lower flex grid to show all the orders recorded for that customer.

Using a hidden key column

To add the second flex grid that lists the order to the text-search form, you need to have a key value in the customer grid that's used to select the corresponding values in the orders grid. That value is quite logically CustomerID, which is the common field between the Customers and the Orders table. The ColListLocal constant, which contains the field list that appears in the CustList grid, now contains an additional field, customerid.

```
Option Compare Database
Dim Cnt As New ADODB.Connection
Dim RS As New ADODB.Recordset
Const ColListLocal = "customerid, Lastname & ', ' & FirstName As Customer, " & _
    "Shipcity & ', ' & ShipState & ' ' & shipzip As Location, " & _
    "DayPhoneNumber As Phone"
```

Although the CustomerID field is an important element in performing the database operations required to define the required recordsets, it isn't necessarily a value that enhances the screen display. You can hide the contents of a column in a flex grid by setting the ColWidth property of that column to zero. In the following BoxSettings procedure, an If structure is used to set column zero to a width of zero:

```
Sub BoxSettings()
    Dim Cust As MSHFlexGrid
    Dim Col
    Set Cust = Me.NameList.Object
    With Cust
        For Col = 0 To 2
            If Col = 0 Then
                .ColWidth(Col) = 0
            Else
                .ColWidth(Col) = (1440 * 1.25)
            End If
        Next
        Cust.SelectionMode = flexSelectionByRow
    End With
End Sub
```

Another important setting in the BoxSettings is the SelectionMode property of the flex grid. The selection mode is important because it's the selection mode that controls what value returns from the flex-grid control when the user clicks in a row in the grid. By default, the selection mode is free. In the free mode, the user can click any cell on the grid. When the user clicks a cell, the value property of the grid returns the data in the selected cell.

However, in this example the value that needs to be returned, the CustomerID, is a hidden column. Because users can't click a column, they can't see that it's necessary to change the SelectionMode property to flexSelectionByRow, as shown in the next example. When flexSelectionByRow is specified, no matter what cell on a given row the user clicks on, the entire row is highlighted. Even more importantly, the value returned by the flex-grid control is the value of the first column in the selected row. Note that the first column doesn't have to be visible. As long as it's the first field in the recordset that was assigned to the flex grid, the value of that field is the value of the flex grid at that moment.

```
Cust.SelectionMode = flexSelectionByRow
```

The procedure that fills the customer-name list is attached to the Change event of the text box, just as it is in the TextSearch form.

```
Private Sub Text4_Change()
    If Text4.Text <> "" Then
        RS.Open "SELECT " & ColListLocal & " from customers " & _
            " where lastname like '" _
            & Me.Text4.Text & "%' Order By Lastname, Firstname", Cnt, _
                adOpenStatic
        Set Me.NameList.DataSource = RS
        RS.Close
    End If
End Sub
```

The new addition to the form is the following procedure. This procedure is linked to the SelChange event of the NameList flex grid. The SelChange event occurs each time that the user selects a different row in the NameList flex grid.

```
Private Sub NameList_SelChange()
    Dim Cmd As New ADODB.Command
    Dim P As New ADODB.Parameter
    Dim RS As New ADODB.Recordset
    Cmd.ActiveConnection = FileDS
    Cmd.CommandText = "Select WineOrderID As OrderNo, " & _
"OrderDate, Format(OrderTotal,'Currency') As Amount, " & _
"Bottles as Items, ShipCity & ', ' & shipState & ' ' &" & _
"shipzip as [Shipped to], " & _
"Format(PaymentVerified,'Yes/No') as Verified, " & _
"Format(not isnull(OrderSentViaEmailAt),'Yes/No') as Email " & _
        "FROM Orders Where Customerid = ?"
    P.Type = adInteger
    P.Value = Me.NameList.Value
    Cmd.Parameters.Append P
    RS.CursorType = adOpenStatic
    RS.Open Cmd
    Me.OrderList.ColWidth(4) = 1440 * 1.25
    Set Me.OrderList.DataSource = RS
End Sub
```

The `NameList_SelChange` procedure has several interesting aspects. Rather than using a recordset object to retrieve the list of orders, a command object is used; the SQL statement that needs to be executed is rather complicated and awkward to read — it's long (broken into many concatenated sections) and contains a number of functions. For example, the `PaymentVerified` field is a Boolean value, True or False. Access stores the Boolean values as 0 or -1. SQL Server stores Boolean values as 0 or 1. In any case, it reads better if the grid shows Yes or No in the column for `PaymentVerified` rather than a numeric value, which makes sense to a programmer but not the average user. One way to avoid numeric results is to use the `Format( )` function (Jet engine only, not supported in SQL Server). However, all of these functions and the required delimiters make the statement a bit of a mess.

Rather than add to the confusion by trying to concatenate the `CustomerID` into this mess, it seems cleaner to insert a ? for a parameter.

```
Cmd.CommandText = "Select WineOrderID As OrderNo, " & _
"OrderDate, Format(OrderTotal,'Currency') As Amount, " & _
"Bottles as Items, ShipCity & ', ' & shipState & ' ' &" & _
"shipzip as [Shipped to], " & _
"Format(PaymentVerified,'Yes/No') as Verified, " & _
"Format(not isnull(OrderSentViaEmailAt),'Yes/No')" & _
"FROM Orders Where Customerid = ?"
```

After the command text has been assigned to the command object, the remainder of the coding is quite simple. In the following fragment, you can see that the value of the `NameList` control is used to assign the value for Parameter zero. Remember that because the `NameList` grid is in the `flexSelectionByRow` selection mode, any click returns the hidden value in the first column of the flex grid, which is `CustomerID`.

```
P.Type = adInteger
P.Value = Me.NameList.Value
Cmd.Parameters.Append P
RS.CursorType = adOpenStatic
RS.Open Cmd
```

The result can be seen by opening the `TextSearch1` form, searching for a customer by entering an ID number, and then clicking on the customer to display the corresponding records.

Chapter 7

Client/Server Databases

● ●

In This Chapter

▶ Retrieving records from a client/server data source

▶ Using views to retrieve data

▶ Creating a new view

▶ Setting user permissions

▶ Using stored procedures

▶ Passing parameters to a stored procedure

▶ Creating recordsets with stored procedures

▶ Displaying data from stored procedures on forms

● ●

*P*eople tend to think of computers as either clients or servers. But from a software point of view, what designates computers as clients or servers are the software applications that they run.

Understanding Client/Server

Client/server computing is one of those techno terms that's become so ingrained into the culture that people take it for granted that everyone knows what it means. However, before I get down to the nuts and bolts of ADO and client/server databases, it may be useful to point out the practical implications of client/server technology for the database programmer.

✔ **Client:** A computer running an application that *requests* information from another computer.

✔ **Server:** A computer providing a service to other computers. A service is an application that *responds* to other computers' requests for information.

It isn't uncommon that a single computer may be both a client and a server at different times or even simultaneously. For example, a computer running SQL Server is a server for database clients but it may also be a client of another machine that's running Exchange for e-mail.

Most of the time, these distinctions don't have much practical meaning. If a computer costs $25,000 and is locked in a room, it's a server. If it costs $500 and sits in a cubicle, it's a client.

However, when it comes to programming, it's important to understand how services work and how your programming strategy must take into account the differences in implementation between non-client/server and client/server database providers.

Ironically, the ADO programming model provides a single programming approach for all types of providers. As you see in this chapter, subtle differences in coding imply significant differences in implementation.

Retrieving records

Consider these two questions when you work with client/server database operations:

- Which computer does what share of the work?
- How much information travels across the network to complete a task?

Figure 7-1 shows the answer to those two questions regarding the operation executed in the CS1 procedure. The key factor isn't the ADO code, but how the selected provider gets the result specified in the code. In CS1, the provider is the Jet database engine.

In Figure 7-1, the Jet database engine produces the required result. First, Jet reads through the data file stored on the remote server and copies the required records into the memory of the client computer. When that is accomplished, the client counter scans the records that have been retrieved to perform the calculation — in this case a count of the record — specified in the SQL statement.

Using Jet, the client computer does the majority of work to find the answer. In terms of services, the server shown in Figure 7-1 provides a file storage service to the client computer, not a database service. The server blindly sends blocks of data across the network, unaware of the purpose of the data retrieval. When the retrieval finishes, the client calculates the result by using a temporary copy of the data obtained from the server.

But if you change the code, what happens on the network changes radically. CS2 is identical to CS1 except that the provider is a SQL Server (see Figure 7-2).

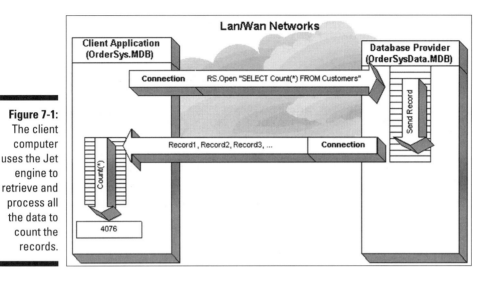

Figure 7-1:
The client computer uses the Jet engine to retrieve and process all the data to count the records.

```
Sub CS2()
    Dim RS As New ADODB.Recordset
    RS.Open "Select Count(*) FRom Customers", _
    "Provider=SQLOLEDB;Data Source=ADODUM;" & _
    "UID=ubad1d1;pwd=21@1n3z"
    MsgBox RS(0)
End Sub
```

Figure 7-2:
A database server analyzes the logic of a request and returns only the result of the query to the client computer.

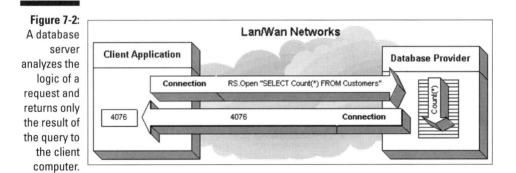

In this scenario, shown in Figure 7-2, the server provides a database, not a file, service. Instead of slavishly sending blocks of data to the client, the server analyzes the logic of the SQL query, carries out the necessary operations (counting the records in the Customer's table), and sends only the result back to the client. This is an example of client/server database operations because the server performs database operations, not just data storage services.

The client/server model has two important advantages:

✔ **Computing:** The database server helps with computing, thus reducing the work the client computer must do. If you further consider that most of the computers running database services are larger, more powerful systems than those typically deployed on desktops, the benefit of having database servers help with the computing tasks is even greater.

✔ **Network:** Because the server returns only the result of the query (not all the raw data used to get that result), the amount of traffic on the network is reduced. Because network communication is typically a computing bottleneck, reducing unnecessary traffic benefits all network users.

It's important to keep in mind that the benefits of client/server computing depend on how you write your application. One of my goals in this chapter is to show you how to write your programs to take advantage of database services. Figure 7-3 shows what happens when the following SQL statement is executed in a client/server environment. Although this query may involve a large number of records (such as 19,779), the query would never return more than 51 records.

```
SELECT ShipState, Sum (OrderTotal),Avg (OrderTotal) FROM Orders
```

Figure 7-3:
Queries that
return a
limited
number of
results use
client/server
architecture.

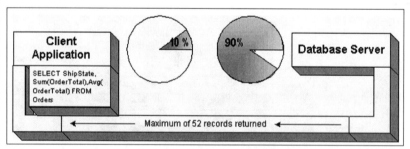

On the other hand, if you submit a loosely structured query (such as the one that follows), you can still strain network resources by moving large numbers of records between the client and the server (see Figure 7-4). In that case, you haven't provided the server any logic that enables it to minimize the traffic. The server has no choice but to dump all the data onto the network.

```
SELECT * FROM Orders
```

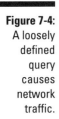

Figure 7-4:
A loosely
defined
query
causes
network
traffic.

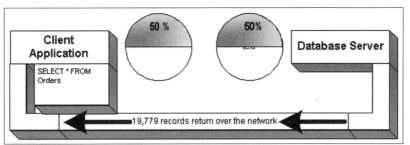

When you design an application, avoid requesting large amounts of data from the server. In most cases, a list of 19,000 records wouldn't be of use to anyone. The goal of the user interface is to focus the data retrieved on the user's task instead of just grabbing huge blocks of data that clog the network and fill up the client computer's memory.

Working with Views

A *view* is a SQL statement that's stored on the database server. Server views are similar to DAO QueryDef objects. Views have these advantages:

✔ **Precompiled/optimized:** Because you define the information available in a view before a user queries the database, the information can be accessed much more quickly than a runtime query.

✔ **Simplify queries:** You can encapsulate complex relationships, calculations, or conditional logic in views. When users need to retrieve data, they can select from the view rather than having to go back to the base tables and enter all of the join information or calculation formulas.

✔ **Security:** Views provide a simple mechanism for restricting access to specific rows and columns within the base tables.

Views are subject to the following limitations:

✔ Views can contain only a single SQL statement.

✔ All calculated fields must be assigned a unique name with the AS clause.

✔ Views must return recordsets. They can't be used to execute Insert, Delete, or Update operations.

✔ Views can't contain ORDER BY clauses. ORDER BY is used to sort records selected by a SQL statement.

✔ If the view contains records from a single table, you can edit data.

✔ If a view contains a `JOIN`, it may be updateable if it follows the rules supported by the data provider.

What is compiling?

It's important to understand that databases don't directly execute SQL statements. A SQL statement expresses a description of the recordset that you want to retrieve. Often, to get that data, the database provider has to execute a number of operations. In most advanced databases, the first step in producing a recordset is analyzing the SQL statement and generating an execution plan. For example, look at the following SQL query. The query is designed to return a list of states with sales averages above the overall average sale.

```
SELECT ShipState, avg(Ordertotal)
FROM Orders WHERE PaymentVerified = 1
GROUP BY ShipState HAVING avg(Ordertotal) >=
(SELECT avg(Ordertotal)FROM Orders
WHERE PaymentVerified = 1)
```

The SQL Server query analyzer program can display the details of the execution plan that SQL Server creates before the creation of the recordset, as shown in Figure 7-5. You can see that a single query can generate dozens of individual steps that must be coordinated to get the desired result.

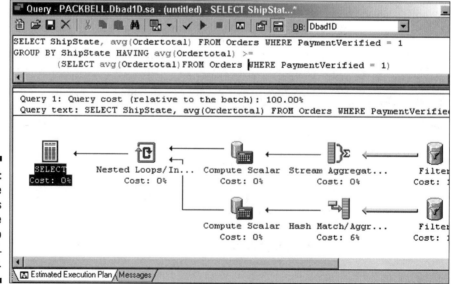

Figure 7-5:
Database servers prepare plans to execute SQL queries.

When you create a view or stored procedure, the database server, in addition to storing the SQL statement, generates and stores the execution plan. When you use an ADO command object to access a view or a stored procedure, the server simply executes its existing plan, saving time and system resources.

Setting permissions with views

In addition to the uses that I describe in the previous section, you can also use views to control access to tables. Although a broad discussion of database administration isn't something that can fit into this book, you may find it useful to know how to use views for security purposes.

For example, in an order-processing application, most users should have access to customer and order information. On the other hand, you may want to limit users' access to sensitive fields, such as credit card numbers. The following SQL Statement displays only selected fields from the customers and orders tables.

```
SELECT FirstName, LastName, OrderDate, OrderTotal
FROM Customers, Order
WHERE Customers.CustomerID = Orders.CustomerID
```

A simple and efficient way to handle security is to provide users access to data through views while restricting direct access to the table to administrators. Figure 7-6 shows how views help you implement security. The average user has permissions to the view but only the sa (system administrator) or other designated administrators can get access to the underlying tables.

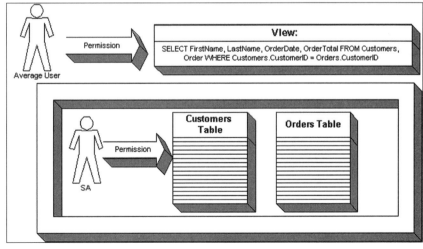

Figure 7-6:
Grant user permissions to views to protect sensitive information stored in the underlying tables.

A bit later in this chapter, you find out how to use the ADO command object to perform tasks, such as setting permissions.

Creating a view

Creating a view is like executing a SQL query except that you precede the SELECT statement with a CREATE VIEW instruction, as shown in the following snippet of code. CREATE VIEW tells the server to save a copy of the SQL statement instead of immediately executing it.

```
CREATE VIEW <name> AS
<SQL Statement>
```

CreateView1 creates a view called v_CustInState, which executes a SQL query that counts the customers in each state. Notice that to execute this procedure successfully, you must have either system administrator (sa) or database owner (dbo) permissions. The SANetDS connection string refers to a connection string that specifies a login with those permissions. The connection string NetDS published in this book is a user (not an owner) login for security reasons. For that reason, you can't execute this procedure over the Internet.

```
Sub CreateView1()
    Dim Cmd As New ADODB.Command
    Cmd.ActiveConnection = SANetDS
    Cmd.CommandText = "CREATE VIEW v_CustInState AS " & _
        "SELECT BillState, Count(*) As CustCount " & _
        "FROM Customers GROUP BY BillState"
    Cmd.Execute
End Sub
```

You use views in SQL statements the same way as tables. You can't tell by reading a SQL statement whether the name in the FROM clause refers to a table. Common practice suggests that you should add some sort of prefix, such as v_, to the names of the views you create so that you can distinguish views from queries quickly.

Dumping a view or table

To check a table's contents or view it, create a generic procedure that simply dumps the contents of any table or view to the Immediate window (in VB, the Debug object).

ShowRS shows you how to do this by using a command object. You can see the result of any new view or stored procedure quickly.

```
Sub ShowRS(RSText, _
       Optional ItemType As Integer = adCmdTable)
    Dim rs As New ADODB.Recordset
    Dim Fld
    rs.Open RSText, NetDS, , , ItemType
    Do Until rs.EOF
        For Fld = 0 To rs.Fields.Count - 2
            Debug.Print rs(Fld) & vbTab;
        Next
        Debug.Print rs(rs.Fields.Count - 1)
        rs.MoveNext
    Loop
End Sub
```

From a coding perspective, you need to look at two elements in ShowRS:

- ✔ **Optional:** The Optional keyword allows you to create a procedure that can use a parameter but does not require the parameter. You can set a default value for the optional parameter by using an equals sign (=), as shown in ShowRS. In this example, the goal is for the procedure to assume that you're querying a table or a view unless you specify something of a different type, such as a stored procedure. Optional parameters enable you to write a procedure that you can use in many situations while still keeping the syntax simple. If you want to use the default value, you can simply call the procedure without a parameter.

- ✔ **Semicolon:** The ";" at the end of the Debug.Print rs(Fld) statement is an old BASIC convention for suppressing a new line. Normally, each Debug.Print prints on a new line. However, what you want to do with this procedure is print all of the fields from one record on one line. By adding the ";" at the end of the line, all of the fields get printed on one line. The vbTab constant inserts a tab character to create the same sort of column alignment (imperfect) normally exhibited in the Immediate window. Notice that the loop continues until the rs.Fields.Count - 2. That means that after the loop, there's still one field left to print. That field's printed without the ";" so that the next record begins on a new line.

Granting permissions

After you create a new view (or stored procedure), you need to set the permissions on that item to determine which users are allowed to access these new items. In addition to using the SQL Server tools for setting permissions, you can set them programmatically by using an ADO command object to issue the SQL language GRANT statement. Perm1 gives the use UBAD1D1 permission to reference v_CustInState in a SELECT statement.

```
Sub Perm1()
    Dim Cmd As New ADODB.Command
    Cmd.ActiveConnection = SANetDS
    Cmd.CommandText = _
    "GRANT SELECT ON v_CustInState TO ubad1d1"
    Cmd.Execute
End Sub
```

Notice that the GRANT statement requires administrator or database owner permissions.

Changing or deleting a view

The database owner or administrator can use the SQL DROP statement to remove an object such as a table, view, or stored procedure from the database. The following example deletes the v_CustInState view from the database. The DROP statement requires administrator or database owner permissions.

```
Sub Kill1()
    Dim Cmd As New ADODB.Command
    Cmd.ActiveConnection = SANetDS
    Cmd.CommandText = _
    "DROP VIEW v_CustInState"
    Cmd.Execute
End Sub
```

Relationship views

One of my favorite uses for views is to see how tables in databases are related (see Figure 7-7).

Figure 7-7:
Sales information is stored in four related tables.

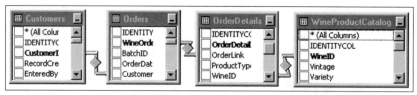

In SQL terms, the four tables are connected when a query contains the following FROM and JOIN clauses:

```
FROM Customers
INNER JOIN Orders
    ON Customers.CustomerID = Orders.CustomerID
INNER JOIN OrderDetails
    ON Orders.WineOrderID = OrderDetails.OrderLink
INNER JOIN WineProductCatalog
    ON OrderDetails.WineID = WineProductCatalog.WineID
```

Because these relationships are basic to the nature of the database, many different queries share the same set of JOIN specifications. One way to avoid having to write out this JOIN syntax over and over again is by to create a generic view — that is, a view that includes all of the field from all of the tables. This is a relationship view because its primary purpose is to provide the JOIN syntax for other more specific queries.

SQL Join syntax

Before I cover using the relationship view, you may want to check out the precise syntax required to perform the JOIN. In many cases, you can avoid writing these complicated statements by using the query builders included in Access, SQL Server 7.0, Visual Basic, or other applications. But there are times when you need to write, edit, or at least understand how these work.

Following is the JOIN syntax used in the v_SalesInfo_1 view stored on the Internet database. The first thing to note is that you need to link four tables. If you need to link four tables, that means you must supply, at a minimum, three expressions that match fields in one table with fields in a related table.

```
(1)    FROM WineProductCatalog
(2)    JOIN OrderDetails
(3)      ON WineProductCatalog.WineID = OrderDetails.WineID
(4)    JOIN Orders
(5)      ON OrderDetails.OrderLink = Orders.WineOrderID
(6)    JOIN Customers
(7)      ON Customers.CustomerID = Orders.CustomerID
```

The trick is to arrange the table names and the expressions in the proper order. What's the proper order? If you write this out, how do you get it right? One simple rule governs how you write the JOIN syntax: You can't join the fields unless you already listed the table. Line 3 can relate the WineProductCatalog and the OrderDetails tables because those tables are listed in Lines 1 and 2. Line 5 can join the Orders and the OrderDetails tables because Line 4 adds Orders to the list of tables.

By following this rule, you may be able to rearrange the names and expressions in a different order that's still valid. The following syntax produces the same results, although it starts with the Customers and Orders tables. You see that each join expression refers to only table names that precede the expression. Because Customers and Orders are listed first, the expression that joins those two tables is placed after the first ON keyword. This syntax is used in the view v_SalesInfo_1.

```
FROM Customers
JOIN Orders
   ON Customers.CustomerID = Orders.CustomerID
JOIN OrderDetails
   ON OrderDetails.OrderLink = Orders.WineOrderID
JOIN WineProductCatalog
   ON WineProductCatalog.WineID = OrderDetails.WineID
```

Keep in mind that only the actual, logical relations among the tables limit the ways that you can rearrange the items. For example, you can determine by reading the following two lines of code that any SQL statement using this JOIN syntax fails. Why? The JOIN expression must use the tables that precede it. In order to retrieve the data you want, it would be necessary to write an expression that joins Customers to OrderDetails. In the sales database, that won't work because those two tables have no common keys. If you start out with two mismatched tables, there's no way to write a JOIN syntax that makes them work correctly.

```
FROM Customers
JOIN OrderDetails ...
```

To complicate the matter further, not all SQL code generators produce the same results. The following syntax was produced by Access 2000. This runs in Access or on SQL Server, although it uses a slightly different style. In the following example, the JOIN expressions are nested inside one another. The OrderDetails and the WineProductCatalog appear first, and the two expressions follow. Access also adds the default JOIN type of INNER explicitly. I find this code harder to follow than the preceding examples. This syntax is used in the view v_SalesInfo_2.

```
FROM
    (Customers INNER JOIN Orders
    ON Customers.CustomerID = Orders.CustomerID)
    INNER JOIN (OrderDetails
    INNER JOIN WineProductCatalog
    ON OrderDetails.WineID = WineProductCatalog.WineID)
    ON Orders.WineOrderID = OrderDetails.OrderLink
```

One last twist: You can write the same code without using the JOIN and ON keywords at all. The following example uses the standard FROM and WHERE keywords without reference to any special join syntax. In this approach, the FROM clause contains a list of all the tables included in the query in no particular order. The WHERE clause contains a series of expressions that relate fields in the different tables to each other. The order of the expressions is not important as long as they are assembled by using the AND operator. The following example is by far the simplest to create if you have to write the query manually. It's also the only Oracle SQL-compatible example that doesn't use the JOIN keyword. This syntax is used in the view v_SalesInfo_3.

```
FROM Customers ,Orders ,OrderDetails ,WineProductCatalog
    WHERE Customers.CustomerID = Orders.CustomerID
    AND OrderDetails.WineID = WineProductCatalog.WineID
    AND Orders.WineOrderID = OrderDetails.OrderLink
```

One argument in favor of the more tedious JOIN syntax is that it distinguishes which expression relates tables and which filters records. The expressions that represent links between tables appear in the JOIN section.

Expressions that select records are listed after the WHERE clause. Look at the following two examples. Both add a criterion that selects a range of dates along with the joins. In the first example, you can easily see which expressions perform what functions. In the second example, the join and the filter expressions are mixed up together. Keep in mind that the result of both cases is the same. Ease and clarity of the SQL code are the issues to consider.

```
FROM Customers  JOIN Orders
    ON Customers.CustomerID = Orders.CustomerID
JOIN OrderDetails
    ON OrderDetails.OrderLink = Orders.WineOrderID
JOIN WineProductCatalog
    ON WineProductCatalog.WineID = OrderDetails.WineID
WHERE Orderdate Between '1/1/99' AND '12/31/99'

FROM Customers ,Orders ,OrderDetails ,WineProductCatalog
    WHERE Customers.CustomerID = Orders.CustomerID
    AND OrderDetails.WineID = WineProductCatalog.WineID
    AND Orderdate Between '1/1/99' AND '12/31/99'
    AND Orders.WineOrderID = OrderDetails.OrderLink
```

You can prove that all three versions produce the same results by using the TestJoins. Note that this dumps out a lot of data, so you may want to take my word for it if you're using a dial-up connection.

```
Sub TestJoins()
    MsgBox "v_saleinfo_1"
    ShowRS "v_salesinfo_1"
    MsgBox "v_saleinfo_2"
    ShowRS "v_salesinfo_2"
    MsgBox "v_saleinfo_3"
    ShowRS "v_salesinfo_3"
End Sub
```

Encapsulating syntax in a view

The relationship view encapsulates the complex JOIN syntax in a single view. You can use that view to select and summarize any of the columns included in the view from any of the tables. Relationship1 uses a SQL query based on the v_SalesInfo_1 view. The query counts the number of bottles of each wine billed in Texas. Notice that the syntax of the SQL statement is significantly reduced because the v_SalesInfo_1 view encapsulates the required joins.

```
Sub Relationship1()
    Dim RS As New ADODB.Recordset
    RS.Open "SELECT WineName, Count(Bottles) " & _
    "FROM v_SalesInfo_1 WHERE BillState = 'TX' " & _
    "AND PaymentVerified = 1 " & _
    "GROUP BY WineName ORDER BY Count(Bottles) DESC", NetDS
    Do Until RS.EOF
        Debug.Print RS(0), RS(1)
        RS.MoveNext
    Loop
End Sub
```

Moreover, you can generalize the query in Relationship1 and create it as a view. CreateView2, which requires administrative or database owner permissions, creates a view based on a view. This is called a *nested view*. Notice that to store an SQL statement as a view, you need to make some changes. First, drop the ORDER BY clause. Then add the BillState field because that's the field that you're going to select.

```
Sub CreateView2()
    Dim Cmd As New ADODB.Command
    Cmd.CommandText = "CREATE VIEW v_BestSell AS " & _
    "SELECT BillState, WineName, Units = Count(Bottles) " & _
    "FROM v_SalesInfo_1 WHERE PaymentVerified = 1 " & _
    "GROUP BY BillState,WineName"
    Cmd.ActiveConnection = SANetDS
    Cmd.Execute
    Cmd.CommandText = _
    "GRANT SELECT ON v_BestSell TO ubad1d1"
    Cmd.Execute
End Sub
```

CreateView2 uses the Cmd object to create the view and then, by changing the CommandText, it sets the permissions on the new view.

Relationship2 now performs a query on the new view v_BestSell, which is itself based on v_SalesInfo_1. Assuming that this query is one that you need to execute over and over again, the nested views provide a greatly simplified top level SQL statement that boils down to you simply selecting the desired state.

```
Sub Relationship2()
    Dim RS As New ADODB.Recordset
    RS.Open "SELECT winename,units " & _
    "FROM v_BestSell WHERE BillState = 'TX'", _
    NetDS
    Do Until RS.EOF
        Debug.Print RS(0), RS(1)
        RS.MoveNext
    Loop
End Sub
```

Combining VB/VBA and SQL

The marriage of VB/VBA code and SQL commands isn't a happy one. VB/VBA code written in code modules is typically readable and easy to enter. SQL statements written in tools specifically designed for accessing client/server databases, such as the SQL Server Query Analyzer, allow you to write the SQL statements in any way you feel comfortable. You can use as many lines and as much white space as you want to arrange the elements in a SQL statement or SQL program you're writing. But when you put SQL into VB/VBA, you get something that's hard to enter and almost impossible to read.

The problem is that the SQL code is treated by VB as string text. To avoid single, long lines of text, you must divide the text into small segments, add line continuation characters, and concatenate all of the segments to form a single string. If the text contains delimiters (such as quotation marks), you must convert them to some other delimiter (such as an apostrophe). This gets incredibly tedious! Changing query text is a torturous process. If you forget to leave a leading or trailing space, an entire query can fail. One alternative is to take a hint from the concept of a server view and create a data table for your application in which the text of the SQL queries is stored.

The `Wine.MDB` file, included on the CD-ROM, contains a SQL Statements table with the following three fields:

- **ID:** An autonumber field.

  ID serves no purpose in an Access-based table. However, if you move the table to a server, it makes the table editable. (Most providers require a primary key in order to make a table editable from a client application using data bound controls.)

- **QName:** A text field used to identify the SQL code.

- **Qtext.** A memo field containing the actual text of the SQL statement or statements you want to execute.

Figure 7-8 shows an Access 2000 form in Wine.MDB called SQL statements. You can enter a multiple-line SQL statement with indents and delimiters just as you do in a SQL Server tool, such as Query Analyzer. Entering your SQL statements in a text field has several advantages:

- You can use as many lines and as much white space as you want.

- You can view the SQL in its normal form — not cut into string segments.

- You can copy and paste SQL created in the Query Analyzer, the view builder, or any other tool directly into the memo field with no changes.

- You can use the same query text in many different places in your application. If you make a change in the SQL code, it flows to all of the procedures that use that query.

Great idea! But how do you get the SQL code into your application? Use a function like `GetQry`. The function starts with the name of query text (the `Qname` field) and uses a command object to extract the text from the `Qtext` field.

```
Function GetQry(QName)
    Dim Q As New ADODB.Recordset
    Dim Cmd As New ADODB.Command
    Dim P As New ADODB.Parameter
    Cmd.ActiveConnection = FileDS
    Cmd.CommandText = "SELECT * FROM SQLStatements WHERE Qname = ?"
    P.Type = adVarChar
    P.Size = 50
    P.Value = QName
    Cmd.Parameters.Append P
    Q.Open Cmd
    GetQry = Q("QText")
End Function
```

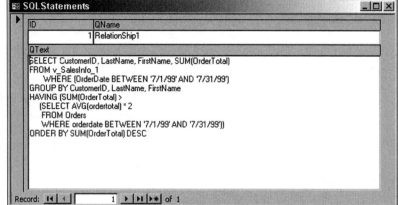

Figure 7-8:
You can
store SQL
statements
in a memo
field.

The following statement entered into the Immediate window returns all of the SQL entered in the corresponding record:

```
? GetQry("Relationship1")

SELECT CustomerID, LastName, FirstName, SUM(OrderTotal)
FROM v_SalesInfo_1
        WHERE (OrderDate BETWEEN '7/1/99' AND '7/31/99')
GROUP BY CustomerID, LastName, FirstName
HAVING (SUM(OrderTotal) >
    (SELECT AVG(ordertotal) * 2
     FROM Orders
        WHERE orderdate BETWEEN '7/1/99' AND '7/31/99'))
ORDER BY SUM(OrderTotal) DESC
```

By using this function, you can enter (or better yet, copy and paste) one or more SQL statements and pass that SQL to any procedure for execution. The procedure `Relationship3`, shown in Figure 7-8, illustrates how you would make use of stored SQL statements to populate a form.

```
Sub Relationship3()
    ShowRS GetQry("Relationship1"), adCmdText
End Sub
```

Of course, there's no reason why you couldn't store the SQL statements on a server and access them remotely.

Going beyond Views

Stored procedures enable you to move beyond the limits imposed by views.

- ✔ **Multiple statements:** A stored procedure can contain any number or type of SQL statements. Most database server SQL languages extend standard SQL (`SELECT`, `INSERT`, `UPDATE`, and `DELETE`) with functions, control flow statements, server based cursors, and other features. You can write entire SQL programs and save them as stored procedure.

- ✔ **Return recordset:** SQL Server-stored procedures can return one or more recordsets as results. Note that Oracle-stored procedures can't return recordsets. In Oracle, you must use a view to return a recordset.

- ✔ **Call other procedures:** Stored procedures can call other stored procedures.

- ✔ **Input and output parameters:** Procedures can receive input through defined parameters. The procedure can also return values through output parameters.

- ✔ **Compiled and optimized:** Like views, the server compiles and optimizes the procedure when it's created.

- ✔ **Security:** Like views, permissions can be granted to execute a stored procedure without allowing the user to have access to the tables, views, or other procedures used by the initial stored procedure.

Stored procedures aren't executed as part of a SQL `SELECT` statement. Stored procedures are executed simply by referencing the procedure name. The `EXECUTE` command is optional. You can also specify a text string that contains the name of the procedure as an argument for the `EXECUTE` command as a way to execute a stored procedure.

```
Sp_spaceused
EXECUTE sp_spaceused
EXECUTE ('sp_spaceused')
```

I can't offer a full explanation of SQL Server programming and the Transact SQL language. My goal in this section is to cover some simple stored procedures and the ADO techniques you need to work with SQL Server-stored procedures. ExecSP shows how you execute a stored procedure: in this case, the sp_who procedure that returns information about the current users in the database. To access a query or a view, you use nearly identical code.

```
Sub ExecSP()
    Dim Cmd As New ADODB.Command
    Dim RS As New ADODB.Recordset
    Cmd.ActiveConnection = NetDS
    Cmd.CommandType = adCmdStoredProc
    Cmd.CommandText = "sp_who"
    RS.Open Cmd
    Do Until RS.EOF
        Debug.Print RS(0), RS(1), RS(2), RS(3)
        RS.MoveNext
    Loop
End Sub
```

Built-in stored procedures with multiple recordsets

SQL Server stores procedures to help in database operations, analysis, management, maintenance, and recovery. These procedures begin with the prefix sp_.

Queries and views are limited by definition to returning a single recordset. The built-in stored procedures typically return information that consists of the results of more than one SQL query. Because each query in the stored procedure generates a recordset, ADO views the result as a data object that contains multiple recordsets.

If you have a recordset object that actually contains more than one recordset, you must use the NextRecordset method of the recordset object to retrieve the full result of the stored procedure.

For example, sp_spaceused stored procedure usually returns two recordsets that summarize the space used by a database. To see all the information a stored procedure generates, use a procedure like BuiltInSP1. The procedure is dynamically linked to three different collections of data that a stored procedure can return.

✓ **Fields:** Each recordset a built-in stored procedure returns has a different number of fields.

✓ **Records:** Each recordset may have one or more records.

✓ **Recordsets:** The stored procedure can return one or more recordsets.

You must treat the collection of recordsets differently than standard ADO collections. The only way to determine if a recordset object contains additional recordsets is to apply the `NextRecordset`.

```
recordsetObj.NextRecordset
```

If the `State` property is zero, as shown in the following statement, no additional recordsets need to be processed.

```
recordsetObj.State = 0
```

`BuiltInSP1` uses loops to process all of the elements in the three collections.

```
Sub BuiltInSP1(sp_Text)
    Dim MultiRS As New ADODB.Recordset
    Dim Fld
    MultiRS.Open sp_Text, NetDS
    Do Until MultiRS.State = 0
        Do Until MultiRS.EOF
            For Fld = 0 To MultiRS.Fields.Count - 2
                Debug.Print MultiRS(Fld) & vbTab;
            Next
            Debug.Print MultiRS(MultiRS.Fields.Count - 1)
            MultiRS.MoveNext
        Loop
        Set MultiRS = MultiRS.NextRecordset
    Loop
End Sub
```

You can test the `BuiltInSP1` procedure with `TestSp1` that executes the `sp_spaceused` SQL Server stored procedure:

```
Sub TestSp1()
    BuiltInSP1 "sp_spaceused"
End Sub
```

The output of the procedure looks like this:

```
DBAD1D  75.00 MB    48.85 MB
26782 KB    25178 KB    930 KB  674 KB
```

Notice that the meaning of the numbers isn't clear because the `BuiltInSP1` procedure retrieves only the data in the recordsets that the stored procedure generated. To get the full picture, you need to output the field names, which end up serving as the column headings. The field names identify the meaning of the data. `BuiltInSP2` corrects this omission by adding code that displays the names of the fields in each recordset before displaying the data.

```
Sub BuiltInSP2(sp_Text)
    Dim MultiRS As New ADODB.Recordset
    Dim Fld
    MultiRS.Open sp_Text, NetDS
    Do Until MultiRS.State = 0
        For Fld = 0 To MultiRS.Fields.Count - 2
            Debug.Print MultiRS(Fld).Name & vbTab;
        Next
        Debug.Print MultiRS(MultiRS.Fields.Count - 1).Name
        Do Until MultiRS.EOF
            For Fld = 0 To MultiRS.Fields.Count - 2
                Debug.Print MultiRS(Fld) & vbTab;
            Next
            Debug.Print MultiRS(MultiRS.Fields.Count - 1)
            MultiRS.MoveNext
        Loop
        Set MultiRS = MultiRS.NextRecordset
    Loop
End Sub

Sub TestSp2()
    BuiltInSP2 "sp_spaceused"
End Sub
```

The following code is the same information you see if you execute the `sp_spaceused` stored procedure in the SQL Server Query Analyzer:

```
database_name    database_size    unallocated space
DBAD1D  75.00 MB      48.85 MB
reserved     data      index_size   unused
26782 KB    25178 KB     930 KB   674 KB
```

Stored procedures with parameters

Stored procedures are the SQL equivalent of procedures in VB/VBA. The SQL language in SQL Server, called Transact SQL, isn't nearly as sophisticated as VB/VBA when it comes to building applications. However, it supports the ability to use parameters to send and receive data from stored procedures. The two types of parameters are

✔ **Input:** A parameter that's passed to the stored procedure

✔ **Output:** A value that's returned by the stored procedure when it completes executing

Using an input parameter

If you have administrator or database owner permissions, you can create a stored procedure on a server. Procedures that use parameters have the following general structure. All the input parameters are listed after the procedure name and before the AS keyword. Following AS, you can list one or more SQL statements or other language elements supported by the provider: in this example, SQL Server. Note that in SQL Server, all parameters and variables begin with an @ character.

```
CREATE PROC <name>
    @param1 datatype,
    @param2 datatype, ...
AS
    Statements...
```

The following is a SQL statement that creates a stored procedure that uses two input parameters — @SDate and @EDate. The parameters are used to select records that fall into a specific date range. The data types used for variables in a stored procedure don't follow ADO conventions, but rather they conform to the date types supported by the database server. As with views, it's usually a good idea to add a prefix, such as usp_ (user stored procedure), to any new procedures you add to a database.

```
CREATE PROC usp_ProductSales
    @SDate datetime,
    @EDate datetime
AS
SELECT Vintage, WineName, Sales = sum(extprice), Units = sum(D.bottles)
FROM Orders O, OrderDetails D, Wineproductcatalog W
WHERE wineorderid = orderlink
AND d.wineid = w.wineid
AND Orderdate between @Sdate and @Edate
GROUP BY Vintage, WineName
ORDER BY sum(extprice) DESC
```

Passing input parameters to a stored procedure

After a procedure has been created on the server, you can access it through a command or recordset object. In a SQL Server application, such as the Query Analyzer, you execute a stored procedure by name followed by a list of the parameters.

```
usp_ProductSales '1/1/99','7/1/99'
```

You can execute the same command via ADO using a recordset object. ExecSpWithParams1 uses the command with parameters as the source text for the recordset object. ADO passes the text to SQL Server and receives the results in the form of a recordset.

```
Sub ExecSpWithParams1()
    Dim Rs As New ADODB.Recordset
    Rs.Open _
    "usp_ProductSales '1/1/99','7/1/99'", _
    NetDS
    Do Until Rs.EOF
        Debug.Print Rs(0), Rs(1), Rs(2), Rs(3)
        Rs.MoveNext
    Loop
End Sub
```

If you want to use ADO parameters to set the parameter values of a stored procedure, use an ADO command object. When using parameters with stored procedures, you need to set the direction to specify which of the parameters is an input or output parameter.

```
parameterObj.Direction = adParamInput
```

ExecSpWithParams2 uses ADO parameters to set the parameters that go to the stored procedure. This approach makes the code considerably more verbose. However, you may find it easier to assign parameters to the command object than to generate command strings that include parameters.

```
Sub ExecSpWithParams2()
    Dim Cmd As New ADODB.Command
    Dim Rs As New ADODB.Recordset
    Dim Sdate As New ADODB.Parameter
    Dim Edate As ADODB.Parameter

    Cmd.ActiveConnection = NetDS
    Cmd.CommandText = "usp_ProductSales"
    Cmd.CommandType = adCmdStoredProc

    Sdate.Direction = adParamInput
    Sdate.Type = adDate
    Sdate.Direction = adParamInput
    Sdate.Type = adDate
    Cmd.Parameters.Append Sdate
    Cmd(0) = "1/1/99"

    Set Edate = Cmd.CreateParameter( _
    Type:=adDate, Direction:=adParamInput, _
    Value:="1999-07-01")
    Cmd.Parameters.Append Edate

    Rs.Open Cmd
    Do Until Rs.EOF
        Debug.Print Rs(0), Rs(1), Rs(2), Rs(3)
        Rs.MoveNext
    Loop
End Sub
```

In ExecSpWithParams2, I use two different approaches to create parameters. In the case of the Sdate parameter, I set individual properties. I create Edate by specifying all the properties with a single CreateParameter function. Both approaches accomplish the same function, so you can use the style that appeals to you.

Output parameters with stored procedures

Although SQL Server allows stored procedures to return recordsets (Oracle doesn't), stored procedures can return data to an application in another way. That method involves using output parameters. An *output parameter* is a variable passed to a stored procedure. During the execution of the stored procedure, the variable is assigned a value. After the execution is complete, the application can retrieve the value assigned to the variable.

Suppose, for example, that you want to calculate the average verified order and the standard deviation for that order. (Although SQL Server 7.0 includes a StDev function, earlier versions don't.) You can use a stored procedure to perform the calculation based on a range of dates (the input parameters). The calculated values are returned not as a recordset but as output parameters.

The following is a stored procedure called usp_OrderStats that uses four parameters. The first two (@SDate and @EDate) are inputs used to set the date range. The last two (@AvgOrders and @StdOrders) are designated as output parameters. When the procedure has completed executing, these variables contain the values generated in the stored procedure.

```
CREATE PROC usp_OrderStats
    @SDate datetime,
    @EDate datetime,

    @AvgOrders money output,
    @StdOrders money Output
AS

SELECT @AvgOrders = avg(ordertotal)
FROM Orders WHERE Paymentverified = 1
AND Orderdate between @SDate and @Edate

SELECT @StdOrders =
SQRT(avg(Power(ordertotal - @avgOrders,2)))
FROM Orders WHERE Paymentverified = 1
AND Orderdate between @SDate and @Edate
```

In Transact SQL, you assign a value to a variable in a SELECT statement. The following example tells SQL Server to assign the value of the expression avg (ordertotal) to the variable @AvgOrders.

```
SELECT @AvgOrders = avg(ordertotal)
```

Within the stored procedure, both the input and output variables can be referenced and modified in any way you like. The distinction between input and output affects only the value of the parameters outside the stored procedure.

To use this stored procedure, create an ADO command object that has four parameters. These parameters must match the data type and direction of parameters in the stored procedure. Note that the output parameters aren't assigned any values. The sequence in which the parameters are appended to the command object is critical because that is the order in which they're fed to the stored procedure. If you append the parameters in a different order than they're defined in the stored procedure, the execution fails.

```
Sub OutputParam()
    Dim Cmd As New ADODB.Command
    Dim Sdate As New ADODB.Parameter
    Dim Edate As ADODB.Parameter
    Dim SalesAvg As ADODB.Parameter
    Dim SaleStDev As ADODB.Parameter

    Cmd.ActiveConnection = NetDS
    Cmd.CommandText = "usp_OrderStats"
    Cmd.CommandType = adCmdStoredProc

    Set Sdate = Cmd.CreateParameter( _
    Type:=adDate, Direction:=adParamInput, _
    Value:="1/1/99")Cmd.Parameters.Append Sdate

    Cmd.Parameters.Append Edate

    Set SalesAvg = Cmd.CreateParameter( _
    Type:=adCurrency, Direction:=adParamOutput)
    Cmd.Parameters.Append SalesAvg

    Set SaleStDev = Cmd.CreateParameter( _
    Type:=adCurrency, Direction:=adParamOutput)
    Cmd.Parameters.Append SaleStDev

    Cmd.Execute
    Debug.Print "Average:", Cmd.Parameters(2)
    Debug.Print "Standard Dev:", Cmd.Parameters(3)

End Sub
```

The result is two values returned by the output parameters and displayed in the Immediate window, as shown in the following example:

```
Average:       54.015
Standard Dev:  113.8427
```

Stored procedures and forms

Use stored procedures with forms in the same manner as with the recordset generated in Chapter 6. Figure 7-9 shows a form (StoredProc in the ClientServer.MDB) that contains two text boxes and a Hflexgrid control. In this example, the goal is to pass the values in the text boxes.

The following code shows that the values from the text boxes are assigned to the parameters of the Cmd command object. The command uses the stored procedure, usp_ProductSales, as the date source. Each time you click the Getdata button, the current dates are passed to the stored procedure, and the corresponding recordset is retrieved for display in the grid.

```
Option Compare Database
Dim Cnt As New ADODB.Connection
```

```
Private Sub Command11_Click()
    Dim Cmd As New ADODB.Command
    Dim P As ADODB.Parameter
    Dim RS As New ADODB.Recordset
    Cmd.ActiveConnection = Cnt
    Cmd.CommandText = "usp_ProductSales"
    Cmd.CommandType = adCmdStoredProc
    Set P = Cmd.CreateParameter( _
    Type:=adDate, Direction:=adParamInput)
    Cmd.Parameters.Append P
    Set P = Cmd.CreateParameter( _
    Type:=adDate, Direction:=adParamInput)
    Cmd.Parameters.Append P
    Cmd(0) = Me.Sdate
    Cmd(1) = Me.Edate
    RS.Open Cmd
    Set Me.Grid1.DataSource = RS
End Sub

Private Sub Form_Load()
    Me.Grid1.ColHeader(0) = flexColHeaderOn
    Cnt.Open NetDS
    Me.Sdate = #1/1/1999#
    Me.Edate = #12/31/1999#
End Sub
```

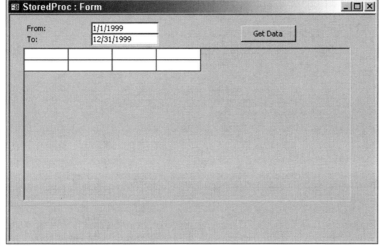

Figure 7-9:
The
StoredProc
form
passes date
parameters.

Adjusting column widths

One useful feature of the code in StoredProc in the ClientServer.MDB is its
capability of adjusting column width to fit the data automatically. In the
recordset returned by the usp_ProductSales, the second column is wider

than the other data columns. Figure 7-10 shows in `StoredProc1` in the ClientServer.MDB the column widths in an active form reset based on the contents of the columns.

You can adjust column widths by using the `AdjustColumns` procedure, which examines the contents of the first records in the recordset and measures the number of characters to adjust column width.

```
Sub AdjustColumns(GSize As ADODB.Recordset)
    Dim GR As MSHFlexGrid, C
    Set GR = Me.Grid1.Object
    GR.ColHeader(0) = flexColHeaderOn
    For C = 0 To GSize.Fields.Count - 1
        If Len(GSize(C)) > 12 Then
            GR.ColWidth(C) = Len(GSize(C)) * 100
        End If
    Next
End Sub
```

Figure 7-10:
The column widths adjust to the length of data in each column.

Vintage	WineName	Sales	Units
1996	North Valley Bordeaux Blend Reserve	53510	1532
1996	South Valley Cabernet Standard	34827.4	1812
1996	Valley Cabernet Standard	29078.5	1153
1994	East Valley Cabernet Standard	20201	2591
1995	South Valley Bordeaux Blend Reserve	15693.52	1677
1997	North Coast Chardonnay Standard	13572	1594
1998	Santa Barbara Chardonnay Reserve	4672	76
1993	Santa Barbara Bordeaux Blend Reserve	4377	194
1996	Santa Cruz Chardonnay Reserve	3223.8	247
1987	East Valley Cabernet Standard	3183.2	159
1996	Valley Zinfandel Standard	2262.4	266
1995	Santa Cruz Merlot Standard	1397	78
1996	Central Valley Chardonnay Standard	1250	97

From: 1/1/1999 To: 7/31/1999   [Get Data]

Of course, the `AdjustColumns` approach isn't perfect. The first record may or may not have an entry that's typical of the size of the entries in the field. If you wanted to expend the effort, you can query the data source to determine the maximum width of the items in a given field and use that value to set the column width. This approach takes extra time, and you may have set a column too wide if the average entry is much small than the widest entry. However, by using some sort of logic to set the column widths, you give the grid a customized look that fits the data better than simply leaving columns at the default width.

One important issue arises in the ADO code when you add an operation such as `AdjustColumns` because of the effect that the flexgrid control has on the recordset object. If you access the data in the recordset before you assign it to the flex control, the control rejects the recordset. Conversely, if you assign the recordset to the flexgrid control and then access the data in a procedure like `AdjustColumns`, you also generate an error.

If you want to use a given recordset as the data source for a flexgrid and as the data for some other operation (such as adjusting the column width), you must requery the recordset to bring it back into the proper state. The following code comes from the form module for `StoredProc1`. In this example, the recordset `RS` is required after `AdjustColumns` uses it. After it has been required, you can assign it to `DataSource` of the flexgrid control.

```
RS.Open Cmd
AdjustColumns RS
RS.Requery
Set Me.Grid1.DataSource = RS
```

Keep in mind that the order of operations doesn't matter. The following example from `StoredProc2` reverses the sequence of operations. Still, it's necessary to requery the recordset after each operation.

```
RS.Open Cmd
Set Me.Grid1.DataSource = RS
RS.Requery
AdjustColumns RS
```

Chapter 8

ADO Services

· ·

In This Chapter

▶ Using the ADO Cursor Service

▶ Invoking client-side cursors

▶ Using the ADO Sort property

▶ Using the ADO Filter property

▶ Using the ADO Data-Shaping service

▶ Creating hierarchical recordsets

▶ Displaying multilevel recordset in a grid

· ·

*O*ne of the major differences between ADO and previous data technologies from Microsoft is that ADO was designed with both the current and future needs of the database programmer in mind. One feature that is aimed at the future is the ADO services. These services are designed to provide standard ADO functionality in areas that Microsoft anticipates will be key technologies in the near future. In this chapter, I look at the Cursor and Data Shaping services now available in ADO.

Note that the Access database for Chapter 8 is an Access 2000 project database. This means that the ADP file connects, via the Internet, to its data source. You need to have setup the ADODUM client for SQL Server and use the reader password. See the introduction for more details.

The ADO Cursor Service

One of the goals of ADO was to create a more consistent level of functionality for the programmer who must deal with a wide variety of data sources. As illustrated in the other chapters of this book, there are inevitably some provider-specific details that require minor code modifications when moving from one data source to another. But by and large, these are the exceptions, and not the rule.

To provide a high level of functionality within ADO, Microsoft has included some ADO features called services. An ADO service is designed to add certain functionality to ADO providers that do not in and of themselves support these features.

One of the most useful services — almost transparent to both the user and the programmer — is called the Cursor Service. The term cursor, within the context of databases, refers to the mechanisms used by a database to manage the data contained in a set of records. When you use ADO to create a recordset, the data provider is given responsibility by default for handling the structure of the recordset. This is called a server-side cursor.

ADO provides an alternative approach to managing recordsets. The alternative is to switch the responsibility for management of the recordset from the server side to the client side, where ADO and your application can control how the recordset behaves.

As an example, take the issue of the sort order of the records contained in a recordset. Using server-side cursors, the sort order of the record is determined by the ORDER BY clause, if one is included in the SQL statement or stored procedure. Want to change the sort order of the recordset after it has been returned to the application by the server? In most cases, you can't change the order of records in the recordset object. Figure 8-1 shows how a server-side cursor does not allow the application to change the sort order of the records once they have been retrieved.

Why not? The answer lies in the mechanisms the server uses to keep track of records as they are manipulated (edited or deleted) by the client application. If you want to see the recordset in a different order, you must send a different data request to the server and have it return a completely new recordset with the requested order. The same limitation applies to record selection using the WHERE clause. If your initial recordset includes all of the customers whose names begin with the letter A, then to get a list of customers' names beginning with the letter B, you must ask the provider to create an entirely new recordset based on the new criteria. This is exactly the approach used in the TextSearch forms used in Chapter 6.

One disadvantage of this approach is the time required to go back to the server and retrieve a new recordset every time the client application wants to sort and/or filter the recordset. The TextSearch forms in Chapter 6 require the provider to generate and return a new recordset every time the user added or removed a single character from the search string.

As networks have gotten physically larger and now extend over the public Internet, server-side operations become an issue. The TextSearch forms (see Chapter 6) are constantly requesting new recordsets as users interact with the forms on their client computers. Over a large or slow network, the users may experience a delay each time that they make a selection requiring a new recordset to be generated by the server and returned to client application.

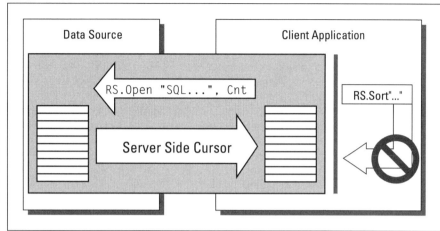

Figure 8-1:
Server-side
cursors limit
the degree
of control
available to
the client
application.

The alternative is a client-side cursor. Figure 8-2 shows how a client-side
cursor works. When a request is made for a recordset, the server returns the
recordset to client and then relinquishes control to the application and the
ADO cursor service. The application can now freely invoke ADO methods,
such as `Sort` or `Filter`, which manipulate the recordset in the same way that
new `WHERE` or `ORDER BY`Mono? clauses changes the recordset on the server.

Of course, the strategy that you employ in building a client-side cursor application is a bit different than in a server-based application. You cannot sort or filter
records that are not already part of the recordset. Suppose that you wanted to
manipulate your customer list by filtering the records based on a search string
(the technique used in the TextSearch forms in Chapter 6). The initial list
extracted from the provider needs to include all of the customer names. Then
use ADO properties to include, exclude, and/or sort those records.

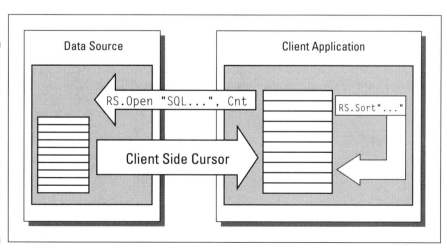

Figure 8-2:
Client-side
cursors use
ADO to
manipulate
the contents
of the
recordset
without
another trip
to the
server.

Wait a minute! If you have to bring over the entire table, whether 4,000 customers or 19,000 orders, won't you experience an even greater delay than with the server-side cursor? The answer is both yes and no. Yes, the time required to populate the recordset increases because you are moving a larger block of records from the server to the client. But once at the client, filter and sort operations takes place rapidly because all of the data need is already stored in the memory of the client computer.

The advantage of the client-side cursor is that it places all of the latency up front, when the recordset is first created. All subsequent recordset operations occur rapidly because there is no need to re-query the server to select subsets of the original recordset. The general rule about user interfaces is that users tolerate a single delay, such as when the form is opening, better than delays that occur after each keystroke or click.

Cursor location

The best way to understand client-side cursors is to put them to use. First, look at some raw coding examples, and then see how I put the code to practical use within some forms.

The code below is an example of a server-side cursor. When it executes, it returns a set of records based on the SQL statement passed to the provider: in this case, SQL Server across the Internet.

```
Sub Sort1()
    Dim RS As New ADODB.Recordset
    RS.Open _
    "SELECT billCity, " & _
    "count(*) As CustCount FROM Customers " & _
    "WHERE billstate = 'MT' GROUP BY billcity", _
    NetDS, adOpenKeyset
    Do Until RS.EOF
        Debug.Print RS(0), RS(1)
        RS.MoveNext
    Loop
End Sub
```

The results are shown below. By default, the records are listed in order under the city name because that was the GROUP BY field.

```
Big Sky        1
Billings       1
Glindive       1
Kalispell      2
Lewistown      1
Whitefish      1
```

But suppose that you want to list the cities according to which one has the most customers. The server-side approach is to request another recordset that specifies a sort order as shown below.

```
SELECT billCity,
count(*) As CustCount FROM Customers
WHERE billstate = 'MT' GROUP BY billcity
ORDER BY count(*) DESC
```

On the other hand, because the records that need to be sorted are already resident in the client application, it is much faster to simply use the Sort property of the recordset object to rearrange the records.

```
RS.Sort = "CustCount DESC"
```

The procedure below attempts to sort the recordset after it has been returned from the server.

```
Sub Sort2()
    Dim RS As New ADODB.Recordset
    RS.Open _
    "SELECT billCity, " & _
    "count(*) As CustCount FROM Customers " & _
    "WHERE billstate = 'MT' GROUP BY billcity", _
    NetDS, adOpenKeyset
    RS.Sort = "CustCount DESC"
    Do Until RS.EOF
        Debug.Print RS(0), RS(1)
        RS.MoveNext
    Loop
End Sub
```

Unfortunately, this generates an error, shown in Figure 8-3. Why? The answer is that once a recordset is opened, its properties are fixed. In Sort2, the default cursor location — server side — is automatically invoked when the record is opened. Following that, any attempt to perform an operation that requires a client-side cursor results in an error.

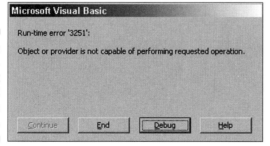

Figure 8-3:
The sort function not supported by the provider.

To take advantage of client cursor features such as sorting or filtering, you must specify that you want a recordset with a client-side cursor prior to opening the recordset using the statement below.

```
RS.CursorLocation = adUseClient
```

Sort3 contains only one change, but it is a significant one. The location of the recordset cursor is specified as the client. This allows the Sort property to be applied to the data at any time after the recordset has been opened.

```
Sub Sort3()
    Dim RS As New ADODB.Recordset
    RS.CursorLocation = adUseClient
    RS.Open _
    "SELECT billCity, " & _
    "count(*) As CustCount FROM Customers " & _
    "WHERE billstate = 'MT' GROUP BY billcity", _
    NetDS, adOpenKeyset
    RS.Sort = "CustCount DESC"
    Do Until RS.EOF
        Debug.Print RS(0), RS(1)
        RS.MoveNext
    Loop
End Sub
```

Further, you can use the properties (such as sort or filter) as many times as you like on the same recordset without having to return to the provider.

Sorting recordsets dynamically

The next step is to apply the concept of client cursors to a practical problem. The Sort1 form (pictured in Figure 8-4) loads a recordset based on the customer's table into a flex grid. Initially, the records are displayed in their natural order. The natural order of a recordset is simply the order in which they are physically arranged in the database table without any sorting. The form has two buttons. Each button rearranges the records into a specific sort order.

Figure 8-4:
You can use the sort property to display the same recordset in different sort orders.

To see how this is accomplished, examine the code in the Sort1 form. Below is the declarations section of the form's code module. Note that the connection and recordset objects are defined in the Declarations section so that they are available to any procedure in the form. This is important because the code in the form allows the user to change the properties of the recordset object (in this case the `sort` property) as many times as they like. Because the SQL statement won't be changed once it has been submitted to the provider, it is defined as a constant.

```
Option Compare Database
Option Explicit
Dim Cnt As New ADODB.Connection
Dim RS As New ADODB.Recordset
Dim HFG As MSHFlexGrid
Const SQLText = "SELECT Lastname, Firstname," & _
    "billcity, billzip From Customers " & _
    "WHERE billstate = 'TX'"
```

The key procedure in the SorHt1 form is the `Form_Load` procedure shown below. The procedure creates the recordset object by opening the connection to the provider and then using the SQL statement to extract the recordset. Note that the cursor location property is set to `adUseClient` before the recordset `Open` method executes. The recordset is then assigned as the `DataSource` property of the flex grid.

```
Private Sub Form_Load()
    Set HFG = Me.DataList.Object
    Cnt.Open NetDS
    RS.CursorLocation = adUseClient
    RS.Open SQLText, Cnt
    With HFG
        .FixedCols = 0
        Set .DataSource = RS
    End With
End Sub
```

The result of the `Form_Load` is pictured in Figure 8-4. The flex grid displays an unsorted recordset that consists of the customers from Texas. The next task is to look at the code that is needed to change the sort order to Lastname when the Sort by Lastname button is clicked.

The procedure below is all that is needed to sort the records. Note that because the flex grid is linked to the recordset object RS, if you change the Sort property of the recordset, the grid automatically changes the records it display to match the current state of the recordset (see Figure 8-5).

```
Private Sub Command1_Click()
    RS.Sort = "Lastname"
End Sub
```

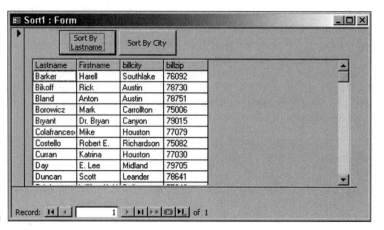

Figure 8-5:
Changing
the sort
property
of the
recordset
automatically
changes the
appearance
of the flex
grid.

Changing to another sort order, such as sort by billcity, is equally simple. The procedure below uses a single statement to rearrange the grid into a different sort order.

```
Private Sub Command2_Click()
    RS.Sort = "billcity"
End Sub
```

If you use the Sort1 form (live, on the Internet), you can see that there is no net-work delay because the client-side cursor avoids accessing the provider when changing the sort order — no matter how often you change the sort order.

Sorting any field in any order

The client-side cursor in Sort1 allows you a fairly sophisticated option with only a few programming statements. But what if you want to broaden the idea to allow the user to sort by any of the fields that appear on the grid and in any order, such as ascending or descending. Sound complicated, right? Sort2, pictured in Figure 8-6, has two buttons for sorting: one for ascending and the other for descending. You can use those to sort any field on the grid in either order.

Expand the idea in Sort1 to the full sorting in Sort2. If you look at the proce-dures in Sort1 that changed the sort order, you see that the only difference between one procedure and the other is the name of the field to be sorted. You can sort any field as long as you know its name.

```
RS.Sort = <any field name>
```

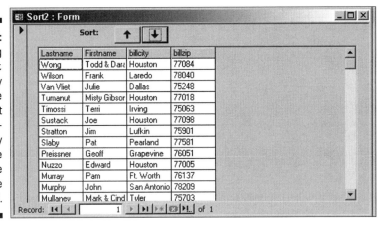

Figure 8-6:
Changing
the sort
property
of the
recordset
auto-
matically
changes the
appearance
of the
flex grid.

Does this mean that you need to add one button for each column that you want to sort? I have a better solution. The names of the fields are already available on the form because each field is assigned to a column in the flex grid. When the user clicks a cell in any of the columns, it sets a property of the flex grid. The ColSel and RowSel properties return a number starting with zero that indicates the currently selected column and row in the grid. In this case, you want to sort on the currently selected column; therefore, you're only interested in knowing which column the selection falls in. The property below gives you that column number.

```
HFG.ColSel
```

Of course, the column number is what is required for sorting. The ADO sort property does not use field ordinal numbers, only field names. However, you can obtain the name of the column from the flex grid by using the ColHeaderCaption property. The expression below returns the name of the column in which the selection is currently located.

```
HFG.ColHeaderCaption(0, HFG.ColSel)
```

To specify a descending sort order, you merely need to add DESC to the field name. The expression below specifies a descending order for sorting the field that corresponds to the location of the selection on the grid. Note that you must separate the field name from the DESC with a space.

```
HFG.ColHeaderCaption(0, HFG.ColSel) & " DESC"
```

All that is needed to go from Sort1 to Sort2 is a little bit of editing — a very little bit. Below are the procedures that correspond to the up- and down-arrow buttons. All that is changed is that name of the sort field is arrived at by examining the properties of the flex grid control. As the user interacts with the grid, the operation performed by the sorting buttons follows the user's current selection.

```
Private Sub Down_Click()
    RS.Sort = HFG.ColHeaderCaption(0, HFG.ColSel) & " DESC"
End Sub
Private Sub UP_Click()
    RS.Sort = HFG.ColHeaderCaption(0, HFG.ColSel)
End Sub
```

This approach is not only simple to code but it provides the user with a much more intuitive user interface. Another advantage is that the sorting feature works with any recordset you choose to display in the grid. There are no changes needed to accommodate recordsets with more columns. The procedures simply draw the required field names from the grid based on the selection location.

Sorting on calculated fields

There is another small but handy benefit in client cursor coding. The client-side cursor uses the field alias as the field name. For example, suppose that instead of using separate firstname and lastname fields, the recordset included a fullname field that was calculated by an expression included in the source SQL statement like the one below.

```
Const SQLText = _
    "SELECT Lastname + ',' + Firstname AS FullName," & _
    "billcity, billzip From Customers " & _
    "WHERE billstate = 'TX'"
```

If you wanted to sort the records by full name on the server side, the syntax does not recognize the alias, FullName, as the name of the field. Instead, you must specify the expression as the sort criterion.

```
SELECT Lastname + ',' + Firstname AS FullName,
billcity, billzip From Customers
WHERE billstate = 'TX' ORDER BY Lastname + ',' + Firstname
```

When you work on the client-side, ADO recognizes the alias as the field name. The form, Sort3, pictured in Figure 8-7, uses a calculated FullName field. However, because ADO works with the alias name, you don't need to change the code to sort by a calculated field.

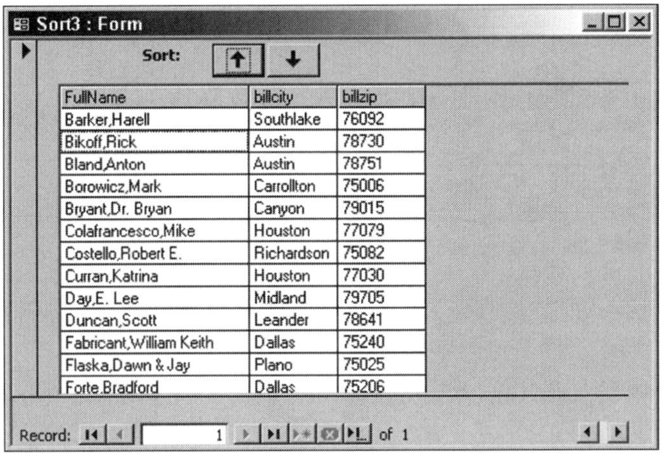

Figure 8-7:
Text boxes
can limit the
names
displayed.

Filtering records

The other key feature available from the ADO cursor service is the ability to apply a logical filter to an existing recordset. The Filter property applies a criterion expression to a recordset the same way that a WHERE clause does in SQL. The statement below filters the records in the RS recordset object for those records whose Lastname field matches the pattern *vin**.

```
RS.Filter = "Lastname LIKE #vin%#"
```

The syntax used by ADO is a bit of a hybrid of SQL and VB/VBA. ADO recognizes either a percent sign (%) or an asterisk (*) as a wildcard symbol. To avoid confusion about the use of quotations and apostrophes, ADO uses the pound sign symbol (#) as a delimiter for text, as well as dates.

The form pictured in Figure 8-8 — Filter — is a reprise of the TextSearch form created in Chapter 6. Both forms use a text box to limit the names displayed in the grid. As the user enters or deletes characters in the search box, a filter is applied to the recordset so that only matching records appear in the grid.

On the surface, Filter and TextSearch are the same. What is significant is that they are implemented differently. TextSearch (see Chapter 6) uses server-side cursors (the default). This means that each time the user enters or deletes a character, a new recordset request is posted to the data provider. The client waits until the provider returns a new recordset before it can repopulate the grid.

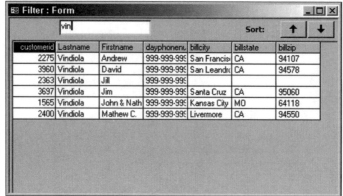

Figure 8-8:
Sorting can
be applied
to calcu-
lated fields
using the
field alias as
the sort
order field
name.

The Filter form uses the same basic approach as TextSearch except that the recordset is located on the client. The code below shows the Declarations section and the `Form_Load` procedure from the Filter form.

```
Option Compare Database
Option Explicit
Dim Cnt As New ADODB.Connection
Dim RS As New ADODB.Recordset
Dim HFG As MSHFlexGrid
Const SQLText = "SELECT customerid, Lastname, " & _
    "Firstname,dayphonenumber," & _
    "billcity, billstate, billzip From Customers " & _
    "order by lastname,firstname"
Private Sub Form_Load()
    Set HFG = Me.DataList.Object
    Cnt.Open NetDS
    RS.CursorLocation = adUseClient
    RS.Open SQLText, Cnt
    With HFG
        .FixedCols = 0
        Set .DataSource = RS
    End With
End Sub
```

There are two areas to note:

✔ **Client-side cursor:** The primary technical difference is the use of a client-side cursor with the recordset object that is used to populate the grid.

✔ **Full recordset:** It is important to understand that switching from the server-side cursor to a client-side cursor changes more than just the value of the `CursorLocation` property. In TextSearch, the grid begins as an empty display (you can't know when the form was opening those records the user wants to display). The recordset is created only after the user enters the first letter in the search box. However, when you use a client-side cursor, you need to apply the opposite logic. Because you are only going to extract data once from the provider, you need to copy all of the potential records into the recordset object when you first open the form. Use the `filter` property to limit the display to a specific subset of the original recordset; you cannot display any records you originally retrieved.

The result is that when you open the Filter form, you experience a delay while the entire recordset is loaded from the data provider to the client. The recordset is assigned to the flex grid as its data source so that the entire customers table is now listed in the grid.

Of course, the key to the form is the ability of the user to quickly narrow the scope of the records displayed by typing one or more characters into the text box as a matching pattern. The code that implements that behavior is shown below in the `Change` event procedure for the Text control. The client-side features of the ADO recordset object greatly simplify the code required to implement this feature. To filter the records, the search pattern is assigned to the `filter` property of the recordset. A second statement sets the sort order. If the pattern is empty, the filter is set to `adFilterNone`, which returns the list to its full, original contents. Recall that because the flex grid is dynamically linked to the recordset when the recordset is using a client-side cursor, any change to the recordset automatically updates the grid display.

```
Private Sub Text6_Change()
  If Text6.Text <> "" Then
      Rs.Filter = "lastname Like #" & Me.Text6.Text & "*#"
      Rs.Sort = "lastname,firstname"
  Else
      Rs.Filter = adFilterNone
  End If
End Sub
```

Not only is the code involved greatly simplified, but the performance is enhanced because the client-side sorting and filtering use the client computer's resource, thus avoiding the need to return to the server for a new recordset each time the criteria is changed on the form.

Note that the filter also retains the sorting by column feature from the previous examples on sorting. All of these features are built on the ADO client-side cursor service.

Opening another form

One of the ways that the grid displays are typically used is as an interface element that provides a wide overview of the data managed by the application. If you need to drill down to the record level, you can link each row in the grid to a form that display the fields for editing. Included in the ADOServices example are generic forms created using the form's wizard for editing the Customers (frmCustomers) and Orders (frmOrders) tables.

You can link each row in the flex grid with a form that allows editing of the full details of each record so that each time the user double-clicks on a row, the customer form is opened displaying the full contents of the record. See Figure 8-9.

Remember that the first column of the flex grid is a hidden column defined in the Form_Load procedure. Because the first column in the recordset is always the CustomerID value, the CustomerID is part of the grid even though the user cannot see it.

```
With HFG
    .ColWidth(0) = 0
End With
```

In opening another form the trick is to know the CustomerID of the row that is being double-clicked. That value is always the first column of the currently selected row. The TextArray property of the flex grid returns the text of the currently selected cell when supplied with the cell number.

```
gridObj.TextArray(<cellNumber>)
```

The cell numbers are simply consecutive numbers that start with 1 and increment for each cell row by row. You can calculate the number of the first column of any row using the formula below.

```
<1st Col Current row> = <# of Cols> * <Selected Row>
```

This formula translates to a statement like the one below. The Cols property returns the number of columns in the grid. The RowSel property returns the numeric values of the currently selected rows below. When you multiply the two, you get the cell number of the first cell on the current row.

```
gridObj.TextArray(gridObj.Cols * gridObj.RowSel)
```

This formula can then be inserted as the argument for the TextArray property, as shown in the DataList_DblClick procedure below. The result is that the CustomerID of the currently selected customer is used to specify the CustomerID of the record that should be displayed in the customers editing form.

```
Private Sub DataList_DblClick()
    With HFG
        DoCmd.OpenForm "frmCustomers", , , _
        "Customerid = " & .TextArray(.Cols * .RowSel)
    End With
End Sub
```

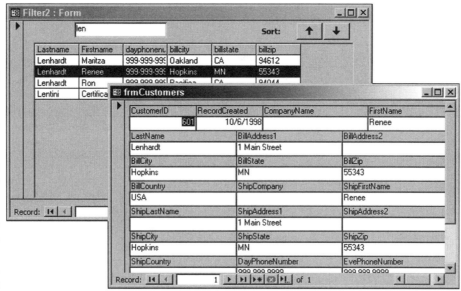

Figure 8-9:
The
CustomerID,
stored in a
hidden
column, is
used to
open the
detail form
when a row
is double-
clicked in
the form.

The interface shown in the form Filter2 in Figure 8-9 is an example of an enhanced use of lists. Instead of simply listing all of the customers or orders in one long list or combo box, the text search style interface working with the flex grid provides several features at one time. The key data about each customer is displayed in the grid itself. For example, by including the telephone number in the flex grid, a user can locate a customer phone number without ever having to open the entire customer record. If that record is needed, the user simply double-clicks the row he located in the list.

Showing one-to-many relationships

Client-side cursors also make it much simpler to create forms in which there are several grids of data that have relationships to each other. Figure 8-10 shows the form Filter3 in which a one-to-many relationship between customers and orders is maintained between the two flex grids on the form.

The strategy in Filter3 is to use recordsets with client-side cursors to supply the data for the grids. The Declarations section of the form's code module, shown below, outlines the basic components. There are two flex grids and two recordsets that correspond to the Customers and Orders tables. Because you are using a client-side cursor, the SQL statements do not have a WHERE clause. You need to load all of the records during the initial creation of the recordset because you to not want to have to return to the data provider while the user is interacting with the form.

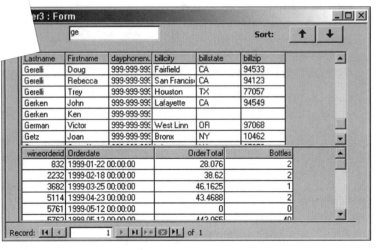

Figure 8-10:
Multiple
data grids
are linked
by filtering
recordsets
that use
client-side
cursors.

```
Option Compare Database
Option Explicit
Dim cnt As New ADODB.Connection
Dim Rs As New ADODB.Recordset
Dim RS1 As New ADODB.Recordset
Dim HFG As MSHFlexGrid
Dim HFG1 As New MSHFlexGrid
Const SQLText = "SELECT customerid, Lastname, " & _
    "Firstname,dayphonenumber," & _
    "billcity, billstate, billzip From Customers " & _
    "order by lastname,firstname"
Const SQLText1 = "SELECT customerid,wineorderid, Orderdate," & _
    "OrderTotal,Bottles FROM Orders"
```

One point to note is that both SQL statements list CustomerID as the first field. This is because this field links the records in the two grids. In these examples, the first field is always placed in a zero width column so that it is hidden from the user but it is available to your procedures. There is no technical reason why this column must be hidden. My reason for doing so is that the customer number is not typically used in business activity to identify a customer. The application needs the value to perform the linking, but there is no reason to crowd the already dense information space with irrelevant data. Conversely, as shown in Figure 8-10, the order numbers are displayed. These order numbers serve as a link to additional information about the order, but they are also typically used in business to refer to the transaction, so it makes sense not to hide that column.

The orders recordset, RS1, is treated a bit differently than the customers recordset that is immediately displayed in the grid. The order grid should initially be empty because when the form first appears, no customer has been selected. In the code below an initial filter, Customerid = 0, is applied to the orders recordset before it is assigned to the grid. Because the CustomerID field is an automatically numbered field, the expression has the effect of creating an empty recordset. Keep in mind that because the cursor location is on the client, the recordset is not really empty but simply temporarily filtered to suppress the display of any records.

```
RS1.CursorLocation = adUseClient
RS1.Open SQLText1, cnt
RS1.Filter = "Customerid = 0"
With HFG1
    .FixedCols = 0
    .ColWidth(0) = 0
    Set .DataSource = RS1
End With
```

All that is needed to link the customers grid to the orders grid is to apply a new filter each time the user changes the selection in the customer grid control (DataList). The SelChange procedure below uses a single statement to apply a filter to the order recordset (RS1), which displays the orders that match the selected customer.

```
Private Sub DataList_SelChange()
    With HFG
        RS1.Filter = "Customerid = " & .TextArray(.Cols * .RowSel)
    End With
End Sub
```

In DataList_SelChange, I use a With...End With structure when I could simply enter the full property references (such as HFG.Cols). I have a reason for doing this. First, because I need to refer to three different properties of the same object (the HFG control), it is a bit simpler to type without having to repeat the object name. Second, by writing out the expression using only the property names but not the object name, I have an expression that I can easily copy and paste into another procedure so that it can apply to a different object. For example, to change the code to work with a flex grid called HFG1, I have to change the object name in just one location and the expression then applies to a different object.

Reducing client-cursor stress

The Sort and Filter forms illustrate that the ADO cursor service can greatly simplify the construction of data-driven user interfaces. The code in this chapter is significantly simpler than similar server-side procedures in Chapter 6. Plus, the form reacts to user interaction quickly enough that they can navigate through a large database quickly and comfortably — something customer service representatives love.

But there is a price to be paid for the client-side benefits. The price is the time it takes to initially populate the form. The argument for client-side cursors is that a single, albeit significant, delay in opening a form is better than constant small delays that occur while interacting with the form.

Nonetheless, you want to minimize the delay as much as possible. One important technique is to limit the number of columns you request to the absolute minimum need to populate the display. You certainly want to avoid using SELECT *, which loads all of the columns in a table.

Another way to reduce the load is to use some logic to limit the number of records that need to be loaded. For example, you can limit the customer names to those that have actually placed orders or placed orders in the last six months. This can be accomplished by adding a JOIN to the query that limits the customers based on the contents of another table like Orders. The SQL statement below retrieves only the customers that have placed an order in the previous six months.

```
SELECT dbo.Customers.CustomerID, dbo.Customers.FirstName,
    dbo.Customers.LastName, dbo.Customers.BillCity,
    dbo.Customers.BillState, dbo.Customers.BillZip,
    dbo.Customers.DayPhoneNumber
FROM dbo.Orders INNER JOIN
    dbo.Customers ON
    dbo.Orders.CustomerID = dbo.Customers.CustomerID
WHERE
    Orderdate >= dateadd(mm, -6 , getdate())
GROUP BY dbo.Customers.CustomerID, dbo.Customers.FirstName,
    dbo.Customers.LastName, dbo.Customers.BillCity,
    dbo.Customers.BillState, dbo.Customers.BillZip,
    dbo.Customers.DayPhoneNumber
ORDER BY dbo.Customers.LastName, dbo.Customers.FirstName
```

Similarly, the next example limits the orders list to only those orders placed in the last six months.

```
SELECT customerid,wineorderid,
    Orderdate,OrderTotal,Bottles
FROM Orders
WHERE Orderdate >= dateadd(mm, -6 , getdate())
```

Form Filter5 uses these queries to load only the relevant records (as defined as occurring in the last six months), which shortens significantly the time it takes for the form to initially load.

Check out the code for Filter5. You see that I avoid coding these rather verbose SQL statements. Instead, I use the strategy discussed in Chapter 6 of creating a table — called Statements — in which I store complex query statements such as those above. When you need to execute one of these queries in a procedure, you can use the GetStatement function, shown below, to extract the required text.

```
Function GetStatement(SName)
    Dim S As New ADODB.Recordset
    S.Open "SELECT QueryText FROM Statements " & _
        "WHERE QueryName = '" & SName & "'", NetDS, adOpenStatic, adLockReadOnly
    GetStatement = S(0)
End Function
```

Using this approach, all that is needed to define a recordset is to use the `GetStatement` function to locate the desired query by name. In this example, Filter5a and Filter5b supply the required SQL.

```
cnt.Open NetDS
Rs.CursorLocation = adUseClient
Rs.Open GetStatement("filter5a"), cnt
RS1.CursorLocation = adUseClient
RS1.Open GetStatement("filter5b"), cnt
RS1.Filter = "Customerid = 0"
```

Another issue is how client-side recordsets deal with local and remote updates, additions, and deletions. This topic is covered in detail in Chapter 13.

The Data-Shaping Service

The display in Filter3 shows two lists that have a one-to-many relationship. In most applications based on relational databases, the one-to-many relationships are the key elements that make the system work. However, storing the data in a relational database does not mean that relational queries are the only, or even the best way, to retrieve that data in an application.

The ADO Cursor Service shows that in some contexts, loading an entire recordset and then applying sort and filter properties provides a better interface than constantly going back to the data provider and extracting new recordsets.

ADO also contains another service, Data Shaping, that is aimed at the issue of display data that is stored in multiple tables that have a series of hierarchical one-to-many relationships. Data Shaping is designed to provide an alternative to standard SQL relational queries. Keep in mind that Data Shaping does not provide any information that couldn't be obtained using ADO and SQL to execute standard relational queries that generate recordsets. This is true of the cursor service, as well. The point of these additional services is to simplify the programming interface and the supporting code required to carry out these operations.

The Data-Shaping service does contain many elements that are identical to standard SQL. Data Shaping organizes all of the elements needed for a group of recordsets with hierarchical one-to-many relationships in a single Data-Shaping statement that defines a master recordset. The master recordset does not merely contain a key field that can establish links. Rather, the master recordset actually contains entire other recordsets.

Figure 8-11 illustrates the special type of recordset object created by a data-shaping query. When you create a master recordset, in addition to the fields you select from the source table, a special field is created with the APPEND keyword that contains a child recordset. The relationship between the Master and Child is defined by the RELATE keyword.

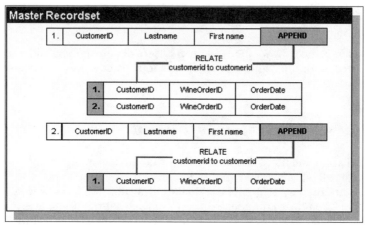

Figure 8-11:
A data-shaped recordset contains multiple objects organized in a hierarchy.

The advantage of creating a data-shaped recordset is that your application needs to manage a single object that contains all of the one-to-many data lists already organized into a hierarchy. If you duplicate the data standard ADO recordsets, you have to write code that individually creates the master and all of its subsequent child records as separate objects.

The data-shaping provider

The Data-Shaping service requires a different provider string than you use with the SQL-oriented ADO services. In fact, Data-Shaping requires two providers:

✔ **Shape service.** The ADO Data-Shaping service is invoked by referencing *MsDataShape* as the provider in the connection string.

✔ **Data provider.** The data provider is the SQL-based data source in which the tables are actually stored.

The example below defines ShapeNetDS as a data-shaping provider that uses the SQL Server ADODUM as the data source.

```
Public Const ShapeNetDS = "Provider=MsDataShape;" & _
    "Data Provider=SQLOLEDB;" & _
    "Data Source=ADODUM;" & _
    "UID=ubad1d1;pwd=21@1n3z"
```

The data-shaping command

The data-shaping provider uses a modified version of the SQL language to generate the master data-shaped recordset. Be aware that the syntax of these commands is complicated. It gets more complicated as you attempt to create more complicated hierarchies with relations expressed in a single statement.

In its simplest form, master and child, it has the following general form:

```
SHAPE
    {<master SQL Statement> }
    APPEND(
    {<child SQL statement> }
    RELATE <master expr> TO <child expr>
    )
```

There are three keywords used in any data-shaping command:

- ✓ **SHAPE:** This clause specifies the SQL statement that defines the contents of the master recordset.

- ✓ **APPEND:** This clause contains the SQL statement that defines the contents of the child recordset.

- ✓ **RELATE:** The RELATE keyword is used to set the relationship between the recordset described with SHAPE to the recordset described with APPEND. Note that you must include in the field list of the SHAPE and the APPEND SQL statements the fields referenced in the RELATE clause.

Suppose that you wanted a data-shaped recordset that lists all of the customers, with orders, who reside in the state of Oregon. This means you need to have two SQL statements that define the master and child recordsets.

```
SELECT CustomerID, LastName, FirstName
FROM Customers WHERE BillState = 'OR'

SELECT WineOrderID, CustomerID, OrderDate, OrderTotal
FROM Orders
```

The first statement forms the argument for the SHAPE clause, while the second is the argument for the APPEND clause. When you put the SQL statements into context in the data-shape command you get the example below.

```
SHAPE
    {SELECT CustomerID, LastName, FirstName
     FROM Customers WHERE BillState = 'OR'}
  APPEND(
        {SELECT WineOrderID, CustomerID,
         OrderDate, OrderTotal
         FROM Orders}
  RELATE CustomerID TO CustomerID
        )
```

Note that I have spread out the statement to clarify where all of the brackets and parentheses should go.

✔ { }: Each of the SQL statements is enclosed in { } brackets.

✔ ( ): The APPEND clause begins and ends with a pair of ( ). The RELATE clause is contained within those parentheses.

The OneToManyExample procedure below shows how to use the data-shaping statement for recordsets and how to display the data contained in those recordsets. To use the data-shaping command in the VB/VBA procedure, it must be entered as a string, which makes the already complex text even harder to enter and read.

```
Sub OneToManyExample()
    Dim cnt As New ADODB.Connection
    Dim Master As New ADODB.Recordset
    Dim Child As ADODB.Recordset
    cnt.Open ShapeNetDS
    Master.Open _
    "SHAPE {SELECT CustomerID, LastName, FirstName " & _
        "FROM Customers WHERE BillState = 'OR'} " & _
        "APPEND( " & _
        "{SELECT WineOrderID,CustomerID,OrderDate,OrderTotal " & _
        "FROM Orders}" & _
        "RELATE CustomerId To CustomerID)", _
        cnt
    Do Until Master.EOF
        Debug.Print Master(0), Master(1), Master(2)
        Set Child = Master("chapter1").Value
        Do Until Child.EOF
            Debug.Print Child(0), Child(1), Child(2), Child(3)
            Child.MoveNext
        Loop
        Master.MoveNext
    Loop
End Sub
```

The key aspects of the procedure involve the way the records are handled. The procedure uses two recordset objects. Master is defined as a new recordset. Child is not. The reason is that the child recordsets are already part of master. The Child recordset object is used to display the contents of the child recordsets already contained in master.

```
Dim Master As New ADODB.Recordset
Dim Child As ADODB.Recordset
```

By default, the data-shaping service assigns the name Chapter1 to the field in the master recordset that contains the child recordset. Thus, the statement below extracts the records in the Chapter1 field of the Master recordset and places then into the Child recordset object. Note that in this case you must specify the Value property of the Master field to have the statement execute properly.

```
Set Child = Master("chapter1").Value
```

When you execute `OneToManyExample`, the procedure dumps a large amount of data into the Immediate window. The example below should be the last set of records displayed.

```
4067        Hobaugh        Ron
796         4067           1/22/1999        28.076
4075        Pellicano      Ken
801         4075           1/22/1999        28.85
2204        4075           2/18/1999        38.65
```

Showing shape results

To experiment with the data shape syntax, it is useful to avoid hard-coding the `shape` statement into the procedure. A better approach, especially considering how complicated a `shape` statement can get, is to enter the `shape` statements in the `Statements` table and simply extract the require command using the `GetStatement ()` function shown earlier in this chapter. Note that you can store `shape` statements in the same way that you store SQL statements in this table.

In addition, it is useful to have a generic procedure that dumps results of a `shape` statement. This generic procedure works with any two-level `shape` statement.

The `ShowOneToManyExample` procedure uses the `Fields` collection to dump the contents of any shape recordset to the Immediate window. The actual text of the data-shape statement is acquired by using the `GetStatement ()` function to get the statement with the name that corresponds to the name furnished as the `Example` variable.

```
Sub ShowOneToManyExample(Example)
    Dim cnt As New ADODB.Connection
    Dim Master As New ADODB.Recordset
    Dim Child As ADODB.Recordset
    Dim F
    cnt.Open ShapeNetDS
    Master.Open GetStatement(Example), cnt
    Do Until Master.EOF
        For F = 0 To Master.Fields.Count - 1
                If Master(F).Type <> adChapter Then
            Debug.Print Master(F);
                End If
        Next
        Debug.Print ""
        Set Child = Master("chapter1").Value
        Do Until Child.EOF
            For F = 0 To Child.Fields.Count - 1
                Debug.Print Child(F);
            Next
            Debug.Print ""
```

```
            Child.MoveNext
        Loop
        Master.MoveNext
    Loop
End Sub
```

The recordsets created with `shape` function like any other recordset with one exception. The chapter field, which is generated by the data-shaping service as a placeholder for the `child` recordset, is assigned the `adChapter` data type (136). This provides a mechanism for handling these special fields differently than ordinary recordset fields. The statement below is used in the `ShowOneToManyExample` to skip the chapter field when the fields in the master recordset are displayed.

```
If Master(F).Type <> adChapter Then
```

You can put the `ShowOneToManyExample` to work by having it execute the `DataShape1` statement. `DataShape1` is identical to the data `shape` statement use earlier. Simply enter this statement below in the Immediate window.

```
ShowOneToManyExample "DataShape1"
```

Using the `ShowOneToManyExample` makes it much simpler to test out the result of data-shaping statements. For example, in the Statements table, the following shaping statement was entered as `DataExample2`. It is identical to the previous example but it selects for verified orders.

```
SHAPE {SELECT CustomerID, LastName, FirstName
    FROM Customers WHERE BillState = 'OR'}
  APPEND({SELECT CustomerID,WineOrderID,OrderDate,
    OrderTotal FROM Orders WHERE paymentverified =1}
  RELATE CustomerId To CustomerID)
```

Once the text has been entered into the Statements table, you can execute it by entering this statement below in the Immediate window.

```
ShowOneToManyExample "DataShape2"
```

You can also control the order of the master recordset using the `ORDER BY` clause.

```
SHAPE {SELECT CustomerID, LastName, FirstName
    FROM Customers WHERE BillState = 'OR'
    ORDER BY Lastname, Firstname}
  APPEND({SELECT CustomerID,WineOrderID,OrderDate,
    OrderTotal FROM Orders}RELATE CustomerId To CustomerID)
```

Execute the above statement by entering the following into the Immediate window.

```
ShowOneToManyExample "DataShape3"
```

Adding summary fields

Another benefit of using data shaping is that it provides an easy way to aggregate totals from the child recordset to the master recordset. For example, suppose that you want to list the number of orders and the total amount of sales for each customer in their customer record.

One way to get this result using only SQL is to `JOIN` customers and orders, group by all of the customer fields, and summarize the `WineOrderId` and `OrderTotal` fields. You then have to issue another query to list the orders.

In the data-shaping language, you can add calculated fields by listing then at the end of the shaping statement. Because the child recordset is assigned the name `Chapter1`, then the summary calculations summarizes the fields using `Chapter1` as the table name. Below is the text of DataShape4, which adds to calculated fields to the master recordset by summarizing fields in the child recordset.

```
SHAPE {SELECT CustomerID, LastName, FirstName
    FROM Customers WHERE BillState = 'OR'
    ORDER BY Lastname, Firstname}
 APPEND( {SELECT CustomerID,WineOrderID,OrderDate,
    OrderTotal FROM Orders}
 RELATE CustomerId To CustomerID),
 Count(chapter1.WineOrderID),
 Sum(chapter1.ordertotal)
```

Execute the above statement by entering the following into the Immediate window.

```
ShowOneToManyExample "DataShape4"
```

The result looks like this fragment. The third and fourth fields in the master recordset are the counts or the orders and sum of order totals.

```
4075 PellicanoKen 2  67.5
4075  801 1/22/1999  28.85
4075  2204 2/18/1999  38.65
```

Forcing server-side processing

The data-shaping service is, by its nature, a significant consumer of data. Depending how wide the scope of the statement, you experience delays while the data is assembled, organized, and returned to the application. In the previous examples, the DataShape service worked by returning the contents of the required recordsets as defined in the SQL statements. The hierarchical recordsets were assembled at the client computer. If you watch the data being written to the Immediate window, there is a long period when nothing happens at all. Then suddenly all of the data is dumped to the window. This is characteristic of the fact that the assembly takes place at the client at a high rate of speed once all of the raw data has been extracted from the data provider.

If you look at the DataShape4 statement in the preceding section, you can see that there is nothing in the child SQL statement that narrows the scope of the child recordset. When this statement is executed, ADO loads the requested fields from the entire Orders table. Once loaded, the orders are matched to the customers in order to produce the result.

In some cases, you may prefer to extract only the child records that are actually required to match the records in the master recordset. In the `DataShape4` example, the goal is to eliminate bringing over to the client any orders that don't match one of the Oregon customers. By doing this, you hope to get improved performance because you have reduced the total amount of information that the provider is sending to the client.

The technique for implementing the mechanism is to write the `shape` statement using a parameter format. The parameter format involves adding a `WHERE` clause to the child SQL statement and altering the field specifications in the `RELATE` clause. The statement below, DataShape5, adds the expression `CustomerID = ?` to the child SQL query. The `CustomerID` reference in the `RELATE` clause is replaced with `PARAMETER 0`.

```
SHAPE {SELECT CustomerID, LastName, FirstName
     FROM Customers WHERE BillState = 'OR'
     ORDER BY Lastname, Firstname}
  APPEND( {SELECT CustomerID,WineOrderID,OrderDate,
     OrderTotal FROM Orders
     WHERE CustomerID = ?}
  RELATE CustomerId To PARAMETER 0)
```

Execute the above statement by entering the following into the Immediate window.

```
ShowOneToManyExample "DataShape5"
```

If you observe the execution of this data-shaping statement, you notice that the first sets of records return much faster than was the case in the previous examples. But you also observe a delay that occurs before each subsequent master/child set is written to the window. The difference in behavior is easy to understand when you realize that using the parameter style syntax causes ADO to issue a separate query to the data provider for the orders that belong to each customer included in the master recordset.

Which is the best approach? This can only be resolved by using both approaches and testing the overall result. Many factors, such as network speed and the relative power of the client and server computers, affect performance. You may find that as with client-side recordsets in general, having the big delay at the beginning is better than lots of little delays throughout the process. There are no hard and fast rules.

Using the FlexGrid with data shaping

One of the purposes of the Hierarchical flex grid is to provide an easy to use way for displaying data generated by a data-shaping statement. Previously, the flex grid has been used to display only standard recordsets. Using the grid control, it is a simple matter to create the form. The DataShape1 form, shown in the background of Figure 8-12, is has a combo box that lists the names of the statements stored in the Statements table, pictured in the foreground of Figure 8-12.

When the user makes a select from the combo box, the name selected is used to execute the correspond statement and the recordset is assigned to the grid. The complete code module for the DataShape1 form is listed below. There are only two ADO objects: a connection and a recordset. The connection to the shape provider is opened when the form is loaded. Each time that a selection is made from the combo box, the corresponding statement is assigned to grid, which then loads and displays the date.

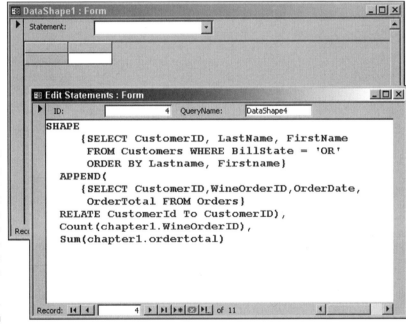

Figure 8-12:
The hierarchical flex grid displays the results of the statements stored in the Statements table.

```
Option Compare Database
Dim cnt As New ADODB.Connection
Dim Rs As New ADODB.Recordset

Private Sub Combo0_AfterUpdate()
    Rs.Open GetStatement(Combo0), cnt
    Set Me.Grid1.DataSource = Rs
    Rs.Close
End Sub

Private Sub Form_Load()
    cnt.Open ShapeNetDS
End Sub
```

Figure 8-13 shows grid displaying the results of the DataShape4 statement. Recall that this statement is the one that calculates the total number of orders and sales total for each customer.

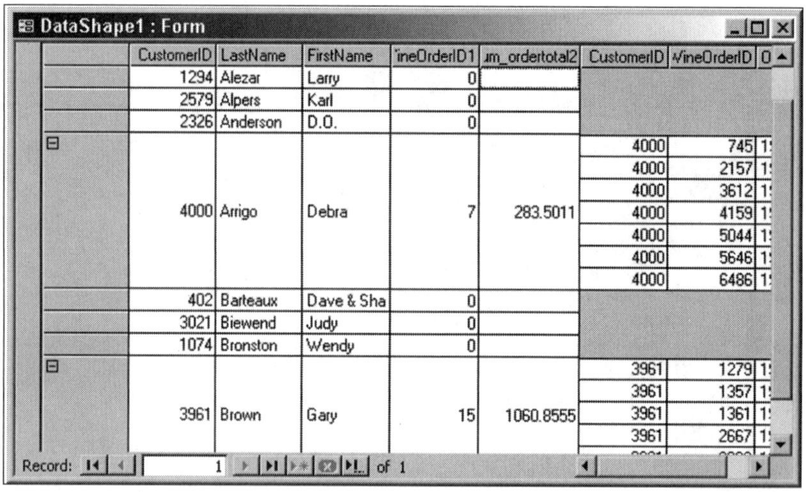

Figure 8-13: The Hierarchical FlexGrid displays the results of the Data Shape4 statement.

Grandchildren

The data-shaping service is not limited to a master/child relationship. You can have as many levels as you need in the data hierarchy. While a full discussion of all of the possible ways to use data shaping is too large to fit into this book, it is useful to at least look at what a data-shaping statement that has three levels (master, child, and grandchild) looks like.

For example, suppose you wanted to show the details of the orders to the data-shape recordset. While it is possible to simply write out the shape statement required to produce these results, even Microsoft admits that shape statements are not easy to read or write. In this case, you can work up to the final statement from the inside out. It is easier to start with the inner relations, such as the lowest level. Then when you have that worked out append that entire shape statement to the Customers list.

First, decide on the SQL query that populates the grandchild level. The SQL statement below creates a list of order details starting with the `OrderLink` field that contains the order number to which the details belong.

```
SELECT OrderLink, WineName, Bottles, Price, ExtPrice
FROM OrderDetails O, WineProductCatalog W
WHERE W.WineID = O.WineID
```

If you place that statement into a `shape` statement that links the order details to each order, you get a statement like the one below, `PartI`. The SQL statement that retrieves the order details is encapsulated as the SQL definition for the recordset appended onto the `Orders` recordset. Note that to make a quick test, the orders in the master recordset are limited to the date 10/8/99. That restriction is removed in the final version.

```
SHAPE {SELECT CustomerID,WineOrderID,OrderDate,
        OrderTotal FROM Orders
        WHERE OrderDate = '1999-10-08'}
    APPEND(
      {SELECT OrderLink, WineName, Bottles, Price, ExtPrice
          FROM OrderDetails, WineProductCatalog
          WHERE OrderDetails.WineID
                =WineProductCatalog.WineID}
    RELATE WineOrderID TO OrderLink)
```

If you select the `PartI` option in the `DataShape` form, the grid displays the orders and their details.

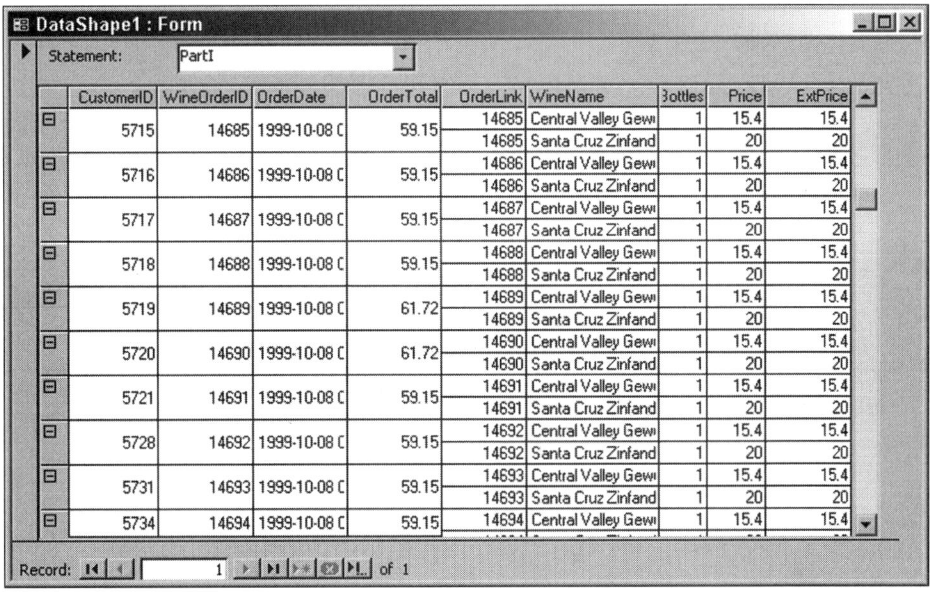

Figure 8-14:
`PartI` uses
a data-
shaping
statement to
link the
orders to
the details.

To arrive at the full statement, the entire `PartI` statement should be inserted as the `APPEND` specification for the original master recordset. This statement is stored as `PartII`.

```
SHAPE {SELECT CustomerID, LastName, FirstName
    FROM Customers}
  APPEND(
      (SHAPE {SELECT CustomerID,WineOrderID,OrderDate,
       OrderTotal FROM Orders}
      APPEND({SELECT OrderLink, WineName,
            Bottles, Price, ExtPrice
            FROM OrderDetails, WineProductCatalog
            WHERE OrderDetails.WineID
            =WineProductCatalog.WineID}
      RELATE WineOrderID TO OrderLink))
    RELATE CustomerId To CustomerID)
```

When you select `PartII`, the results (as shown in Figure 8-15), display the customers, orders, and order details recordsets in a hierarchical structure. Note that you can click the "-@" in the left column of the grid to collapse the expanded levels to change the appearance of the data in the grid.

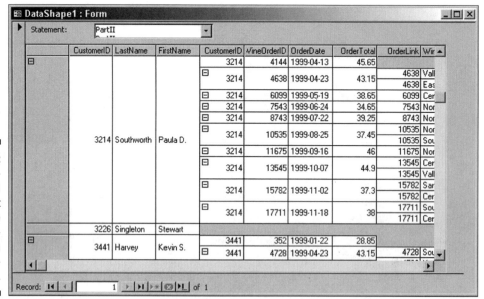

Figure 8-15:
A data-shaped recordset with three levels is displayed in the hierarchical grid.

Part IV

Using ADO to Access Data through the Web

The 5th Wave   By Rich Tennant

Before installing Windows 95, Dwayne prepares to partition the hard drive.

In this part . . .

Unless you have been living in a cave for quite a few years, it won't surprise you that Web-based applications are a critical element in any computer technology. One of the main reasons that Microsoft created ADO was because its previous database technologies were inadequate for use with Web-based and Internet-based applications.

In Part IV, I show you how ADO can be used to add data and database operations to Web documents. We begin with the most generic techniques — ones that apply to all Web users and browsers — and move on to special features that currently run only under Microsoft's Internet Explorer.

Chapter 9

The Internet Information Server and ADO

*A*DO can be used to develop data-enhanced applications using a wide variety of tools. In fact, one of the primary reasons for the creation of ADO was to provide a replacement for older database technologies, such as ODBC and DAO, in the belief that Web and Internet applications are the wave of the future. In this chapter, I turn to the subject of using the Web for accessing database information.

You can execute all of the Active Server Pages described in this chapter, live on the Web, by opening the following document in your browser.

```
http://www.wbase2.com/cgi-bin/ado/chp9exp.asp
```

Click on the name of the example that you want to run, such as simple1.asp, and it is displayed. You can also go directly to the specific ASP that you want to run by entering its name, instead of `chp9exp.asp`, as the following shows:

```
http://www.wbase2.com/cgi-bin/ado/simple1.asp
```

The Web versus the Internet

The growth of the Internet over the past few years has put networking terminology in the mouths of all sorts of people who may or may not be grounded
in these technologies. One of the fuzzy areas is the difference between
Internet technologies and Web technologies.

The term *Internet* refers to a type of networking that uses devices called
routers to move data between client and server computers. Figure 9-1 illustrates how the public Internet network can be used to convey data between
client and server computers. The specific applications that communicate can
be any applications capable of using the Internet network protocol. In Figure
9-1, the client computer is running both a Visual Basic 6.0 application and
Access 2000. The server in this example is running SQL Server 7.0, but it can
just as well be Oracle, Sybase, or an e-mail server. The point that I want to
stress is that the Internet refers to the underlying communication structure
that is used to send information between clients and servers. It does not
mean that you are using any specific client or server applications.

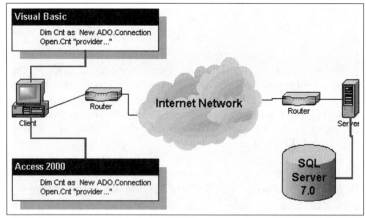

Figure 9-1:
An internet
is a type of
network that
uses routing
to connect
client com-
puters to
servers.

The World Wide Web, on the other hand, refers to a number of very specific
applications that closely define the way that clients and servers communicate. Figure 9-2 shows how a database application typically works on the
Web. The client computer always uses the same generic software application:
that is, the Web browser application. The server is always running a specific
type of software called a *Web server*. When you refer to Web programming,
you are usually referring to the action of accessing the Web service with a
Web browser. An application is a Web application not because it runs on an

Internet network (although that is usually the case), but because it utilizes a specific software service — the World Wide Web service.

Web clients are not limited to just the Web browser. You can write a Web-enabled application in Visual Basic, C++, or Java. However, within the context of this book, I make the assumption that the purpose in building a Web-based application is to provide the application for use with a browser — an application that Web clients already have on their desktops. The alternative is to distribute your own Web-based client application to each user's desktop. This is a possible, but not typical, scenario, and is outside the scope of this book.

Figure 9-2:
When accessing Web services, the client computer typically uses a browser application.

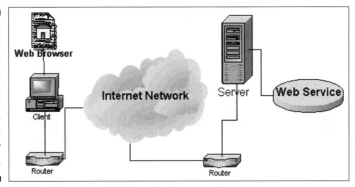

Remember that, despite all of the hype, a Web server is primarily designed to do one simple task. The Web server receives requests for files from Web clients, like a browser application. The Web server then sends the requested documents to the clients. How then can you build database applications using a Web server?

Figure 9-3 shows an approach that uses Web ASP (Active Server page) documents. Unlike a standard Web document that interacts only with the Web server, the ASP contains commands that call into play other services, such as ADO, to connect to data sources. The result is that the document that the user sees is the sum of all the services (Web, database, etc.) that are specified in the ASP.

Web servers can typically support several different types of document-retrieval protocols, such as FTP, Gopher, and HTTP. The term *Web* has become synonymous with the HTTP (Hypertext Transfer Protocol). This protocol allows the user to request a document by entering the document name and location in the form of a URL (Uniform Resource Locator). The following example uses the HTTP protocol to retrieve the EXAMPLE1.HTM document from the server named WWW.WBASE2.COM in the /CGI-BIN/ADO folder.

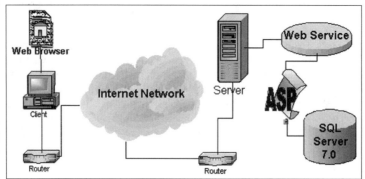

Figure 9-3:
Web appli-
cations are
enhanced
by adding
services to
the Web
server to
supplement
the Web
service.

`http://www.wbase2.com/cgi-bin/ado/example1.htm`

Initially, the content of a document that was retrieved by using the HTTP protocol from a Web server was a *static document*. A static document is like a
word-processing document in that, after it is saved, its content remains
exactly the same until you edit and save it again.

The HTTP protocol does not directly provide a way to access relational database information, which can change from moment to moment, through Web
documents. In order to achieve this means of access, it is necessary to have
some technology at work at the Web server — technology that can dynamically alter the content of the requested document by filling it with the latest
data from the database each time that a user requests that document from
the Web server.

Active Server Pages

Microsoft provides just such a technology in the form of an ASP, or *Active
Server Pages*. An ASP document is a hybrid of static Web content and programming instructions in the form of VBScript (JScript is also support),
which is embedded in the document.

Figure 9-4 shows what happens when an ASP document is retrieved from a
Web server such as Microsoft's IIS (Internet Information Server). Unlike static
Web documents, the requested ASP is not directly returned to the requesting
user. Instead, the Web server examines the content of the document. If one or
more parts of the document contain script instructions, the server extracts
these instructions and passes then to the VBScript engine (installed as a
component on the IIS). The VBScript engine executes the commands in the
script, including any ADO instructions contained in the script.

After all of the script statements have been executed, the Web server inserts any output from the script, such as a recordset retrieved using ADO, into the ASP document in the form of standard text. The Web server now has a newly created Web document that consists of the initial static content plus anything returned by the script. This combined document is then sent back to the requesting user's browser.

Figure 9-4:
Active server pages use VBScript to interact with other services on the server side in order to return an enhanced document to the client.

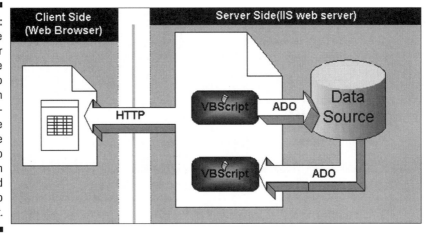

An ASP document is dynamic because the script portions of the document are replaced every time that the document is requested, so that the combined content always reflects the latest data changes in the data source.

Another important concept reflected in Figure 9-4 is that ASP is a server-side technology. This means that the dynamic transformation of the document takes place at the server between the time that the user requests a document and the time that document is returned to the user. This has several important implications:

✔ **Pure HTML.** Regardless of which programming code is used in the ASP, the result of the server-side processing is pure HTML. When the user requests an ASP from a Web server, the server submits the page to the specified scripting engine (in this case, VBScript) before returning the page to the user. The scripting engine translates the programming code into a result set, which consists of HTML text. The requesting user never receives the actual ASP. Instead, the user gets an HTML document that is the combination of the HTML and the script contained in the ASP.

 ✔ **Secure.** Because requesting users never have direct access to the ASP, they can't view any of the coding stored in the original ASP. You don't have to worry about users reading your code and seeing things such as logins and passwords.

 ✔ **Universal.** Because ASPs are server-based and return only HTML, they can be displayed in any browser. Although your ASP may take advantage of NT and IIS features, the requesting users are insulated from these specific products. The users receive only the HTML output from the Web server and server-side programs with which the HTML interacts. Of course, differences exist among different versions of HTML, so it is possible that some of the HTML tags aren't recognized by some versions of some browsers. But that is an HTML issue — not an ASP issue.

HTML and VBScript

Keep in mind that VBScript can be used in a number of different platforms for different purposes. For example, the SQL Server DTS (Data Transformation Service) uses VBScript as part of its extensive data import and export services. I discuss DTS in Part V of this book.

This chapter and the remainder of Part IV deal specifically with the combination of VBScript and HTML that creates ASP applications. When you create an ASP, you have to deal with both of these languages all mixed up together. If you are new to both HTML and VBScript, then things can quickly get pretty confusing. Although a full treatment of both languages can fill two more books, here is quick summary of the two.

HTML

HTML, which stand for *Hypertext Markup Language*, is a text-based coding system designed to display documents in an HTML-compliant application, such as Netscape Communicator or Internet Explorer. The term *text-based* means that you don't need any special applications to create HTML documents. You can use any program that is capable of creating a standard text document to create an HTML document. For example, the Windows Notepad program or the DOS Edit program can be used to create an HTML document as complex as you desire.

Applications that are specifically designed for creating Web sites (such as FrontPage or Visual Interdev) have functions that make it easier to design and update HTML documents, but these applications are not a required for creating HTML documents.

An HTML document consists of two types of items:

> ✔ **Text.** Text is simply the text that appears in the HTML document exactly as it appears when it is displayed in the browser.

> ✔ **Tags.** Tags are pre-defined text items that are added to the text in order to create a formatted document. When the HTML text is loaded into the browser, the tags are treated as formatting instructions.

HTML tags have a common structure. A tag consists of a keyword or character enclosed in angle brackets (< >). Tags typically (but not always) have a beginning and an end. The ending tag includes a backslash (/) before the tag name or letter. The following example shows the use of the B tag (bold text). When displayed in the browsers, the text *Go Away* appears in bold because it falls between the beginning and ending bold tags. The phrase *That means you!* is normal text because it is located after the end of the bold tag.

```
<B>Go Away!</B>That means you!
```

Many tags have additional parameters and settings that are included within the tag. Furthermore, many tags work in relation to other tags so that the overall meaning can't be understood unless you include all of the elements. The following example shows how tables are created in HTML. The TABLE tag sets the beginning of the table and its attributes, such as the width of the borders and the amount of space (padding) between the border and the contents of the table. However, in order to actually display information in the table, two other sets of tags — TR for table rows and TD for table details (cells) — are used inside the TABLE tags. When displayed in a browser, the HTML in the following example shows a 2-row x 2-column table.

```
<TABLE border=2 cellpadding=3>
<TR><TD>1.</TD><TD>Smith, John</TD></TR>
<TR><TD>2.</TD><TD>Jones, Walter</TD></TR>
</TABLE>
```

The relationship between the HTML and the document displayed in the browsers is determined by the logic of the HTML tags — not their layout. This means that elements such as line breaks, paragraph ends, or spaces between items that are entered into the HTML document may look different in the browser. For example, the following HTML appears to be two lines of text.

```
<B>Welcome to Rob Krumm Publications
ADO Reader's Web Site</B>
```

However, the browser displays this as a single line, as shown in the following example, because logically no tag is present to indicate a line break. Without explicit instructions, the browser has no reason to put the text on two separate lines.

```
Welcome to Rob Krumm Publications ADO Reader's Web Site
```

Spacing is created with tags like P for *paragraph* or BR for *line break*. In addition, HTML recognizes character entities that are text codes for white space or special characters. These codes begin with an ampersand (&) and end with a semicolon. The following example shows you how to code two names joined by an ampersand in an HTML document.

```
Rob &amp; Carolyn ===> Rob & Carolyn
```

VBScript

VBScript is a subset of the VB/VBA language. The purpose of VBScript is to add programming logic to applications such as ASPs, which create documents on either the server-side or the client-side of a network operation. In an ASP, VBScript co-exists with HTML in two ways:

✔ **Script blocks:** Script blocks use special tags to identify the scripting language and to specify the script code. This type of scripting is used primarily for client-side scripting. Client-side scripting is not a universal approach because it relies on features supported by the client's browser, such as DHTML. I cover client-side scripting in Chapters 12 and 13.

```
<SCRIPT LANGUAGE='vbscript'>
<!-- document.write Date () --->
</SCRIPT>
```

✔ **Server Scripts:** Server scripts are not dependent on browser features. Instead, the server scripts are executed by the IIS server before the document is returned to the user. Server scripts can be inserted into any part of an HTML document using the <% %> tags. The following example shows the value of the VBScript function Date( ) being inserted into flow of the HTML document.

```
<B>Today is <% =date() %></B>
```

Note that IIS assumes that server-side scripts are written in VBScript; therefore, no special mention of VBScript is required in an ASP. If you prefer JScript, you can specify that as the scripting language by using the LANGUAGE keyword.

```
<%@ LANGUAGE="jscript"%>
```

Basic server-side scripting

A *server-side script* is any code that you insert into an ASP that the IIS server can execute. The simplest way to get started with server-side scripts is to explore the built-in capabilities of the VBScript language and the IIS server.

One of the easiest, but most useful abilities that VBScript provides is the ability to use scripting logic to insert information into the HTML stream, which is then returned to the user when requesting an ASP. This is accomplished by using the `Write` method of the IIS server's Response object:

- ✔ **The Response object:** The Response object refers to the information that the IIS server returns to the client's browser when a page is requested. In a static HTML document, the Response object consists purely of HTML text as it was stored on the server. In an ASP document, VBScript operations can add to or alter the HTML stream before it is returned to the requesting user.

- ✔ **The Write method:** The `Write` method of the Response object provides a scripting mechanism for inserting data into the HTML that is being sent back to the user. The `Write` method inserts text into the HTML stream at the exact location in the document where the `Response.Write` script statement appears in the original ASP.

For example, VBScript contains `Date( )` and `Now( )` functions (like VB/VBA) that return the current date or date/time from the system on which it is executing. The following VBScript statement displays the value of the `Now( )` function on the current page.

```
Response.Write Now()
```

In addition to any script, an ASP file must include two tags in the ASP:

- ✔ `<HTML></HTML>`: These tags define the section of the document that contains HTML.

- ✔ `<BODY></BODY>`: These tags define the section of the HTML area that appears in the main window of the browser.

These three elements, the script and the two tags, can be combined in the following code to create a simple but dynamic ASP. This text is stored in the file Simple1.Asp. Note that the ASP file extension is required by the IIS Web server. When a requested file has an ASP extension, the IIS server sends it to the scripting engine for processing.

```
<HTML><BODY>
It is now <% Response.Write Now() %>
</BODY></HTML>
```

If you want to write text that is not part of a procedure, you can replace the `Response.Write` object with an equal sign (=). The following example shows the file Simple2.Asp. It produces the same result as Simple1.Asp using the equal sign as an abbreviation for the `Response. Write` object.

```
<HTML><BODY>
<P>It is now <% =Now() %></P>
</BODY></HTML>
```

The Request object

The complement to the Response object is the *Request object*. The Request object of the IIS Web server contains information about the server and its current state. The Request object keeps track of the requests that users make for documents stored on the Web server. In this capacity, the Request object plays a critical role in building Web applications because it is the repository for any user inputs, such as any data entered into a Web form. Most Web applications involve manipulating the Response and the Request objects. To create an interactive Web application, you write code that takes user input stored in the Request object. In turn, this input modifies the Response object, which is what is returned to the user.

For now, the subject is information about the Web server that the Request object is always maintained in the form of server variables. For example, the server variable SERVER_SOFTWARE contains the name and version of the software running on the Web server. The following expression extracts the server software information:

```
Request.ServerVariables("SERVER_SOFTWARE")
```

The following shows the file ServerVar1.ASP. The purpose of this Web document is to retrieve the name and version of the Web server software. Note that the single line of VBScript code involves both the Response and Request objects. The statement submits a request to the server for information about the running software by using the Request object. This is added to the HTML page that is being returned to the user by applying the Write method in the Response object.

```
<HTML><BODY>
IIS Server Software version:
<%
Response.Write Request.ServerVariables("SERVER_SOFTWARE")
%>
</BODY></HTML>
```

When you open the ServerVar1.ASP document, you see the text shown in the following example. In this case, the server is running Version 3.0 of IIS.

IIS Server Software version: Microsoft-IIS/3.0

Recall from the previous examples that the script block contains only Response.Write operations You can use the equal sign (=) in place of the full object name. The code below, contained in ServerVar2.Asp, produces the information as ServerVar1.ASP.

```
<HTML><BODY>
IIS Server Software version:
<% =Request.ServerVariables("SERVER_SOFTWARE")%>
</BODY></HTML>
```

Of course, Version 3.0 is not the latest version of IIS. If you open ServerVar3.ASP, you get the following response:

```
IIS Server Software version: Microsoft-IIS/5.0
```

Why is this different? The answer is that ServerVar3.ASP is located on a different Web server than ServerVar1.ASP. ServerVar3.ASP is actually located in my office and is running Windows 2000, which is supplied with IIS 5.0. ServerVar1.ASP is running at my ISP, where evidently the server is running NT 4.0 with an older version of IIS.

Connecting to a Data Source

The next step in building ASPs is to use the Web server to connect to a data source. You are justified in thinking that getting access to data sources through the Web requires special Web-oriented techniques that don't apply to other types of programming environments. This was exactly the case before ADO. One of the reasons for the creation of ADO was to put into place a data access programming approach that uses the same objects, methods, and properties — regardless of the environment. This approach holds true with environments as different as VB and ASP. The following example shows a VB/VBA statement that initializes an ADO connection object in VB/VBA.

```
Dim Cnt as New ADODB.Connection
```

In an ASP, the same statement is used, but with a small yet important change in syntax. The change is due to the fact that when you work with a Web server, you add a middle layer of software to the application structure. In Chapters, I tell you how the VB/VBA code connects directly to the ADO library. In a Web application, the browser connects to the Web server and the server, in turn, must establish any required connections to additional services (like ADO) as part of its response to the user's request for a document.

The IIS Server object supports the `CreateObject` method that provides a channel by which VBScript contained in a Web document can access services available to the Web server. In this case, the Web server needs to use ADO to create a connection object. The following statement is the VBScript syntax used in an ASP to create an ADO connection object.

```
Set Cnt = Server.CreateObject("ADODB.Connection")
```

Keep in mind that in order to use ADO to construct the Response object, the Web server must have ADO installed. This is an important distinction between Web applications and VB/VBA applications. The VB/VBA examples shown in Chapters require that the computer running the application (the client desktop) have ADO installed. When you use ADO in a Web application, the client computers (the ones using the browsers) do not need ADO installed. Only the Web server needs ADO because the Web server needs to include the ADO data in the Response object. The client computer receives only the final HTML output of the Response object. This is one of the great advantages of using a Web application. In order to upgrade your application, you only need to upgrade the server, so all of the users coming through the Web see the update application.

The really handy part is that after you use the correct syntax to create the object, the VBScript statements are identical to those you use in VB/VBA when writing an ADO application. The ASP shown in the following example, Connect1.Asp, uses a standard OLE DB connection string to specify the data provider. After they are connected, the name of the default database is inserted into the Response object.

```
<HTML><BODY>
<%
Set Cnt = Server.CreateObject("ADODB.Connection")
Cnt.Open "Provider=SQLOLEDB;Data Source=208.222.107.6;" & _
"UID=ubad1d1;pwd=21@1n3z"
Response.Write "Data Source Database: " & _
Cnt.DefaultDatabase
%>
</BODY></HTML>
```

When you open Connect1.Asp, you see the response shown in the following example. The name of the database is dynamically acquired by the ADO code in the ASP.

```
Data Source Database: DBAD1D
```

I want to emphasize that the provider string used in the ASP refers to resources available to the Web server, and not necessarily available to the Web client. Figure 9-5 illustrates how the Web server functions as a *middle-ware application* that indirectly connects the client to a data source. When you create an ASP, the code in the ASP can access any resource that the Web server can access, even if that resource is not exposed to the Internet. In Figure 9-5, the database server at address www.xxx.yyy.zzz can't be directly accessed through the Internet. The Web server interacts with the database server and then includes the results in the Response object that is sent back to the user. The middleware role of the Web server allows the client to access information from the data source without having to expose the data source provider on the Internet.

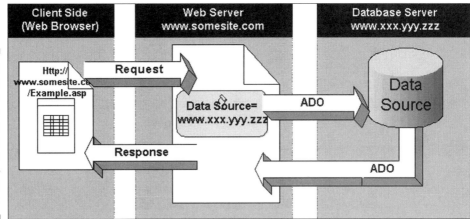

Figure 9-5:
Connections inside an ASP refer to resources available to the Web server — not the Web client.

Checking the source response

While you have the Connect1.Asp document displayed in the browser, use the View⇨Source command to display the source HTML code for the displayed page. When you open that window, you see the HTML shown in the following example:

```
<HTML><BODY>
Data Source Database: DBAD1D
</BODY></HTML>
```

Notice that the portion of the VBScript that includes the provider string information appears in the source text. This is because the Web server does not return the ASP to the user. Rather, the Web server returns the `Response` object based on the specified ASP. Your ASP code is protected from the Web server. This means that you don't need to be concerned about users seeing passwords, logins, or other sensitive elements in your ASP code.

Using provider names and DSNs

You are not required to use the IP address of the data source provider. You are free to use either a network name or an ODBC DSN for a provider, assuming that these are available to the Web server. (See Chapter 2 for a full discussion of provider connection strings — DSN and ODBC.)

The following example, Connect2.Asp, connects to an NT server called PACK-BELL. The name is available on my LAN but not on the Internet. However, you can still access the data source indirectly by loading the ASP and having the ASP talk to the NT sever on the local LAN.

```
<HTML><BODY>
<%Set Cnt = Server.CreateObject("ADODB.Connection")
Cnt.Open "Provider=SQLOLEDB;Data Source=PACKBELL;" & _
"UID=adoreader;pwd="
Response.Write "Data Source Database: " & _
Cnt.DefaultDatabase%>
</BODY></HTML>
```

When you open Connect2.Asp, you get the following result, which shows the default database for the AdoReader login.

```
Data Source Database: dummies
```

Displaying recordset data

After you have established a connection to a data source, you can write ADO code in your ASP to access recordset. The ASP syntax for creating a record-set object is shown in the following example, using the CreateObject method.

```
Set RS = Server.CreateObject("ADODB.Recordset")
```

Rs1.Asp, shown in the following example, uses the Cnt connection object to open a recordset that summarizes the number of records in the Customers table. What is remarkable about the code is just how unremarkable it is; in other words, the objects, properties, and methods used are exactly the same when writing ADO code in VB/VBA. The only differences between the two occur when you want to insert ADO data into the Response object. In those cases, the ADO object references are intermingled with HTML. However, within each block of script (between the <% %> tags), the code can be copied and pasted from a VB/VBA application.

```
<HTML><BODY>
<%
Set Cnt = Server.CreateObject("ADODB.Connection")
Cnt.Open "Provider=SQLOLEDB;Data Source=208.222.107.6;" & _
"UID=ubad1d1;pwd=21@1n3z"
Set RS = Server.CreateObject("ADODB.Recordset")
RS.ActiveConnection = Cnt
Rs.Open "SELECT Count(*) As CustCount FROM Customers"
%>
<H1>Database: <%=Cnt.DefaultDatabase%></H1>
<H2><% =Rs.Fields(0).Name %>: 
<%=rs(0)%></H2>
</BODY></HTML>
```

Rs1.Asp returns the data shown below.

```
Database: DBAD1D
CustCount:  4143
```

Connecting to an Access MDB

Although client/server databases like SQL Server and Oracle are typically the data sources used by large companies for their Web applications, you can also use Access MDB files as the source for ASPs. And, although Access is not nearly as powerful as these client/server applications, you may be pleasantly surprised at how much you can do with an MDB file — especially when you use ADO to connect to the file.

I have noticed that many of the documents from Microsoft that discuss the use of Access and ASPs show the use of an ODBC DSN (Data Source Name) as the means by which you can connect to an Access MDB database. This approach has two drawbacks:

- **DSN Setup**. ODBC DSNs require you to have access to the Web server in order to run the ODBC manager, so you can set up the DSN connection to your Access MDB file.

- **Performance.** ODBC typically performs database operations much more slowly than ADO. If you are building a Web application and you don't have access to a client/server database, then you must make sure that your application is running as fast as possible.

You can use ADO to connect to an Access MDB file as a data source by using the Jet engine as the ADO provider. If the Web server is available on your LAN, you can check for which version of ADO is installed, or you can run the latest MDAC update (available at www.microsoft.com/data/download_250rtm.htm). If you are using space on an IPS's Web server, you have to try either the Jet 3.5 or 4.0 providers to see which one works.

To see an example of the Access 2000 MDB file WineOnWeb.MDB, go to the ADO folder on the www.wbase2.com Web site. It is possible to use ADO to connect to this file as a Web-based data source.

The key problem that you have to deal with is the difference between the directory structure of the Web server and the directory structure of the NT Server. The directory system used by the NT Sever is the familiar DOS/Windows system of drive letters and folders based on the actual, physical drives and partitions. However, when you expose network resources through a Web server, you have the ability to present the resources in any way you like. Figure 9-6 shows how the directory of a Web server hides the actual physical organization of the network. On the NT server, the ADO Exp folder on the Web site is actually located in the folder d:\ADO Exp, even though it appears to the Web user to be one level below the site's home directory.

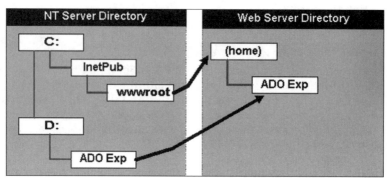

Figure 9-6:
The Web
server
presents the
Web user
with a differ-
ent view of
the physical
resources
available on
the network.

When you use ADO to access a database service, the physical location of the data source is not an issue. All you need to do is specify the IP or the name of the server, and the network locates the resource. However, when the provider is a file-based data source, the physical location of the file becomes an issue.

As it turns out, ADO requires the location of the database file to be specified in terms of its NT directory location — not its location in the Web server directory. Fortunately, you can acquire the required path information from the Web server by using the `MapPath` method of the Server object. In order to use `MapPath`, you enter the name of the Web folder that you need to have translated into a physical location. The following example is ServerVar4.Asp, which displays the physical path for the `/ADO` folder.

```
<HTML><BODY>
<P>MapPath: <% =Server.MapPath("/ADO") %></P>
</BODY></HTML>
```

When you open ServerVar4.Asp, the document returns the path. Note that in this case, the folder is located on drive D on the server. This is the information that ADO requires in order to locate and access the MDB file as a data provider.

```
MapPath: d:\209.237.129.67\ADO
```

You can put the `MapPath` method to work by using it to provide the full path name of the data source in the ADO connection string. The following expression evaluates to the physical path needed by ADO in order for ADO to locate the `WineOnWeb.MDB` file.

```
"Data Source=" & server.MapPath("/ADO/wineonweb.mdb")
```

The following ASP, rsMDB.Asp, uses the `MapPath` method to open the access database file and to create a recordset based on the contents. Note that the procedure is identical to RS1.Asp, which accessed an SQL Server data source, with the exception of the connection string.

```
<HTML><BODY>
<%
Set Cnt = Server.CreateObject("ADODB.Connection")
Cnt.Open "Provider=Microsoft.Jet.OLEDB.4.0;" &_
"Data Source=" & server.MapPath("/ADO/wineonweb.mdb")
Set RS = Server.CreateObject("ADODB.Recordset")
RS.ActiveConnection = Cnt
Rs.Open "SELECT Count(*) As CustCount FROM Customers"
%>
<H2><% =Rs.Fields(0).Name %>: <%=rs(0)%></H2>
</BODY></HTML>
```

If you open Rs1.Asp and RsMDB.Asp, you notice a slight but detectable delay when RsMDB.Asp executes. This is due to the fact that an MDB file data source can't respond as quickly as a client/server data source responds. On the other hand, you can run the Access MDB from any Web site hosted on an NT Server with the latest service packs installed.

Handling recordsets

The first examples of data retrieval in Web documents returned only a single value. However, it is more common for recordsets to consist of multiple records and fields. You can see how to handle these in an ASP by checking out the following SQL query, which is stored on the database server as the view, `v_CustOrderList`. This query lists some key information about the orders for each customer.

```
SELECT Customers.CustomerID, LastName, FirstName,
OrderDate, WineOrderID, Bottles, OrderTotal,
Verified = CASE Orders.PaymentVerified
WHEN 1
THEN 'Yes'
ELSE 'No'
END
FROM Orders INNER JOIN
Customers ON Orders.CustomerID = Customers.CustomerID
```

The `v_CustOrderList` takes advantage of the SQL Server's CASE structure to convert a Boolean value, `PaymentVerified`, into either Yes or No text. This is the SQL Server equivalent of the `IIF( )` function in Access. Note that the CASE structure ends with the `END` keyword.

For example, you can pick a customer ID number at random, such as 4110, with the goal of displaying the orders for that customer in a Web page by creating an ADO recordset based on the following statement:

```
SELECT * FROM v_CustOrderList WHERE Customerid = 4110
```

You can create the recordset by using the following block of VBScript. Note that in this case, because the ASP requires only a single recordset, you can use ADO to create the recordset without creating a separate connection object. This is consistent with the behavior of ADO in VB/VBA.

```
<%Set RS = Server.CreateObject("ADODB.Recordset")
Rs.Open
"SELECT * FROM v_CustOrderList WHERE Customerid = 4110"
,"Provider=SQLOLEDB;Data Source=208.222.107.6;" & _
"UID=ubad1d1;pwd=21@1n3z"%>
```

HTML does not have a single display mechanism that can display a recordset in a row and column format. If you want a table style layout, you must include all of the HTML tags needed to create a table in your ASP and then arrange the items in a table, like the one shown in the following example:

```
<TABLE>
<%Do Until RS.EOF%>
<TR>
<%For F = 0 To Rs.Fields.Count -1%>
<TD><%=RS(F)%></TD>
<%Next%>
</TR>
<%Rs.MoveNext%>
<%Loop%>
</TABLE>
```

The arrangement of the two loops is typical of the code that you use to display a recordset. The `<TR>` tag starts a new row. Then the `Fields` collection is used to display each field in a cell on that row by enclosing the field in `<TD>` and `</TD>` tags. When the `MoveNext` method of the recordset is applied, a `</TR>` tag is required to end the current table row. Rs2.Asp uses the preceding code to display the data below the browsers.

```
4110   Tugel   Tammy   1/22/99   823    2   28.076   Yes
4110   Tugel   Tammy   2/18/99   2223   2   38.62    Yes
```

Column headings

The simplest way to add column headings to your table is to use the names of the fields. You can use a For . . . Next loop to print out the names of the fields in the first row of the table as shown in the following example. Note that this loop should be inserted after the `<TABLE>` tag but before the first record is added to the table. In this example, some additional HTML formatting tags have been added to the heading row. The text is formatted as bold, and the cell background color is set to light-gray.

```
<TABLE>
<%For F = 0 To Rs.Fields.Count -1%>
<TD bgcolor=LightGrey><B><%=RS(F).Name%></B></TD>
<%Next%>
<%Do Until RS.EOF%>
   ...
</TABLE>
```

Open Rs3.Asp to see the results pictured in Figure 9-7.

Figure 9-7:
Field names
appear as
column
headings in
Rs3.Asp.

CustomerID	LastName	FirstName	OrderDate	WineOrderID	Bottles	OrderTotal	Verified
4110	Tugel	Tammy	1/22/99	823	2	28.076	Yes
4110	Tugel	Tammy	2/18/99	2223	2	38.62	Yes

Embedding HTML

The Rs2.Asp and Rs3.Asp examples generate the data-enhanced HTML display by inserting VBScript code mixed in with HTML coding. An alternative approach is to write all of the code necessary to generate the table as VBScript by using the Response.Write method to insert both the ADO data and any HTML coding into the Web server's Response object using a single block of VBScript code.

The code below, used in Rs4.Asp, eliminates the need to have multiple script tags inserted through the code. Instead, the entire table is generated with a single script block. Any HTML code required is inserted into the Response object by using the Response.Write method as literal text, which is included with ADO recordset field information.

```
<%
Set RS = Server.CreateObject("ADODB.Recordset")
Rs.Open "SELECT * FROM v_CustOrderList WHERE Customerid = 4110",_
"Provider=SQLOLEDB;Data Source=208.222.107.6;" & _
"UID=ubad1d1;pwd=21@1n3z"
Response.Write "<TABLE>"
For F = 0 To Rs.Fields.Count -1
Response.Write "<TD bgcolor=LightGrey><B>" & _
RS(F).Name & "</B></TD>"
Next
Do Until RS.EOF
Response.Write "<TR>"
For F = 0 To Rs.Fields.Count -1
Response.Write "<TD>" & RS(F) & "</TD>"
Next
```

```
Response.Write "</TR>"
Rs.MoveNext
Loop
Response.Write "</TABLE>"
%>
```

The result of Rs4.Asp is identical to Rs3.Asp. The only difference is the style of coding. Both approaches have advantages and disadvantages. Using `Response.Write` reduces the number of separate script tags that you have to insert into the page. On the other hand, each HTML element must be inserted as a text literal, enclosed in quotation marks. Of course, you are not required to use either approach consistently. You may find that some sections of an ASP are simpler with a single script block while other sections are more easily written by inserting smaller script fragments within the HTML.

Request collections

Of course, the current examples don't have much practical application the way they are coded because they always return the same recordset. The ASP is much more valuable if you can specify which customer's orders should be displayed each time the page is displayed.

Normally, the Request object of the Web server consists of the document that the user wants to load. The request is made by entering a URL in the browser Address box.

HTML provides two ways in which additional data can be sent to the IIS Request object:

  ✔ **Querystring:** HTML allows you to add one or more values to the URL that you are using in order to request a page. The values are attached to the end of the URL using a question mark (?). The Web server stores the value or values added to the URL in the `queryString` collection of the Request object.

  ✔ **Forms:** HTML allows you to create entry forms. When you fill out a form and click the Submit button, the data in the form is sent to the Web server and is stored in the Request objects `Form` collection.

This chapter looks at the ways in which querystrings can be used to place values in the Request object and how those values can be used to retrieve data. Forms are discussed in Chapter 10.

Querystrings are useful when you only need to store a few simple values in the Request object. You can easily extract the values from the `queryString` collection. On the other hand, because the values must be appended onto the end of the URL, it can be awkward to fill out a complex querystring that has several different values. Querystrings can be integrated into hyperlinks so that when a user clicks on a link, they can send values as well as request-specific pages.

Forms allow the user to enter data directly onto the displayed page. A user can easily enter data into the text boxes displayed on a form. Forms can also allow users to make selections from list boxes or choose among several radio buttons. However, forms are significantly more complicated to design and program.

Passing values with querystrings

Querystrings are created as part of the URL address that is used to request a document from a Web server. Querystrings are created by placing a question mark (?) at the end of the URL and following it with one or more expressions in the form <name>=<Value>. If you want to create more than one querystring value, you can add on additional expressions using an ampersand (&) before each one.

```
Http://address?<Name>=<Value>&<Name>=<value>...
```

The following URL tells the Web server named `www.wbase2.com` to load the document `cgi-bin/ado/qs1.asp` and store the value 4110 as qs in the Request object's `queryString` collection.

```
http://www.wbase2.com/cgi-bin/ado/qs1.asp?qs=4110
```

Adding a querystring has no direct effect on the document retrieved from the Web server, unless the document contains instructions that retrieve the value from the `queryString` collection and use that value to alter the content of the Response object before the page is returned to the user.

You can retrieve the querystring data from the Request object by using a VBScript statement like the one in the following example. In this example, the value stored in the `queryString` — qs — is inserted into the response being returned to the user.

Response.Write Request.Querystring ("QS")

The ASP Qs1.Asp contains the code shown in the following example. This code simply displays in the response the value, if any, specified in the URL that requested the page.

```
<HTML><BODY>
QueryString: <% =Request.QueryString("QS")%>
</BODY></HTML>
```

To test this code, enter the following URL in your browser.

```
http://www.wbase2.com/cgi-bin/ado/qs1.asp?qs=4110
```

The result, shown in the following example, indicates that the Response document can reflect the value sent to the Web server as part of the URL:

```
QueryString: 4110
```

Using the querystring with a SQL query

You can use the value in the querystring as part of any of the VBScript coding in the ASP. For example, you can alter the VBScript used in Rs4.Asp to insert a querystring value as the CustomerID in the SQL statement (as shown in the following example), which is contained in Rs5.Asp.

```
Rs.Open
"SELECT * FROM v_CustOrderList WHERE Customerid = " _
& Request.QueryString("CID")
```

This one change makes it possible to use Rs5.Asp to display the order history of any customer. The following URL displays the orders for customer 4110.

```
http://www.wbase2.com/cgi-bin/ado/rs5.asp?cid=4110
```

The contents returned by Rs5.Asp vary dynamically based on the value assigned to the CID querystring. The result, pictured in Figure 9-8, shows the order history of customer 3756.

```
http://www.wbase2.com/cgi-bin/ado/rs5.asp?cid=3756
```

Figure 9-8:
The contents of the page are determined by the value of the querystring.

CustomerID	LastName	FirstName	OrderDate	WineOrderID	Bottles	OrderTotal	Verified
3756	Boaz	Barbara	1/22/99	584	2	28.076	Yes
3756	Boaz	Barbara	2/18/99	2015	2	38.62	Yes
3756	Boaz	Barbara	3/25/99	3482	1	46.1625	Yes
3756	Boaz	Barbara	4/13/99	4132	2	83.635	Yes
3756	Boaz	Barbara	4/23/99	4921	2	43.4688	Yes

Multiple querystring values

You are not restricted to passing a single value by using the querystring format. You can pass multiple values in two ways.

✔ **Multiple Querystrings:** You can create multiple querystrings, each with its own unique name by appending additional querystring specifications to the URL.

```
http://test.asp?first=Walter&Last=Lafish
```

Each of the querystrings can be retrieved from the Request object using the names of the individual querystrings.

```
Request.Querystring("Last")
Request.Querystring("First")
```

✔ **Multiple Values:** You can assign a series of values to the same. In the following example, three customer ID values are assigned to the same querystring, qs.

```
http://www.wbase2.com/cgi-bin/ado/qs2.asp?qs=4110&qs=3756&qs=3063
```

You can retrieve the individual values by using the Index property of the querystring item. The following example retrieves the first value assigned to the qs querystring.

```
Request.QueryString("QS").Item(1)
```

The document Qs2.Asp shows how a loop can be used to extract all of the values assigned to a querystring. The following code shows two methods. The first method uses a For . . . Next loop to numerically increment through the items in the qs querystring. The second method uses a For . . . Each loop to accomplish the same thing, but using a slightly simpler syntax.

```
<HTML><BODY>
<% For Q = 1 To Request.QueryString("QS").Count %>
Query Item: <% =Request.QueryString("QS").Item(Q)%><BR>
<% Next %>
<HR>
<%
For Each I In Request.QueryString("qs")
Response.Write "Query Item: " & I & "<BR>"
Next
%>
</BODY></HTML>
```

You can pass multiple values to the Qs2.Asp document by using a URL like the following one:

```
http://www.wbase2.com/cgi-bin/ado/qs2.asp?qs=4110&qs=3756&qs=3063
```

When you execute Qs2.Asp with multiple querystring values, the result looks like the following text in which each value is displayed individually.

```
Query Item: 4110
Query Item: 3756
Query Item: 3063
Query Item: 4110
Query Item: 3756
Query Item: 3063
```

This principle can be applied to the display of the orders related to each customer ID. The following example shows the code for Rs6.Asp. This code is identical to Rs5.Asp with the addition of a loop that repeats the output of customer orders for each customer ID in the querystring collection. The additional code is shown in bold.

```
<% For Q = 1 To Request.QueryString("CID").Count %>
<%
Set RS = Server.CreateObject("ADODB.Recordset")
Rs.Open "SELECT * FROM v_CustOrderList WHERE Customerid=" _
& Request.QueryString("CID").Item(Q) , _
"Provider=SQLOLEDB;Data Source=208.222.107.6;" & _
"UID=ubad1d1;pwd=21@1n3z"
Response.Write "<TABLE>"
For F = 0 To Rs.Fields.Count -1
Response.Write "<TD bgcolor=LightGrey><B>" & _
RS(F).Name & "</B></TD>"
Next
Do Until RS.EOF
Response.Write "<TR>"
For F = 0 To Rs.Fields.Count -1
Response.Write "<TD>" & RS(F) & "</TD>"
Next
Response.Write "</TR>"
Rs.MoveNext
Loop
Response.Write "</TABLE>"
%>
<HR>
<% next %>
```

You can display the order history of as many customers as you want by entering a URL, like the following one, that lists multiple values for the CID querystring.

```
http://www.wbase2.com/cgi-bin/ado/rs6.asp?cid=4110&cid=3756&cid=3063
```

The result, shown in Figure 9-9, is a Web page that displays the orders for three different customers on one page.

Using hyperlinks with querystrings

Querystrings are widely used on the Web to pass values from one Web page to another. But the querystrings are not usually entered manually on the address line. More often, the querystrings are automatically generated when a user clicks on a hyperlink that is embedded in a Web page.

CustomerID	LastName	FirstName	OrderDate	WineOrderID	Bottles	OrderTotal	Verified
4110	Tugel	Tammy	1/22/99	823	2	28.076	Yes
4110	Tugel	Tammy	2/18/99	2223	2	38.62	Yes

CustomerID	LastName	FirstName	OrderDate	WineOrderID	Bottles	OrderTotal	Verified
3756	Boaz	Barbara	1/22/99	584	2	28.076	Yes
3756	Boaz	Barbara	2/18/99	2015	2	38.62	Yes
3756	Boaz	Barbara	3/25/99	3482	1	46.1625	Yes
3756	Boaz	Barbara	4/13/99	4132	2	83.635	Yes
3756	Boaz	Barbara	4/23/99	4921	2	43.4688	Yes

CustomerID	LastName	FirstName	OrderDate	WineOrderID	Bottles	OrderTotal	Verified
3063	Burgarino	James & Karen	1/22/99	178	2	28.076	Yes
3063	Burgarino	James & Karen	2/18/99	1645	2	38.62	Yes
3063	Burgarino	James & Karen	3/25/99	3133	1	46.1625	Yes
3063	Burgarino	James & Karen	4/23/99	4579	2	43.4688	Yes
3063	Burgarino	James & Karen	5/19/99	6040	2	38.62	Yes
3063	Burgarino	James & Karen	6/24/99	7486	2	34.31	Yes
3063	Burgarino	James & Karen	7/22/99	8684	2	39.2665	Yes
3063	Burgarino	James & Karen	8/25/99	10470	2	37.327	Yes
3063	Burgarino	James & Karen	9/16/99	11629	2	46.578	Yes
3063	Burgarino	James & Karen	10/7/99	13501	3	45.3928	Yes
3063	Burgarino	James & Karen	11/2/99	15739	3	37.8658	Yes
3063	Burgarino	James & Karen	11/18/99	17668	3	38.62	Yes

Figure 9-9:
Output from multiple querystring values.

Hyperlinks are created with the HTML anchor tag, <A>, using the general form shown in the following example. The beginning <A> tag contains the Href parameter. This parameter specifies the URL that is requested when the user clicks the link text. Note that the link text becomes whatever text that appears between the <A> and the </A> tags. The user only sees the link text. The document specified in the href parameters does not appear on screen, although it appears on the status line of most browsers.

```
<A href="filename">hyperlinktext</A>
```

The hyperlink HTML code shown in the following example, QSLink1.Asp, opens the Rs5.Asp document with a specific querystring value. The result is that you see the order history of a different customer depending upon which of the hyperlinks that you select.

```
<HTML><BODY>
 <A href="rs5.asp?CID=4110">Cust #4110</A><BR>
 <A href="rs5.asp?CID=3687">Cust #3687</A><BR>
 <A href="rs5.asp?CID=3941">Cust #3941</A><BR>
 <A href="rs5.asp?CID=3044">Cust #3044</A><BR>
 </BODY></HTML>
```

Dynamically building hyperlinks

QSLink1.Asp shows how hyperlinks allow a Web document to function as a menu of items. However, writing out the HTML codes for all of the links that you need for the customers in a single statement is a tedious and costly exercise. The solution is to use ADO and VBScript to generate the hyperlinks dynamically. If you look at the hyperlinks used in the previous example, the code falls into a pattern. Each link differs from the others only with respect to the specific CustomerID. Of course, the CustomerID values are all stored in the data source along with the other data. You can use ADO to obtain a list of the CustomerID and customer names. You can then use VBScript to dynamically generate a unique hyperlink for each record in the customer list recordset.

The starting point is a view added to the SQL Server database that generates a list of customer names and IDs called v_CustList.

```
SELECT Customers.CustomerID, Customers.BillState,
Customers.LastName + ', ' + Customers.FirstName AS FullName,
COUNT(Orders.WineOrderID) AS Orders
FROM Orders INNER JOIN
Customers ON
Orders.CustomerID = Customers.CustomerID
WHERE (Customers.BillState IS NOT NULL)
GROUP BY Customers.CustomerID, Customers.BillState,
Customers.LastName + ', ' + Customers.FirstName
```

The data generated by this view can be used to create a Web document that contains hyperlinks that display the order history for any of the listed customers. To narrow the scope of the document, the recordset is limited to customers from a particular state, such as MO.

The first block of code in the QSLinks2.Asp file uses ADO to open the v_CustList view and selects records from the state of MO.

```
<%
Set Cnt = Server.CreateObject("ADODB.Connection")
Cnt.Open "Provider=SQLOLEDB;Data Source=208.222.107.6;" & _
"UID=ubad1d1;pwd=21@1n3z"
Set Cust = Server.CreateObject("ADODB.Recordset")
Cust.ActiveConnection = Cnt
Cust.Open "SELECT * FROM v_CustList Where billstate ='MO' ORDER BY Fullname"
%>
```

The interesting part of the ASP is shown in the following example. Hyperlinks are automatically generated in this section. The hyperlink URL is created by combining a static reference to the Rs5.Asp document with the contents of the Cust ("CustomerID") field. The hyperlink text is created by inserting the Cust ("FullName"). The code here can be a bit hard to read because the VBScript (in bold) is all tangled up with the HTML code. You may easily leave out a parenthesis or a quotation mark when you are combining VBScript and HTML so closely. One common mistake is to forget to include the closing quotation mark following <%=Cust("CustomerID")%>. The quotation mark is needed because it is the closing quotation mark around the hyperlink's URL.

```
<H1>State: MO</H1>
<%Do Until Cust.EOF %>
<A href="rs5.asp?CID=<%=Cust("CustomerID")%>">
<%=Cust("FullName")%></A><BR>
<% cust.MoveNext
Loop %>
</BODY>
</HTML>
```

When you open Qslinks2.Asp, the VBScript loads the recordset using ADO and then proceeds to generate a list of hyperlinks — one for each customer in the recordset, as shown in Figure 9-10. When you click on any of the hyperlinks in the QSLinks2.Asp document, the URL is submitted to the Web server with a querystring value that corresponds to the CustomerID of the customer named in the hyperlink text. This means that each link opens a document that lists the order history for that customer.

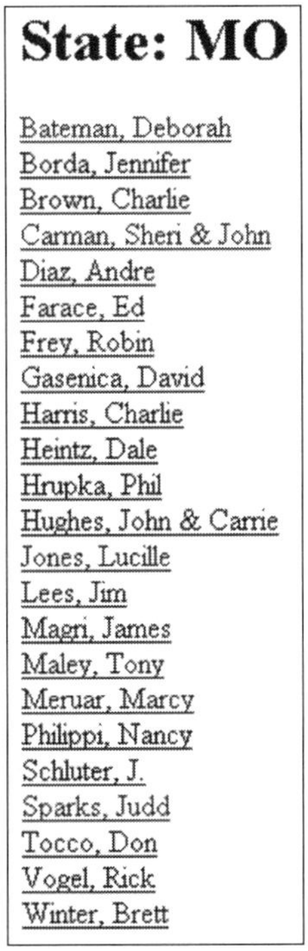

Figure 9-10:
A list of
hyperlinks is
dynamically
generated
from the
contents of
a recordset.

State: MO

Bateman, Deborah
Borda, Jennifer
Brown, Charlie
Carman, Sheri & John
Diaz, Andre
Farace, Ed
Frey, Robin
Gasenica, David
Harris, Charlie
Heintz, Dale
Hrupka, Phil
Hughes, John & Carrie
Jones, Lucille
Lees, Jim
Magri, James
Maley, Tony
Meruar, Marcy
Philippi, Nancy
Schluter, J.
Sparks, Judd
Tocco, Don
Vogel, Rick
Winter, Brett

Multiple-level hyperlinks

Although QSLinks2.Asp demonstrates how you can use ADO to generate hyperlinks, the recordset displayed in Figure 9-10 is arbitrarily limited to a specific state, such as MO. To build something more practical, you need to be able to access a list for any state.

This can be accomplished using the same concepts and applying them to a recordset of states. The following example shows the code used in StatesList.Asp. In this document, the recodset is created containing a list of all of the states in which there are customers with an order history.

```
<HTML><BODY>
<%
Set Cnt = Server.CreateObject("ADODB.Connection")
Set States = Server.CreateObject("ADODB.Recordset")
Cnt.Open "Provider=SQLOLEDB;Data Source=208.222.107.6;" & _
"UID=ubad1d1;pwd=21@1n3z"
States.Open "SELECT BillState FROM v_CustList Group By BillState", _
cnt
%>
```

After the recordset is created, the state list is used to create a series of hyperlinks for each state. Each link makes a request for the document QSLink3.Asp, which had not been created yet, and passes the state abbreviation to QSLink3.asp in the form of a querystring named State.

```
<H1>States</H1>
<%Do Until States.EOF %>
<A href="QSLink3.asp?State=<%=States(0)%>">
<%=States(0)%></A><BR>
<% States.MoveNext
Loop %>
</BODY></HTML>
```

Figure 9-11 shows the StateList.Asp document as it appears in the browser.

The final piece of the puzzle is to modify the code used in QSLinks2.Asp to work not just with the state abbreviation MO, but with any state abbreviation passed to it as a querystring.

In this case, I decided to use an ADO command object so that I can create a parameterized query to generate the recordset. While the code could have been written using a recordset alone, this example provides an opportunity to show that ADO command and parameter objects function within an ASP in exactly the same way they function in a VB/VBA procedure. After the recordset is created, the code that creates the hyperlinks can function without modification.

A difference between ASP and VB/VBA occurs in the code. The Type property of the Parameter object is defined by the numeric value 200, not the constant adVarChar, which is what you typically use in VB/VBA. The reason for this is that the type of library used for ADO, which contains the list of constants, is not available to the VBScript engine. Therefore, it's necessary to use the numeric values when you are setting properties.

```
<HTML><BODY>
<%
Set Cnt = Server.CreateObject("ADODB.Connection")
Set Cmd = Server.CreateObject("ADODB.Command")
Set Cust = Server.CreateObject("ADODB.Recordset")
set Param = Server.CreateObject("ADODB.Parameter")
```

```
Cnt.Open "Provider=SQLOLEDB;Data Source=208.222.107.6;" & _
"UID=ubad1d1;pwd=21@1n3z"
cmd.ActiveConnection = Cnt
cmd.CommandText = _
"SELECT * FROM v_CustList Where billstate = ? ORDER BY Fullname"
Param.Type = 200
Param.Size = 2
Param.Value = Request.QueryString("State")
cmd.Parameters.Append Param
Cust.Open cmd
%>
<H1>State: <%=Request.QueryString("State")%></H1>
<%Do Until Cust.EOF %>
<A href="rs5.asp?CID=<%=Cust("CustomerID")%>">
<%=Cust("FullName")%></A><BR>
<% cust.MoveNext
Loop %>
</BODY></HTML>
```

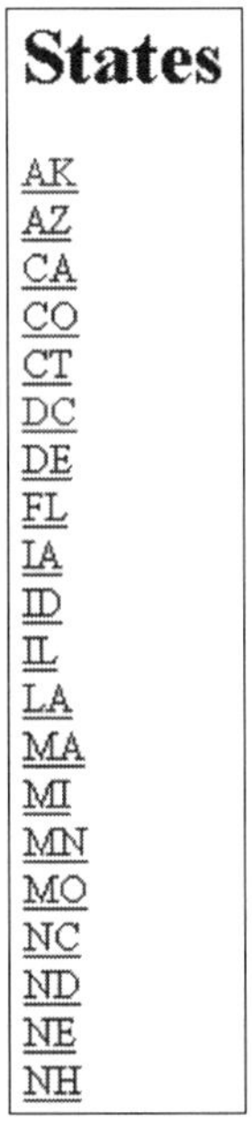

States

AK
AZ
CA
CO
CT
DC
DE
FL
IA
ID
IL
LA
MA
MI
MN
MO
NC
ND
NE
NH

Figure 9-11: The StateList.Asp document displays a series of hyperlinks for each state in the recordset.

The result is a series of documents — StateLinks.Asp, QSLinks3.Asp, and Rs5.Asp — that are related to each other by dynamically created hyperlinks. The hyperlinks are, in turn, dependent upon the data stored in the ADO provider. The hyperlinks in StateLinks.Asp establish the criteria that selects the contents of the QSLinks3.Asp which, in turn, narrow the content of the Rs5.Asp to the order history of a selected customer.

To test how these ASP files interact, open the StateList.Asp and use the hyperlinks to display order information for as many customers as you like.

Chapter 10

Data Forms on the Web

*W*hen the HTML language was created, it included the ability to displays forms on Web pages into which the user could enter data. However, there's nothing in the HTML language that accounts for what, if anything, happens to the data entered into the form on the Web page. In this chapter, you find out how to use ADO to store and retrieve data based on Web page forms.

Sending Data to the Server with a Form

HTML forms provide Web pages with a simple, easily recognized structure for both input and display of data. Although the querystrings discussed in Chapter 9 are useful ways to relate different pages running on a Web site, they do not offer an efficient way to get user input. A *querystring* is an expression that's added to the URL of a Web page that sends a data value to the Web server.

Forms support standard data entry controls, such as text boxes, list boxes, drop-down lists, radio buttons, and command buttons. As any Web user knows, the Submit button performs a special function on a Web form; it sends the user entry to the Web server.

Forms allow Web pages to have a look and feel that is consistent with the conventions for data display and entry that are common among Windows applications.

Unlike forms in Access or Visual Basic, standard HTML forms aren't bound to data elements like fields in a recordset. The data entered into a form has no built-in relationship to any ADO object. To handle database tasks such as entry, display, and editing of data with HTML forms, you must add VBScript code to your Web page. The VBScript, utilizing ADO objects, can add data to the HTML form and then store any new or edited data in ADO data source.

User Input and Forms

Technically, HTML forms operate in roughly the same manner as querystrings. When a user clicks the Submit button, a request is made for a Web document. If the Web page contains a form, the contents of the form are passed to the Web server using the HTTP protocol. The process is similar to what's used to pass a querystring to a Web server. From the Web server's point of view, the only difference is that form values contained in a request are stored in the Form collection instead of the QueryString collection (see Figure 10-1).

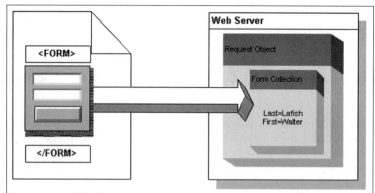

Figure 10-1: Forms submit the user entries to the Form collection of the Request object on the Web server.

You can construct most HTML forms by using the following four tags. Figure 10-2 shows HTML input elements that you can create by using these tags, as displayed in the SampleForm.Asp document.

✔ <FORM></FORM>: The Form tags bracket all the elements in the form. The beginning Form tag specifies what should happen when the Submit button is clicked. If you specify POST as the METHOD parameter, all the elements in the form, and any user entry in those elements, are passed to the Web server. When the Web server receives the form data, it stores the information in a collection within the Request object. After it's stored in the Request object, that data can be extracted from the server for use in another Web page. If you have also included an `ACTION` parameter, the Web server automatically returns the specified Web page to the user who had just submitted the form.

```
<FORM METHOD=POST ACTION="document.asp">
```

Note that `POST` and `ACTION` work together to facilitate the creation of forms that have an interactive look and feel. When the Web server is responding to the `ACTION` (creating a Response object to return to the user), any data entered into the form is available to the scripting engine through the `Request.Form` collection. Using VBScript, you can modify the Response object to reflect the data the user entered into the form. In terms of ADO, this means you can create a recordset, or update or insert records based on the user input captured in the form.

✔ `<INPUT>`: This tag creates text boxes, radio buttons, check boxes, password boxes, and command button elements depending on the `Type` parameter.

✔ `<TEXTAREA>`: This tag creates a multiple line text entry area.

✔ `<SELECT>`: This tag creates the list-oriented elements: drop-down list boxes and list boxes.

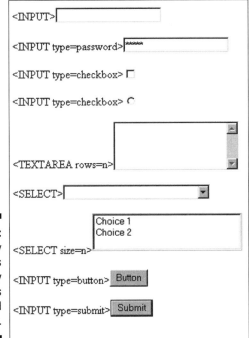

Figure 10-2: Form entry elements defined by HTML tags and parameters.

It's possible to use the ACTION parameter to request the same document that contains the form. This enables you to use a simple ASP to perform a variety of tasks by using the same layout. For example, you can use VBScript to handle the display, update, and insert operations using a single ASP. You see how this is accomplished in this chapter. For now, you work with pairs of documents: one with the form, and one that shows the response.

A simple form

The first issue in working with forms is to see how entries made to a form can be accessed by another document. One of the simplest forms that you can create is the Form1.Asp, as shown in Figure 10-3. In this example, each element in the form is assigned a unique name by using the Name parameter of the INPUT tag.

```
<HTML><BODY>
<FORM METHOD="post" ACTION="ShowForm1.asp">
<INPUT Name="First"><BR>
<INPUT Name="Last"><BR>
<INPUT Type="submit" value="Submit Form">
<FORM></BODY></HTML>
```

Figure 10-3:
A simple HTML-based form.

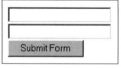

If a form document, such as Form1.Asp, does not contain any VBScript, but merely contains HTML form tags, it can be stored with an HTM or HTML extension. But when you set up the folders on a Web server, you can designate a folder as having execute permissions and not read permissions. This means that you can load ASP documents, which pass through the VBScript engine even if they don't have any script commands, because the operation is considered an execute operation by the Web server. Conversely, if reading documents isn't allowed in that folder, then you aren't permitted to view HTM or HTML documents because they don't pass through the script engine. The CGI-BIN folder setup on most Web servers is usually set up with execute permissions but no read permissions. I have found it simpler to make all the documents ASP. In theory, however, this can result in slower Web server response time because every document in the folder must pass through the VBScript engine.

On the other end of the operation is the document, ShowForm1.Asp, which is requested when you click the Submit button in Form1.Asp. That document needs to examine the contents of the Request object's Form collection in order to react to the specific data, if any, that the user entered into Form1.Asp. The code below shows how the ShowForm1.Asp document extracts the values entered in Form1.Asp from the Form collection of the Request object. The form information is stored in the request object because it was sent to the Web server along with a request for a document (ShowForm1.Asp). Because Form1.Asp assigned a unique name to each element, ShowForm1.Asp extracts each value by using the name of the element in the Request.Form( ) expression.

```
<HTML>
<BODY>
First name: <%=Request.Form("first")%> <BR>
Last name: <%=Request.Form("Last")%>
</BODY>
</HTML>
```

When you run Form1.Asp, any text that you enter into the entry boxes appears in the ShowForm1.Asp document. If you enter **Morgan** and **Krumm** into Form1.Asp, you see the following in ShowForm1.Asp:

```
First name: Morgan
Last name: Krumm
```

Accessing form collection elements

You don't need to know the names of all the elements in a form in order to extract data from a form. You can use the For Each statement to extract each element in the form collection without having to code each element name. The following statement assigns to the variable E the name of each element in the form collection:

```
For Each E In Request.Form
```

The statement below inserts the name of the element into the document:

```
Response.Write E ===> First
```

If you want to insert the user entry for that item, you use:

```
Request.Form(E) ===> Morgan
```

ShowForm2.Asp, shown next, displays the data entered into Form2.Asp without requiring the VBScript to specifically list the form element names:

```
<HTML><BODY>
<% For Each E In Request.Form
    Response.Write _
        E & ": " & _
        Request.Form(E) & "<BR>"
Next%>
</BODY></HTML>
```

Using a single form collection

The two previous examples, ShowForm1.Asp and ShowForm2.Asp, use forms in which each element is given a unique name in the <INPUT> tags used to create the form. But this doesn't have to be the case. The next example, Form3.Asp, uses the same name, *Enter*, for each of the elements in the form.

```
<HTML><BODY>
<FORM METHOD="post" ACTION="ShowForm2.asp">
<INPUT Name="Enter"><BR>
<INPUT name ="Enter"><BR>
<INPUT Type="submit" value="Submit Form">
<FORM></BODY></HTML>
```

When ShowForm2.Asp displays the entry, the results appear as a comma-separated list of items for the single named element, ENTER:

```
ENTER: Morgan, Krumm
```

You can still deal with each data item as a separate element if you modify the method of retrieval from the form collection. The values contained in the Web page form are stored on the Web server as elements in an array. You can refer to individual data items within the array by their position, starting at 1.

```
Response.Form("Enter")(1)
Response.Form("Enter")(2)
Response.Form("Enter")(...)
```

ShowForm4.Asp extracts the individual data items entered into Form4.Asp, even though each element in the form uses the same name, Enter.

```
<HTML><BODY>
<% For Each element In Request.Form
    For I = 1 To Request.Form(element).Count
    Response.Write _
        element & "-" & I & ": " & _
        Request.form(element)(I) & "<BR>"
    Next
Next%>
</BODY></HTML>
```

ShowForm4.Asp displays the same entry as shown below.

```
ENTER-1: Morgan
ENTER-2: Krumm
```

Generating forms automatically

Why spend so much time exploring the minutia of forms elements? The answer is that although it's common to code forms (or create them with an HTML form builder such as FrontPage or Visual InterDev) in which each element has a unique name, it's also possible and useful to automatically generate forms by using VBScript and an ADO recordset. The advantage of automatically generating a form is that you can display and retrieve data items without having to hard-code the element names in advance.

To see how this idea works, begin with ASP GetCustData1.Asp (see the next grouping of code), which creates the form shown in Figure 10-4. This form enables the user to enter a CustomerID.

```
<HTML><BODY>
<FORM METHOD=POST ACTION="ShowCustdata1.Asp">
Enter Customer ID: <INPUT Name="CID">
<INPUT type="submit" value="Submit" name=submit1>
</FORM>
</BODY></HTML>
```

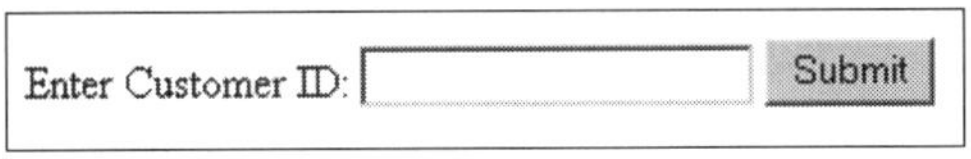

Figure 10-4:
HTML form
enables
the user
to enter a
Customer ID.

Enter Customer ID: [   ] [Submit]

The ShowCustdata1.Asp ASP is designated as the document that uses the CustomerID to display data from the corresponding record in the Customers table. In this case, the data appears in a form. The form isn't created in advance but generated on-the-fly by a combination of VBScript and the ADO recordset that contains the Customer data.

The first block of VBScript uses the techniques discussed in Chapter 9 to create an ADO recordset. In Chapter 9, the CustomerID was stored in the queryString collection. In this instance, the CustomerID is stored in the form collection.

```
<% Set Cnt = Server.CreateObject("ADODB.Connection")
cnt.Open "Provider=SQLOLEDB;Data Source=208.222.107.6;" & _
   "UID=ubad1d1;pwd=21@1n3z"
 Set Cust = Server.CreateObject("ADODB.Recordset")
 Cust.Open "SELECT * FROM v_Custdata WHERE CustomerID = " _
   & Request.Form("CID"), Cnt%>
```

After you create the recordset, you can display the information. Instead of manually coding each <INPUT> tag pair, the HTML is combined with VBScript in the following code. The For . . . Each loop cycles through all the fields in the recordset. VBScipt is used to insert the name of the field — col.Name — and the value of the field — Cust (col.name) — to the HTML tag that generates a text and text box combination when the Web page is displayed.

```
<H1>Customer: <%=Cust("Last") & ", " & Cust("First")%></H1>
<FORM>
   <%For Each col In Cust.Fields%>
   <%=col.Name%>
     <INPUT Name="Data" Value="<%=Cust(col.name)%>"><BR>
   <%Next%>
</FORM>
```

Figure 10-5 shows the form that is generated in the ShowCustData1.Asp. To see how this works, load the Web document GetCustData1.Asp and enter **4110** into the Customer ID box; then submit the form. The browser shows the page pictured in Figure 10-5.

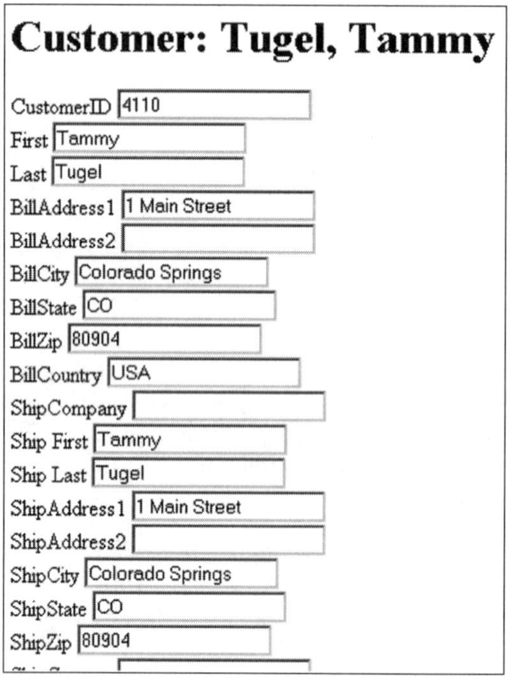

Figure 10-5:
An entire form is generated using VBScript.

Customer: Tugel, Tammy

CustomerID	4110
First	Tammy
Last	Tugel
BillAddress1	1 Main Street
BillAddress2	
BillCity	Colorado Springs
BillState	CO
BillZip	80904
BillCountry	USA
ShipCompany	
Ship First	Tammy
Ship Last	Tugel
ShipAddress1	1 Main Street
ShipAddress2	
ShipCity	Colorado Springs
ShipState	CO
ShipZip	80904

You can greatly improve the appearance of the form in Figure 10-5 by aligning the text and text boxes vertically in columns. The HTML tool to handle alignment is a `<Table>` tag pair. ShowCustData2.Asp adds `<Table>` tags to the `For . . . Each` loop that generates the form. The HTML generated by the following code places the text labels in the first column of the table and the text boxes are placed in the second column of the table.

```
<FORM>
<TABLE>
<%For Each col In Cust.Fields%>
<TR>
   <TD><%=col.Name%></TD>
   <TD>
      <INPUT Name="Data" Value="<%=Cust(col.name)%>">
   </TD>
</TR>
<%Next%>
</TABLE>
</FORM>
```

If you load GetCustData2.Asp into your browser and enter the CustomerID 4110 into the Customer ID box, ShowCustData2.Asp generates the form elements within the cells of a table structure creating a neat vertical alignment of the form into two vertical columns (see Figure 10-6).

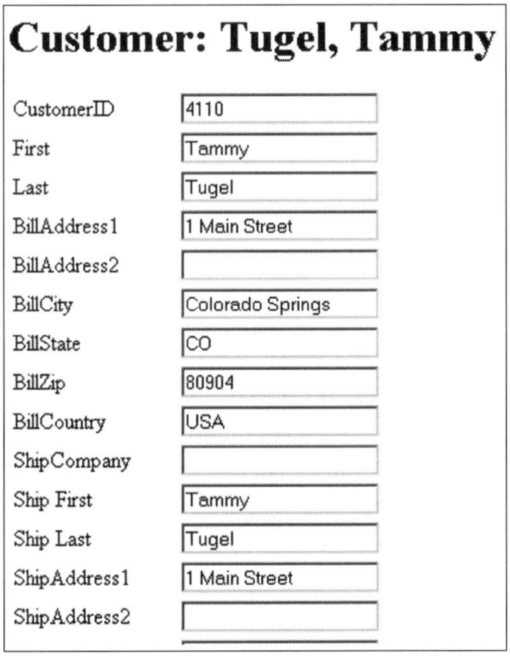

Figure 10-6: Placing form elements inside a table structure enables you to line up items in columns.

Customer: Tugel, Tammy

CustomerID	4110
First	Tammy
Last	Tugel
BillAddress1	1 Main Street
BillAddress2	
BillCity	Colorado Springs
BillState	CO
BillZip	80904
BillCountry	USA
ShipCompany	
Ship First	Tammy
Ship Last	Tugel
ShipAddress1	1 Main Street
ShipAddress2	

Using an Include file

You may have noticed that many of the ASPs used as examples in this and the previous chapter often have blocks of code that are identical to one or more other ASP documents. For example, all the variations of the ShowCustData ASP use exactly the same block of VBScript to create the recordset.

VBScript enables you to store blocks of VBScript and/or HTML code in text files. You can have VBScript automatically insert the text stored in these files when it's processing the ASP by using the Include instruction. The following example instructs the VBScript engine to insert the contents of the file CustCnt.inc into the ASP at the location where the Include tag is located.

```
<!--#include file ="CustCnt.inc"-->
```

The CustCnt.inc contains the following VBScript:

```
<% Set Cnt = Server.CreateObject("ADODB.Connection")
cnt.Open "Provider=SQLOLEDB;Data Source=208.222.107.6;" & _
"UID=ubad1d1;pwd=21@1n3z"
Set Cust = Server.CreateObject("ADODB.Recordset")
Cust.Open "SELECT * FROM v_Custdata WHERE CustomerID = " _
& Request.Form("CID"), Cnt%>
```

Include files can have any filename or extension. Using the INC extension is customary but not required. The following code, ShowCustData3.Asp, uses an Include instruction to insert the VBScript that creates the recordset. The ASP GetCustData3.Asp invokes ShowCustData3.Asp.

```
<HTML>
<BODY>
<!--#include file ="CustCnt.inc"-->
<H1>Customer: <%=Cust("Last") & ", " & Cust("First")%></H1>
<FORM id=form1 name=form1>
<TABLE>
<%For Each col In Cust.Fields%>
<TR>
    <TD><%=col.Name%></TD>
    <TD>
        <INPUT Name="Data" Value="<%=Cust(col.name)%>">
    </TD>
</TR>
<%Next%>
</TABLE>
</FORM>
</BODY>
</HTML>
```

Forms that load themselves

No restrictions exist on what page you specify in the ACTION parameter of
the FORM tag. In fact, the current page often reloads itself when you click the
Submit button.

Why do that? The primary reason for reloading the same page is to reduce
the number of different documents needed to perform a task. For example, in
order to load Customers information, you use GetCustdata3.Asp to obtain the
user input and you use a second page, ShowCustData3.Asp, to display the
results.

You may want to consolidate both functions on a single ASP page, which provides both the input box and the output of the customer data recordset.
Figure 10-7 shows the ShowCustData4.Asp example, which combines the
input function of GetCustdata3.Asp and the output function of
ShowCustData3.Asp into a single ASP.

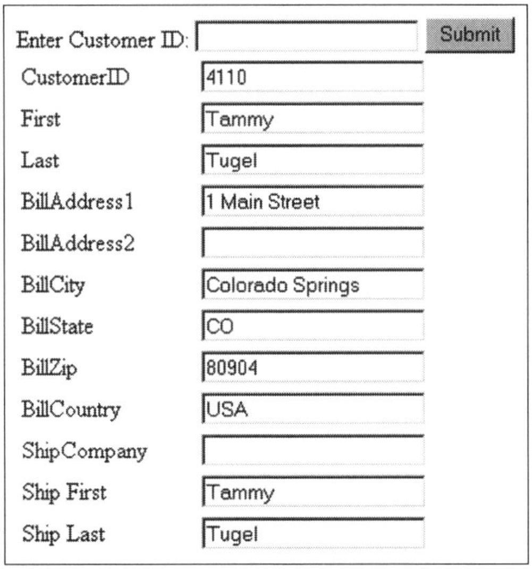

Figure 10-7:
A single
ASP page
can be used
to enter
requests
and displays
responses.

Because you use the same page for more than one function, you need to add
code to the ASP that evaluates which operations should take place. In this
example, the most significant problem occurs when a user loads the page for
the first time during a session. At that point, the form collection is empty. If
you attempt to refer to any item in the form collection, an error results.

The first thing your VBScript needs to do is determine whether the form collection is empty. Unfortunately, no built-in property exists that can provide this data. You have to write some code to do it. The following code assigns the variable HasForm a value equal to the number of elements, if any, currently stored in the form collection:

```
HasForm=0
For Each E in Request.Form
    HasForm=HasForm+1
Next
```

The following ASP, ShowCustdata4.Asp, specifies itself as the document to load when you press the Submit button. The ASP uses the HasForm variable to determine what sort of display should appear on the Web page.

If the form collection is empty, the HasForm variable remains zero the first time that the ASP loads. Any variable with a value of zero is the logical equivalent of a false value.

After the user actually enters a value in the form on the page, the HasForm variable has a value greater than 0, which is equivalent to true. The following code creates a recordset with no records if there are no values in the form collection:

```
If hasform then
    if Request.Form("CID")<> "" Then
        Cust.Open "SELECT * FROM v_Custdata WHERE CustomerID = " _
        & Request.Form("CID"), Cnt
    Else
        Cust.Open "SELECT * FROM v_Custdata WHERE CustomerID = 0" _
        , Cnt
    end if
else
    Cust.Open "SELECT * FROM v_Custdata WHERE CustomerID = 0" _
    , Cnt
end if%>
```

You can also use conditional statements such as If, Else, and End. You can use If in combination with HTML elements. In the following code, VBScript code fragments use If and End If. Even though the HTML elements aren't part of the VBScript code, they are affected by the placement of VBScript conditional instructions. In this case, the fragment that contains If not cust.EOF Then controls the inclusion or exclusion of all the items, VBScript, and HTML, up to the locations of the End If statement. The result is that the code that displays the recordset on the ASP operates only if you have a valid record in the Cust recordset.

```
<FORM METHOD=POST ACTION="ShowCustdata4.Asp">
Enter Customer ID: <INPUT Name="CID">
<INPUT type="submit" value="Submit" name=submit1>
<TABLE>
<%If not cust.EOF Then
    For Each col In Cust.Fields%>
    <TR><TD>
    <%=col.Name%></TD>
    <TD><INPUT Name="Data" Value="<%=Cust(col.name)%>"><BR>
    </TD>
    <%Next
End if%>
</TABLE></FORM></BODY></HTML>
```

When you load ShowCustdata4.Asp the first time, you see only the input box for the CustomerID. After you enter an ID (such as 4110) and click Submit, the same form reloads because it is the page specified in the ACTION parameter of the FORM tag. But due to the effect of the conditional statements in the VBScript, the reloaded form shows both the entry box and the full contents of the customer record for the previously entered CustomerID. You can continue this cycle by entering a different ID, such as 3579, and have the contents of that record displayed in the ASP. You can continue to submit as many entries as you desire using only a single ASP.

Lists in Forms

HTML supports the use of lists within a form. The list can be a drop-down list box style or a list box style. You can create both of these lists by using the SELECT and OPTION tags. These tags work together as shown in the following code:

```
<SELECT name='???'>
  <Option>Item 1</Option>
  <Option>Item 2</Option>
</SELECT>
```

Writing out a series of OPTION tags makes sense when you have a short list of items to display. But suppose you want to have a form that includes a drop-down list of state abbreviations. It's certainly possible to write out OPTION tags for all the states, but that's tedious and unproductive work.

An alternative approach would be to use VBScript to automatically generate the OPTION tags based on the recordset that contains a list of the state abbreviations. Suppose that you have a recordset called States that contained a list of the state abbreviations. You could insert each state abbreviation into an OPTION tag in order to generate each item for the list.

The PickStateFromList1.Asp uses VBScript to automatically generate a list of states. The page begins by defining as recordset called `States` using the VBScript code below. The `States` recordset lists each state that has at least one order:

```
<%Set States = Server.CreateObject("ADODB.Recordset")
States.Open "SELECT BillState FROM v_CustList Group By BillState", _
cnt
%>
```

After you have a recordset that contains the items you want to use to populate the list, you need to use VBScript to generate the `OPTION` tags. The tags are generated by combining text for the tag with the value in the `BillState` field of the `States` recordset. The following statement uses the `Response.Write` method to generate a tag:

```
Response.Write "<OPTION>" & States("BillState") & "</OPTION>"
```

When the Web server processes the VBScript, it returns an HTML tag in which the state AK is inserted from the `States` recordset:

```
<OPTION>AK</OPTION>
```

In order to fill the entire list, you would place the statement that writes the `OPTION` tag inside a loop so that there would be one tag written for each state in the list. The remainder of PickStateFromList1 consists of a form that contains a loop that writes the `OPTION` tags using the `States` recordset to supply the names of the states.

```
<FORM METHOD=POST ACTION="PickCustFromState.Asp">
<SELECT Name="StateAbbr">
<%Do Until States.EOF
    Response.Write "<OPTION>" & _
      States("BillState") & "</OPTION>"
    States.MoveNext
  Loop
  Response.Write "</SELECT>" & _
  "<INPUT type='submit' value='Continue'>"%>
</FORM>
```

When you load PickStateFromList1, you can select a state from the list, as shown in Figure 10-8. You can open the drop-down list and select any of the state abbreviations. Although it would've been possible to create the list in PickStateFromList1 using HTML only, VBScript greatly simplified the coding required. In addition to making it easier to code, the recordset made sure that only states that actually had one or more orders were included. States that have no order activity do not appear on the list.

In order to use the list displayed on PickStateFromList1 to list the customers from that selected state, you need to create another ASP called PickCustFromState.Asp.

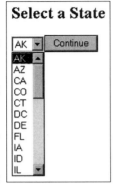

Figure 10-8:
An ADO
recordset
used to
populate an
HTML
drop-down
list.

How will PickCustFromState.Asp know which state was selected in PickStateFromList1? The answer is that the selected state abbreviation is stored in the Web server's form collection when the user clicks the submit button. Note that the Continue button (refer to Figure 10-8), is a submit-type button even though it uses a label other than submit.

The following code is the code for PickCustFromState.Asp. Like PickStateFromList1, PickCustFromState.Asp uses a loop to write a series of OPTION tags, which create a list of customer names in a list box. The VBScript code in PickCustFromState.Asp uses Request.Form("StateAbbr") to insert the state selected on the PickStateFromList1 page to control which records will be included in the Cust recordset.

This code produces a list box because the Size parameter of the SELECT tag is set at a value greater than 1. In HTML, sizes greater than 1 change the display from a drop-down list box to a list box.

```
<%@ Language=VBScript %>
<HTML><BODY>
<!--#include file ="AdoDumCnt.inc"-->
<%   Set Cust = Server.CreateObject("ADODB.Recordset")
    Cust.Open _
    "SELECT * FROM v_CustList Where billstate ='" & _
    Request.Form("StateAbbr") & "' ORDER BY Fullname", _
    cnt
%>
<H2>Select a Customer From <%=Request.Form("StateAbbr")%> </H2>
<FORM action="ShowCustData3.Asp" method=post>
<SELECT Name="CID" Size=10>
<%Do Until Cust.EOF%>
<OPTION Value=<%=Cust("CustomerID")%>>
<%=Cust("Fullname")%>
</OPTION>
<%Cust.MoveNext
Loop%>
</SELECT>
<P><INPUT type=submit value=Submit></P></FORM>
</BODY></HTML>
```

After you create and save PickCustFromState.Asp, you can use PickStateFromList1 to select lists of customers based on their state location. Load PickStateFromList1 and select a state from the list. Click the Continue button.

The result is that PickCustFromState.Asp displays a list of customers from the state selected on the previous page.

Lists with hidden values

PickCustFromState provides you with a list of customers on a state-by-state basis. Suppose that you want to display a list of the order history of a customer by making a selection from the customer list and loading another page that shows all the orders for the selected customer.

Getting a list of customer orders requires the use of hidden values in the customer list. In PickStateFromList1, the state abbreviation list displayed the two-letter state abbreviations such as AZ, PA, and so on. The displayed abbreviations were the exact criteria needed to construct the customer list recordset because the BillState field contained the same two-letter abbreviations.

But when the task is to locate the orders for an individual customer, you do not want to use the text that appears on the list as your criterion. Because it's possible for two different customers to have the same name, order retrieval is always based on the CustomerID field rather than the first and last name fields. On the other hand, it wouldn't be very useful to display a list of CustomerID's on the Web page.

The solution: Display the customer names on the page, but assign each name a value that corresponds to the CustomerID of each customer. This means that when the page is submitted, the CustomerID, not the customer name, is stored in the Form collection.

To see how you can create an ASP that will display customer names but submit the CustomerID, the code begins with VBScript that creates a recordset that contains all the information about the customers from the selected state:

```
<% Set Cust = Server.CreateObject("ADODB.Recordset")
   Cust.Open _
   "SELECT * FROM v_CustList Where billstate ='" & _
   Request.Form("StateAbbr") & "' ORDER BY Fullname", _
   cnt%>
```

After the recordset is created, the next task is to use VBScript to generate a list of customers from the selected state as OPTION tags in a SELECT drop-down list.

You can create a hidden column for an HTML list by using the Value parameter of the OPTION tag. The goal is to create a series of OPTION tags, like the following, which have the CustomerID defined as the value, and the customer name is the text that will appear in the list.

```
<SELECT Name=CustomterID>
<OPTION Value=1000>Smith, John</OPTION>
<OPTION Value=2010>Glass, Ruth</OPTION>
</SELECT>
```

This principle is put into practice in the following code, which appears in PickCustFromState. In this example, VBScript is used to insert the CustomerID as the OPTION value and then a text of the customer's name as the text that appears on the Web page.

```
<FORM action="ShowCustData3.Asp" method=post>
<SELECT Name="CID" Size=10>
<%Do Until Cust.EOF%>
<OPTION Value=<%=Cust("CustomerID")%>>
<%=Cust("Fullname")%>
</OPTION>
<%Cust.MoveNext
Loop%>
</SELECT>
<P><INPUT type=submit value=Submit></P></FORM>
```

Figure 10-9 shows the list of customers for the state abbreviation OR. Note that in this case the visual display is a list box rather than a drop-down list. The difference in appearance is controlled by the Size parameter of the SELECT tag. By default, the size is set at 1, which results in a drop-down-list-style display. In PickCustFromState, the Size parameter is set at 10, which creates a list box with up to ten items displayed at one time.

What happens when the user makes a selection? In this case, the ACTION parameter of the form calls ShowCustData3.Asp, an ASP that you created earlier in this chapter. ShowCustData3.Asp reads the CustomerID from the Web server's form collection, which it uses to display a complete list of customer orders. The only requirement is that you use the name CID as the name of the SELECT tag because that is the form collection item that ShowCustData3.Asp was designed to look for when it loads. Figure 10-10 shows ShowCustData3.Asp, which displays the data for a customer like Gary Brown, selected in the list box displayed on the ASP PickCustFromState.

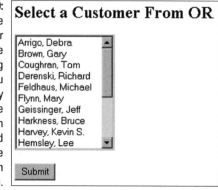

Figure 10-9:
The value parameter of the OPTION tag allows you to display one value and store an associated value in the form collection.

Select a Customer From OR

Arrigo, Debra
Brown, Gary
Coughran, Tom
Derenski, Richard
Feldhaus, Michael
Flynn, Mary
Geissinger, Jeff
Harkness, Bruce
Harvey, Kevin S.
Hemsley, Lee

Submit

Figure 10-10:
Customer Gary Brown is retrieved when his name is selected in the list box on the ASP PickCust-FromState.

Customer: Brown, Gary

CustomerID	3961
First	Gary
Last	Brown
BillAddress1	1 Main Street
BillAddress2	
BillCity	Bend
BillState	OR
BillZip	97701
BillCountry	USA
ShipCompany	Bend Chamber of Comr
Ship First	Gary
Ship Last	Brown
ShipAddress1	1 Main Street
ShipAddress2	

One side issue involved in this example is the way in which VBScript and HTML are combined to create the ASP. Figure 10-11 shows the routines used in both PickStateFromList1 and PickCustFromState. In PickStateFromList1, the drop-down list was created by a single block of VBScript. The HTML elements were inserted as text literals combined with other data, such as fields from the recordset, using the `Write` method of the Web server's Response object. In PickCustFromState, the VBScript elements occur as a series of fragments interspersed with HTML.

```
<SELECT Name="StateAbbr">
<%Do Until States.EOF
    Response.Write "<OPTION>" &
       States("BillState") & "</OPTION>"
    States.MoveNext
 Loop
 Response.Write "</SELECT>" & _
 "<INPUT type='submit' value='Continue'>"
%>
```

```
<SELECT Name="CID" Size=10>
<%Do Until Cust.EOF%>
<OPTION Value=<%=Cust("CustomerID")%>>
<%=Cust("Fullname")%>
</OPTION>
<%Cust.MoveNext
Loop%>
</SELECT>
```

Figure 10-11:
You can
combine
HTML with
VBScript in
a variety of
programming
styles.

Which is the best way? Again, the answer lies in the mind of the individual programmer. Using a single VBScript block is simpler in the sense that the number of VBScript fragments in the ASP is reduced. But the individual statements inside the block are more complicated because they must concatenate the HTML text with other items and objects. Conversely, the PickCustFromState uses a larger number of VBScript fragments. The HTML elements are a bit easier to read in that case because they don't have to be enclosed in quotations or concatenated onto other items. The net result of either style is the same because the user in both cases is sent the pure HTML that results from the coding. As you create more ASPs on your own, you may evolve a style of your own with which you feel comfortable.

queryString actions

Another way to use one ASP to call another is to use a queryString as part of the Action parameter of the FORM tag. For example, suppose that you want to add a button (see Figure 10-12) to the customer information screen that displays the order list for the current customer. In this case, you know the value of the CustomerID when you load the customer information page. You can use VBScript to add a queryString value to the hyperlink specified in the ACTION parameter of the FORM tag as shown in the following code. Specifically, this code calls the Rs5.Asp created in Chapter 9 with a queryString that corresponds to the currently displayed customer. The code appears in ShowCustData5.asp. To test the operation, start by loading PickStateFromList2.asp.

```
<FORM METHOD =POST
ACTION="rs5.asp?CID=<%=Cust("CustomerID")%>">
```

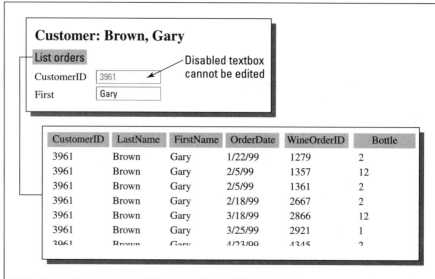

Disabled text boxes

Another small but useful addition that appears in Figure 10-12 is the use of a disabled control to display the CustomerID while preventing the user from actually typing in the text box. At this point, there is no connection between the text boxes on the form and the data source. Any editing performed by the users is simply discarded when they request another page. (You find out how to issue updates from an ASP in the next section.)

It makes sense, however, to indicate that the user cannot change the CustomerID because that value may be utilized by another ASP that reads the CustomerID from the form collection. If you allow the user to edit the CustomerID, even accidentally, it can result in getting an invalid CustomerID placed into the servers form collection.

The `disabled` parameter is included in HTML version 4.0, which is supported by all the versions of Netscape and Internet Explorer released since 1998. The following example creates a text box that displays 2010 but can't be edited by the user due to the addition of the `disabled` parameter. This parameter does not take any arguments.

```
<INPUT Name="CustomerID" Value=2010 disabled>
```

The next code fragment, from PickStateFromList2.asp, shows how the disabled effect illustrated in Figure 10-12 is achieved by using a VBScript `If . . . End If` structure inside a loop that displays the contents of the `Cust` recordset as a series of text boxes. The `If` condition checks the name of the field, `col.name`, and determines whether the name of the field is `CustomerID`. If it matches CustomerID, then the VBScript code inserts the `disabled` parameter into the `INPUT` tag.

```
<TABLE><%For Each col In Cust.Fields%>
<TR>
   <TD><%=col.Name%></TD>
   <TD>
      <INPUT Name="Data" Value="<%=Cust(col.name)%>"
      <% If col.name = "CustomerID" Then%>
      disabled
      <%End if%>
      >
   </TD>
</TR>
<%Next%></TABLE>
```

The result, shown in Figure 10-12, is a text box whose contents are grayed out. In addition, the user isn't able to place the cursor inside the box or edit any of the contents.

Changing the Recordset Contents

As I discussed in the previous section, the practical effect of editing the data displayed in INPUT tags on an HTML form is to change the contents of the form collection being stored temporarily in the memory of the Web server. No connection exists between the `INPUT` tags on the HTML form and the fields in the ADO recordset. This is true even though the ADO recordset was used to initially create the `INPUT` tags.

None of the VBScript statements, including the ones that involve ADO objects, ever get sent to the user when you are executing server-side scripts in ASPs. All the ADO operations take place at the Web server. The result of all the VBScript operations is to modify or enhance the flow of HTML back to the user. After the user gets the HTML, no link or connection exists between the page displayed in the user's browser and the data source that was used to fill in that page.

If you want to use the data in the HTML form to update an existing record or insert a new record into the data source, you must create an ASP page that takes the data stored in the Web server's form collection and stores that data in an ADO data source (see Figure 10-13).

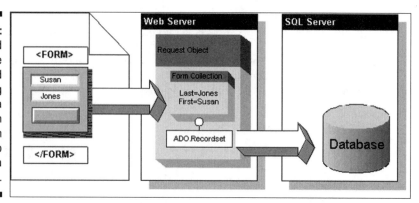

Figure 10-13:
Updates and inserts are accomplished by writing the data contained in the form collection to an ADO data source.

In order to create an example with which you can actually interact, live on the Internet, I have created a GuestBook table in the SQL Server database, which is available to readers of this book (see the "About the CD"appendix for info about how to connect to the Internet database). The table has the following structure:

```
GuestID, Integer
FirstName, Varchar
LastName, Varchar
DateEntered, DateTime
City, Varchar
State, Varchar
Country, Varchar
Comment, Varchar
DateChanged, DateTime
```

The goal is to create ASP pages that allow guests, like you, to add their names to the guest book or edit the entry they have already made. Because the data stored in this table changes as new readers use the Internet database, the displays are more populated than the screen images shown in the text picture.

Multiple Submit buttons

The main page for the guest book, GbookMain.Asp, appears in Figure 10-14. The page consists of a list box, which shows the guests that have made an entry into the guest book.

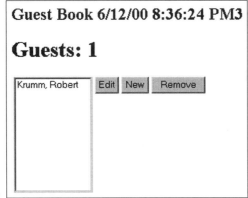

In addition to the list, there are three buttons: Edit, New, and Remove. You can create each of these buttons by using an INPUT tag that has the Submit type. HTML enables you to include as many Submit-type buttons as you like within a FORM tag. You trigger the form's ACTION whenever any of the Submit-type buttons are clicked.

```
<TD valign=top>
<INPUT Name="Action" type=submit value="Edit">
<INPUT name="Action" type=submit value="New">
<INPUT name="Action" type=submit value="Remove">
</TD>
```

All the Submit buttons perform the identical function. Then what good is having more than one Submit button?

When you click a Submit button, the value of the button, as indicated by the Value parameter, is stored in the Web server's Form collection. If you assign each Submit button a different value you can figure out which button was clicked by the user by checking the value stored in the Web server's Form collection. You can use the expression below in VBScript to determine which button in the requesting page was the one that was clicked by the user.

The following VBScript statement shows how you would check the Form collection to determine if the user has clicked the Edit button on the previously displayed page:

```
If Request.Form(Action)="Edit" Then
```

You apply this technique in the coding for the Gbookaddedit.Asp page, which begins in the next section.

VBScript procedures

Before moving on to create the Gbookaddedit.Asp ASP page that perform the Edit, New, and Remove operations, I cover some useful changes in the way that I constructed the VBScript used in the GBookMain.Asp.

One of the issues that I discuss in this book is the style in which various programming problems are implemented. If you compare the VB/VBA code written in Chapters 3, 4, and 5 with the ASP page coding in Chapters 9 and 10, you find that each ASP page is written as one big procedure without any procedure sections. When the Web server processes the HTML and VBScript code in an ASP, it starts with the first line of code and works straight through to the last line in the order the code was entered.

In contrast, VB/VBA is always divided into specifically named procedures by using the Sub or Function statements. A procedure is executed only when a statement in a different procedure explicitly calls the Sub or Function by name.

The advantage of the VB/VBA approach is that you can divide a large operation into smaller units of logic that can be reused by other procedures. VB/VBA also makes it easier to write and debug your code because you can isolate problems to specific Sub or Function procedures.

Even through server-side VBScript isn't as fully featured a language as VB/VBA, you can choose to write your VBScript in a more structured way by creating Sub and Function procedures at the top of the ASP. When the Web server processes the ASP, any named procedures encountered aren't immediately executed but defined and stored temporarily in memory. After all of the named procedures are defined, the code in the unstructured part of the ASP begins to execute. This process is diagrammed in Figure 10-15.

The advantage of using procedures is that the unstructured section of the ASP can reference the Sub and Function routines defined within the ASP as often as needed. Your purpose in organizing your ASP in this way is to separate, as much as possible, your VBScript code from the HTML code. While this cannot be accomplished completely, you can greatly reduce the clutter in your ASP that occurs when you need to insert VBScript within HTML code. Calling a function, such as Call InsertList (Guest), is a much more compact instruction than writing out all of the code.

One of the messiest coding tasks covered in this chapter is the code required to create a list box populated from a recordset. You can improve the coding style of the ASP by breaking the tasks involved in that process into one or more named procedures. You can simply call a function in order to insert the entire list box.

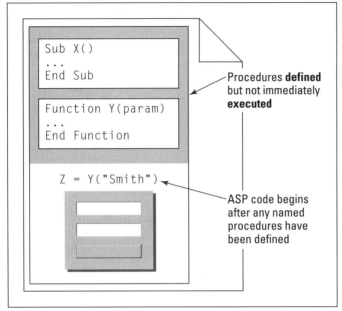

Figure 10-15:
Named
procedures
can be
included in
an ASP.

The first procedure defined in the GbookMain.Asp follows. `WriteOption` is a function that composes the required HTML needed for adding an option to a list box. The function takes two values as arguments. The `ID` argument is the ID number of the record, which you use to set the `Value` parameter of the `ACTION` tag.

```
<%
Function WriteOption(ID,Display)
    WriteOption = "<OPTION value=" & _
    ID & ">" & _
    Display & "</OPTION>"
End Function
```

You can utilize the `WriteOption` function by another routine that constructs the HTML needed for the entire `SELECT` tag. The `InsertList` procedure shown in the following code is designed to take any recordset (`RS`) and build a list box based on the first two fields where field 0 is the ID and field 1 is the display text.

```
Sub InsertList(RS)
    Response.Write "<SELECT Name='" & RS(0).name & _
    "' Size=10>"
    Do Until guest.EOF
        Response.Write writeoption(RS(0),RS(1))
        Guest.MoveNext
    Loop
    Response.Write "</SELECT>"
End Sub
```

Another advantage of writing out the code as named procedures that pass parameters is that your VBScript becomes more easily reusable. When you mix VBScript with HTML, copying and pasting the code into another ASP is difficult. Using Gbookaddedit.Asp as a model, you can easily copy the code used to create the list box (`WriteOption` and `InsertList` procedures) to another ASP or store it in an include file.

One more function, `RSCount`, used in GbookMain.Asp page appears in the following code. This function returns a count of the number of records in any recordset.

```
Function RSCount(R)
    Do Until R.eof
        RSCount = rscount+1
        r.movenext
    Loop
    R.movefirst
End Function
%>
```

Note that all the code shown for the `RSCount` function comprises a single VBScript block that is inserted into the ASP page before the `<HTML>` tag. This makes sense because no explicit HTML code is involved.

After the HTML section of the document begins, you can write VBScript statements that reference the procedures you have defined at the beginning of the page. For example, suppose that you wanted to insert a list box control that shows the items in a recordset called `Guest` into you ASP. The following statement is all the VBScript required:

```
<%Call InsertList(Guest)%>
```

If you want that list box inserted into a cell within a table, your code looks like this:

```
<TR><TD><%Call InsertList(Guest)%></TD>
```

You can see that the preceding example reduces a great deal of clutter from your ASP. The code required to insert a complete list box is reduced to a single VBScript fragment which makes coding the HTML table much easier.

The remainder of the GbokkMain.Asp follows:

```
<HTML><BODY><!--#include file ="AdoDumCnt.inc"-->
<%    Set Guest = Server.CreateObject("ADODB.Recordset")
    Guest.Open _
    "SELECT GuestID, LastName + ', ' + FirstName As GuestName" & _
    " FROM GuestBook ORDER BY LastName + ', ' + FirstName", _
    cnt,3,1
%>
```

```
<H2>Guest Book <%=FormatDateTime(now())%>  <%=vbLongTime%></H2>
<H1>Guests: <%=rscount(Guest)%>
<FORM action="Gbookaddedit.asp" method=post>
<TABLE>
<TR><TD><%Call InsertList(Guest)%></TD>
<TD valign=top>
<INPUT Name="Action" type=submit value="Edit">
<INPUT name="Action" type=submit value="New">
<INPUT name="Action" type=submit value="Remove">
</TD></TABLE></FORM></BODY></HTML>
```

Reacting to Submit buttons

The GbookMain.Asp contains three INPUT tags (Edit, Insert, and Delete) that define Submit buttons, each with a different value. When a user clicks any one of the three buttons, that submits a request to the Web server for the document specified in the ACTION parameter of the FORM tag. Because the FORM tag permits only one m parameter, the same document (Gbookaddedit.Asp) is requested regardless of which button is clicked.

How can you implement the three different operations from the same ASP page? You need to structure the VBScript code in the ASP to perform different tasks based on the value of the Submit item in the Web server's form collection. Gbookaddedit.Asp contains the upcoming code. The code uses a select case structure, which evaluates the value of the action item in the form collection. Recall that in the GbookMain.Asp page all the Submit buttons were given the same Name parameter of Action. The value of Action varies depending upon which Submit buttons the user clicked.

The amount of code listed under each case consists of only two statements. The first statement opens the Guest recordset. If the action is Edit or Remove, then the Guest recordset consists of the record that matches the GuestID item in the form collection. If you go back to GbookMain.Asp, you see that the list box is assigned the name of the first field in the list box recordset, such as GuestID. If the action is New, the recordset uses GuestID 0 because, by definition, a new record isn't already contained in the table.

```
Select Case Request.Form("Action")
    Case "Edit"
        Guest.Open "SELECT " & Flist1 & _
        " FROM GuestBook WHERE Guestid = " _
        & Request.Form("Guestid"),cnt
        ListRS2Col Guest, "Edit"
    Case "New"
        Guest.Open "SELECT " & Flist2 & _
        " FROM GuestBook WHERE Guestid = 0",cnt
        ListRS2Col Guest, "New"
    Case "Remove"
        Guest.Open "SELECT " & Flist1 & " _
        FROM GuestBook WHERE Guestid = " _
    & Request.Form("Guestid"),cnt,1,3
        DropGuest Guest
End Select
```

Each case calls a VBScript procedure (either `ListRS2Col` or `DropGuest`) that is defined in the ASP before the HTML tag. The most complex procedure is `ListRS2Col`. Its function is to provide a screen form for editing an existing recordset or adding a new record to the GuestBook table. Figure 10-16 shows the form generated for editing the Rob Krumm guest book entry. Notice that instead of using the strictly vertical form layout shown in the previous examples, this form creates two parallel columns of fields and labels. This layout takes better advantage of the Web browser page display by spreading the information horizontally as well as vertically on the page.

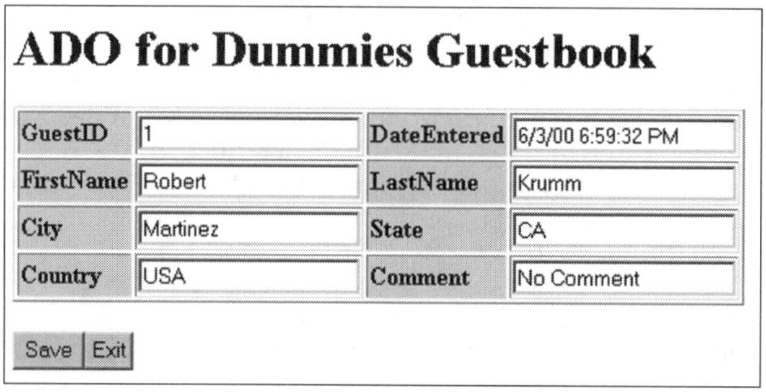

Figure 10-16:
VBScript generates a two-column form that displays the fields from a recordset.

ADO for Dummies Guestbook

GuestID	1	DateEntered	6/3/00 6:59:32 PM
FirstName	Robert	LastName	Krumm
City	Martinez	State	CA
Country	USA	Comment	No Comment

Save | Exit

Of course, this modified layout has programming implications. The basic technique is to provide a slightly different coding for even-numbered fields than for odd-numbered fields. For example, if you have an even-numbered field (assuming that zero is considered an even number), then you start a new row in the table (`<TR>` tag) but do not include an end-of-the-row tag (`</TR>`). Conversely, the odd-numbered fields have an end-of-the-row tag (`</TR>`) but no beginning-of-the-row tag (`<TR>`). The result is that the two fields appear on the same row of the table creating the two-column effect shown in Figure 10-16.

You can use the `Mod` operator to distinguish even from odd numbers. The following expression is false for even numbers but true for odd numbers.

```
If f mod 2 Then
```

The `Mod` (modulus) operator returns the remainder when one number is divided by another. Any number `Mod 2` yields either a zero (0; false) or a one (1; true) remainder. You can use the `Mod` operator to distinguish between odd and even numbers.

The `ListRS2Col` procedure shown in the following code creates a table that lists fields in the recordset `RS` in the two-column display shown in Figure 10-16. The function generates not only a table, but also a complete `FORM` tag including the `ACTION` parameter, which specifies the GBookSaveData.Asp as the document to request when the Submit button is clicked.

```
<%Sub ListRS2Col(RS, RsType)
    Response.Write "<FORM METHOD=Post ACTION = 'GBookSaveData.Asp'>" & _
    "<TABLE Border=1>"
    For F = 0 To RS.Fields.Count -1
        If f mod 2 Then
        Response.Write "<TD bgcolor=#d3d3d3><B>" & RS(f).Name & _
           "</B></TD><TD><INPUT Name='" & rs(f).Name & "' value='"
        If RsType = "Edit" Then
          Response.Write RS(f) & "'></TD></TR>"
         Else
          Response.Write "'></TD></TR>"
         End if
        Else
        Response.Write "<TR><TD bgcolor=#d3d3d3><B>" & RS(f).Name & _
           "</B></TD><TD><INPUT Name='" & rs(f).Name & "' value='"
        If RsType = "Edit" Then
          Response.Write RS(f) & "'></TD>"
         Else
          Response.Write "'></TD>"
         End if
        End If
    Next
    Response.Write "</TABLE><P><INPUT Name='Action' type=submit value='Save'>"
    Response.Write "<INPUT name='Action' type=submit value='Exit'>"
    Response.Write "<INPUT Name= 'DataTask' type='hidden' value='" & RsType &
              "'>"
    Response.Write "</P></FORM>"
End Sub
```

The form generated by the ListRS2Col procedure is used for both editing an
existing record and adding a new record. The only difference between editing
an existing record and inserting a new record is the section of the procedure
shown next. This section controls the value parameter of the INPUT tag for
each field. If the user clicks the Edit button on the GBookMain.Asp page, the
current value of the field is inserted into the tag. If the user clicks the New
button, the text box is assigned an empty value. This simple distinction
makes it possible for a single form to perform all three operations.

```
If RsType = "Edit" Then
    Response.Write RS(f) & "'></TD></TR>"
Else
    Response.Write "'></TD></TR>"
End if
```

Saving form data

Keep in mind that while the form on the ASP appears to provide the impres-
sion that it is linked to the corresponding records in the database, there is no
actual connection. When the user edits data or enters new data in the displayed text boxes, those changes have no effect on the data source.

How can you get the new or changed data back into the corresponding
records in the data source? The answer is that you need to create an ASP that
contains VBScript code that reads the values submitted to the Web server's

form collection and writes them back to the data source. In the Gbookaddedit.Asp page, the specified document for Edit and New is the GBookSaveData.Asp page.

GBookSaveData.Asp reverses the processes performed by Gbookaddedit.Asp, which places database information in an HTML form. GBookSaveData.Asp takes that in an HTML form and uses ADO to write it to a data source.

One of the interesting characteristics of GBookSaveData.Asp is that none of its tasks generate any HTML. Saving new or edited data to the data source requires only VBScript. There's no HTML to be displayed in the browser. Put another way, the operation of this page is invisible. When the data is saved, you can simply return to an appropriate page, like GbookMain.Asp.

The IIS Web server supports an operation called *redirection*. Redirection is a VBScript instruction that causes the Web server to load a specified page just as if the user had entered the URL onto the address line of the browser. The redirection feature is executed by calling the Redirection method, which is part of the Web server's Response object. The following statement is equivalent to a user clicking a hyperlink to GbookMain.Asp:

```
Response.Redirect "GbookMain.Asp"
```

You must insert Redirect into the ASP before the <HTML> tag. In this case, GBookSaveData.Asp contains only VBScript and no HTML at all. The contents of GBookSaveData.Asp are shown in the upcoming code. The last statement is the Redirect method. From the users' point of view, they go from the Gbookaddedit.Asp back to the GbookMain.Asp page because GBookSaveData.Asp produces no HTML. Of course, it's GBookSaveData.Asp that actually forms the connection between the HTML forms and the data source.

```
<% Set Cnt = Server.CreateObject("ADODB.Connection")
   cnt.Open "Provider=SQLOLEDB;Data Source=208.222.107.6;" & _
   "UID=ubad1d1;pwd=21@1n3z"
 If Request.Form("Action") = "Save" Then
   Set Guest = Server.CreateObject("ADODB.Recordset")
   If Request.Form("datatask") = "New" Then
      Guest.Open "GuestBook",cnt,1,3
      Guest.addnew
      For Each F in Request.Form
          Select case f
          Case "ACTION","DATATASK","GUESTID"
             'do Nothing
          Case Else
              Guest(F) = Trim(Request.Form(F))
          End Select
      Next
      Guest("DateChanged") = Now()
      Guest("DateEntered") = Now()
      Guest.Update
```

```
    Else
        Guest.Open "SELECT * FROM GuestBook WHERE Guestid=" _
        & Request.Form("GuestID"),cnt,1,3
        For Each F in Request.Form
            Select case f
              Case "ACTION","DATATASK","GUESTID"
                    'do Nothing
              Case Else
                    Guest(F) = Trim(Request.Form(F))
            End Select
        Next
        Guest("DateChanged") = Now()
        Guest.Update
    End if
  Guest.Close
  Cnt.Close
  End if
  Response.Redirect "GbookMain.Asp"%>
```

Because the preceding code is somewhat complex, it may be useful to break down some of the functions and look at how they're accomplished. First, the procedure checks the value of the `Action` form item to determine whether the user wants to save the changes or additions they have made.

```
If Request.Form("Action") = "Save" Then
```

Next, the datatask form item determines whether form data represents a new record to be added to the data source or editing changes made to an existing record. If the record is a new insert, then you use the `AddNew` method to create a record in the data source.

```
If Request.Form("datatask") = "New" Then
    Guest.Open "GuestBook",cnt,1,3
    Guest.addnew
```

Conversely, if the task is editing, you create the recordset by locating the records in the data source that have the same `GuestID` as the `GuestID` item in the form collection.

```
Guest.Open "SELECT * FROM GuestBook WHERE Guestid=" _
& Request.Form("GuestID"),cnt,1,3
```

Loop structure performs the actual field updates as shown in the following code. Note that the loop cycles through the elements in the form collection. You can perform an update by using the form item name as the field name for the `Guest` recordset. Some elements in the form collection, like the buttons included in the HTML form, don't correspond to recordset fields. The first case statement lists the items that shouldn't be used to update the recordset. Included in this list is the `GuestID`. While this does correspond to a field, you don't want to allow the user to change the ID number during an edit. In addition, the `GuestID` field for new records is automatically generated by the data source.

```
For Each F in Request.Form
   Select case f
      Case "ACTION","DATATASK","GUESTID"
         'do Nothing
      Case Else
         Guest(F) = Trim(Request.Form(F))
   End Select
Next
```

Deleting a record

The final operation needed to complete the guest book is the ability to delete a record. You don't need to use the Gbookaddedit.Asp page to display the recordset data in order to delete a record. Instead, all you need to do is add a Remove button to the GbookMain.Asp.

The following procedure deletes the selected guest record and skips the field display. The code is associated with the Remove button. DropGuest deletes the current record and displays the messages, as shown in Figure 10-17. The Back hyperlink returns the user to the GbookMain.Asp.

The procedure is executed of the Remove button on GbookMain.Asp is clicked.

Figure 10-17:
The
DropGuest
procedure
removes a
record from
the
database.

ADO for Dummies Guestbook

Hart, Heather removed.

Back

```
Sub DropGuest(RS)
   Response.Write "<H2>" & Guest("LastName") & ", " & Guest("FirstName") & "
               removed." & "</H2><BR>"
   Rs.Delete
   Rs.Close
   Response.Write "<A href='gbookmain.asp'>Back</A>"
End Sub
```

Chapter 11

Server-Side Custom Database Objects

* *

In This Chapter

▶ Building ActiveX Server components

▶ Writing class modules

▶ Installing an ActiveX component on a server

▶ Accessing custom components from an ASP

▶ Building components that return ADO recordsets

▶ Building components that return HTML streams

* *

*B*uilding ActiveX components that encapsulate common business objects, such as the summary statistic shown in this chapter, can improve both the performance and coding issues associated with data-oriented ASPs.

The techniques in this chapter feel like a giant leap in complexity from the ASPs created in Chapters 9 and 10. That feeling is only partially justified. The actual ADO programming is on about the same level of complexity as the other examples in this book. The difference is that creating and deploying ActiveX components require more precision than placing the same ADO code into an Access form or an ASP.

Creating Server-side Objects

Chapters 9 and 10 explain how to use ADO within Active Server Pages (ASPs) to produce Web pages that draw some or all of their content from interactions with a data source such as a SQL Server database.

If you look at the code examples in Chapters 9 and 10, you notice that the code examples have evolved. The first ASP examples combined HTML and VBScript in an ad hoc, unstructured way. Wherever a VBScript statement was needed, it was inserted into the HTML code using the <% %> tags. The guest book example at the end of Chapter 10 provides a more structured example. In the GbookMain.Asp, Gbookaddedit.Asp, and GBookSaveData.Asp documents, as much of the VBScript as possible was placed into structured procedures that were placed outside the HTML tags within the ASP document.

The programming techniques shown in Chapters 9 and 10 illustrate how easily ADO can create Web pages with content that is closely controlled by and linked to ADO data sources.

On the other hand, the coding issues that arise indicate a simple fact. ADO isn't Web oriented. Because ADO can be used in so many different contexts (such as VB, VBA, and ASP), the data returned by ADO is simply unformatted text or date or numeric data. It is up to the programmer to place this data in a display structure, such as a Visual Basic form or a Web-server HTML page.

In general, this approach makes a lot of sense. The tools for creating user interfaces, such as Access and Visual Basic forms, are powerful and easy to use. As shown in Chapter 8, you can use ActiveX controls to easily display complex data structures with a minimal amount of coding.

However, when coding ASPs, it is difficult to easily separate operational logic (create a recordset with a certain content) from the user interface code. For example, suppose you want to display the contents of a recordset in a row and column display. In an HTML document, there is no easy way to get this done. The only way to get this done is to write code that processes the recordset field by field, record by record, adding HTML coding as needed to generate tables, rows, and cells required.

Chapters 9 and 10 show that you can do this two ways:

- ✔ **Insert script:** Do the primary coding in HTML and insert fragments of VBScript into the HTML code when needed using the <% %> tags. When you take this approach, coding a loop that processes a recordset may require a dozen or more separate VBScript fragments inserted among various HTML tags.

- ✔ **Response.Write script statements:** Code primarily in VBScript. When you need to generate HTML, you add the HTML as text and send the result to the page using the Response.Write method.

In addition, you may notice that many of the coding issues tend to be repetitions of frequently used data/display combinations, such as showing a recordset in a table and editing a record in a form.

ADO Programming For Dummies®

Cheat Sheet

ADO 2.5 Objects, Methods, and Properties

Connection

Properties	Methods
Attributes	BeginTrans
CommandTimeout	Cancel
ConnectionString	Close
ConnectionTimeout	CommitTrans
CursorLocation	Execute
DefaultDatabase	Open
Errors	OpenSchema
IsolationLevel	RollbackTrans
Mode	
Properties	
Provider	
State	
Version	

Command

Properties	Methods
ActiveConnection	Cancel
CommandText	CreateParameter
CommandTimeout	Execute
CommandType	
Name	
Parameters	
Prepared	
Properties	
State	

Recordset

Properties	Methods
AbsolutePage	AddNew
AbsolutePosition	Cancel
ActiveCommand	CancelBatch
ActiveConnection	CancelUpdate
BOF	Clone
Bookmark	Close
CacheSize	CompareBookmarks
CursorLocation	Delete
CursorType	Find
DataMember	GetRows
DataSource	GetString
EditMode	Move
EOF	MoveFirst
Fields	MoveLast
Filter	MoveNext
Index	MovePrevious
LockType	NextRecordset
MarshalOptions	Open
MaxRecords	Requery
PageCount	Resync
PageSize	Save
Properties	Seek
RecordCount	Supports
Sort	Update
Source	UpdateBatchCommand
State	
Status	
StayInSync	
Supports	

ADO Programming For Dummies®

Cheat Sheet

Parameter

Properties	Methods
Attributes	AppendChunk
Direction	
Name	
NumericScale	
Precision	
Properties	
Size	
Type	
Value	

Stream

Properties	Methods
Charset	Cancel
EOS	Close
LineSeparator	CopyTo
Mode	Flush
Position	LoadFromFile
Size	Open
State	Read
Type	ReadText
	SaveToFile
	SetEOS
	SkipLine
	Write
	WriteText

Field

Properties	Methods
ActualSize	AppendChunk
Attributes	GetChunk
DataFormat	
DefinedSize	
Name	
NumericScale	
OriginalValue	
Precision	
Properties	
Status	
Type	
UnderlyingValue	
Value	

Record

Properties	Methods
ActiveConnection	Cancel
Fields	Close
Mode	CopyRecord
ParentURL	DeleteRecord
Properties	GetChildren
RecordType	MoveRecord
Source	Open
State	

For Dummies®: Bestselling Book Series for Beginners

It is very useful if, instead of getting unformatted data from an ADO recordset object, server-based objects can return both the HTML tags and the data source data. This makes creation of ASP applications simpler and faster. In addition, if you want to change the display style of an object (such as a recordset in table), you just modify the server object and the ASPs that use that object.

It turns out that Visual Basic 6.0 provides just the tool to move your ASP coding to the next level. The tool comes in the form of ActiveX DLL projects. An ActiveX DLL is a Visual Basic program that can be installed on an IIS Web server to provide customer designed objects for ASPs.

Because Visual Basic can use ADO to perform database operations, you can build ActiveX DLLs that provide data-enhanced objects for use with ASPs. In this chapter, you create custom-designed Web-server objects.

Component objects

When you add ADO statements to an ASP, you are adding a layer of complexity to the process that generates the HTML that is returned to the Web browsers. ADO isn't part of the Web server. It isn't part of Visual basic or Access for that matter. Then what is it?

ADO is an example of a *COM object*. COM stands for Component Object Model. It refers to method of creating executable programs that are modular in nature. A COM program is capable of interacting with other COM-compliant applications, typically in a client/server fashion.

The diagram in Figure 11-1 shows what takes place when an ASP creates a recordset:

1. **When the Web server finds a reference to an ADOBE object within the VBScript of an ASP, the Web server loads a program called MSADO15.DLL into memory (if it isn't already there).**

2. **MSADO15.DLL passes the ADO instructions to the program for processing.**

3. **The DLL carries out the operations and returns the data to the Web server.**

4. **The data server converts the data into HTML and returns it to the user's browser window.**

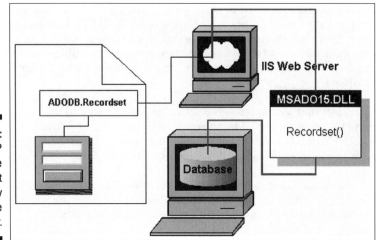

Figure 11-1:
An ASP
employs the
ADO object
indirectly
through the
Web server.

What is significant about the process shown in Figure 11-1 is that the MSADO15.DLL program is the same program that is used by such programs as Access, Visual Basic, and Excel when those programs perform ADO data operations. The reason that all of these different applications can utilize the same DLL is that it was designed to fit the COM object standards. Once installed on a computer, such as a Web server, any COM-compliant application can use the functions provided by the COM object:

✔ **You can build your own custom-designed COM objects, install them on a Web server, and utilize the functions provided by the object in ASPs.**

✔ **The COM standard isn't language dependent.**

  In practical terms, it means that you don't need to program in C++ to create your own customized object DLLs. Visual Basic 6.0 can create COM objects that you can deploy on your Web server and take advantage of in any ASPs running on that server.

✔ **COM objects can interact with each other.** If you build your own custom-designed object, you can include code in that object that interacts with other objects, such as ADO.

The example in this chapter is a new version of the Guest Book ASP application created at the end of Chapter 10. The example uses custom designed objects that provide fully formatted HTML directly to your Active Server Pages.

Enhanced date information

In most of the applications I develop, there is often a need to work with certain specific types of dates. For example, if you are reporting, you often need the first and last days of any given month as the default values.

It is easy to find today's date using the `Date` or `Now` functions. But what is the first day of the current month? Or the last? Or the first business day of the week? Or the last business day of the week?

The following expression written in Visual Basic calculates the first day of the current month.

```
DateSerial(Year(Date),Month(Date), 1)
```

The last day gets a bit trickier because the length of the months varies. The following expression shows how you can calculate the last day of the current month in VB/VBA.

```
DateAdd("m", 1, DateSerial(Year(vInitDate), Month(vInitDate), 1)) - 1
```

These date calculations, and others like them, come up so frequently that I decided to create a reusable object to provide the date information.

ActiveX DLL projects

If you want to enhance your Web server by adding custom-designed objects, you can use Visual Basic 6.0 to create ActiveX DLLs. ActiveX DLL is a special type of Visual basic program that isn't designed as a stand-alone application. Instead, it creates a DLL file that can be registered as a component object on any computer. If you install the DLL on a Web server, you can use the VBScript `Server.CreateObject( )` method to access the properties and methods from within an ASP.

While a full explanation of Visual Basic ActiveX programming is outside the scope of this book, it is a fairly simple matter to create small but useful objects. The example here creates a DLL called `AdoDum` that has an object called `DateValues`.

The first step is to create an ActiveX DLL project.

1. **Start Visual Basic.**

   In the New Project dialog box, click the ActiveX DLL icon and then click Open.

2. **Open the Project Explorer window by pressing Ctrl+R.**

3. **Click the default project name Project1.**

4. **Open the properties dialog box by pressing F4.**

5. **Change the Name property to AdoDum.**

6. **In the Project Explorer window, click the default name, Class1.**

7. **In the Properties dialog box, change the Name property to DateValues.**

The project explorer should not show the project and class names (see Figure 11-2).

Figure 11-2:
The
AdoDum
ActiveX DLL
project
contains a
class called
DateValues.

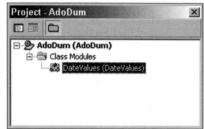

When you create an ActiveX DLL, the project contains one or more classes. A *class* is the programming code that creates an object. When the program runs, each class module provides an object that you can use in your ASP.

The names you create here are the names you use in your ASP later when you want to access the properties and methods of the object. The name of the project is the prefix to the object name. The object name is the name of the class. The following statement shows how you create an object based on the DateValues class in the AdoDum project.

```
Set DI = Server.CreateObject("AdoDum.DateValues")
```

Property procedures

Programming ActiveX DLLs is a bit different than writing standard VB/VBA code. ActiveX DLLs operate under the COM object model in which objects provide information in the form of properties.

When you create your own DLL, you write special procedures called *property procedures.* Property procedures come in two types:

✔ **Property Let:** A Let procedure is used to assign a value to a property. The data specified for the property is assigned to the variable VnewValue. Typically, the new value is assigned to a module level variable (vInitDate in this example) so it is available to other procedures in the same class.

```
Public Property Let InitDate(ByVal vNewValue As Variant)
    vInitDate = vNewValue
End Property
```

In an application, such as an ASP, you assign an InitDate value to the object with a statement like the one below.

```
DI.InitDate = #12/31/00#
```

✔ **Property Get:** A Get procedure determines what information the object provides when a reference is made to the property. The following procedure, FirstofMonth, uses the value of the vInitDate variable to calculate the first day of the month in which the vInitDate falls.

```
Public Property Get FirstofMonth() As Variant
    FirstofMonth = DateSerial(Year(vInitDate), _
        Month(vInitDate), 1)
End Property
```

The following statement shows how you use the FirstofMonth property to insert a date into the Response object of an ASP.

```
Response.Write DI.FirstOfMonth
```

The initialize event

Another feature of class modules is the Initialize and Terminate events. The Initialize event takes place when an instance of the object is created. The Terminate event takes place when the object is closed.

The Initialize event is useful for setting initial conditions or values that server as defaults for the object. In the case of the DateValues object, you can use the Initialize event to assign the current systems date as the vInitdate so that as soon as a DateValues is created, it already has a valid date. Following is the Initialize procedure used in the DateValues class.

```
Private Sub Class_Initialize()
    vInitDate = Date
End Sub
```

Creating a method

An object method is an instruction that causes the object to perform some action. In ADO, the Command object has an Execute method that executes the specified command against the data provider.

You can create a method for your own objects by adding Sub or Function procedures to your class module. The following procedure adds a method called NextMonth to the DateValues object. The purpose of this method is to increment the vInitDate date value forward by one month. Because all of the date properties in the dateValues class are calculated relative to the vInitDate value, then using the NextMonth method moves all of the date properties forward one month.

```
Sub NextMonth()
    vInitDate = DateAdd("m", 1, vInitDate)
End Sub
```

The following sample code displays the last day of the current month and then the last day of the next month because the NextMonth method changes the vInitDate of the DateValues object to the next month.

```
Response.Write DI.LastofMonth
DI.NextMonth
Response.Write DI.LastofMonth
```

Entering the class module code

To begin entering the code for the class module, simply double-click DateValues in the Project Explorer. The full code of the DateValues class is shown below.

```
Option Explicit
Dim vInitDate
Private Sub Class_Initialize()
    vInitDate = Date
End Sub
Public Property Get FirstofMonth() As Variant
    FirstofMonth = DateSerial(Year(vInitDate), _
        Month(vInitDate), 1)
End Property
Public Property Get LastofMonth() As Variant
    LastofMonth = DateAdd("m", 1, _
                  DateSerial(Year(vInitDate), _
                  Month(vInitDate), 1))- 1
End Property
Public Property Get InitDate() As Variant
    InitDate = vInitDate
End Property
Public Property Let InitDate(ByVal vNewValue As Variant)
    vInitDate = vNewValue
End Property
Public Property Get LastofBizWeek() As Variant
    LastofBizWeek = vInitDate + (6 - Weekday(vInitDate))
End Property
```

```
Public Property Get FirstofBizWeek() As Variant
    FirstofBizWeek = vInitDate - (Weekday(vInitDate) - 2)
End Property

Sub NextMonth()
    vInitDate = DateAdd("m", 1, vInitDate)
End Sub
Sub PreviousMonth()
    vInitDate = DateAdd("m", -1, vInitDate)
End Sub
Sub NextWeek()
    vInitDate = DateAdd("ww", 1, vInitDate)
End Sub
Sub PreviousWeek()
    vInitDate = DateAdd("ww", -1, vInitDate)
End Sub
```

Testing your class module

It is important to keep in mind that, unlike standard programs, class modules do not have a starting point. There is no direct way to run the class module. If you want to test the code you have written, you must access the properties and methods of your class by using another application. To facilitate testing, Visual Basic allows you to have multiple projects open so that you can test one project by using another.

To test an ActiveX project, do the following:

1. **Choose File⇨Add Project.**

2. **Select Standard.EXE from the New Project dialog box and then click Open.**

3. **Click the Form1 form.**

4. **Right-click anywhere on the form and select View Code from the pop-up menu that appears.**

   The Form_Load Procedure appears.

5. **Open the Reference dialog box by choosing Project⇨References.**

   The references dialog box, pictured in Figure 11-3, now shows an object library called AdoDum. This is a reference to the ActiveX DLL that you have created in the AdoDum ActiveX DLL project.

6. **Select the reference you want.**

   Figure 11-3 shows selecting the AdoDum reference.

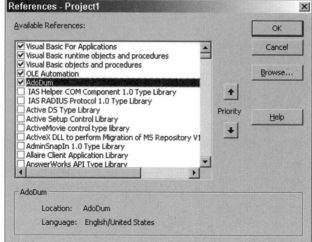

Figure 11-3:
The
References
dialog box
shows the
ActiveX
project as
an object
library.

You can now enter code that refers to the properties and methods of the object you have created, AdoDum. The following procedure tests the code in the ActiveX project to see if it can produce the desired date values.

As you enter the code, Visual Basic displays autocomplete lists. The list shows the properties and methods of the ActiveX project, as shown in Figure 11-4.

```
Private Sub Form_Load()
    Dim DI As New AdoDum.DateValues
    MsgBox DI.LastofMonth
    DI.NextMonth
    MsgBox DI.LastofMonth
End Sub
```

Figure 11-4:
The AdoDum
project
contains its
own list of
properties
and
methods.

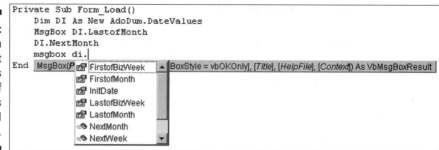

To run the test code, you must designate the test project, Project1, as the Start project.

1. **In the Visual Basic Project Explorer, click the project that you want to test.**

   For this example, select Project1.

2. **Right-click and choose Select as Start Up from the pop-up menu that appears.**

3. **Press F5 to run the test.**

   Two consecutive message boxes show an end-of-the-month date. The two dates are one month apart due to the effect of the NextMonth method.

4. **End the program by choosing Run➪End.**

Installing the DLL

To use an ActiveX DLL such as AdoDum:

✓ Create a Setup package for the program.

✓ Use that Setup package to install the DLL on the IIS Web-server computer that processes the ASPs for the object you created.

When you finish coding and testing the ActiveX DLL project, exit Visual Basic and save the project files in the desired location.

If you build the components on the Web server, they are automatically installed on the system in the testing process. You need an installation package when you build the code on one machine, and then you need to transfer it to the Web server.

You can create an installation package using the Package & Deployment Wizard. Follow these steps:

1. **Choose Start➪Microsoft Visual Studio 6.0 Tools➪Package & Deployment Wizard.**

   Wait for the Package & Deployment Wizard to load.

2. **Click Browse to locate the project you want to create a package for.**

3. **Click Package.**

   If a DLL file hasn't been compiled for the project, click Compile and wait for the DLL to compile.

4. **Select Standard Setup Package, and then click Next.**

5. **Select the location to store the Setup package.**

You should select a location that is accessible by the Web server computer on which you want to install the DLL.

6. **Click Next in the Included Files screen.**

7. **Select Single Cab, and then click Next.**

8. **Accept the default name for the installation title, and then click Next.**

9. **Click Next on the Start Menu Items screen.**

10. **Click Next on the Install Locations screen.**

11. **Click Next on the Shared Files screen.**

12. **Click Finished to create the package.**

Wait for the package to be created.

13. **Click Close twice to exit the Package & Deployment wizard.**

You are now ready to install the DLL on the Web server. Access the Web server that processes the ASPs so you can run the Setup package. (In many cases, your access to the server is via a remote control program, such as PCAnyWhere.)

Follow these steps to install the DLL:

1. **Open the folder that contains the Setup program for the project.**

2. **In the folder, double click the Setup icon.**

3. **Follow the prompts to install the DLL.**

The ActiveX project is installed on the Web server. It can now be accessed through the ASPs processed by that computer.

Using the AdoDum object

Once you have run the Setup program on your IIS Web server, the new object, AdoDum, is available for use in ASP pages. Following is the code for the DataInfo1.Asp. The VBScript code in this document uses the CreateObject method to create an instance of the AdoDum object created earlier.

```
<HTML><BODY>
<H1>Data Information Object</H1>
<% Set DI = Server.CreateObject("AdoDum.DateValues")%>
Today is <% =date %><BR>
Month Begins: <% =DI.FirstOfMonth%><BR>
Month Ends:   <% =DI.LastofMonth%>
</BODY></HTML>
```

The custom object is treated exactly like any other available object. Once created, the code

- ✔ References properties of that object
- ✔ Places the properties into the Response object of the Web server by using VBScript fragments

The `Initialize` event of this object automatically sets the default date for the object to today's date. When you load DataInfo1.Asp, you see the beginning and ending month dates for the current month, as shown in Figure 11-5.

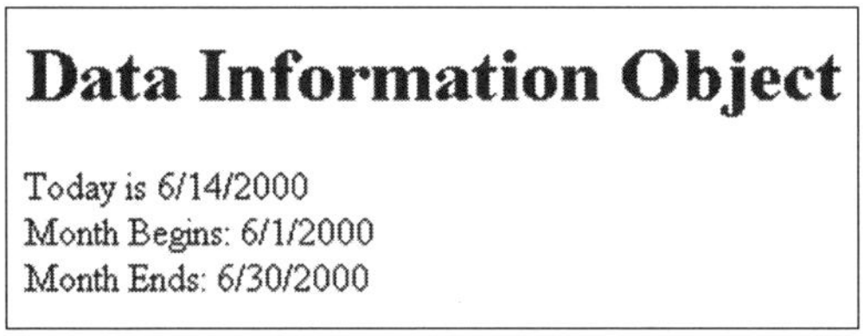

Figure 11-5:
Custom object AdoDum provides date values to an ASP.

Data Information Object

Today is 6/14/2000
Month Begins: 6/1/2000
Month Ends: 6/30/2000

Components That Return Recordsets

Some of the most frequently used ADO components access database information. The `DateInfo` component furnishes date values that you may often use in an application:

- ✔ By placing the detailed code into a component, you can get to the desired values without duplicating the code in every application or Web page that you create.
- ✔ Components make other design and programming tasks simpler and less tedious.

Someone creating a Web page does not need to know how to calculate the last day of the month. They can reference the `LastofMonth` property.

When you use ADO to access a data provider, the item returned is typically a recordset object. You can apply the same logic used with the `DateInfo` component to commonly used set of records. For example, this logic is applied in the data displayed in Figure 11-6. The data summarizes the sales history of a specific product SKU, as shown in Figure 11-7.

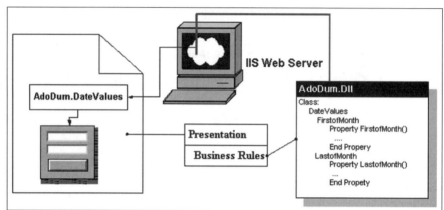

Figure 11-6: A business process returns a particular set of records.

Figure 11-7: A Web page displays the sales history for a specific product, SKU.

Sales History for SKU 15

Year	Month	Period	Units	Amount
1999	4	1999-April	1	16
1999	5	1999-May	12	192
1999	6	1999-June	8	128
1999	7	1999-July	12	192

How do you create a Web page like Figure 11-7? There are three basic steps. Each choice uses a different type of technology:

- ✔ **SQL relational query:** The rows and columns of data shown in Figure 11-7 are not part of any table in the database. Rather, they are the result of a SQL statement that performs operations such as `JOIN` and `GROUP BY` to arrive at the desired data set. The data provider performs this task.

- ✔ **Create a recordset:** The SQL statement itself isn't an object. The statement itself does not provide anything that your VB, VBA, or VBScript code can manipulate. ADO transforms the SQL statement into a data object that can be manipulated by an application.

- ✔ **Merge data with HTML:** The final step is to combine the data with the appropriate HTML coding to display the information on a Web page.

In Chapters 9 and 10, all three of these operations are coded together. In a component-oriented approach, you isolate each task in its own level of component operation.

SQL relational query

You start the component-oriented approach with the SQL component. Following is a SQL statement that returns the sales summary data shown in Figure 11-7.

```
SELECT  DatePart(Year,OrderDate) AS Year,
    DatePart(Month,OrderDate) As Month,
    Convert(Varchar(4),DatePart(Year,OrderDate))
    + '-' + DateName(month,OrderDate) As Period,
    Sum(D.Bottles) As Units,
    Sum(D.ExtPrice) as Amount
  FROM WineProductCatalog P, OrderDetails D, Orders O
  WHERE P.WineID = D.WineID
    AND D.OrderLink = O.WineOrderID
    AND P.WineID = @WID
  GROUP BY DatePart(Year,OrderDate),
    DatePart(Month,OrderDate),
    Convert(Varchar(4),DatePart(Year,OrderDate))
    + '-' + DateName(month,OrderDate)
```

 While it is possible to insert the text of the preceding statement into an ASP (that is how you have been doing it), the most efficient way to execute this statement is to turn it into a SQL Server stored procedure called WineProdSalesHist. The @WID in the statement indicates where a WineID parameter should be inserted. Once created as a SQL server procedure, you can access the data with a much simpler statement, like this:

```
WineProdSalesHist 15
```

Create a recordset

A server-based object can handle the ADO details and return the completed recordset to the application.

The following three statements show how this is processed. The first line creates an instance of an ActiveX component called OrderInfo1.SalesInfo. To obtain the data displayed in Figure 11-7, do the following:

🗸 Set the WineID value to the correct product.

🗸 Use the ProductSalesHistory property to return a complete ADO recordset that contains the specified data.

```
Set S = Server.CreateObject("OrderInfo1.SalesInfo")
S.WineID = 15
Set Prod = S.ProductSalesHistory
```

This approach

- ✔ Simplifies development of data-enhanced pages by placing another level of service between the data consumer (the ASP) and the data provider.

- ✔ Changes the terminology of ADO concepts to such business process terms as Products, Sales, and Customers.

- ✔ Allows someone assembling a Web page to insert ADO data without dealing with ADO coding.

Creating a recordset property

When you create a VB/VBA class module, all of the Property procedures are defined by default as a Variant data type. However, you can change that designation so that you can return any sort of object as a property. In this case, the goal is to create Property procedures that provide complete ADO recordsets as their values. As shown in the preceding example, this type of procedure copies a complete recordset to an application without writing the complete ADO code. The ProductSalesHistory procedure is defined as an ADO recordset.

In this example, the data for the recordset is extracted using the preceding SQL Server stored procedure, WineProdSalesHist:

```
Public Property Get ProductSalesHistory() _
    As ADODB.Recordset
    Dim Cmd As New ADODB.Command
    Cmd.ActiveConnection = vCnt
    Cmd.CommandText = "WineProdSalesHist " & vWineID
    Set ProductSalesHistory = Cmd.Execute
End Property
```

Because the procedure returns an object, not a value, the Set command is used to assign the result of the Execute method against the Cmd command object. The procedure uses a variable, vWineID, to set the parameter for the stored procedure. That value is obtained by the following standard property procedure:

```
Public Property Let WineID(ByVal vNewValue As Integer)
    vWineID = vNewValue
End Property
```

Another variable in ProductSalesHistory is vCnt, which is used as the connection object for the command. Because all of the ADO operations in the OrderInfo1.SalesInfo component will use the same data provider, the connection can be established once (when the object is first referenced), and then are used by all of the procedures within the component. This is accomplished through the use of the `Initialize` procedure. This procedure, a part of every class module, automatically fires with each new instance of the object I created. This creates an ADO connection when the object is initialized.

```
Dim vCnt As New ADODB.Connection
Dim vWineID, vCustomerID

Private Sub Class_Initialize()
    vCnt.Open "Provider=SQLOLEDB;" & _
    "Data Source=ADODUM;UID=UBAD1D1;PWD=21@1n3z"
End Sub
```

In addition to the properties already defined, the `SalesInfo` class has four additional properties that return recordsets. Each recordset is associated with a stored procedure:

- ✔ `CustomerProductHistory` lists what products that were purchased by a customer.
- ✔ `ActiveCustomerList` lists all customers that have at least one order.
- ✔ `ActiveProductList` lists all products that have been sold.
- ✔ `CustomerSalesHistory` lists the orders for each customer.

The following code creates these recordsets:

```
Public Property Get CustomerProductHistory() As Recordset
    Dim Cmd As New ADODB.Command
    Cmd.ActiveConnection = vCnt
    Cmd.CommandText = "ProdCustSalesHist " & vCustomerID
    Set CustomerProductHistory = Cmd.Execute
End Property
Public Property Get ActiveCustomerList() As Recordset
    Dim Cmd As New ADODB.Command
    Cmd.ActiveConnection = vCnt
    Cmd.CommandText = "ActiveCustomers"
    Set ActiveCustomerList = Cmd.Execute
End Property
Public Property Get ActiveProductList() As Recordset
    Dim Cmd As New ADODB.Command
    Cmd.ActiveConnection = vCnt
    Cmd.CommandText = "ActiveProducts"
    Set ActiveProductList = Cmd.Execute
End Property
Public Property Get CustomerSalesHistory() As Recordset
    Dim Cmd As New ADODB.Command
    Cmd.ActiveConnection = vCnt
    Cmd.CommandText = "CustomerSalesHist " & vCustomerID
    Set CustomerSalesHistory = Cmd.Execute
End Property
```

The code for this ActiveX component is found in `OrderInfo1.Vbp`.

Using the recordset in an ASP

Once the ActiveX component DLL has been installed on the Web server, you can use the object and its properties to create ASPs.

Following is RSActiveX1.Asp. In the following example, there are no ADO objects explicitly mentioned. The `SalesInfo` object stores an ADO recordset in the `Prod` variable, which is then used to fill a table. The `WineID` number is supplied through a querystring, variable so this page can display the statistics for any product.

```
<%@ Language=VBScript %>
<HTML><BODY>
<% Set S = server.CreateObject("OrderInfo1.SalesInfo")
    S.WineID = Request.QueryString("WID")
    Set Prod = S.ProductSalesHistory
%>
<H1>History SKU <% = Request.QueryString("WID")%></H1>
<TABLE Border=1><TR>
<TD>Year</TD><TD>Month</TD><TD>Period</TD>
<TD>Units</TD><TD>Amount</TD></TR>
<%Do Until Prod.eof%>
<TR>
<%  For Each F in Prod.Fields%>
    <TD><%=F.Value%></TD>
<%  Next%>
</TR>
<%Prod.movenext
loop%>
</TABLE></BODY></HTML>
```

When you load RSActiveX1.Asp with the querystring `WID=15`, as shown in the following code, you produce a table like the table in Figure 11-7.

```
http://208.185.177.211/chp11X/RSActiveX1.Asp?WID=15
```

You can use the object returned by the `SalesInfo` methods in any way that you use an ADO recordset. The following example of this is RSActiveX2.Asp. This page uses the `ActiveProductList` of the ActiveX component to generate a series of hyperlinks. Each link shows the name of a product. When clicked, the link calls RSActiveX1.Asp with a querystring that corresponds to the product's `WineID`.

```
<%@ Language=VBScript %>
<HTML><BODY>
<%Set S = server.CreateObject("OrderInfo1.SalesInfo")
  Set CList = S.ActiveProductList
  Do Until CList.Eof
  Response.Write "<A Href='RSActiveX1.Asp?WID=" & _
    CList("WineID") & "'>" & CList("Vintage") & " " & _
    CList("WineName") & "</A><BR>"
  CList.MoveNext
  Loop
%></BODY></HTML>
```

When you load RSActiveX2.Asp (see Figure 11-8) and click a link, the RSActivex1.Asp loads the corresponding product's statistics.

Figure 11-8:
Custom
component
returns a
recordset
that lists
active
customers.

1987 East Valley Cabernet Standard
1988 Santa Cruz Cabernet Reserve
1988 North Valley Chardonnay Reserve
1989 South Valley Cabernet Reserve
1989 North Coast Cabernet Standard
1990 North Coast Cabernet Reserve
1991 South Valley Cabernet Reserve
1992 South Valley Cabernet Reserve
1993 Santa Barbara Bordeaux Blend Reserve
1993 Santa Barbara Bordeaux Blend Reserve
1993 South Valley Cabernet Standard
1993 South Valley Cabernet Standard
1994 East Valley Bordeaux Blend Reserve
1994 South Valley Bordeaux Blend Reserve
1994 East Valley Cabernet Standard
1994 North Coast Cabernet Standard
1994 North Valley Cabernet Standard

You can do the same thing with the `ActiveCustomerList` property. RSActiveX3.Asp displays a list of hyperlinks for the active customers, as shown in the following example:

```
<%@ Language=VBScript %>
<HTML><BODY>
<%Set S = server.CreateObject("OrderInfo1.SalesInfo")
  Set CList = S.ActiveCustomerList
  Do Until CList.Eof
    Response.Write "<A Href='RSActiveX4.Asp?WID=" & _
      CList("CustomerID") & "'>" & CList("Fullname") & " " & _
      CList("ShipState") & "</A><BR>"
    CList.MoveNext
  Loop%></BODY></HTML>
```

The RSActiveX4.Asp, which follows, is called by the hyperlinks in RSActiveX.Asp3 for each customer on the list. In this page, the `SalesInfo` component provides two recordsets.

```
<%@ Language=VBScript %>
<HTML><BODY>
<% Set S = server.CreateObject("OrderInfo1.SalesInfo")
   S.Customerid = Request.QueryString("WID")
   Set C1 = S.CustomerSalesHistory
   Set C2 = S.CustomerProductHistory%>
<H1>Customer # <%  = Request.QueryString("WID")%></H1>
<H3>By Period</H3>
<TABLE Border=1><TR>
<TD>Year</TD><TD>Month</TD><TD>Period</TD>
<TD>Units</TD><TD>Amount</TD></TR>
<%Do Until C1.eof%><TR>
```

```
<%  For Each F in C1.Fields%>
    <TD><%=F.Value%></TD>
<%  Next%></TR>
<%C1.movenext
loop%></TABLE>
<H3>By Period</H3>
<TABLE Border=1><TR>
<TD>Vintage</TD><TD>WineName</TD>
<TD>Units</TD><TD>Amount</TD></TR>
<%Do Until C2.eof%><TR>
<%  For Each F in C2.Fields%>
    <TD><%=F.Value%></TD>
<%  Next%></TR>
<%C2.movenext
loop%></TABLE></BODY></HTML>
```

In the preceding code, C1 is sales by month and C2 is sales by product.

When you open RsActiveX3.Asp, the ActiveX component generates the data for a list of customer hyperlinks. Each link that you click displays RsActiveX4.Asp for the selected customer. Figure 11-9 shows an example of RsActiveX4.Asp, which uses two recordsets for the selected customer:

✔ Sales by period

✔ Sales by product

Customer # 3088

By Period

Year	Month	Period	Units	Amount
1999	6	1999-June	6	112.87
1999	7	1999-July	6	95.41
1999	8	1999-August	2	37.33
1999	9	1999-September	2	46.58
1999	10	1999-October	3	45.39
1999	11	1999-November	6	76.49

By Period

Vintage	WineName	Units	Amount
1994	East Valley Cabernet Standard	1	78.56
1995	North Coast Bordeaux Blend Reserve	2	83.91
1995	Santa Barbara Cabernet Reserve	1	37.87
1996	North Valley Bordeaux Blend Reserve	2	90.46
1996	South Valley Cabernet Standard	2	117.82

Figure 11-9:
The ActiveX component creates multiple recordsets.

A custom-designed ActiveX component to provide commonly used record-sets significantly reduces the coding and errors involved in creating data-enhanced ASPs. By dividing the tasks into three separate processes, you achieve significant performance benefits:

- ✔ **Stored procedures:** Executing the SQL tasks as stored procedures is the fastest way to perform the SQL because the procedures are compiled and optimized when they are stored on the server. This approach has the added benefit of disentangling the SQL statement from the VBScript. If you need to make a change in the SQL, you merely edit the stored procedure and the changes flow through to the ASP.

- ✔ **Executable Dll:** The ADO code stored in the ActiveX component is also compiled and optimized for execution. This code runs much faster than the equivalent VBScript. Each time the page is loaded, VBScript must be parsed out of the ASP and interpreted by the scripting engine before it can be executed.

- ✔ **Less VBScript:** When you remove the SQL and ADO code from the ASP, you produce a light version of the ASP that requires less system resources to process.

Objects That Return Formatted Results

You can simplify the last element in the ASP that requires repetitive coding: HTML.

An ActiveX component can return the completed HTML (including recordset data) efficiently. A single property can add a data-populated table to an ASP. The result is a much faster response time because all of the code that produces the formatted table text is running on the server as compiled, optimized code.

Create a table template

For the most part, the method by which a recordset is combined with HTML to generate a table display on a Web page consists of repetitive coding. <TR> tags for records and <TD> tags for fields are presented again and again.

The first task is to write functions inside a class module that produce an HTML table from any recordset.

The `TableHeader` function in the following example uses the `Fields` collection of the supplied recordset to generate the HTML code that creates column headings.

```
Private Function TableHeader(R As ADODB.Recordset)
    Dim HTMLText
    Dim F As ADODB.Field
    For Each F In R.Fields
        HTMLText = HTMLText & _
        "<TD align=center bgcolor=#DDDDDD><B>" & _
        F.Name & "</B></TD>"
    Next
    TableHeader = "<THEAD><TR>" & HTMLText & _
    "</TR></THEAD"
End Function
```

The `TableBody` function produces the body of the table by looping

✔ Through the recordset

✔ Within each record in the fields collection

```
Private Function TableBody(R As ADODB.Recordset)
    Dim HTMLText
    Dim F As ADODB.Field
    Do Until R.EOF
        HTMLText = HTMLText & "<TR>"
        For Each F In R.Fields
            HTMLText = HTMLText & "<TD align=center>" & _
            F.Value & "</TD>"
        Next
        HTMLText = HTMLText & "</TR>"
        R.MoveNext
    Loop
    TableBody = "<TBODY>" & HTMLText & "</TBODY>"
End Function
```

The `HTMLTable` function puts the `TableHead` and `TableBody` functions together with the `TABLE` tags to complete the table template.

If you supply a recordset object to the `HTMLTable` function, the result is a block of pure HTML code that displays the data-populated table. Whatever the recordset, the following functions generate the required HTML.

```
Private Function HTMLTable(R As ADODB.Recordset)
    HTMLTable = "<TABLE Border=1>" & _
        TableHeader(R) & TableBody(R) & _
        "</TABLE>"
End Function
```

All that remains is to produce the recordsets and feed them as parameters to the `HTMLTable` function when you need to display a table of data. You can add ADO code to the class module to produce the recordsets, as was done when the `OrderInfo1.SalesInfo` component was created for this example.

ActiveX components work with

- ✔ ASPs
- ✔ VB and VBA
- ✔ Another component, like the one built in this section

If the `OrderInfo1.SalesInfo` component is available to ASPs, it is also available to other ActiveX components running on the same server. This is an example of the advantages of building applications as modular, reusable components.

The following code begins by adding a reference to the `OrderInfo1.SalesInfo` component in the current class module. The `SalesInfo` object is used to supply the various recordsets, which in turn are converted into streams of HTML text by the `HTMLTable` function. The results are properties like `ProductSalesHistory` that return a complete data-populated, formatted HTML table to the calling application, which in this example is an ASP. Note that the data type of the properties is Variant this time because this component returns HTML text, not ADO recordsets.

```
Dim SInfo As New OrderInfo1.SalesInfo
Public Property Get ProductSalesHistory() As Variant
    ProductSalesHistory = HTMLTable(SInfo.ProductSalesHistory)
End Property
Public Property Get CustomerProductHistory() As Variant
    CustomerProductHistory = HTMLTable(SInfo.CustomerProductHistory)
End Property
Public Property Get ActiveCustomerList() As Variant
    ActiveCustomerList = HTMLTable(SInfo.ActiveCustomerList)
End Property
Public Property Get ActiveProductList() As Variant
    ActiveProductList = HTMLTable(SInfo.ActiveProductList)
End Property
Public Property Get CustomerSalesHistory() As Variant
    CustomerSalesHistory = HTMLTable(SInfo.CustomerSalesHistory)
End Property
```

Two final items are the property procedures that set the values for the `WineId` and `CustomerId` within the class module.

```
Public Property Let CustomerID(ByVal vNewValue As Variant)
    SInfo.CustomerID = vNewValue
End Property
Public Property Let Wineid(ByVal vNewValue As Variant)
    SInfo.Wineid = vNewValue
End Property
```

When compiled and installed on the server, you can build ASPs that utilize the components. By building separate components for the recordsets and the HTML output, you retain the flexibility to use both recordsets and HTML objects in your ASPs.

The code for this ActiveX component is found in HTMLOrderInfo.Vbp.

Using a component that generates HTML

The HTMLOrderInfo.HTMLTables component can insert complete tables into an ASP. The following code, RSActiveX5.Asp, produces the table shown in Figure 11-10. Only three statements are needed to generate the table:

- Create an instance of the HTMLOrderInfo.HTMLTables component.

- Set the WineID property.

- Insert the complete, formatted table.

```
<%@ Language=VBScript %>
<HTML><BODY>
<% Set S = server.CreateObject("HTMLOrderInfo.HTMLTables")
   S.WineID = Request.QueryString("WID")
   Response.Write "<H1>Product #" & _
      Request.QueryString("WID") & "</H1>"
   Response.Write S.ProductSalesHistory
%>
</BODY></HTML>
```

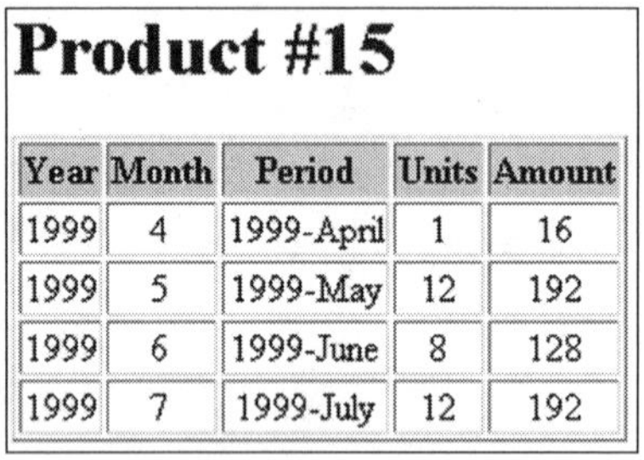

Figure 11-10:
The HTML code used to display the table is generated directly from an ActiveX component.

Product #15

Year	Month	Period	Units	Amount
1999	4	1999-April	1	16
1999	5	1999-May	12	192
1999	6	1999-June	8	128
1999	7	1999-July	12	192

RSActiveX6.Asp produces the identical product list as RSActiveX2.Asp, but calls RSActiveX5.Asp to display the tables.

Building the ASP for the Customer display requires only four statements related to the HTMLOrderInfo.HTMLTables object. (See Figure 11-11.) The following example code is RSActivex8.Asp. When you load the customer list, RSActivex7.Asp, each hyperlink calls RSActivex8.Asp for the linked CustomerID.

```
<%@ Language=VBScript %>
<HTML><BODY>
<% Set S = server.CreateObject("HTMLOrderInfo.HTMLTables")
    S.Customerid = Request.QueryString("CID")
    Response.Write "<H1>Customer #" & _
        Request.QueryString("CID") & "</H1>"
    Response.Write "<H3>By Period</H3>"
    Response.Write S.CustomerSalesHistory
    Response.Write "<H3>By Product</H3>"
    Response.Write S.CustomerSalesHistory
%></BODY></HTML>
```

Customer #3542

By Period

Year	Month	Period	Units	Amount
1999	1	1999-January	2	31.9
1999	2	1999-February	2	41.5
1999	3	1999-March	1	48.5
1999	4	1999-April	2	46
1999	5	1999-May	2	41.5
1999	6	1999-June	2	37.5

Figure 11-11: The customer page is populated using only four VBScript statements.

By Product

Year	Month	Period	Units	Amount
1999	1	1999-January	2	31.9
1999	2	1999-February	2	41.5
1999	3	1999-March	1	48.5
1999	4	1999-April	2	46
1999	5	1999-May	2	41.5

Chapter 12

Client-Side Recordsets

· ·

· ·

Dynamic HTML

Dynamic HTML (DHTML) refers to browser features that are implemented within the browser client rather than on the server. All the ASPs created in Chapters 9, 10, and 11 result in a pure HTML document being sent to the user's browser.

DHTML is an extension of the HTML code. HTML offers only the limited interactions supported by the form-based INPUT and SELECT tabs. The primary goal of DHTML is to create Web pages that have the same type of interactive characteristics as common windows applications.

DHTML implements these additional features by treating the contents of the browser as a structured object, which has properties, method, events and collections. This is in sharp contrast to HTML, which doesn't have any overall object structure.

However, because the DHTML model is a superset of HTML, not all Web browsers support DHTML. In this chapter, the pages use features that are fully supported by IE version 4.0 or higher.

DHTML limits the number of users that can take advantage of the application. However, sometimes you may know in advance that your application is only being deployed to users who have browsers capable of working with DHTML.

If you wish to deploy your application on the public Internet, you may have to settle for creating pages with server-side scripting only in order to have the application remain compatible with the widest range of users. Keep in mind that if you use server scripts with ASPs, only the Web server needs features like ADO because the requesting browser receives only pure HTML.

In this chapter, I give you a brief introduction to the concepts of DHTML and see how these concepts can be integrated with ADO scripting on both the client and server sides of a Web application.

Client-side scripting

The Web server doesn't implement DHTML operations. Instead, they're implemented by the Web client: that is, the browser application that receives the requested document from Web server.

When you use server-side scripts, the Web server reads and executes the script code before anything is returned to the user. When the script processing is complete, the resulting document, which consists of only HTML code, is returned to the browser.

When you write DHTML code, that code isn't aimed at the Web server. Rather, the code's designed to enhance the behavior of the page after it is returned to the requesting user. These are called *client-side scripts* because the script code is sent through the network to the browser right along with any HTML code in the document. The execution of the DHTML code doesn't take place until all the data reaches the client's browser.

Client-side scripts are organized into event procedures. Procedures can be related to specific objects and events that may take place after the Web page has arrived at the client. Need an example of an event? If a user clicks a button or enters text into a text box, that is an event.

When an event for which a procedure is defined takes place in the browser, the browser then executes the associated code. It's important to keep in mind that it isn't necessary for the browser to re-request the page in order to execute the script. Because the script was downloaded to the browser along with the static HTML, the browser can immediately execute the client-side script.

Further, a client-side script can modify how the document is displayed in the browser. Figure 12-1 shows a Web page that displays two date/time values. A server-side script creates the first value. Its value is fixed at the moment when the Web server executes the server-side script and doesn't change unless the user makes a request to reload the page.

On the other hand, the second date/time, which appears in the box, is updated each time the user clicks the DoSomething button. Because this update takes place on the client, the server's date/time remains unchanged. Figure 12-1 shows the result of both server-side and client-side scripting. The server-side script is executed once — when the page is requested. The client-side script can be executed any number of times, depending on how the user chooses to interact with the page.

Figure 12-1:
A DHTML
page can
update the
displayed
page
without
making an
additional
request to
the server.

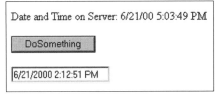

Another client/server characteristic that appears in Figure 12-1 is the three-hour difference between the server and the client times. Remember that when the server inserts the current date and time, it uses the date and time setting on the server computer. Conversely, when the client script inserts the date and time, it uses the date and time setting on the client's computer. The page shown in Figure 12-1 was loaded from a sever located in the eastern time zone and was received by a computer located in the Pacific time zone.

DHTML code

You can write server-side code in a structured or unstructured way. You can, but aren't required to, create structured code in the form of VBScript procedures within an ASP. Server-side script can simply be embedded at the desired locations with the HTML code.

Client-side scripts are more structured. If you want to execute client-side script, you must associate a script with an object within the Web page and event that represents some interaction with that object.

For example, the page shown in Figure 12-1 contains an HTML textbox and a button. *Note:* This isn't a Submit button, but a *button*-type button. Button-type buttons can be clicked without triggering the submission of a form. Each HTML element becomes an object that DHTML can manipulate. DHMTL recognizes the browser window and the entire document as objects, as well as small elements, such as INPUT and SELECT tags.

Changing a textbox with DHTML

The page displayed in Figure 12-1 is initially generated by the following code. The document's almost completely HTML with one server-side script element, =Now( ), used to insert the server's date and time into the HTML stream sent to the user.

```
<HTML><BODY>
Date and Time on Server: <% =now()%><P>
<INPUT type="button" value="DoSomething" name=DoSomething><P>
<INPUT type="text" name=ShowDateTime>
</BODY></HTML>
```

You can add the DHTML components by using the SCRIPT tab. The language parameter can be used to specify VBScript or JScript as the language. The code is inserted between the <!– –> tags.

```
<SCRIPT LANGUAGE=vbscript>
<!--
-->
</SCRIPT>
```

You can use the <SCRIPT> tag to create either server-side or client-side code. By default, the <SCRIPT> tag is assumed to define client-side code. You must add the RUNAT parameter and specify server as the location for the code.

```
<SCRIPT LANGUAGE=vbscript RUNAT=Server>
</SCRIPT>
```

In this case, you want the code to be a client-side script. The following example defines a procedure that's related to the OnClick event of the ShowDateTime HTML element. The name of an event procedure is always written using the name of the element (as defined by the Name parameter of the tag), an underscore, and the name of the event. Because the code is supposed to run each time that someone clicks the DoSomething button, the procedure name should be DoSomething_onclick.

In this case, each time the DoSomething button is clicked, the procedure changes the Value property of the ShowDateTime text box.

```
<SCRIPT LANGUAGE=vbscript>
<!--
Sub DoSomething_onclick
    ShowDateTime.value = now()
End Sub
-->
</SCRIPT>
```

The code for the entire page is as follows:

```
<%@ Language=VBScript %>
<SCRIPT LANGUAGE=vbscript>
<!--
Sub DoSomething_onclick
    ShowDateTime.value = now()
End Sub
-->
</SCRIPT>
<HTML><BODY>
Date and Time on Server: <% =now()%><P>
<INPUT type="button" value="DoSomething" name=DoSomething>
<P><INPUT type="text" name=ShowDateTime>
</BODY></HTML>
```

Changing images

Of course, there isn't room in this book for a complete tour around DHTML, but you can do many neat tricks with client-side scripting, including tricks with images.

Everyone knows that graphics are big part of the appeal of any Web page or application. Because this book is about ADO programming, the Web pages are very sparse in their appearance to avoid making the coding any more cluttered than it has to be.

However, now that the topic has turned to DHTML, it may be interesting to see how you can manipulate an element, like an image, using client-side scripts. Figure 12-2 displays one of the graphics I created for the example menus available at www.wbase2.com.

Figure 12-2:
You can use
DHTML to
modify
images.

Click on the image

In HTML, the <IMG> tag is used to load a graphic image into a Web page. The HTML used to create the page is quite simple, as the following code shows. The only item to note is the use of the ID parameter of the <IMG> tag. This parameter establishes a name for the <IMG> tag. You need this name if you want to reference the HTML element in DHTML code. Although it's common to use names with form elements, you need to add IDs to elements, such as <IMG> tags, which normally aren't named, to manipulate the element with DHTML.

```
<HTML><BODY>
<H2>Click on the image</H2>
<IMG src="/ado/chp9exp.gif" id="Pix">
</BODY></HTML>
```

Note: You can also use the Name parameter in place of ID if you prefer, as the following example shows. In either case, the Web browser can identify the <IMG> element as the element referenced in the DHTML code.

```
<IMG src="/ado/chp9exp.gif" name="Pix">
```

But what about clicking the image? It's interesting to use DHTML to change the image from Chapter 9 to Chapter 10. In HTML, you use the following <IMG> tag to show the graphic for Chapter 10:

```
<IMG src="/ado/chp10exp.gif" id="Pix">
```

But in this case, you don't want to make that change in the static HTML. Rather, you want to include DHTML code in the page that makes the change at the client when the user clicks the image. The script that accomplishes this trick is shown in the following example. The code changes the SCR parameter to a different graphic when the current image is clicked.

```
<SCRIPT LANGUAGE=vbscript>
<!--
Sub pix_onclick
    Pix.src = "/ado/chp10exp.gif"
End Sub
-->
```

The entire code is shown next. When you load the Dhtml2.Asp and click the graphic, it immediately changes to a different image. *Note:* The change takes place without reloading the document, as shown in Figure 12-3. In fact, if a request is made to reload, the graphic doesn't appear to change because the reloaded document returns to the original graphic.

```
<SCRIPT LANGUAGE=vbscript>
<!--
Sub pix_onclick
    Pix.src = "/ado/chp10exp.gif"
End Sub
-->
</SCRIPT>
<HTML><BODY>
<H2>Click on the image</H2>
<IMG src="/ado/chp9exp.gif" name="Pix">
</BODY></HTML>
```

Figure 12-3:
DHTML
changes the
displayed
image
without
reloading
the page.

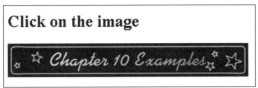

Entry validation

In terms of database operations, the primary value of DHTML is that it enables you to place code into the browser that can perform logical operations without having to submit a request to the server. Often, the logic involves small elements of the entire page, such as checking the validity of an entry.

Validation can be performed on either the client or server side. Although both can execute the same logic (such as the validity of the e-mail address), the look, feel, and performance characteristics are different.

In addition, the code you need to write has a different level of complexity depending on whether all the operations have to be performed on the server side or whether client-side scripts handle part of the task.

Server-side validation

Before looking at how client-side scripts can be used for data validation, it may be useful to see how you perform validation using server-side scripts. Look at the form shown in Figure 12-4. The example has a single entry for the e-mail address of the customer. I list the code for the page, ValidE-mailServer1.asp, here. The form calls the page ValidE-mailServer2.asp when the entry's submitted.

```
<%@ Language=VBScript %>
<HTML><BODY>
<% Set CustE-mail = server.CreateObject("ADODB.Recordset")
   CustE-mail.Open "SELECT Firstname + ' ' + LastName," & _
 "e-mailaddress FROM Customers WHERE Customerid = 1", _
"Provider=sqloledb;datasource=adodum;database=dbad1d;uid=ubad1d1;pwd=21@1n3z;"%>
<H1>Enter an E-mail Address</H1>
Customer: <% =CustE-mail(0)%>
<FORM Method=Post Action="ValidE-mailServer2.asp">
E-mail:
<Input type=textbox name=e-mail value=<% =CustE-mail(1)%>>
<P><INPUT type="submit" value="Submit" id=submit1 name=submit1>
</FORM></BODY></HTML>
```

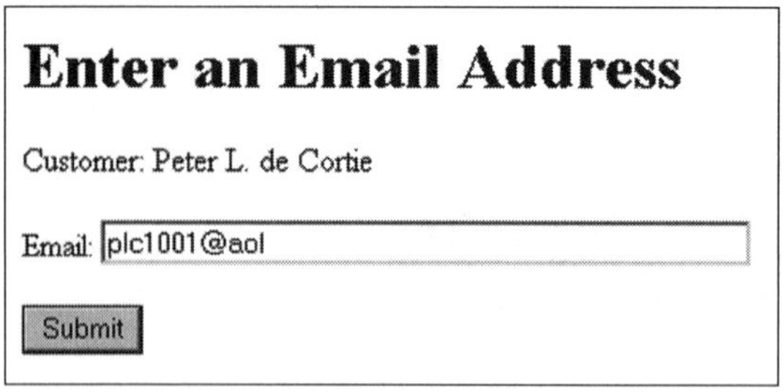

Figure 12-4:
Data entry
requires
that a valid
e-mail
address be
entered.

Enter an Email Address

Customer: Peter L. de Cortie

Email: plc1001@aol

Submit

The goal in this example is to ensure that a valid e-mail address is acquired from the user before moving on to other issues. Without a validation check, you can store an obviously invalid e-mail address. Further, if a user makes a typing mistake or deletes the address accidentally, the code, without a validation check, may end up overwriting good data with bad data.

But how to validate? Aside from trying to send mail to an e-mail address and waiting to see if you get a valid response, you can try some obvious tests to weed out the majority of bad entries. First, check to see if the entry is blank because that's obviously invalid. You also know that e-mail address must have an @ symbol and at least one period. Further, there shouldn't be any spaces in the address.

The following VBScript function, IsValidSMPT, applies a series of logical tests to the value stored in the request object's Form collection for the e-mail address. The function operates on a scoring system. The function gives the item one point if it isn't blank, another for having an @ symbol, and another for a period. If spaces exist, a point's deducted. At the end of the function, the address must score a 3 to be valid — simple, but effective in weeding out bad data.

```
<%@ Language=VBScript %>
<%
    Function IsValidSMPT(e-mail)
        If len(e-mail) > 0 Then
            points = 1
        End if
        If instr(e-mail,"@") > 0 Then
            points=points+1
        end if
        If instr(e-mail,".") > 0 Then
            points = points+1
        End if
        if instr(e-mail," ") > 0 Then
            points = points -1
        end if
        If points = 3 then
        IsValidSMPT = True
        Else
            IsValidSMPT = False
        End if
    End Function
%>
```

The rest of ValidE-mailServer2.Asp is divided by an If statement into two sections. If IsValidSMPT returns True, which indicates a valid-looking e-mail address, ADO is used to write the new e-mail address into the customer's record. A hyperlink is displayed that returns the user to ValidE-mailServer1. In practice, you may choose to continue with another page that has some additional function.

If the IsValidSMPT function returns False, the data isn't written to the data source. Instead, a message and hyperlink direct the user back to ValidE-mailServer1.Asp to reenter the required item.

```
<HTML><BODY>
<% if IsValidSMPT(Request.Form("e-mail")) Then
    Set CustE-mail = server.CreateObject("ADODB.Recordset")
    CustE-mail.Open "SELECT Firstname + ' ' + LastName," & _
      "e-mailaddress FROM Customers WHERE Customerid = 1", _
      "Provider=sqloledb;data
               source=208.222.107.6;database=dbad1d;uid=ubad1d1;pwd=21@1n3z;",1,
               3
    CustE-mail("E-mailAddress") = Request.Form("e-mail")
    CustE-mail.Update
        Response.Write "User Entry is Valid. Database Updated."
        Response.Write "<BR><A href='ValidE-mailServer1.asp'>Back</A>"
Else
        Response.Write Request.Form("e-mail") & " is not a valid e-mail
               address."
        Response.Write "<BR><A href='ValidE-mailServer1.asp'>Please re-
               enter</A>"
End if
%></BODY></HTML>
```

The preceding server-side validation accomplishes the goal of requiring valid (as best you can tell) entries for critical fields on a form. However, the process requires that the form be submitted to the server, which needs to process the page before returning a response to the user.

Client-side validation

In cases where DHTML is an appropriate tool (for example your users have IE supplied by your company), you can place the validation code on the client side. Two advantages to this approach are the following:

- **Client responds to entry.** Client-side DHTML coding exists within the object and event model of the IE. You can check validity at various points in the interaction between the page and the user. You don't have to wait until the Submit button is clicked. If you desire, you can validate entries every time an element in the form is updated, in addition to validating the entire form when it's submitted.

- **Simpler server coding.** In the server-side validation example, it's necessary to code the page that saves the user's entries to first evaluate the data before making the ADO update. When you validate on the client side, you control when the user is enabled to submit. This means that when a submission's made, you can be assured that it contains valid data. The need to code and process validation on the server side is eliminated.

Changing from server-side to client-side validation is simply a matter of moving the script logic out of the server-side script model and into the client-side model. In this example, that means you can copy the IsValidSMPT() function from ValidE-mailServer2.asp and place it in the client script <Script> tags in a new document, ValidE-mailClient1.Asp. As the following example shows, the code for this function is identical to the IsValidSMPT used on the server side:

```
<SCRIPT ID=clientEventHandlersVBS LANGUAGE=vbscript>
<!--
Function IsValidSMPT(e-mail)
    If len(e-mail) > 0 Then
        points = 1
    End if
    If instr(e-mail,"@") > 0 Then
        points=points+1
    end if
    If instr(e-mail,".") > 0 Then
        points = points+1
    End if
    if instr(e-mail," ") > 0 Then
        points = points -1
    end if
    If points = 3 then
        IsValidSMPT = True
    Else
        IsValidSMPT = False
    End if
End Function
```

The difference between the server and client sides is how and when this function is used. On the server side, the function's used after submission but before the changes are written to the data source. On the client side, you can use the IE object and event model to use the IsValidSMPT in order to check the e-mail address as the entry is made and before the user is enabled to submit the form.

The e-mail_onchange procedure fires (the hip term for executes) each time the user updates the e-mail INPUT tag text box. The procedure displays a message box that warns the user that the entry isn't a valid e-mail address, if that's the case. Figure 12-5 shows an example of what the user sees if they make an invalid e-mail entry.

In addition, you can use the Select method to place the selection highlight back on the e-mail box to encourage the user to correct the entry. If the address is valid, the procedure does nothing.

```
Sub e-mail_onchange
    If not IsValidSMPT(DataEntry.e-mail.value) Then
        MsgBox DataEntry.e-mail.value & " does not appear " & _
        "to be a valid e-mail address." & chr(10) & chr(13) & _
        "Please Re-enter. A valid e-mail address is required.", _
        48,"Data validation"
        DataEntry.e-mail.select
    end if
End Sub
```

Figure 12-5:
Client-side
script
catches
invalid
entries as
they are
entered.

When the Submit button is clicked, a final check is required. *Note:* This isn't a submit-type button. It is an ordinary button that is labeled *Submit.* This difference is important. Clicking an ordinary button doesn't initiate a submission to the server. In this case, it merely fires off the submit1_onclick procedure, shown in the following example. This procedure repeats the validation check because the user may have simply ignored the previous warning and left an invalid entry on the form.

If the form entry passes the validation text, the data's ready to be submitted. In this case, the Submit method of the form is executed from VBScript. The form, named DataEntry in this case, can be programmatically manipulated with VBScript to produce the same effect as actually clicking a Submit button.

```
Sub submit1_onclick
   If not IsValidSMPT(DataEntry.e-mail.value) Then
      MsgBox DataEntry.e-mail.value & " does not appear " & _
      "to be a valid e-mail address." & chr(10) & chr(13) & _
      "Please Re-enter. A valid e-mail address is required.", _
      48,"Data validation"
      DataEntry.e-mail.select
   Else
      DataEntry.submit
   end if
End Sub
```

Using the pseudo-submit button enables you to perform operations, such as validity checks, before you actually enable the form to be submitted. The remainder of the code remains as it was in ValidE-mailServer1.Asp with the exception that the form is no longer needed. ValidE-mailClient2.Asp is shown in the following example. Because the client-side script ensures that only valid data is submitted, the coding of the page requested by the form submission can be simplified.

```
<HTML><BODY><%
  Set CustE-mail = server.CreateObject("ADODB.Recordset")
  CustE-mail.Open "SELECT Firstname + ' ' + LastName," & _
  "e-mailaddress FROM Customers WHERE Customerid = 1", _
  "Provider=sqloledb;data
source=208.222.107.6;database=dbad1d;uid=ubad1d1;pwd=21@1n3z;",1,3
  CustE-mail("E-mailAddress") = Request.Form("e-mail")
  CustE-mail.Update 'line in active for testing
  Response.Write "User Entry is Valid. Database Updated."
  Response.Write "<BR><A href=ValidE-mailClient1.asp'>Back</A>"
%></BODY></HTML>
```

Data Binding in Internet Explorer

As part of its feature set, IE supports client-side binding of data to standard HTML elements such as text boxes, list boxes, or even tables. *Data binding* enables you to display data on Web pages without having to write code that explicitly handles the mechanics of HTML layout.

Instead, you can connect a data source with a display element and have the browser generate the appropriate display. Furthermore, you can manipulate the data displayed on the page by executing client-side scripts that sort, filter, and navigate through data sources. When you manipulate the data source, the display elements automatically update to reflect changes in the data set.

Ultimately, through the use of Remote Data Services (RDS), (discussed in Chapter 13), client-side operations can display, insert, delete, and update the data source directly.

You first need a data source to use data binding on a Web page. Ideally, creating a data source for a Web page uses the same techniques as adding data recourse to a VB/VBA application: that is, by using ADO to create data objects, like recordsets, within the Web page.

Unfortunately, because of the nature of the Web service and Web browsers, no simple mechanism is available to connect client- and server-side activities. The HTTP protocol was created without any way of connecting the server- and client-side objects. After the Web server supplies a page to the browser, it doesn't keep track of any changes or user interaction with the page. Conversely, the page displayed in your browser has no direct connection to the server from which it was loaded. This is called a *stateless connection* because the server doesn't keep track of the document after it's passed to the client.

Most client/server applications keep track of what sort of operations the client is performing on the server. When you use ADO to access a data provider like SQL Server, the provider maintains a connection between the objects being manipulated by the client computers (such as recordsets) and the data source stored on the server (tables). For example, SQL Server manages locks, which prevent more than one user from altering the same record at the same time.

Web servers are asynchronous and stateless. A stateless server does not attempt to maintain ongoing control over the interactions of multiple users with the server. Instead, each request received for data is processed independently of any other request from the same or different users. An asynchronous server is one that does not maintain a constant flow of information between the client and server. After a requested page is sent to the requesting client, the process is ended as far as the Web server is concerned. Anything that the user does to the data in the Web page isn't a concern of the Web server.

This works well when the Web server publishes only HTML documents. But when you want to use the Web service as a front end for a database application, a stateless server is less than ideal. There's no link between the data object used to populate a Web page and any manipulation that takes place on the client end.

When you combine IE features and DHTML client scripts, you can create more useful data-enhanced Web pages. Data binding enables you to eliminate a great deal of tedious coding that otherwise is required.

XML as a data source

Even in the latest versions of IE 5.x), no direct connection exists between client-side operations and data providers. That connection can be achieved only with the introduction of additional element, such as RDS.

For the moment, I put aside the issue of creating a recordset that exists both on the client and server at the same time in order to look at how data can be manipulated on the client side of a Web application. In order to use data binding on a Web page, you first need a data source.

One of the hottest topics today is XML. Although a complete discussion of XML is beyond the scope of this book, be aware that you cannot deal with Web-based data today without encountering XML in some form.

XML was created to provide exactly what is needed for the example pages you are about to work with. Put as simply as possible, XML is a protocol for creating text-based data sources for use in Web applications. Like HTML, XML doesn't require any binary objects, such as ActiveX controls or OLE DB drivers. It's composed of pure text, like HTML.

To get an idea of how XML works, look at Figure 12-6.

Figure 12-6:
A simple
table with
data.

| Morgan | Krumm |
| Heather | Hart |

The HTML that produces the table shown in Figure 12-6 is shown here:

```
<TABLE BORDER=1 >
<TR>
 <TD>Morgan</TD>
 <TD>Krumm</TD>
</TR>
<TR>
 <TD>Heather</TD>
 <TD>Hart</TD>
 </TR>
</TABLE>
```

HTML has two significant problems worth mentioning here:

- The data is all mixed in with the formatting. If you want to add more data, you must add or remove the formatting code along with it.
- HTML doesn't provide any defining structure to the data. Is Morgan a first or last name? A company perhaps?

The server-side code used in Chapters 9, 10, and 11 don't address these issues. Server-side code produces pure HTML, like the preceding code, from ADO data objects such as recordsets. Even if you wanted to write client-side code, there are no defined elements on the HTML page to reference. The fact that the data was extracted from a table with fields and records is information that was left at the server and not sent to the Web client.

In order to use DHTML to logically manipulate data on the client side, you must provide the client with a structured data object that retains characteristics such as field and record organization when sent to the client.

XML provides just such a structure. And, it does so in a pure text format. Like HTML, XML relies on a combination of tags and untagged text to create its structures. However, unlike HTML (with structures aimed at displaying text on a page), XML is purely concerned with defining data structure relationships similar to records and fields. Like client-side script, XML is inserted into a document using the following XML tags. Anything entered between these tags is ignored by the HTML processing of the browser, but it enters the memory of a XML-enabled browser, such as IE 5.0 or higher.

```
<?xml version="1.0" ?>
</xml>
```

XML uses tags to approximate structures such as tables, records, and fields. Using the table in Figure 12-6 as a starting point, the first set of tags you need to create are equivalent to a table or recordset. The Customers tags added to the XML structure indicate that you're defining a set of records and calling it Customers. The XML tags that define data structures aren't predefined. You can make up any names you like. The only requirement? You must use the names you create consistently.

```
<?xml version="1.0" ?>
  <Customers>
  </Customer>
</xml>
```

The example record block consists of two records. In XML, you define a record with a set of tags. Because the record block is called Customers, each record can be tagged as a Customer:

```
<?xml version="1.0" ?>
  <Customers>
    <Customer>
    <Customer>
  </Customer>
</xml>
```

Records consist of fields. In this example, each record has two fields, First and Last. Each field requires a set of beginning and ending tags:

```
<?xml version="1.0" ?>
  <Customers>
    <Customer>
      <First></First>
      <Last></Last>
    <Customer>
  </Customer>
</xml>
```

The structure is complete. The final addition is the assignment of data to the field-level tags. This is done by placing the data between the field tags.

```
<?xml version="1.0" ?>
  <Customers>
    <Customer>
      <First>Morgan</First>
      <Last>Krumm</Last>
    <Customer>
  </Customer>
</xml>
```

If you want to add another record to the record block, you must include a complete set of tags along with the data. Because a new record represents a new customer, you have to add the record and field-level tags along with the new First and Last name. The following code is the XML equivalent of the data displayed in Figure 12-6:

```
<?xml version="1.0" ?>
  <Customers>
    <Customer>
      <First>Morgan</First>
      <Last>Krumm</Last>
    <Customer>
    <Customer>
      <First>Heather</First>
      <Last>Hart</Last>
    <Customer>
  </Customer>
</xml>
```

XML provides a way to pass a highly structured data block to a client using a Web server. Because Web protocols are designed for text transmission, having a text-based data structure simplifies the process of sending data to a Web client. An ADO recordset is also a highly structured data object, but moving it between a Web server and a Web client requires some additional support. These techniques are discussed in detail in Chapter 13.

Binding display elements to data structures

In and of itself, an XML structure contained within a Web document doesn't place any information on the page. In order to place that data on the page, you need to link a display element like a text box, list box, or table with the data structure.

In IE, this is accomplished using the DATASRC (data source) and DATAFLD (data field) parameters that IE supports for display tags, such as INPUT, SELECT, and TABLE.

In order to connect a data source, such as an XML structure, to elements in the document, you must assign a name to the XML object. The xml id tag assigns the name Cust to the XML data structure:

```
<xml id = Cust>
<?xml version="1.0" ?>
  ...xlm elements
</xml>
```

You can then use the data structure name to content a display element, like a TABLE tag, with the data. The following tag links the XML record block with a TABLE:

```
<TABLE border=1 datasrc=#cust>
```

Individual fields can then be displayed in the table using the SPAN tag and the DataFld parameter. The SPAN tag is a sort of generic TAG that is used for client specific operations. In this case, SPAN is used to specify the location where a field should be inserted into the table. The following SPAN tag inserts the First field into a table column:

```
<TD><SPAN datafld="First"></SPAN></TD>
```

The XMLTable1.Asp page, listed here, generates the same displays as the HTML displayed in Figure 12-6 by using an XML data block bound to a TABLE tag:

```
<xml id = Cust>
<?xml version="1.0" ?>
    <Customers>
    <customer>
    <First>Morgan</First>
    <Last>Krumm</Last>
    </customer>
    <customer>
    <First>Heather</First>
    <Last>Hart</Last>
    </customer>
    </Customers>
</xml>
<%@ Language=VBScript %>
<HTML>
<BODY>
<TABLE border=1 datasrc=#cust>
<TR>
    <TD><SPAN datafld="First"></SPAN></TD>
    <TD><SPAN datafld="Last"></SPAN></TD>
</TR></BODY></HTML>
```

Most of the coding in XMLTable1.Asp is XML code used to define the data object. The code used to display the data is significantly reduced from the equivalent HTML. When the TABLE is bound to a DSO, you need define only a single row of tags. The table expands to include all the records in the DSO. Regardless of the number of records included in the XML DSO, your table code remains the same.

Generating XML from ADO

The XML example is interesting because it shows the advantages of separating the data coding from the display coding in Web pages. But XML is a verbose format. If you create XML data sources manually by writing out the XML code, XML is of little practical use.

Of course, you can easily write code in VB/VBA that can take an ADO recordset and write it out as XML code. Fortunately, you don't have to go through all that the trouble. ADO recordsets include a Save method, which converts an ADO Recordset object (which exists only in memory) and writes that recordset to a file.

When you save the data from memory to a file structure, the recordset becomes a Persistent object. Persistent objects are objects that are stored in their own separate files. These files, once created, can be used as data sources even when the connection to the data provider isn't available. ADO can save the data in two formats:

✔ **Advanced Data Tablegram (ADTG).** A proprietary format created by Microsoft to provide offline storage and retrieval of ADO data.

✔ **XML.** An industry standard format. Unlike ADTG, which contains binary information, XML is pure text.

The Save method has the following form:

```
Recordsetobjcet.Save filename, format
```

In this context, the XML option is of primary interest because XML is pure text and Web services are designed to deal with text. The WriteXML procedure shows how the Save method can be used to generate XML files that contain the XML equivalent of the ADO Recordset object:

```
Sub WriteXML()
    Dim R As New ADODB.Recordset
    R.Open "SELECT DISTINCT Variety FROM WineProductCatalog", _
      "Provider=sqloledb;data source=208.222.107.6;" & _
      "database=dbad1d;uid=ubad1d1;pwd=21@1n3z;"
    R.Save "C:\XMLTest.txt", adPersistXML
End Sub
```

Adding XML to the Response object

Although the ability to generate XML text files from an ADO recordset may be useful in some circumstance, ADO 2.5 added a new feature that enables ADO data to be saved to a data stream object.

What is a stream object? Why is that important? To answer these questions, you need to think about what happens when a Web server responds to a request for a document. The Web server sends the data contained in the requested document, not to a file in another location, but directly to the Web browser. Unless the user specifically goes through the trouble of saving a file on a local drive, the document returned to the user by the Web server isn't saved in a file. It exists in memory and then is discarded as soon as another document is requested. To put it in ADO terms, a Web document accessed by a browser isn't persistent but only temporary.

The flow of information between the Web server and the browser client represents a stream of data flowing from point to point over a network. In ADO 2.5, streams of data, such as the response made by a Web server to a request for a document, can be treated as an object — a stream object.

In all the client-side scripting shown so far in this book, ADO data has been inserted into the response stream object on a field-by-field basis where VBScript statements are used to convert individual fields into text that becomes part of the Response object. The recordset itself, being a complex binary object, cannot be directly inserted into the response stream because that stream is, by definition, a text-only object.

However, the Save method provides a means of converting an ADO recordset into a pure text structure, XML. It's possible to insert the XML equivalent of an entire ADO recordset into the response object data stream so that the entire recordset is passed to the browser. This is an easy way to eliminate the need to manually code XML data. All you need to do is generate an ADO recordset and insert the XML equivalent into the Response object.

In order to prepare the Response object to accept the XML data, you need to set the ContentType property to text/XML. The default is text/HTML. If you don't change this property, the XML isn't captured in the Response object.

```
Response.ContentType = "text/xml"
```

The following is the code for a page called WineVarietyXML.Asp. This procedure creates a recordset that lists the variety of wines stored in the WineProductCatalog table. The Save method is used to convert the ADO recordset to an XML data structure. The tricky part is that, instead of using a file name as the destination parameter of the Save method, a stream object (in this case, the Response object) is specified as the destination. The result of loading this page is shown in Figure 12-7. The XML data structure is displayed as part of the response text displayed in the browser.

```
<%@ Language=VBScript%>
<%    Set WList = server.CreateObject("ADODB.Recordset")
    Response.ContentType = "text/xml"
    WList.Open "SELECT DISTINCT variety " & _
      "FROM WineProductCatalog", _
      "Provider=sqloledb;data source=208.222.107.6;" & _
      "database=dbad1d;uid=ubad1d1;pwd=21@1n3z;",1,3
    wlist.Save response,1
%>
```

Note: The value 1 is used with the Save method because it's the numeric equivalent of the constant adPersistXML, which isn't available in an ASP.

The XML generated by ADO is more complicated than is necessary just to list the names of the wine varieties. The format used by ADO is designed to be a generic format that can handle all types of data sets and provide information about the recordset schema as well as the data.

Note: In IE 5.x, XML data is automatically treated as a hierarchical tree structure. If you look carefully as the display generated by WineVarietyXML.Asp is displayed, you will notice dash (-) characters in front of some tags, such as s:schema and rs:data. If you click the dash (-) characters, the built-in DHTML features in IE 5.0 automatically collapse that section of the XML structure and change the character to a plus sign (+).

```
- <xml xmlns:s="uuid:BDC6E3F0-6DA3-11d1-A2A3-00AA00C14882"
    xmlns:dt="uuid:C2F41010-65B3-11d1-A29F-00AA00C14882"
    xmlns:rs="urn:schemas-microsoft-com:rowset" xmlns:z="#RowsetSchema">
  - <s:Schema id="RowsetSchema">
    - <s:ElementType name="row" content="eltOnly">
      - <s:AttributeType name="variety" rs:number="1" rs:nullable="true"
          rs:writeunknown="true">
          <s:datatype dt:type="string" rs:dbtype="str"
            dt:maxLength="50" />
        </s:AttributeType>
        <s:extends type="rs:rowbase" />
      </s:ElementType>
    </s:Schema>
  - <rs:data>
      <z:row variety="Bordeaux Blend" />
      <z:row variety="Cabernet" />
      <z:row variety="carmenere" />
      <z:row variety="Chardonnay" />
      <z:row variety="Dolcetto" />
      <z:row variety="Gewurztraminer" />
      <z:row variety="Merlot" />
      <z:row variety="Pinot Noir" />
      <z:row variety="Proprietary Blend" />
      <z:row variety="Sauvignon Blanc" />
      <z:row variety="Syrah" />
      <z:row variety="Zinfandel" />
    </rs:data>
  </xml>
```

Figure 12-7:
An ADO
recordset is
converted to
XML and
included in
the
response.

Another point to note: Despite the apparent complexity of the XML generated by ADO, it can be worse. Using tags, it takes all of the following text to define one item in the recordset as an XML record with one field.

```
<Wines>
  <Wine>
    <Varierty>Bordeaux Blend</Variety>
  </Wine>
```

The ADO format, starting with the `rs:data` tag, writes one tag for each record. All the fields in that record are written as properties of the row tag. This eliminates a significant amount of text from the XML structure, which means that the total amount of text sent from the server to the browsers is reduced.

```
<rs:data>
  <z:row variety="Bordeaux Blend" />
```

Using an XML stream as a data source object

Of course, displaying the XML on the browser page isn't of much practical use. The goal is to have the XML data returned in the stream function as a DSO for the page.

The solution to this problem is to use the SRC (source) parameter with an XML DSO definition tag. The SRC parameter enables you to specify another document as the XML data source. If that document is an ASP, such as WineVarietyXML.Asp, the Web server processes the ASP and returns the entire response stream to the XML tag.

The following XML tag loads the XML data generated by WineVarietyXML.Asp as the DSO. The document behaves exactly as if the static XML were part of the document itself. The result is that the Web page contains a block of XML data commonly referred to as a data island. The term *data island* refers to the fact that the data set is isolated from its original source, the ADO recordset set.

```
<XML ID="WList" SRC="WineVarietyXML.asp"></XML>
```

The difficult part of this technique? You have to deal with a rather complex XML data source.

XML is hierarchical in nature: To get down to the data stored in the Z:Row variety tags, you must move through three outer layers of information. The following example, XMLTable2.asp, uses three layers of nested tables. The first layer binds the Wlist DSO structure to the table. The second TABLE tag accesses the rs:data section of the XML structure, which is the part that holds the actual data. The third accesses the z:row structure, which then exposes the actual field data — in this case, the Variety field. Because multiple z:row elements exist in the XML data, the tags contained within the TABLE tags bound to the z:row element repeat for each z:row. This means that table automatically expands to accommodate all the records drawn from the original ADO recordset.

```
<HTML>
<BODY>
<XML ID="WList" SRC="WineVarietyXML.asp"></XML>
<TABLE DATASRC="#WList">
  <TR><TD>
    <TABLE DATASRC="#WList" DATAFLD="rs:data">
      <TR><TD>
        <TABLE DATASRC="#WList" DATAFLD="z:row">
          <THEAD>
            <TR>
              <TD><B>Variety</B></TD>
            </TR>
          </THEAD>
          <TBODY>
            <TR>
              <TD><SPAN DATAFLD="variety"></SPAN></TD>
            </TR>
          </BODY>
        </TABLE>
      </TD></TR>
    </TABLE>
  </TD></TR>
</TABLE>
</BODY>
</HTML>
```

When you load XMLTable2.asp, ADO and XML work together to pass an entire recordset from the server side to the client side and bind the resulting DSO to an DHTML element, as shown in Figure 12-8.

Figure 12-8:
ADO and
XML enable
entire
recordsets
to be
passed from
the server
side to the
client side.

Variety
Bordeaux Blend
Cabernet
carmenere
Chardonnay
Dolcetto
Gewurztraminer
Merlot
Pinot Noir
Proprietary Blend
Sauvignon Blanc
Syrah
Zinfandel

Building applications with XML data islands

XML data islands greatly simplify the creation of Web pages that display data stored in ADO data sources. By combining ADO, XML, and DHTML data binding, you greatly reduce the amount of HTML code you have to write in order to display a recordset on a Web page. You can use the same general approach to quick-build pages that do all sorts of publishing tasks.

On the other hand, XML data islands are less appropriate for data base tasks that involve adding or updating existing records or recordsets because the data island is isolated from the source of the data. In Chapter 13, you learn how to handle these tasks using ADO and Remote Data Services.

Displaying recordset using XML

Using ADO, XML, and DHTML, you can build Web applications like the ones shown in Chapters 9 and 10 much more easily than you can using ADO and HTML.

For example, suppose you want to display an informational table about all the wines in the catalog of a certain variety, as shown in Figure 12-9 (which lists the zinfandels in the wine catalog).

Zinfandels Available

Vintage	Wine	Quality
1995	South Valley Zinfandel Standard	Standard
1996	Central Coast Zinfandel Standard	Standard
1996	Valley Zinfandel Standard	Standard
1997	Central Valley Zinfandel Standard	Standard
1997	East Valley Zinfandel Reserve	Reserve
1997	Santa Cruz Zinfandel Standard	Standard
1997	Valley Zinfandel Standard	Standard

Figure 12-9:
You can use
XML to
display a
detailed
recordset.

To build a page that displays a recordset, create an ASP that creates an ADO recordset and save that object to the Response object stream. This is the basic technique for generating the XML data island.

The following code, WineProductsXML.Asp, adds a twist to the previous XML island generators. In this case, VBScript is used to insert a `queryString` value called *Variety* into the SQL text used to create the ADO recordset.

```
<%Set WList = server.CreateObject("ADODB.Recordset")
  Response.ContentType = "text/xml"
  WList.Open "SELECT DISTINCT vintage, winename, quality " & _
    "FROM WineProductCatalog where variety = '" & _
    Request.QueryString("Variety") & "'", _
    "Provider=sqloledb;data source=208.222.107.6;" & _
    "database=dbad1d;uid=ubad1d1;pwd=21@1n3z;",1,3
  wlist.Save response,1%>
```

You can always use server-side script instructions with an ASP regardless of what client-side operations you also perform with that page. The Web server processes the server-side script before the document returns to the client. In this case, the server-side VBScript instruction modifies the SQL statement before it's used to create the recordset.

The following URL, which can be executed from the Chapter 12 examples page, returns the XML equivalent of the zinfandel product list:

```
WineProductsXML.Asp?variety=zinfandel
```

ADO generates an XML record that looks like this one. Each field in the recordset is written as a property of the `z:row` object:

```
<z:row vintage="1995" winename="South Valley Zinfandel Standard"
                quality="Standard" />
```

In order to display the data, you add one SPAN tag for each field. The following is XMLTable3.Asp, which uses the same basic table structure to display the contents of the XML data island generated automatically from the ADO recordset:

```
<HTML><BODY>
<XML ID="WList" SRC="WineProductsXML.Asp?variety=zinfandel"></XML>
<H1>Zinfandels Available</H1>
<TABLE DATASRC="#WList">
<TR><TD><TABLE DATASRC="#WList" DATAFLD="rs:data">
<TR><TD><TABLE DATASRC="#WList" DATAFLD="z:row" Border = 1>
   <THEAD><TR>
      <TD><B>Vintage</B></TD>
      <TD><B>Wine</B></TD>
      <TD><B>Quality</B></TD>
   </TR></THEAD>
   <TBODY><TR>
      <TD><SPAN DATAFLD="vintage"></SPAN></TD>
      <TD><SPAN DATAFLD="winename"></SPAN></TD>
      <TD><SPAN DATAFLD="quality"></SPAN></TD>
   </TR></BODY>
   </TABLE>
   </TD></TR></TABLE></TD></TR></TABLE>
</BODY></HTML>
```

Of course, in the previous example, the queryString value was hard-coded into the ASP. However, a simple change enables you to use the code in XMLTable3.Asp to display the list of any variety. XMLTable4.Asp adds server-side VBScript to two statements in the ASP. The server-side script inserts a queryString value into two locations in the DHTML code where the name of the variety should appear.

```
<XML ID="WList" SRC="WineProductsXML.Asp?variety=<% =Request.QueryString("vari-
            ety")%>"></XML>
<H1><% =Request.QueryString("variety")%>s Available</H1>
```

After you make this change, you can use the same page, XMLTable4.Asp, to display a list of any variety in the catalog by entering the name as a queryString in the URL.

```
XMLTable4.asp?variety=Merlot
```

The result is a list of the merlots in the wine catalog table.

Creating hyperlinks using XML fields

Of course, the valid values for the querystring in XMLTable4.asp are themselves the result of a recordset — in fact, the recordset displayed by XMLTable2.asp, as shown in Figure 12-7.

You can combine the variety list with the product list pages by using the ADO/XML data to create hyperlinks to the XMLTable4.asp page that include the various variety names as queryString values.

IE 5.x enables you to use other tags beside SPAN with data fields: INPUT, BUTTON, and IMG tags with the DATASRC and DATAFLD parameters.

The first step is to add a new column to the ADO recordset that produces the required hyperlink URL. In this case, the literal text *'XMLtable4.asp?variety=* is combined with the Variety field to create a server of URLs with the appropriate queryString values.

```
'XMLtable4.asp?variety=' + variety AS Link
```

The WineVarietyXMLLinks.asp is shown here. It adds the Link fields to the ADO recordset, which is then included in the XML data island:

```
<%    Set WList = server.CreateObject("ADODB.Recordset")
      Response.ContentType = "text/xml"
      WList.Open "SELECT DISTINCT variety " & _
        ",'XMLtable4.asp?variety=' + variety AS Link " & _
        "FROM WineProductCatalog", _
        "Provider=sqloledb;data source=208.222.107.6;" & _
        "database=dbad1d1;uid=ubad1d1;pwd=21@1n3z;",1,3
    wlist.Save response,1
%>
```

The next step is to change the variety list to a list of hyperlinks. Each hyperlink opens the XMLTable4.Asp page using a querystring that specifies a wine variety that corresponds to the text of the hyperlink. The following DHTML code shows how the hyperlinks are created. The Link field, generated in the ADO recordset and included in the XML data island, is used as the DATAFLD parameter for an A (anchor) tag. In DHTML, a field inserted into an A tag is treated like an HREF parameter so that the field text becomes a hyperlink reference. The SPAN tag is used to insert the Variety name (without the URL text) as the visible link name.

```
<Td><A Datafld = "link"><Span Datafld ="variety"></Span></A></Td>
```

The following is the XMLTable5.Asp that implements the hyperlink coding:

```
<HTML><BODY>
<XML ID="WList" SRC="WineVarietyXMLLinks.asp"></XML>
<TABLE DATASRC="#WList">
<TR><TD><TABLE DATASRC="#WList" DATAFLD="rs:data">
<TR><TD><TABLE DATASRC="#WList" DATAFLD="z:row">
    <THEAD> <TR>
       <TD><B>Variety</B></TD>
    </TR> </THEAD>
    <TBODY> <TR>
        <TD><A DATAFLD = "link">
        <SPAN DATAFLD="variety"></SPAN>
        </A></TD>
    </TR> </BODY>
    </TABLE>
    </TD></TR></TABLE></TD></TR></TABLE>
</BODY></HTML>
```

The result, shown in Figure 12-10, is a page that lists hyperlinks, which display the catalog pages for each variety of wine.

Figure 12-10:
XML is used
to generate
a series of
hyperlinks to
other XML
data
displays.

Variety
Bordeaux Blend
Cabernet
carmenere
Chardonnay
Dolcetto
Gewurztraminer
Merlot
Pinot Noir
Proprietary Blend
Sauvignon Blanc
Syrah
Zinfandel

Figure 12-11 shows the catalog contents for the sauvignon blanc wines. **Note:** You didn't have to explicitly create this catalog page. The page was the result of the ADO, XML, and DHTML code interacting with the data in the SQL Server data source. If you add more varieties and wines to the catalog, the code creates the hyperlinks and catalog pages for you.

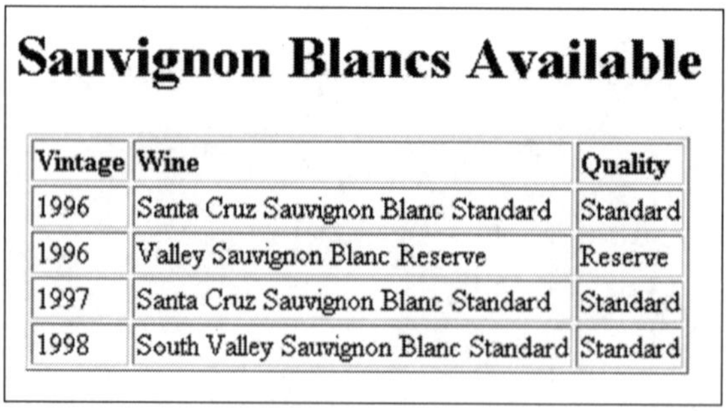

Figure 12-11:
ADO, XML,
and DHTML
combine to
dynamically
generate
catalog
page
displays
based on the
contents of
a SQL
Server table.

Sauvignon Blancs Available

Vintage	Wine	Quality
1996	Santa Cruz Sauvignon Blanc Standard	Standard
1996	Valley Sauvignon Blanc Reserve	Reserve
1997	Santa Cruz Sauvignon Blanc Standard	Standard
1998	South Valley Sauvignon Blanc Standard	Standard

Using Data Shaping with XML

So far, all the XML data you work with resembles traditional relation database tables. However, XML, like ADO, is designed to support a broader category data than relational database.

XML is specifically designed to support hierarchical data structures and to facilitate their use. Hierarchical data is tree-structured data in which blocks of information are arranged in a parent/child relationship.

ADO also supports hierarchical data sets. In Chapter 8, I discuss the ADO Data-Shaping provider. The Data-Shaping provider generates a special type of recordset, which can contain other recordsets in a parent/child relationship.

For example, suppose you want to generate a catalog display like the one in Figure 12-12, in which the items are organized into a two-level hierarchy. The top level creates groups based on the color of the wine. Within each color, the varieties are listed.

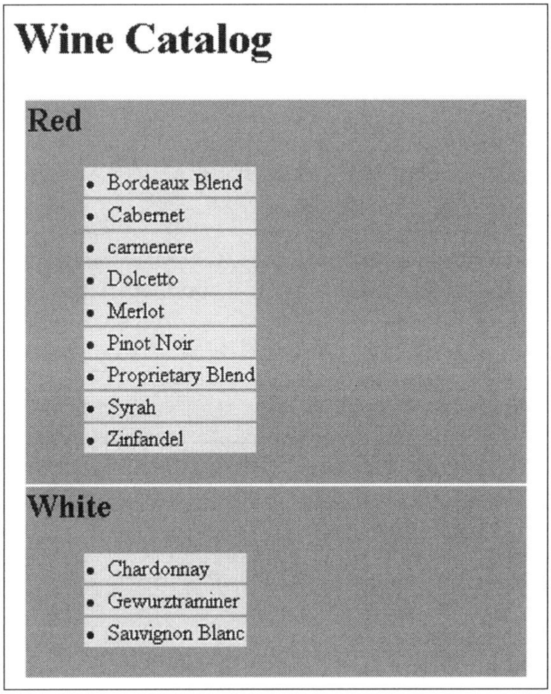

Figure 12-12: The wine catalog displays a two-level hierarchy.

Figure 12-12 is an example of a hierarchical recordset. You use the ADO shape provider to generate a Recordset object that is organized into hierarchical levels. After you have that recordset, you can use the `Save` method to convert the ADO data into a hierarchical XML data island. The XML data island can then be bound to `TABLE` tags in order to produce the catalog, as shown in Figure 12-12.

The following code is a data-shaping statement that generates the list of wine colors and wine varieties required to create the document shown in Figure 12-12. (For more information about data shaping, see Chapter 8.)

What's interesting in this case is that both levels of data are drawn from the same table, `WineProductCatalog`. The `DISTINCT` keyword eliminates duplicates from the list. Note that the `AS` keyword is used to assign the name `WineType` to the child recordset. If you do not specify a name, ADO generates the name Chapter1 for a child recordset.

```
SHAPE {SELECT DISTINCT WineColor FROM WineProductCatalog}
APPEND( {SELECT Distinct WineColor,Variety
FROM WineProductCatalog} AS WineType
RELATE winecolor to winecolor)
```

The preceding data-shaping statement is complicated and tedious to code directly into VBScript code. It may be better to use the same technique discussed in Chapter 8: that is, storing the shaping statement in a table called *statements*. You can then use an ADO recordset to extract the shape command text as part of the server-side script that creates the XML stream. If you need to edit the text of the shaping statement, you can edit the text in the Statements table without having to change your VBScript code.

In this case, the shape statement is stored in the Statements table with the QueryName `XMLWineShap`. The following ASP code, stored in ShapedXML.Asp, first retrieves the shape statement from the Statements table. The expression `Shapecmd(0)Value` is then used to insert the shape statement as the `Source` property for the `Sh` recordset. **Note:** It's necessary to specify the `Value` property of the `Shapecmd(0)` object in order to avoid confusing ADO as to the exact nature of the `Source` argument even though the `Value` property is usually assumed to be the default property of a field object.

ADO accepts a variety of objects as `Source` arguments. Using `Shapecmd(0)` by itself results in an error.

```
<% Set cnt = Server.CreateObject("ADODB.Connection")
   Set Sh = Server.CreateObject("ADODB.Recordset")
   Set Shapecmd = server.CreateObject("ADODB.Recordset")
   cnt.Open "provider=MSDataShape;Data Provider=sqloledb;data
             source=208.222.107.6;" & _
      "database=dbad1d;uid=ubad1d1;pwd=21@1n3z;"
   Shapecmd.Open _
   "SELECT querytext FROM statements WHERE queryname = 'XMLWineShape'", cnt
```

```
Response.ContentType = "text/XML"
Sh.Open Shapecmd(0).Value, cnt
Sh.Save Response, 1%>
```

The rs:data section of the resulting XML structure is shown in the following
example. XML expresses the hierarchical relationship between WineColor
and WineType. Each z:row tag represents a top-level record. Below each top-
level record are one or more WineType tags, which represent child records.

```
<rs:data>
  <z:row WineColor="Red">
    <WineType WineColor="Red" Variety="Bordeaux Blend" />
    <WineType WineColor="Red" Variety="Cabernet" />
    <WineType WineColor="Red" Variety="carmenere" />
    <WineType WineColor="Red" Variety="Dolcetto" />
    <WineType WineColor="Red" Variety="Merlot" />
    <WineType WineColor="Red" Variety="Pinot Noir" />
    <WineType WineColor="Red" Variety="Proprietary Blend" />
    <WineType WineColor="Red" Variety="Syrah" />
    <WineType WineColor="Red" Variety="Zinfandel" />
  </z:row>
  <z:row WineColor="White">
    <WineType WineColor="White" Variety="Chardonnay" />
    <WineType WineColor="White" Variety="Gewurztraminer" />
    <WineType WineColor="White" Variety="Sauvignon Blanc" />
  </z:row>
</rs:data>
```

In order to display this XML data island in a table structure, you need to bind
two levels of tables that place data on the screen. The DHTML code form
XMLtable6.Asp is as follows:

```
<HTML><BODY>
<XML ID="WList" SRC="ShapedXML.asp"></XML>
<H1>Wine Catalog<H2>
<TABLE width = 75% DATASRC="#WList"><TR><TD>
<TABLE width = 75% DATASRC="#WList" DATAFLD="rs:data">
<TR><TD>
<TABLE width = 100% DATASRC="#WList" DATAFLD="z:row">
  <TR bgcolor="violet"><TD><H2><SPAN
            DATAFLD="rs:data.z:row.winecolor"></SPAN></H2>
  <OL>
    <TABLE DATASRC="#WList" DATAFLD="rs:data.z:row.winetype">
    <TR bgcolor ="mistyrose">
      <TD><LI><SPAN DATAFLD="variety"></SPAN></TD>
    </TR>
    </TABLE>
  </OL>
</TD></TR></TABLE>
</TD></TR></TABLE>
</TD></TR></TABLE>
</BODY></HTML>
```

The code used in XMLtable6.Asp looks a bit bewildering at first glance.
Although DHTML is a vast improvement over the equivalent HTML coding,
it's still a bit hard to see what's going on in terms of accessing the XML

structure through TABLE tags. The TABLE tags correspond directly to the structural levels in the XML data island. In this case, you need to work with four levels of data in order to construct the catalog display. Table 12-1 shows how the XML structure breaks down into levels. *Note:* Some levels don't have any data that will be displayed on the page. However, because of the hierarchical nature of XML, these levels, which act as containers for the levels that have displayable data, must be bound to TABLE tags in order to access the lower levels.

Table 12-1	XML Structure Levels	
Level	*Description*	*Displays Data*
1	The entire XML island structure	No
2	schema and rs:data tags	No
3	z:row under rs:data	Yes
4	winetype under z:row	Yes

If you extract just the TABLE tags from XMLTable6.Asp, you get an outline of the DHTML code that shows these are four TABLE tags used in the code which correspond to the four levels of the XML structure.

```
<TABLE #1 bind to XML structure>
<TABLE #2 select the rs:data section>
<TABLE #3 select the z:row section>
    show winecolor property of z:row
    <TABLE #4 select winetype element below z:row>
    show variety property of winetype
    </TABLE #4>
</TABLE #3>
</TABLE #2>
</TABLE #1>
```

It's important to remember that when you code a TABLE structure like the preceding one, each TABLE must have at least one row and cell even if that level does not actually place any data on the page. If you look at the code for XMLTable6.Asp, you notice <TR><TD> tags following each TABLE tag even when there are no SPAN tags used. If you do not remember to include the <TR><TD> on non-displaying levels (such as Levels 1 and 2 in this example), the data displayed in the lower levels doesn't appear on the document page. To put it another way, the TABLE tags for the non-displaying levels do affect the DHTML formatting of the page.

The catalog is still a bit incomplete. It needs one more level of detail, which shows the actual wines under their color and variety, as shown in Figure 12-13.

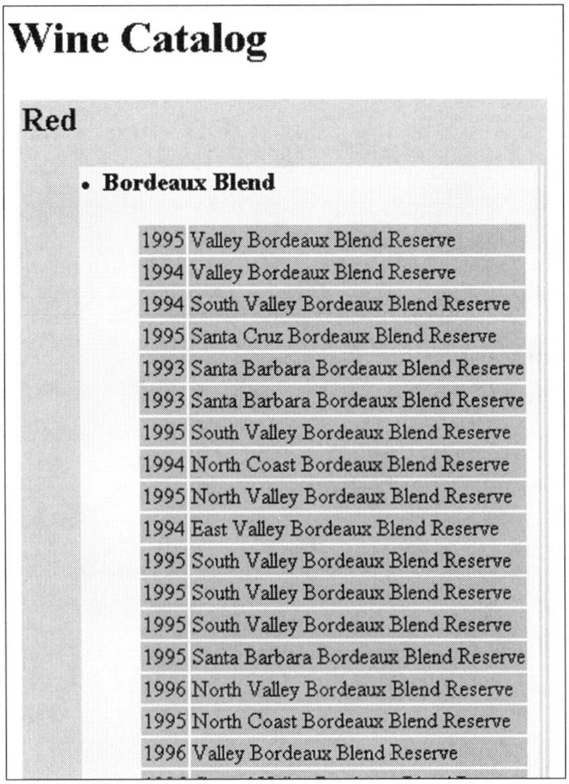

Figure 12-13:
A three-level catalog is generated by using the Data-Shaping provider to generate hierarchical XML.

After you have the basic structure from XMLTable6.Asp, it's a fairly simple process to nest additional levels of details. The most difficult step is writing the data-shaping statement that generates the ADO recordset. The following statement adds a third level of information: the wine product details below the variety level. This statement is stored as `Queryname XMLWineShape1` in the Statements table:

```
SHAPE {SELECT DISTINCT WineColor FROM WineProductCatalog}
APPEND(
 (SHAPE
  SELECT Distinct WineColor,Variety
    FROM WineProductCatalog} as WineType
 APPEND({SELECT winecolor, variety,vintage,winename
    FROM wineproductcatalog ORDER BY vintage, winename}
      As Product
    RELATE variety TO variety))
  RELATE winecolor To winecolor)
```

ShapedXML1.Asp is identical to ShapedXML.Asp with the exception that it uses `XMLWineShape1` as its shape command because the code simply exports the ADO recordset to an XML data island. You don't have to be concerned with the mechanics involved in building either the multiple level ADO recordset (that is done by the Data-Shaping provider) or the multiple level XML structure (that is done by ADO).

The DHTML code for XMLTable7.Asp simply nests one more TABLE tag inside the four that were used in XMLTable6.Asp.

```
<HTML><BODY>
<XML ID="WList" SRC="ShapedXML1.asp"></XML>
<H1>Wine Catalog<H2>
<TABLE DATASRC="#WList"><TR><TD>
<TABLE DATASRC="#WList" DATAFLD="rs:data"><TR><TD>
<TABLE DATASRC="#WList" DATAFLD="z:row">
  <TR bgcolor="peachpuff"><TD><H2><SPAN DATAFLD="winecolor"></SPAN></H2>
  <OL>
  <TABLE DATASRC="#WList" DATAFLD="winetype">
    <TR bgcolor ="lightyellow">
      <TD><LI><H3><SPAN DATAFLD="variety"></SPAN></H3>
      <OL>
        <TABLE DATASRC="#WList" DATAFLD="Product">
        <TR  bgcolor="lightblue">
          <LI><TD><SPAN DATAFLD="vintage"></TD>
          <TD><SPAN DATAFLD="winename"></TD>
        </TR>
        </TABLE>
        </OL>
      <TD></TR></TABLE>
    </OL></TD></TR></TABLE>
    </TD></TR></TABLE>
  </TD></TR></TABLE>
</BODY></HTML>
```

The combination of data shaping, ADO, XML, and DHTML create a significantly improved development environment for publishing data through Web pages. This combination of technologies can handle simple data sets or, as you see in this chapter, complicated multi-level hierarchical data structures quite easily. In many ways, it is easier creating these displays in the development context than it is using tools like Access or Visual Basic 6.0.

However, one important area of database work cannot be easily handled with this technology. The XML data islands are essentially a read-only data provider. XML Islands work well when you are building applications that publish data. But what if you wanted to enter or edit the data? In order to do that, you need a technology that's able to maintain a two-way relationship between the data being manipulated on the client side and the original data source. But, that's the topic of Chapter 13.

Chapter 13

Client-Side ADO

Client-Side Objects

Chapter 12 showed that in circumstances such as a company intranet, where you knew that your users were using Internet Explorer 5.x (IE), you can simplify programming and increase features by using client-side scripting and Dynamic HTML (DHTML) display elements in your Web pages.

The Web pages created in Chapter 12 took advantage of the ability of IE 5.x to read XML text and store that data structure provided by the XML text as a data island. The data island can be bound to DHTML display elements to produce a data-enhanced Web page with a minimum of coding. The diagram in Figure 13-1 illustrates how data binding works with Web pages. The point to note is that the ADO objects operate only on the server side. ADO sends XML, a pure text format, to the browser because the browser has no built-in facility for handling a complex, binary object such as an ADO recordset. XML becomes the common denominator between the server and the client, enabling them to share a common set of data.

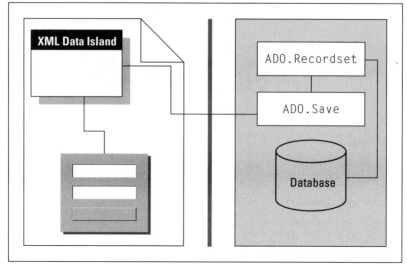

Figure 13-1:
ADO sends
XML text to
create an
XML data
island in the
Web
browser.

However, an XML island lacks many of the features provided by a more robust object like an ADO recordset. You can get around the limitation of the browser by using the OBJECT tag to insert a reference to an ActiveX component that is already installed on the client. The object is called a *DataControl*. The DataControl is installed automatically with Office 2000 or any version of the Microsoft Data Access Components (MDAC). The latest MDAC is available at www.microsoft.com/data/download.htm.

Adding a client-side object

The OBJECT tag is used to add ActiveX objects to a Web page so that client-side scripts can work with binary objects that enhance the feature set of the browser. Unlike most VB/VBA compatible applications, you cannot add objects to a Web page using a reference to the name of the object, such as CreateObject("ADODB.Recordset").

Instead you must refer to the class id of the object. Windows uses a system of Globally Unique Identifier (GUID) to uniquely identify components. The GUID is a 128-bit unique identification string that is created during the development process. When a new component is installed on a Windows system, the GUID is added to the system registry. After added to the registry, the software component registry entry contains several important pieces of information, including:

✓ **DLL file name:** Windows components are supplied in the form of a DLL file. This entry indicates the name of the DLL and where it's stored.

✓ **Object name:** The object name is the name by which an application, such as a ASP, can reference the component. For example, when you install Microsoft Word, the name `Word.Application` is added to the registry. In VB/VBA or in an ASP, you would refer to Word using the name `Word.Application`.

GUID is created by an algorithm that takes into consideration elements such as current date and time and the Media Access Control identifier on the network adapter of the system. The result is a universally unique number that can identify a component on any PC. Microsoft Visual Basic or Visual C++ automatically generates GUIDs for any ActiveX components generated by so that independent software developers can distribute or sell their own software components.

Most components have a descriptive name as well as a GUID. However, in DHTML you must use the GUID to refer to any installed component. The following tag shows the GUID for the DataControl component. This GUID is always the same on all systems unless Microsoft specifically changes it. For now, simply assume that all updates to the DataControl will use this GUID.

```
<OBJECT classid="clsid:BD96C556-65A3-11D0-983A-00C04FC29E33"
</OBJECT>
```

If you add this `OBJECT` tag to a Web page, you have the ability to create a recordset object on the client side of your Web application. The DataControl component creates an Active Data Object Remote (ADOR) recordset on the client side. ADOR is a subset of ADO that omits server-oriented ADO features that aren't be needed on the client side of an application.

Figure 13-2 shows the use of the DataControl object on a Web page. Instead of sending text (XML format) to the browser, the server sends an ADO object to the client. The client then uses the DataControl (which contains the recordset) to bind the data to the display elements on the page.

The ADOR recordset supports all of the operations that an XML data island supports, but adds ADO features such as navigation (`MoveNext`, `MovePrevious`), filter, and sort. Furthermore, it enables you to edit that data in the ADOR recordset and have the changes updated as a batch to the original data source on the server. This enables you to create Web pages that have many of the features you expect from an Access or Visual Basic application.

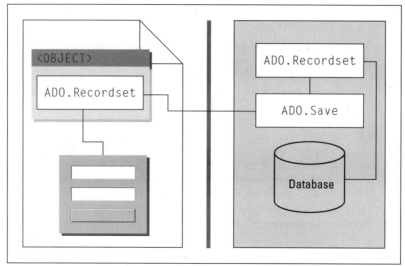

Figure 13-2:
ADO sends
data to a
client-side
object that
creates a
recordset
object on
the client.

Using the OBJECT tag

The `DataControl` object is typically inserted with the `OBJECT` tag shown below. The `ID` attribute of the `OBJECT` tag is very important because it is the name of the DataControl that you use in your script to refer to the control and its properties and methods.

```
<OBJECT classis="clsid:BD96C556-65A3-11D0-983A-00C04FC29E33"
ID="VList" HEIGHT=1 WIDTH = 1>
```

One oddity is the use of the `HEIGHT` and `WIDTH` attributes. The DataControl, like the XML island, has no visible characteristics. However, the `OBJECT` tag generates some blank space on the page. To suppress this blank space, set the `HEIGHT` and `WIDTH` to 1.

Object parameters

When you use an `OBJECT` tag, you specify the parameters by using a `PARM` tag for each parameter you need to set. Valid parameters are determined by the specific object that you are referencing.

```
<PARM NAME="parameter name" VALUE = "value">
```

Using the ADTG format

You can use the DataControl to create a client-side recordset in a very similar manner to the way you used XML tags to create an XML data island on the client.

✔ **Save format:** Instead of using the `Save` method to generate an XML equivalent of the ADO recordset, you can use the Advanced Data Tablegram (ADTG) format. This format contains all of the information required to create a corresponding recordset on the client. The ADTG format has a value of 0 for the `Save` method.

✔ **ContentType:** The ADTG format, unlike XML, contains a mixture of binary and text. To add this data to the response stream, set the `ContentType` to multipart/mixed, as shown below.

```
Response.ContentType = "multipart/mixed"
```

✔ **URL parameter:** The `URL` parameter is used with the `DataControl` object when you want insert data from a specific document into the client. This is similar to the way that you specified the ASP that generated the XML as the XML source in Chapter 12.

Keep in mind that you aren't directly linking the client to the server-side recordset. Rather, you are using ADO to create an ADOR equivalent of the server's ADO recordset on the client. The ADOR recordset is independent of the server's original ADO recordset. However, the ADOR recordset on the client contains references to the records in the server's data source tables. Having a client-side recordset object enables you to reconnect to the server and update the records with any changes made to the client-side ADOR recordset.

Loading the variety list as a recordset

The first step in using a DataControl is creating an ASP that generates the required ADO recordset using server-side scripting. The following procedure is stored in the RsSource1.Asp. This procedure is identical to the one used in Chapter12, WineVarietyXML.Asp, with two small but important changes. First, the `ContentType` is changed to enable transmission of binary and text in the Response object. Also, the format type parameter of the `Save` method is changed to 0, which specifies the ADTG format.

```
<%  Set List = server.CreateObject("ADODB.Recordset")
  List.Open "SELECT DISTINCT variety " & _
    "FROM WineProductCatalog", _
    "Provider=sqloledb;data source=208.222.107.6;" & _
    "database=dbad1d;uid=ubad1d1;pwd=21@1n3z;",1,3
  Response.ContentType = "multipart/mixed"
    List.Save response,0
%>
```

After it's created, the RsSource1.Asp page functions as the source for the recordset in the Data Control object. The following code is stored in the ClientRs1.Asp page. It duplicates the wine variety listing in Chapter12. The URL parameter of the DataControl object references the ASP RSSource1.Asp, which generates the ADTG data stream. Keep in mind that the ADTG data isn't a recordset. It's a data format that can be loaded by ADO to create a recordset. In this case, the ADTG data isn't stored in a file but is contained in the Response data stream. The DataControl is named `Vlist` by the `ID` attribute.

```
<HTML><BODY>
<OBJECT CLASSID="clsid:BD96C556-65A3-11D0-983A-00C04FC29E33" ID="VList" HEIGHT=1
          WIDTH = 1>
   <PARAM NAME="URL" VALUE="http://208.185.177.211/chp13/RSSource1.Asp">
</OBJECT>
<H1>Client Side Recordset</H1>
<TABLE Name="Wine Variety" DATASRC="#VList">
<TR><TD><SPAN DATAFLD="Variety"></SPAN></TD></TR>
</TABLE>
</BODY></HTML>
```

The DataControl can be used as the `DATASRC` parameter of the DHTML display elements. The preceding code shows that the variety field is bound to a `TABLE` tag. Note that the DataControl eliminates the need to navigate through various layers, as is the case with XML. You can write the DHTML code for the table using just three lines.

Figure 13-3:
The DataControl can be bound to TABLE tags to display data contained in a recordset.

Client Side Recordset

Bordeaux Blend
Cabernet
carmenere
Chardonnay
Dolcetto
Gewurztraminer
Merlot
Pinot Noir
Proprietary Blend
Sauvignon Blanc
Syrah
Zinfandel

Recordset navigation

The DataControl is an object that functions in two ways. The DataControl itself functions as a data source for DHTML controls. In RsSource1.Asp, the DataControl is bound to a table that displays all of the records contained in the DataControl's recordset.

It also functions as a container for a recordset that supports ADO recordset properties and methods. For example, a records navigation method such as MoveNext or MovePrevious can be used to change the current record.

To see how this works, remove the TABLE tag from the Web page and replace it with an INPUT tag bound to the same data source and fields, as shown below.

```
Wine Variety: <INPUT Name=Variety DATASRC=#VList DATAFLD=Variety>
```

Because an INPUT tag text box can display only one field from one record at a time, you need a way for users to move to the next record. The following INPUT tag creates a button on the page named Next that shows the greater than sign (>) indicating "next record."

```
<INPUT type="button" value=">" id=Next>
```

The button needs to be linked to a client side script procedure that applies the MoveNext method to the recordset contained in the DataControl. The following SCRIPT applies the MoveNext method each time the Next button is clicked.

```
<SCRIPT LANGUAGE=vbscript>
<!--
Sub Next_onclick
    VList.Recordset.MoveNext
End Sub
-->
</SCRIPT>
```

Note that in the script, you cannot apply the MoveNext method to the DataControl, Vlist, because a DataControl isn't a recordset object. It contains a recordset. By using the Recordset method you can access the ADOR recordset inside the DataControl.

When you put the pieces together, ClientRS2.Asp, shown below, displays the first variety in the recordset when the page is loaded. When the user clicks the button, the Next value, as shown in Figure 13-4, appears in the box.

```
<HTML>
<SCRIPT LANGUAGE=vbscript>
<!--
Sub Next_onclick
    VList.Recordset.MoveNext
End Sub
-->
</SCRIPT>
<BODY>
<OBJECT CLASSID="clsid:BD96C556-65A3-11D0-983A-00C04FC29E33"
ID="VList" HEIGHT=1 WIDTH = 1>
    <PARAM NAME="URL" VALUE="http://208.185.177.211/chp13/RSSource1.Asp">
</OBJECT>
<H1>Client Side Recordset</H1>
Wine Variety: <INPUT Name=Variety DATASRC=#VList DATAFLD=Variety>
<P>
<INPUT type="button" value=">" id=Next>
</BODY></HTML>
```

Figure 13-4:
You can apply methods to the DataControl's recordset to manipulate the data displayed on the page.

When you load these pages, you may need to wait a moment for the boxes to fill because they are running off my office server.

You can expand the concept to include buttons for all four of the standard navigation methods — MoveFirst, MoveLast, MoveNext, and MovePrevious. ClientRS2.Asp, shown in the following example, adds buttons and the corresponding client-side script to implement four navigation buttons, pictured in Figure 13-5.

```
<HTML>
<SCRIPT LANGUAGE=vbscript>
<!--
Sub Next_onclick
    VList.Recordset.MoveNext
End Sub
Sub First_onclick
    VList.Recordset.MoveFirst
End Sub
Sub Last_onclick
    VList.Recordset.MoveLast
End Sub
Sub Previous_onclick
    VList.Recordset.MovePrevious
End Sub
-->
</SCRIPT>
<BODY>
<OBJECT CLASSID="clsid:BD96C556-65A3-11D0-983A-00C04FC29E33"
ID="VList" HEIGHT=1 WIDTH = 1>
    <PARAM NAME="URL" VALUE="http://208.185.177.211/chp13/RSSource1.Asp">
</OBJECT>
<H1>Client Side Recordset</H1>
Wine Variety: <INPUT Name=Variety DATASRC=#VList DATAFLD=Variety>
<P>
<INPUT type="button" value="|<" id=First>
<INPUT type="button" value="<" id=Previous>
<INPUT type="button" value=">" id=Next>
<INPUT type="button" value=">|" id=Last>
</BODY></HTML>
```

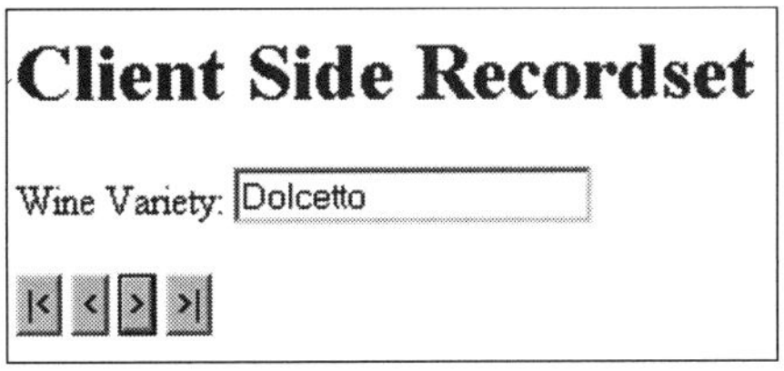

Figure 13-5:
A client-side
script
implements
navigation
buttons.

Client Side Recordset

Wine Variety: Dolcetto

|◁ ◁ ▷ ▷|

Populating lists

In Part III of this book, recordsets are used extensively for user interface
enhancements, such as for populating combo and list boxes. After you have a
recordset in a DataControl, you can do the same thing on a Web page.

In Access 2000 and Visual Basic 6.0, list controls have both data binding properties and display list properties, both of which can be bound to different
recordsets. In DHTML, the SELECT tag, which is used to create drop list and
list boxes, uses data binding only to define the value of element. The contents of the list, defined in HTML by OPTION tags, cannot be directly linked to
a field in a recordset.

However, you can use client-side script to add options to a SELECT tag programmatically. To populate a list from a recordset, start by adding an empty
list to the Web page, as shown below.

```
<SELECT ID="VarietyList"></SELECT><P>
```

If you want to add an option to that SELECT tag, you must write a VBScript
procedure. Remember that in a Web document, there is a significant difference between an attribute or property of an existing element and adding a
element to the current page. In Access 2000 and Visual Basic 6.0, the items
listed in a combo box or list box are considered properties of the control. In a
Web page, each item listed is created by a separate OPTION tag.

This means that if you want to add an option to a SELECT tag, you must
create and add a new OPTION tag and add it to the current document. To do
this, begin with a statement that creates a new OPTION tag object. The following statement uses the DHTML method CreateElement to create a new
OPTION tag object. The Document object refers the entire Web page.

```
Set O = document.CreateElement("OPTION")
```

Then you can define the attributes of that OPTION. An OPTION object requires
a Text property. You also have the option to add a Value property if desired.
The SELECT element returns the Text as its value if no specific value is
assigned.

```
O.Text = "Cabernet"
O.Value = 1000
```

At this point, the OPTION object exists in memory, but it has not yet been
added to the Web page. The Add method of the SELECT object adds the
OPTION to the list. MakeList1.Asp, as shown in the following example, applies
this technique to the recordset in the DataControl. When the page loads, the
list is initially empty. Clicking the Get Variety List button executes the
VBScript code, which adds the first items in the DataControl recordset to the
list, as shown in Figure 13-6. Note that the Text property is assigned a value
from the Recordset property of the Vlist object. Vlist, the DataControl, is
the container for the recordset.

```
VarietyList.Add O
<SCRIPT LANGUAGE=vbscript>
<!--
Sub GetList_onclick
    Set O = document.createElement("OPTION")
    O.Text = VList.Recordset(0)
    VarietyList.add O
End Sub
-->
</SCRIPT>
<HTML><BODY>
<OBJECT CLASSID="clsid:BD96C556-65A3-11D0-983A-00C04FC29E33"
ID="VList" HEIGHT=1 WIDTH = 1>
    <PARAM NAME="URL" VALUE="http://208.185.177.211/chp13/RSSource1.Asp">
</OBJECT>
<SELECT ID="VarietyList"></SELECT><P>
<INPUT type="button" value="Get Variety List" id=GetList>
</BODY></HTML>
```

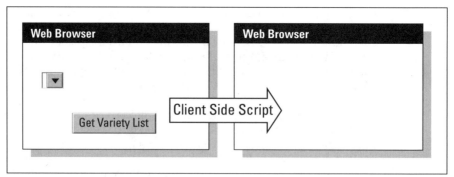

Figure 13-6:
VBScript
adds an
option to a
drop list.

Of course, MakeList1.Asp added only a single item to the list. What about adding the entire recordset to the list? MakeList2.Asp shows how you to modify the procedure to add one OPTION for each record in the recordset. This is accomplished by using a loop. You must destroy the OPTION object O before you create each new OPTION.

```
<!--
Sub GetList_onclick
    Set R = VList.Recordset
    Do Until R.Eof
        Set O = document.createElement("OPTION")
        O.Text = R(0)
        VarietyList.add O
        Set O = Nothing
        R.MoveNext
    Loop
End Sub
-->
```

When you load MakeList2.Asp and click on the button, the script procedure produces the result shown in Figure 13-7. The drop-down list shows the entire contents of recordset.

Figure 13-7:
The entire recordset is used to populate a drop-down list.

Running script onloading

In many cases, operations such as populating the contents of a drop-down list should take place as soon as the Web page is loaded rather than waiting for the user to click a button. The DHTML object model supports events related to the entire Window object. The OnLoad event, similar to the OnLoad event of a VB/VBA form, takes place automatically when the Web page is being loaded into the browser.

MakeList3.Asp places the list populating code into a separate procedure, as shown below, and then calls that procedure as part of the Window_OnLoad event procedure.

```
<SCRIPT  LANGUAGE=vbscript>
<!--
Sub FillVarietyList
Set R = VList.Recordset
Do Until R.Eof
      Set O = document.createElement("OPTION")
      O.Text = R(0)
      VarietyList.add O
      Set O = Nothing
      R.MoveNext
   Loop
End Sub
Sub window_onload
   FillVarietyList
End Sub
```

Disabling an element

You may have noticed that when the page is loading, it first shows an unpopulated drop-down list element. Then after a few seconds, the box expands indicating that the list has been populated and is ready for display. If you got impatient and tried to open the list before the loading was complete, you may have generated an error in the browser.

Part of the reason for the delay is that my server (at the time of writing this book) is badly in need of a new motherboard, a faster processor, and more memory, which I hope to be able to afford by writing this book. Regardless of server improvements, it is useful to prevent a user from using the screen elements before they are fully populated.

DHTML display elements in IE 5.x support the DISABLED attribute, which grays out the display element on the page. The following tag sets the initial state of the VarietyList drop-down list as disabled.

```
<SELECT ID="VarietyList" DISABLED></SELECT>
```

After the list is populated, you can enable the element by setting the Disabled property of the element to False using a VbScript statement.

```
VarietyList.disabled = false
```

In MakeList4.Asp, the preceding statement is added to the FillVarietyList procedure so that the list becomes enabled as soon as it has been filled.

```
Sub FillVarietyList
    Set R = VList.Recordset
    Do Until R.Eof
        Set O = document.createElement("OPTION")
        O.Text = R(0)
        VarietyList.add O
        Set O = Nothing
        R.MoveNext
    Loop
    VarietyList.disabled = false
End Sub
```

When you load MakeList4.Asp, notice that the unpopulated drop-down list is grayed out until it is fully populated.

Direct Access to Datasources

In the preceding examples, the ADO data source was accessed indirectly. The source ADO recordset was created by a SQL statement stored in the RSSource1.Asp page. This page saved a copy of the recordset created on the server as a stream of ADTG data, which flowed through the DataControl on the client side.

Although this method works perfectly well, in may cases it has the disadvantage of requiring you to create a page like RSSource1.Asp for each recordset you want to use. This becomes even more cumbersome when you create pages that require multiple recordset in a single document.

You can directly access a data source from the browser client using the features of the DataControl. Figure 13-8 illustrates how a DataControl can be used to establish a connection between a Web client and a data provider.

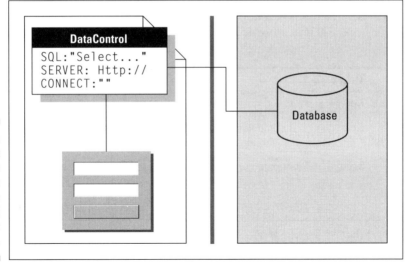

Figure 13-8:
Direct connections between a client-side DataControl and the data provider.

The direct connection approach eliminates the need to create a special document that creates the recordset on the server and then passes a copy to the client. Instead, the SQL and Connection string information are sent directly from the client to the server.

The DataControl requires three parameters to create a recordset by directly accessing a data provider.

- ✔ **SQL:** This parameter contains the text of the statement that is executed by the data provider. Although this is usually a SQL statement, it can be any statement from which the ADO provider can create a recordset, such as a Data-Shaping command.

- ✔ **SERVER:** This the name of the server that acts as the gateway for processing the query. Remember this is the name of the Web server to which you connect. The database server may be a completely different computer. The examples in this chapter use one computer as the Web server and a different computer, located some 3,000 miles from the Web server, as the database server. The DataControl uses the HTTP protocol to connect to a Web server. This means that the computer running the Web browser does not have to have any special client protocols setup. It is only required that the computer specified in the SERVER parameter be able to access the data provider.

- ✔ **CONNECT:** This is the OLE DB connection string that the Web server uses to connect to the data source. The connection string is used by the computer named in the SERVER parameter to connect to an ADO data source.

The networking issues can get a bit confusing because there are potentially several computers acting as servers and clients of different types. Table 13-1 illustrates the task request flow of the wine variety list box — which computers are asked to do what tasks in order to get the list of options.

Table 13-1			Task Request Flow
Order	**Client**	**Asks This Server**	**For This Task**
First	Your computer	Web server (my office)	Send requested Web page to client.
Second	Your computer	Web server (my office)	Client-side object (DataControl) sends SQL, SERVER, and CONNECT parameters to the Web server using http protocol.
Third	Web server	Database server (wbase2.com)	Web server request a recordset from the database server using the SQL, SERVER, and CONNECT parameters sent by your computer.
Fourth	Your computer	Web server (my office)	Web server returns the recordset to the client browser.
Fifth	Your computer	No server	Client-side script uses the recordset to create OPTION tags for SELECT tag.

Sounds complicated, doesn't it? But there are good reasons why this approach actually is efficient. First, the total amount of data (actual bytes) that are exchanged is very small — a few kilobytes for each transmission. Also, the overall task is divided among several different computers rather than having one computer perform all the work. Third, the client computer does not need to have a direct connection to the database server. The client (your computer) only needs to connect to the Web server. The Web server, in turn, contacts the database server, acquires that recordset, and returns that recordset to the client browser. The only tools that must be on the client desktop are the IE 5.x and the DataControl ActiveX component.

In practice, the weak link in this scenario is my office Web server, which was never meant to be a Web host (but is good enough for you to see how these examples work). In some ways, building applications on less-than-ideal computers has some advantages in that they magnify slow points in the process so that it is easier to tell when there is a bottleneck in your application during the testing period. If you develop on powerful machines, they may mask weaknesses in your code that won't be revealed until you get a lot of real traffic. At least that is my rationalization.

Following is a Remote Data Services (RDS) DataControl OBJECT tag that sends a request to the Web server for an ADOR recordset.

```
<OBJECT classid="clsid:BD96C556-65A3-11D0-983A-00C04FC29E33"
ID="VList" HEIGHT=1 WIDTH = 1>
   <PARAM NAME="SQL" VALUE="SELECT DISTINCT variety FROM WineProductCatalog">
   <PARAM NAME="SERVER" VALUE="http://208.185.177.211">
   <PARAM NAME="CONNECT" VALUE="Provider=sqloledb;data
             source=208.222.107.6;database=dbad1d1;uid=ubad1d1;pwd=21@1n3z;">
</OBJECT>
```

Note that when you issue the data request from the client, the source document at the client shows all of the client-side code including the connection string details. When you use the URL method, as in MakeList4.Asp, the SQL and CONNECT information is stored in a separate ASP and isn't exposed to the client.

Changing the method by which the DataControl acquires its recordset is transparent to the rest of the code in the ASP that utilizes those objects. This means that the only change needed to convert MakeList4.Asp into DirectConnect1.Asp is to modify the PARM tags in the DataControl object.

When you load DirectConnect1.Asp, you get the identical result as MakeList4.Asp on the screen. The difference between the two pages is invisible to the user.

Implicit server naming

The SERVER parameter used with the DataControl is usually the same server from which the ASP was loaded. It is possible, but not typical, for a one Web server to load the ASP and a different Web server to handle data requests made by the embedded DataControl.

You often see ASP code in which the SERVER parameter isn't explicitly written. Instead, the code takes advantage of server variables to insert the name of the server.

The following example shows how to use the Request objects server variables to insert the name of the server from which the page was loaded as the DataControl server.

```
<PARAM NAME="SERVER"
        VALUE="http://<%=Request.ServerVariables("server_name")%>">
```

Using the variable in place of the actual server name makes it simpler to move an ASP application to a different Web server. If you use the actual name or IP address of the server in your ASP, then you must recode the pages if they are moved to a different server. Because it is common to develop applications on a development server and then move them to a production server when you deploy the application, you may want to use this technique to avoid recoding later on.

Pages with multiple recordsets

One of the primary reasons for switching from the ADTG method to the direct connection method is that the direct connection method makes it easier to load multiple recordsets into a single page. Using the ADTG method, you have to create a separate source ASP for each recordset. The direct-connect method enables you to simply add another DataControl to the page when you need additional recordsets.

Look at the page displayed in Figure 13-9. The page contains a drop-down list and a table, both populated from recordsets drawn from the WineProductCatalog table.

Figure 13-9:
Data
from two
separate
recordsets
displayed on
one page.

Following is the code for DirectConnect2.Asp. This page uses two separate DataControl objects given the Ids, Wines, and Vlist. Although Vlist is used to populate the drop-down list, the Wines DataControl is bound to a table. When you load DirectConnect2.Asp, each DataControl opens a connection to the designated server, which in turn queries the specified database server in order to create the recordset objects in the displayed page.

```
<SCRIPT LANGUAGE=vbscript>
<!--
Sub FillVarietyList
    Set R = VList.Recordset
    Do Until R.Eof
        Set O = document.createElement("OPTION")
        O.Text = R(0)
        VarietyList.add O
        Set O = Nothing
        R.MoveNext
    Loop
End Sub
Sub window_onload
    FillVarietyList
End Sub
-->
</SCRIPT>
<HTML>
```

```
<OBJECT CLASSID="clsid:BD96C556-65A3-11D0-983A-00C04FC29E33"
ID="Wines" HEIGHT=1 WIDTH = 1>
   <PARAM NAME="SQL" VALUE="SELECT variety,vintage,winename,quality FROM
             WineProductCatalog">
   <PARAM NAME="SERVER" VALUE="http://208.185.177.211">
   <PARAM NAME="CONNECT" VALUE="Provider=sqloledb;data
             source=208.222.107.6;database=dbad1d1;uid=ubad1d1;pwd=21@1n3z;">
</OBJECT>
<OBJECT CLASSID="clsid:BD96C556-65A3-11D0-983A-00C04FC29E33"
ID="VList" HEIGHT=1 WIDTH = 1>
   <PARAM NAME="SQL" VALUE="SELECT DISTINCT variety FROM WineProductCatalog">
   <PARAM NAME="SERVER" VALUE="http://208.185.177.211">
   <PARAM NAME="CONNECT" VALUE="Provider=sqloledb;data
             source=208.222.107.6;database=dbad1d1;uid=ubad1d1;pwd=21@1n3z;">
</OBJECT>
Wine Variety: <SELECT ID="VarietyList"></SELECT><P>
<TABLE Name="Wines" DATASRC=#Wines Border = 1 >
<TR bgcolor="lightblue">
<TD><SPAN DATAFLD="Vintage"></SPAN></TD>
<TD><SPAN DATAFLD="Winename"></SPAN></TD>
<TD><SPAN DATAFLD="Quality"></SPAN></TD>
</TR></TABLE>
<P></BODY></HTML>
```

Sorting

One of the advantages of using the DataControl is that the recordset objects it contains can be manipulated with client-side script without having to connect to the server. For example, the wine list recordset added to the ASP in DirectConnect2.Asp isn't retrieved in any particular sort order from the server. Figure 13-10 shows a similar ASP, DirectConnectSort.Asp, that has added a drop-down list and a button that can be used to change the sort order of the recordset in the wine list.

Figure 13-10: DataControl recordsets can be sorted within the client.

Wine Variety: Bordeaux Blend ▾		

Sort By: Vintage ▾	Sort	

1997	Santa Cruz Sauvignon Blanc Standard	Standard
1996	North Coast Chardonnay Standard	Standard
1997	North Coast Chardonnay Standard	Standard
1994	South Valley Dolcetto Standard	Standard
1996	East Valley Proprietary Blend Reserve	Reserve
1996	Santa Cruz Sauvignon Blanc Standard	Standard
1995	Valley Bordeaux Blend Reserve	Reserve
1995	Santa Cruz Merlot Standard	Standard

Keep in mind that this is a client-side operation. Instead of using the server to generate a new, sorted recordset, client-side scripting is used to sort the data already loaded into the client. Sorting the records on the client side is much faster than requesting a new recordset from the server. It also eliminates the need to tax network resources just to change the order of an existing record-set. On the other hand, sorting is limited to using a single column as the sort criterion. If you need a multiple-column sort, you have to requery the server in order to return a new, sorted recordset.

The ADOR recordset uses two properties to set the sort order of a recordset.

- **SortColumn:** This is the name of the column in the recordset used as the sort order key.
- **SortDirection:** This property is either True for ascending or False for descending order.

When you have set the sort properties, the changes are applied to the record-set by using the `DataControl Reset` method. Note that the DataControl supports both a `Reset` and a `Refresh` method. `Reset` is used to apply sort (and also filter) properties to the current recordset without involving the server. `Refresh`, on the other hand, does connect to the server and requery the data provider to create a new recordset in the same DataControl.

The following HTML code adds the drop-down list and Sort buttons shown in Figure 13-10.

```
Sort By: <SELECT ID="zOrder">
<OPTION>Vintage</OPTION>
<OPTION>WineName</OPTION>
<OPTION>Quality</OPTION>
</SELECT>
<INPUT type="button" value="Sort" id=DoSort><P>
```

The instructions to perform the actual sorting are contained in the `OnClick` procedure for the `DoSort` button shown below.

```
Sub DoSort_OnClick
    Wines.SortColumn = zOrder.options(zOrder.selectedIndex).Text
    Wines.SortDirection = True
    Wines.Reset
End Sub
```

The expression used as the `SortColumn` property value may require some explanation. The purpose of this expression is to use the item selected in the `zOrder` drop-down list. You may think that you can get the value of the drop-down list by referring to the `Value` of the `SELECT` tag like the statement below.

```
Zorder.Value
```

But this won't work. The reason is that HTML/DHTML options listed in a drop-down list are a collection of elements that are separate from the SELECT tag element. The following statements refers to properties of the first option, in this case Vintage, in the zOrder SELECT tag.

```
ZOrder.Options(1).Text
Zorder.Options(1).Value
```

Of course, in the sorting script you don't know in advance which of the options is selected. The SelectedIndex property of a SELECT tag returns the number of the currently selected item.

```
zOrder.selectedIndex
```

When you put these elements together, you get the following expression that returns the text of the current selected item. Anytime you need to use a selection from a list box you use a similar expression.

```
zOrder.options(zOrder.selectedIndex).Text
```

Note that if you have OPTION tags that have both a text and a value property, you can get the value using the following expression from the selected option.

```
zOrder.options(zOrder.selectedIndex).Value
```

When you load DirectConnectSort.Asp, you can use the drop-down list and button to resort to the wine list as many times as you desire without causing the browser to connect to the server.

Client-side filtering

In addition to sorting records on the client side, you can also apply filters to the recordset. For example, DirectConnect2.Asp and DirectConnectSort.Asp both contain a drop-down-list, which shows each variety of the wine in the WineProductCatalog table.

It seems logical that if you select a variety from the list, you can filter the wine list to show only wines of the same variety. You can accomplish this by requerying the server to return a new recordset for each variety you want to display.

However, client-side filtering enables you to start by downloading the entire recordset to the client and apply filters without having to requery the server.

The DataControl has three properties that are used to define a filter for the current recordset.

✔ **FilterColumn:** This is the name of the column on which the filter is applied.

✔ **FilterCriterion:** This property specifies the logical operator that is used for filtering, such as =, <, >, >=, <=.

✔ **FilterValue.** This is value to which the sort column data is compared.

It is important to remember that if you want to apply a filter to a recordset, the recordset must include a column that contains the data you want to select by. In the `DirectConnect` examples, the wine list does not contain the wine variety. However, if you want to use `Variety` as the criterion for selecting a subset of the entire table, you need to include that field in the recordset even though it isn't visible on the page. The following DataControl tag adds the `Variety` field to the `Wines DataControl` recordset.

```
<OBJECT CLASSID="clsid:BD96C556-65A3-11D0-983A-00C04FC29E33"
ID="Wines" HEIGHT=1 WIDTH = 1>
    <PARAM NAME="SQL" VALUE="SELECT variety,vintage,winename,quality FROM
             WineProductCatalog">
    <PARAM NAME="SERVER" VALUE="http://208.185.177.211">
    <PARAM NAME="CONNECT" VALUE="Provider=sqloledb;data
             source=208.222.107.6;database=dbad1d1;uid=ubad1d1;pwd=21@1n3z;">
</OBJECT>
```

To filter a recordset contained in a DataControl, use a series of statements like the ones below. The order isn't important with the exception that the `Reset` method, which actually applies the filter to the data, is the last item.

```
    Wines.FilterColumn = "Variety"
    Wines.FilterCriterion = "="
    Wines.FilterValue = "Cabernet"
    Wines.Reset
```

In this example, the criterion is taken from the page in the form of the currently selected item in the `VarietyList SELECT` tag. The following procedure is linked to a change in the `VarietyList` selection. Because the ASP enables users to change the variety as many times as they desire, it is necessary to first remove the current filter, if any, before a new filter is applied. The `Reset` method, by default, applies a new filter to the already filtered recordset. If you want to apply the new filter to the original, unfiltered recordset, you must use the parameter `False` with the `Reset` method as shown below.

```
Sub VarietyList_onchange
    Pick = VarietyList.options(varietylist.selectedIndex).Text
    Wines.FilterColumn = "Variety"
    Wines.FilterCriterion = "="
    Wines.FilterValue = pick
    Wines.Reset False
End Sub
```

When you load DirectConnect3.Asp, you can use the drop-down list to limit the wines listed wines to those that match the selected variety as pictured in Figure 13-11.

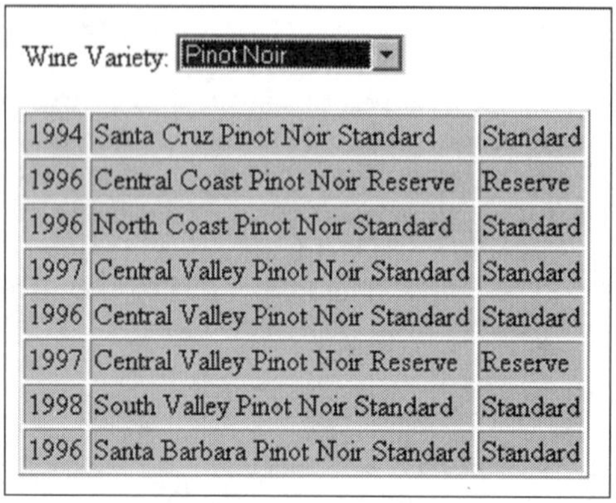

Figure 13-11:
Client-side
scripting
can apply
data filters
to
DataControl
recordsets.

Wine Variety:	Pinot Noir ▾		

1994	Santa Cruz Pinot Noir Standard	Standard
1996	Central Coast Pinot Noir Reserve	Reserve
1996	North Coast Pinot Noir Standard	Standard
1997	Central Valley Pinot Noir Standard	Standard
1996	Central Valley Pinot Noir Standard	Standard
1997	Central Valley Pinot Noir Reserve	Reserve
1998	South Valley Pinot Noir Standard	Standard
1996	Santa Barbara Pinot Noir Standard	Standard

You can apply a filter and a sort order at the same time. DirectConnect3a.Asp adds a sort order, descending by Vintage, to the procedure that filters the recordset. The result is a list that is both filtered and sorted.

```
Sub VarietyList_onchange
    Wines.FilterColumn = ""
    Wines.FilterCriterion = ""
    Wines.FilterValue = ""
    Wines.SortColumn = ""
    Wines.Reset
    Pick = VarietyList.options(varietylist.selectedIndex).Text
    Wines.FilterColumn = "Variety"
    Wines.FilterCriterion = "="
    Wines.FilterValue = pick
    Wines.SortColumn = "Vintage"
    Wines.SortDirection = False
    Wines.Reset False
End Sub
```

Perform filtering on load

Currently, the DirectConnect pages load and display the entire wine catalog when the page is first displayed. By default, the first item in the VarietyList drop-down list is the first item in the recordset used to populate the list, such as Bordeaux Blend.

It may make more sense to the user if the page automatically filtered the wine list to match the initial display in the drop-down list. This can be accomplished quite simply by adding the name of the procedure that filters the wine list, VarietyList_onchange, to the window_onload procedure as shown below.

```
Sub window_onload
    FillVarietyList
    VarietyList_onchange
End Sub
```

Keep in mind that event procedures such as VarietyList_onchange can be called from any procedure in the ASP client-side script in addition to being automatically fired off when the specified interaction, such as changing the VarietyList value, takes place. DirectConnect4.Asp immediately filters the wine list to match the value displayed in the VarietyList control when the page is loaded. You can then use the to change the displayed list.

Relating list contents

When you build a user interface, it is often necessary to have the user make a selection and then use that selection to perform some other task. The problem is that often the list from which the user must make a selection — such as products or customers — contains so many items that choosing from it is cumbersome. The alternative is using two or more related lists. When the user makes a selection from the first list, it automatically narrows the choices on the second list to the category indicated by the first list.

This approach reduces the length of each drop-down list but still enables the user access to the entire list of items. As an example, look at the page displayed in Figure 13-12. This page shows two drop-down lists and a table of data. To display the sales history, the user must select a wine product. To keep the wine product list to a manageable size, a wine variety list is used to filter the wine product list so it lists a single variety of wine product.

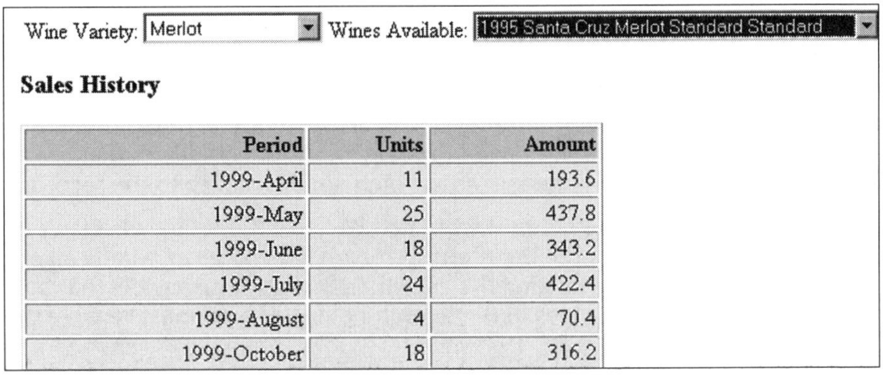

Figure 13-12:
A Web page reports sales history of individual products.

Wine Variety: Merlot	Wines Available: 1995 Santa Cruz Merlot Standard Standard

Sales History

Period	Units	Amount
1999-April	11	193.6
1999-May	25	437.8
1999-June	18	343.2
1999-July	24	422.4
1999-August	4	70.4
1999-October	18	316.2

Populating multiple Lists

The first step in creating the page shown in Figure 13-12 is to create a document in which you populate more than one SELECT tag with data from different recordsets.

Begin by removing the TABLE tag for the wine list and replacing it with a blank SELECT tag.

```
Wines Available: <SELECT ID="WineList"></SELECT>
```

Recall, that unlike TABLE tags, SELECT tags do not support data binding for the option list. The options have to be created with VBScript. The following code populates the new SELECT tag, WineList, with the records from the Wines DataControl. This procedure is then called from the window_onload procedure so that both lists populate when the page RelatedList1.Asp loads.

```
Sub FillWineList
    Set R = Wines.Recordset
    Do Until R.Eof
        Set O = document.createElement("OPTION")
        O.Text = R("Vintage") & " " & R("winename") & " " & _
        R("Quality")
        WineList.add O
        Set O = Nothing
        R.MoveNext
    Loop
End Sub

Sub window_onload
    FillVarietyList
    FillWineList
End Sub
```

Linking lists

The preceding example does populate both lists but it does so independently. The value of the VariertyList does not affect the contents of the WineList. To build the page shown in Figure 13-12, you need to dynamically link changes in the VarietyList with the contents of the WineList.

To write the code needed, it is helpful to outline what needs to happen when the user makes a select in the VarietyList drop-down list.

 ✔ **Filter wines recordset:** The first step is to use the new selection as the criterion for filtering the recordset in the Wines DataControl. The code for this is the same (VarietyList_onchange) as that used in DirectConnect4.Asp, which applies a filter to the recordset.

 ✔ **Erase the current wine list:** Because the options list isn't dynamically bound to the DataControl recordset, you must handle all of the mechanics of populating the list with VBScript. This means that before you can add the wines in the filtered recordset, you must remove the current items.

✔ **Remove:** This method of the SELECT object deletes individual OPTION objects from the Options collection based on the index number of the item. The following statement deletes the first item in the Options collection.

```
WineList.Remove(0)
```

✔ **Length:** This property of the Options collection returns the number of items in the collection. Length is equvalent to the Count property typically found in Microsoft collection objects.To clear the entire collection, you can use a For . . . Next loop as shown below.

```
For ONum = 0 To WineList.options.length
    WineList.remove(0)
Next
```

There is one curious aspect to the code used in the loop that may look odd at first glance. The code removes the same item, Remove(0), over and over. What is happening is that the Options collection is dynamic; as soon as you delete an item, all of the other items are renumbered. In this case, when you delete item 0, the item that was 1 changes to 0. Although the code appears to be removing the same item each time, it's actually working its way through the collection, eliminating each entry until the list is empty.

✔ **Populate the wine list:** After the list is cleared, you can use the filtered recordset to add the wines that match the selected variety.

The following procedure adjusts the contents of the WineList drop-down list to match the variety in the VarietyList.

```
Sub FillWineList
    For ONum = 0 To WineList.options.length
        WineList.remove(0)
    Next
    Set R = Wines.Recordset
    Do Until R.Eof
        Set O = document.createElement("OPTION")
        O.Text = R("Vintage") & " " & R("winename") & " " & _
        R("Quality")
        WineList.add O
        Set O = Nothing
        R.MoveNext
    Loop
    WineList.value = null
End Sub
```

The desired effect, linking the data in the two lists, is achieved by first running the code that filters the Wines recordset and then refilling the WineList SELECT object with the filtered wine list. The following VarietyList_onchange procedure ensures that these two procedures are executed each time the user makes a change in the VarietyList.

```
Sub VarietyList_onchange
    FilterWineList
    FillWineList
End Sub
```

When you load RelatedList2.Asp, you can make selections in the
`VarietyList` and then open the `WineList` drop-down list. The `WineList` is
limited to wines that match the selected variety as shown in Figure 13-13.

Figure 13-13:
The wine
drop-down
list is
related to
the value of
the variety
drop-down
list.

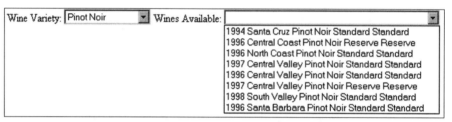

Executing stored procedures with DataControls

To complete the programming needed to create the page shown in Figure
13-13, you need to use the selection made in the wine list to query the data
source so that you can summarize the sales history for the product.

The query needed to find the desired information is a bit complicated
because it requires relating information from three tables:
`WineProductCatalog`, `Orders`, and `OrderDetails`. A query of this complexity is beyond the ability of client-side recordset operations.

The best way to calculate the required recordset is to run the query on the
server and return the completed recordset to a DataControl on the form for
display. In Chapters 9 and 10, server-side scripts were used to execute
queries (`SELECT` statements) and stored procedures on the database server,
and return the results as HTML to the Web page. However, in this example,
the required recordset changes each time the user makes a different selection in the variety drop-down list.

In theory, it is possible to use client-side operations to achieve the desired
result. You create a list of all the sales for all of the products and load that list
as a recordset into a DataControl. You then select the data for individual
products by applying a filter to the downloaded recordset. In practice this
isn't a very efficient way to attack this problem. It is probably the case that
most of the downloaded data is never displayed.

It is much more efficient to use the DataControl to requery the data source for the exactly set of records that match the selected wine.

The most efficient way to query a database server is to create a stored procedure on the server and use it to extract the required recordset. Following is a statement that creates a SQL Server stored procedure that calculates the sales history for any specified wine product. The procedure uses one parameter, @WID, which is the WineID of the product being summarized.

```
Create Procedure WineProdSalesHist
        @WID int
As    SELECT  DatePart(Year,OrderDate),
        DatePart(Month,OrderDate),
        Convert(Varchar(4),DatePart(Year,OrderDate))
        + '-' + DateName(month,OrderDate) As Period,
        Sum(D.Bottles) As Units,
        Sum(D.ExtPrice) as Amount
    FROM WineProductCatalog P, OrderDetails D, Orders O
    WHERE
        P.WineID = D.WineID
        AND D.OrderLink = O.WineOrderID
        AND P.WineID = @WID
    GROUP BY
        DatePart(Year,OrderDate),
        DatePart(Month,OrderDate),
         Convert(Varchar(4),DatePart(Year,OrderDate))
        + '-' + DateName(month,OrderDate)
```

When you want to execute the stored procedure, all you need to do is end a command, like the one below, to the SQL Server. The command is the name of the stored procedure followed by the value you want to assign to the @WID parameter. This simplifies your page coding because you don't have to store this complicated SQL statement in your ASP. All you need is the name of the stored procedure. The following statement would execute the WineProdSalesHist procedure with a parameter of 15.

```
WineProdSalesHist 15
```

In order to use the stored procedure, you need to add a DataControl to the page that will serve as the container for the recordset returned by the stored procedure. However, unlike the other DataControls, the SQL parameter of this object isn't specified because you do not yet know which wine the user will select.

```
<OBJECT CLASSID="clsid:BD96C556-65A3-11D0-983A-00C04FC29E33"
ID="Sales" HEIGHT=1 WIDTH = 1>
    <PARAM NAME="SERVER" VALUE="http://208.185.177.211">
    <PARAM NAME="CONNECT" VALUE="Provider=sqloledb;data
            source=208.222.107.6;database=dbad1d1;uid=ubad1d1;pwd=21@1n3z;">
</OBJECT>
```

In this application, you have to use VBScript to specify the SQL code for the DataControl and then use the `Refresh` method of the DataControl to acquire a new recordset from the servers.

Although this may sound like a complicated task, the code required is rather simple. The following `WineList_onchange` procedure uses the SQL property of the DataControl to specify the stored procedure and parameters that define the required recordset. This time, the `Refresh` (not the `Reset`) method is used. `Refresh` forces the IE to reconnect to the server, execute the SQL statement, and load the recordset that is returned into the DataControl. The result is that each time the user makes a selection from the `WineList`, a new recordset is defined for the Sales DataControl.

```
Sub WineList_onchange
    Sales.SQL = "WineProdSalesHist " & _
        WineList.options(Winelist.selectedIndex).Value
    Sales.Refresh
End Sub
```

In the `WineList_onchange` procedure, it is the `Value` property of the `WineList SELECT` object that is used as the parameter for the stored procedure, instead of the `Text` property. To use the `Value` property, you need to modify the `FillWineList` procedure so that the `WineID` field is assigned to the `Value` of each `OPTION`. The following procedure adds a statement that assigns the `WineID` field to the `Value` property.

```
Sub FillWineList
    For ONum = 0 To WineList.options.length
        WineList.remove(0)
    Next
    Set R = Wines.Recordset
    Do Until R.Eof
        Set O = document.createElement("OPTION")
        O.Text = R("Vintage") & " " & R("winename") & " " & _
        R("Quality")
        O.Value = R("Wineid")
        WineList.add O
        Set O = Nothing
        R.MoveNext
    Loop
    WineList.value = null
End Sub
```

To display the summarized sales information, bind the Sales DataControl to a table using the DHTML shown here:

```
<TABLE ID="SalesHist" Border=1 DATASRC=#Sales width=50%>
    <THEAD>
        <TR bgcolor = #CCCCCC>
        <TD Align=right><B>Period</B></TD>
        <TD Align=right><B>Units</B></TD>
        <TD Align=right><B>Amount</B></TD>
        </TR>
    </THEAD>
```

```
    <TR bgcolor = #EEEEEE>
        <TD Align=right><SPAN DATAFLD="Period"></SPAN></TD>
        <TD Align=right><SPAN DATAFLD="Units"></SPAN></TD>
        <TD Align=right><SPAN DATAFLD="Amount"></SPAN></TD>
    </TR>
</TABLE>
```

The result can be seen by loading RelatedLists3.Asp and making a selection first from the `VarietyList` and then from the `WineList`. The result is a recordset that shows the sales history, if any, for that product. Figure 13-14 shows the sales history of the 1996 East Valley Proprietary Blend Reserve.

Figure 13-14:
The sales history of the 1996 East Valley Proprietary Blend Reserve.

Wine Variety: Proprietary Blend ▼ Wines Available:	1996 East Valley Proprietary Blend Reserve Reserve ▼

Sales History

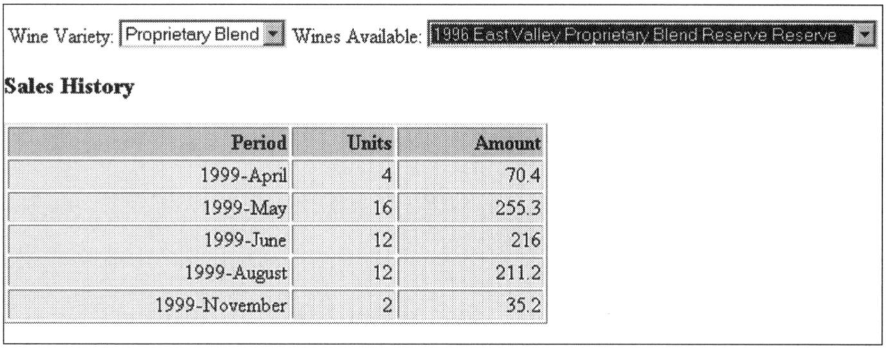

Period	Units	Amount
1999-April	4	70.4
1999-May	16	255.3
1999-June	12	216
1999-August	12	211.2
1999-November	2	35.2

Updating Recordsets

When you create a recordset in a DataControl, you can edit, delete, and add records on the client sides and then submit the changes as a batch to the original data source. These features make it relatively easy to use DHTML Web pages to do data entry and editing in addition to the other operations covered so far in this chapter.

Editing records

The DataControl makes is simple to deal with changes made to the recordset contained in the DataControl. There are two methods for dealing with changes made to the recordset:

- **SubmitChanges:** When this method is applied to a DataControl, any changes made to any of the records in the current recordset for that control are replicated on the original data provider.

- **CancelUpdate:** This method is used to discard changes made to one or more records. This method returns the recordset to its original contents based on the last time the DataControl was refreshed.

As a simple example of how to use these method, RSEdit1.Asp (shown in Figure 13-15), displays a single customer record from the Customers table.

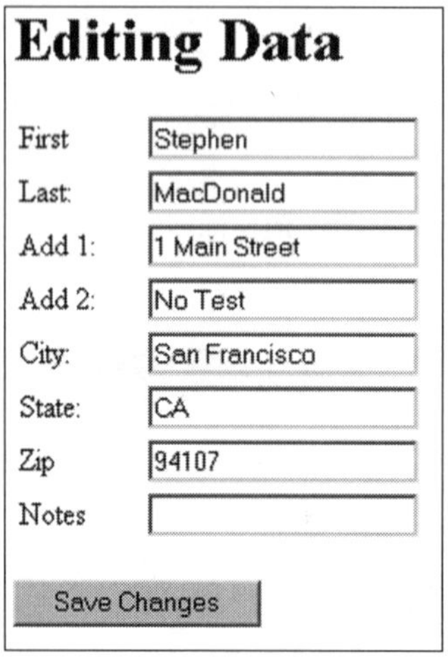

Editing Data

First	Stephen
Last:	MacDonald
Add 1:	1 Main Street
Add 2:	No Test
City:	San Francisco
State:	CA
Zip	94107
Notes	

Save Changes

Figure 13-15: Editing a single record with a DataControl.

The customer record is loaded from a DataControl named Cust. The OBJECT tag for this control is shown below. No special parameters are required to edit a recordset. All recordsets created with a DataControl are editable. Keep in mind that some SQL queries produce recordsets that various providers refuse to update due to the underlying relational structure of the source database. The DataControl accepts edits and attempts to post these edits back to the source provider.

```
<OBJECT CLASSID="clsid:BD96C556-65A3-11D0-983A-00C04FC29E33"
ID="Cust" HEIGHT=1 WIDTH = 1>
   <PARAM NAME="SQL" VALUE="SELECT * FROM Customers WHERE CustomerID=1000">
   <PARAM NAME="SERVER" VALUE="http://208.185.177.211">
   <PARAM NAME="CONNECT" VALUE="Provider=sqloledb;data
            source=208.222.107.6;database=dbad1d;uid=ubad1d1;pwd=21@1n3z;">
</OBJECT>
```

The fields are displayed in INPUT tags that are bound to the fields in the DataControl. You are free to edit the data in any of the INPUT tags. The DataControl saves these changes as they are entered in memory assigned to the Web browser. However, the changes are not permanent. The changes are immediately discarded if you load a different page, refresh the current page, or issue the CancelUpdate method in VBScript.

```
<INPUT TYPE=BUTTON ID="Save" VALUE="Save Changes">
```

To save any editing changes, you must explicitly execute the SubmitChanges method in a VBscript procedure. The procedure below, linked to the OnClick event of the Save button, saves the changes to the current record and then displays a message box to confirm the action to the user.

```
Sub Save_onclick
    Cust.SubmitChanges
    Msgbox "Change to Customer #" & Cust.Recordset("Customerid") & _
    " saved."
End Sub
```

You can test this page by loading RSEdit1.Asp and editing the Notes field. Click the Save Changes button and then reload the page. You see that your edits to the Notes field have been retained by the data provider, which in this example is a SQL Server database.

Editing multiple records

Chapter 10 includes an example, GbookMain.Asp, of record updating using server-side scripting. In that example, individual records were edited and updated using an interface that looked like the one shown in Figure 13-14.

However, editing multiple records on a single page using server side scripting is quite complicated because after the server converts the server-side scripts to pure HTML, the relationship among the fields and records is lost.

However, using DHTML and client-side scripting, you can create a page that enables you to edit as many records in the data set as you desire on the same page. Figure 13-16 shows the RSEdit2.Asp displaying the order history for customer 5501. You can edit any of the records and then save all of the changes by clicking the Save Changes button. Clicking Discard Changes returns the entire recordset to its original contents.

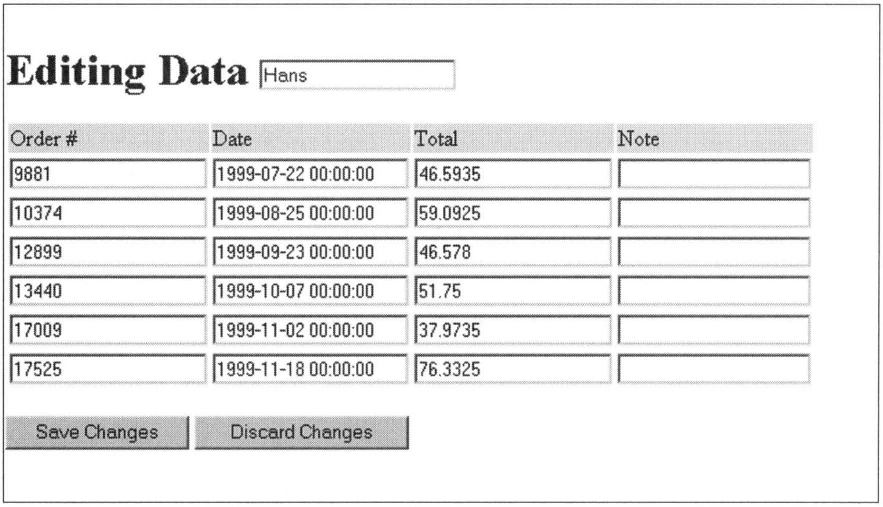

Figure 13-16: Editing of multiple records on one page is support by the DataControl.

Order #	Date	Total	Note
Editing Data Hans			
9881	1999-07-22 00:00:00	46.5935	
10374	1999-08-25 00:00:00	59.0925	
12899	1999-09-23 00:00:00	46.578	
13440	1999-10-07 00:00:00	51.75	
17009	1999-11-02 00:00:00	37.9735	
17525	1999-11-18 00:00:00	76.3325	

Save Changes   Discard Changes

Creating the table of records is a relatively simple matter due to the advantages of DHTML binding. To make an editable display, the SPAN tags, used in other examples to display a recordset in a table, are replaced with INPUT tags, which are bound to the fields in the recordset.

When the page is loaded, IE generates a set of bound INPUT tags for each record contained in the DataControl's recordset. Each row in the table is bound to a different record, which enables you to edit any of the displayed records and save the changes with a single SubmitChanges method linked to the Save Changes button.

```
<TABLE DATASRC="#Orders"Width=50%>
<THEAD><TR bgcolor ="#DDDDDD"><TD>Order
              #</TD><TD>Date</TD><TD>Total</TD><TD>Note</TD></TR></THEAD>
<TR>
    <TD Align=right><INPUT ID="WineOrderID" DATASRC=#Orders
            DATAFLD="WineOrderID" READONLY></TD>
    <TD Align=right><INPUT ID="OrderDate" DATASRC=#Orders
            DATAFLD="OrderDate"></TD>
    <TD Align=right><INPUT ID="OrderTotal" DATASRC=#Orders
            DATAFLD="OrderTotal"></TD>
    <TD><INPUT ID="Notes" DATASRC=#Orders DATAFLD="SpecialInstructions"></TD>
</TR>
</TABLE><P>
```

The only other addition to the page is the Discard Changes button.

```
<INPUT TYPE=BUTTON ID="Drop" VALUE="Discard Changes">
```

This button is linked to a procedure that executes the CancelUpdate method. This enables you to discard edits and start again with a clean copy of the recordset.

```
Sub Drop_onclick
    Orders.CancelUpdate
    Msgbox "Changes Discarded"
End Sub
```

Note that the specific customer that is displayed is determined by the querystring variable CID. The SQL parameter of the DataControl contains a server-side script fragment that inserts the query string as the criterion for selecting orders.

```
<PARAM NAME="SQL" VALUE="SELECT * FROM Orders WHERE
            CustomerID=<%=Request.QueryString("CID")%>">
```

When you load RSEdit2.Asp, you can make changes to the Notes fields in one or more records. If you click the Save Changes button and then reload the document, you see that your edits in all of the records have been saved on the data provider.

Combining lists and edits

As a way of pulling together all of the techniques covered in this chapter, look at the page shown in Figure 13-17. This page combines the use of DataControl to populate lists and the ability of DataControl to expose sets of records for editing.

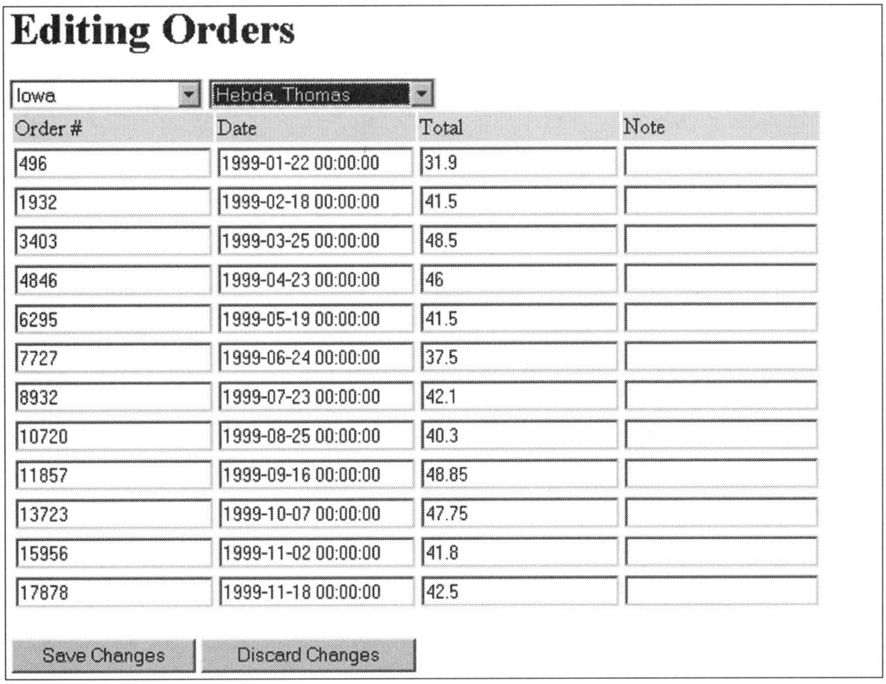

Editing Orders

Order #	Date	Total	Note
496	1999-01-22 00:00:00	31.9	
1932	1999-02-18 00:00:00	41.5	
3403	1999-03-25 00:00:00	48.5	
4846	1999-04-23 00:00:00	46	
6295	1999-05-19 00:00:00	41.5	
7727	1999-06-24 00:00:00	37.5	
8932	1999-07-23 00:00:00	42.1	
10720	1999-08-25 00:00:00	40.3	
11857	1999-09-16 00:00:00	48.85	
13723	1999-10-07 00:00:00	47.75	
15956	1999-11-02 00:00:00	41.8	
17878	1999-11-18 00:00:00	42.5	

Save Changes   Discard Changes

Figure 13-17: RDS DataControl is used to populate lists and edit records.

To understand how this document is put together, begin with the first drop-down list that lists the states in which there have been orders. The list is generated by the SQL Server-stored procedure shown below. This procedure uses a JOIN to ensure that only states that actually have orders are listed. This makes sense because there is no point in cluttering up the list with states that don't have any customers.

```
Create Procedure ActiveStates AS
SELECT States.STATE_ABBR, States.STATE_NAME
FROM States INNER JOIN
    Orders ON States.STATE_ABBR = Orders.ShipState
GROUP BY States.STATE_ABBR, States.STATE_NAME
```

The stored procedure is used as the SQL value of the DataControl.

```
<OBJECT CLASSID="clsid:BD96C556-65A3-11D0-983A-00C04FC29E33"
ID="States" HEIGHT=1 WIDTH = 1>
    <PARAM NAME="SQL" VALUE="ActiveStates">
    <PARAM NAME="SERVER" VALUE="http://208.185.177.211">
    <PARAM NAME="CONNECT" VALUE="Provider=sqloledb;data
            source=208.222.107.6;database=dbad1d;uid=ubad1d1;pwd=21@1n3z;">
</OBJECT>
```

The States recordset returns both the state abbreviation and the full state name. By assigning the state name to the Text property of the Option, and the state abbreviation to the Value property, the drop-down list can display the full name of the state using the FillStateList procedure.

```
Sub FillStateList
    Set R = States.Recordset
    Do Until R.Eof
        Set O = document.createElement("OPTION")
        O.Text = R(1)
        O.Value = R(0)
        StateList.add O
        Set O = Nothing
        R.MoveNext
    Loop
    StateList.value = Null
    CustomerList.value = Null
End Sub
```

The second drop-down list is an example of a filtered recordset. The source for the data is also a stored procedure, ActiveCustomers, which returns the CustomerId and Name of those customers that have orders in the database.

```
Create Procedure ActiveCustomers AS
SELECT Orders.ShipState, Orders.CustomerID,
    Customers.LastName + ', ' + Customers.FirstName AS FullName
FROM Orders INNER JOIN Customers ON
    Orders.CustomerID = Customers.CustomerID
GROUP BY Orders.ShipState, Orders.CustomerID,
    Customers.LastName + ', ' + Customers.FirstName
ORDER BY  Customers.LastName + ', ' + Customers.FirstName
```

The Customers list is logically controlled by the state selected in the States drop-down list. The strategy in this case is to use the following DataControl tag to download the entire customer list and then use client-side filtering to relate the customers to the state.

```
<OBJECT CLASSID="clsid:BD96C556-65A3-11D0-983A-00C04FC29E33"
ID="Customers" HEIGHT=1 WIDTH = 1>
    <PARAM NAME="SQL" VALUE="ActiveCustomers">
    <PARAM NAME="SERVER" VALUE="http://208.185.177.211">
    <PARAM NAME="CONNECT" VALUE="Provider=sqloledb;data
            source=208.222.107.6;database=dbad1d;uid=ubad1d1;pwd=21@1n3z;">
    <PARAM NAME="FetchOptions" VALUE="adcFetchUpFront">
</OBJECT>
```

The contents of the `Customer` drop-down list are created by the `StateList_onchange` and the `FillCustomerList` procedures, which fire each time that the user selects a state. First, the `Customers` DataControl is filtered for customers that have the same `ShipState` as the selected item in the `State` drop-down list. The `FillCustomerList` procedure then clears and refills the list of `Customer` names based on the filtered recordset.

```
Sub StateList_onchange
    Customers.FilterColumn = "ShipState"
    Customers.FilterCriterion = "="
    Customers.Filtervalue = StateList.options(StateList.selectedIndex).Value
    Customers.Reset false
    FillCustomerList
    Orders.SQL = ""
    Orders.Refresh
End Sub
Sub FillCustomerList
    For ONum = 0 To CustomerList.options.length
        CustomerList.remove(0)
    Next
    Set R = Customers.Recordset
    Do Until R.Eof
        Set O = document.createElement("OPTION")
        O.Text = R(2)
        O.Value = R(1)
        CustomerList.add O
        Set O = Nothing
        R.MoveNext
    Loop
    CustomerList.value = Null
End Sub
```

One other detail in the `StateList_onchange` is that it sets the `Orders` SQL value to a blank. This is done to clear the order list when no new customer has been selected.

The `Orders` DataControl isn't initially assigned a SQL parameter.

```
<OBJECT CLASSID="clsid:BD96C556-65A3-11D0-983A-00C04FC29E33"
ID="Orders" HEIGHT=1 WIDTH = 1>
    <PARAM NAME="SERVER" VALUE="http://208.185.177.211">
    <PARAM NAME="CONNECT" VALUE="Provider=sqloledb;data
            source=208.222.107.6;database=dbad1d1;uid=ubad1d1;pwd=21@1n3z;">
</OBJECT>
```

The SQL parameter is assigned to the `Orders` DataControl dynamically through the `CustomerList_onchange` procedure. When the user selects a customer name, this procedure uses the value of that `OPTION`, such as the `CustomerID`, to define a new SQL statement for the DataControl. The Refresh method connects to the server and retrieves the corresponding recordset.

```
Sub CustomerList_onchange
    Orders.SQL = "SELECT * FROM Orders WHERE CustomerID=" & _
    CustomerList.options(CustomerList.selectedIndex).Value
    Orders.Refresh
    Orders.Reset
End Sub
```

When you put these pieces together, you get the page RSEdit3.Asp shown in Figure 13-16. You can use the drop-down lists to display and/or edit the orders for customer.

Inserting new records

In addition to editing existing records, you can add new records to the DataControl's recordset (see Figure 13-18). Like editing changes, any new records appended onto the recordset remain in memory on the client. If you execute a SubmitChanges method, all of the edits and additions are saved to the server-side data provider. If you execute CancelUpdate or simply load a different page, the client-side edits are lost.

Editing Orders

Colorado ▼	Cambell, Michael ▼		
Order #	Date	Total	Note
428	1999-01-22 00:00:00	28.85	
1874	1999-02-18 00:00:00	38.65	
3347	1999-03-25 00:00:00	45.65	
4790	1999-04-23 00:00:00	43.15	
6244	1999-05-19 00:00:00	38.65	
7680	1999-06-24 00:00:00	34.65	
8882	1999-07-22 00:00:00	39.25	
10672	1999-08-25 00:00:00	37.45	
11810	1999-09-16 00:00:00	46	
13677	1999-10-07 00:00:00	44.9	
15912	1999-11-02 00:00:00	37.3	
17834	1999-11-18 00:00:00	38	
Save Changes	Discard Changes	Add New Record	

Figure 13-18: New records can be added to a DataControl recordset.

The DataControl itself does not have an AddNew method. The AddNew method is applied to the Recordset property of the DataControl object. The new record becomes part of the DataControl's recordset when an Update method is executed against the DataControl object. If you do not perform a recordset level update, the new record is discarded as it is in a normal ADO recordset object.

You must write code that maintains any logical relationships between data-base elements. In this case, that means that every order must be assigned a valid `CustomerID` so that the order is linked to a customer. The DataControl isn't aware of this relationship, so you must specifically insert the correct linking value. In this case, the `CustomerID` is the `Value` of the current selection in the `Customers` drop-down list. By adding this value, you insure that when you requery the `Orders` for this customer, the new record is included.

```
Sub AddNew_onclick
  Set R = Orders.Recordset
  R.Addnew
  R("Customerid") = CustomerList.options(CustomerList.selectedIndex).Value
  R.Update
  Orders.Reset
End Sub
```

You can test the Add New Record button by loading the RSEdit4.Asp and using the Add New Record button.

You also notice that the `WineOrderID` of the new record is empty. The `Customer` table uses the SQL Server Identity feature to automatically insert a unique value into each new record added to the table. However, in this case you aren't directly adding the new records to the SQL Server table but to a DataControl recordset. This means that the Identity feature isn't available for generating a new `WineOrderID`. The problem is resolved when the new record or records are submitted to the provider data source. At that point, the SQL Server Identity feature comes into play and assigns each order a `WineOrderID`.

Part V

Using ADO and Non-Relational Data Sources

The 5th Wave   By Rich Tennant

"We're here to clean the code."

In this part . . .

*W*hile most of the heavy lifting in the world of data management is performed by traditional relational databases, more and more data is now being stored in sources that aren't organized as a relational model.

In Part V, I show you how ADO can be used to work with data stored in these non-relational sources.

Chapter 14

ADO and OLAP

. . . .

In This Chapter

▶ Analyzing databases using OLAP

▶ Creating OLAP cubes

▶ Using Excel 2000 with OLAP cubes

▶ Using Recordsets with OLAP servers

▶ Using the MDX Query language

▶ Populating a Tree control

▶ Creating Web pages that use OLAP data

. . . .

*I*n this chapter, the subject is multidimensional data structures generated by the SQL Server OLAP Analysis Services. The subject of building, maintaining, and using OLAP services is enough to fill a book on its own. The focus of this chapter is on how you can use ADO to access already existing analytical data structures.

Online Analytical Processing

Before getting into the details of accessing multidimensional data, it is probably useful to look at an overview of what a multidimensional database is.

The development of relation databases was a great advance in computing. They provided an approach to data storage that was both reliable and flexible. At the core of relational databases are two operations:

> ✔ **Transactions:** The data obtained from a relation provider is subject to change at any moment. If you are extracting a summary of the orders table and another user is editing one of the orders, the result may change as soon as the edited order is saved. In some cases, you may choose to postpone a report if any of the records is in the process of being edited by using a feature called *locking*.

✓ **Joins:** In a relational database, there are not fixed relationships between data in different tables. The relationships are established on-the-fly when a JOIN instruction is executed that links records in one table with records in another table by some logical criteria.

These core feature mean that business operations that require constant updates, additions, and deletions can be carried out by multiple users without damaging the integrity of the data store or limiting the ways in which the data can be manipulated.

But there are many business activities that use the data that is stored in the relational database that do not require either transactional or relational features. These activities fall into the broad classification of data analysis. Activities such as sales reports and profitability analysis represent activities can be carried out without the need to rearrange the relationship between data elements or to have instant access to edit, addition, and updates.

Most analytical tasks work with historical data that is infrequently subject to revision, additions, or deletions. Further, in many cases where the task is analytical, it is easier to work with flat, spreadsheet-like lists of data than to have to constantly execute joins to assemble the desired lists.

Today, it is becoming more common to distinguish between two types of system that work with the basic business data contained within the data providers in an organization:

✓ **OLTP (Online Transactional Processing):** This refers to the traditional, transaction-oriented relational databases from Access to SQL Server, Oracle or other client/server databases.

✓ **OLAP (Online Analytical Processing):** This refers to a data provider that does not follow the strict relational model. Instead, the OLAP system transforms the data stored in the OLTP system into a hierarchical structure called a multidimensional database. This database is designed to summarize transactional data by a set of pre-defined characteristics, such as date/time factors, geographical factors, product categories, departmental operations, or other ways by which an organization analyzes its activities.

What is OLAP?

To understand what an OLAP system does, look at a simple analytical question that might be asked by people running the wine business used as the example database for this book: "Where do we sell the most product?"

This is a simple question that immediately begs other questions. Over what time period? By month? By quarter? By state? By city? By zip? Which products? What varieties? What vintages?

If you attempt to answer these questions with an OLTP system such as an SQL-based database, you have to compose each question in the form of an individual SQL statement. For example, the statement below calculates the sales by state.

```
SELECT ShipState, Sum(OrderTotal)
FROM Orders
GROUP BY ShipState
```

What if you wanted to summarize these state totals by month? You have to compose a slightly different statement.

```
SELECT DatePart(Year,OrderDate), DatePart(Month,OrderDate),
ShipState, Sum(OrderTotal)
FROM Orders
GROUP BY DatePart(Year,OrderDate),
DatePart(Month,OrderDate)ShipState
```

But what you really need are sales by quarter, broken down by state and city. Hey, wait a minute — this can go on forever! Not only that, what happens if you (or your users) want to go back and look at the data the first way again? Are you going to create views or stored procedures for every possible way of summarizing the data?

OLAP seeks to address these needs while at the same time relieving the OLTP system from having to process all of these requests for analytical data.

Analytical data sources

An OLAP system works by answering the question about creating views for every possible combination in the affirmative. Keep in mind that by definition, analysis involves data that is historical in nature. Therefore, it needs to be updated or changed infrequently, usually at some set time, such as the end of the month when a new batch of transactions need to be added to the historical database.

Because the data is not subject to frequent changes, it make sense to take some time up front and generate all of the totals for all of the possible combinations of the desired factors. Then store that data in a special hierarchical format that is optimized for locating and displaying the already calculated summary values.

This type of database is called a multidimensional database because it consists of a series of layered structures arranged in a top-to-bottom hierarchy with the broader categories on top and the narrower ones on the bottom. It does not consist of related tables.

For example, take a date field like `OrderDate` field in the `Orders` table. If you want to calculate the total amount of the order on each `OrderDate`, you execute a SQL statement like the one below.

```
SELECT OrderDate ,sum(OrderTotal)
FROM Orders
GROUP BY Orderdate
```

An OLAP database takes a different approach to the same task. Instead of simply summing a total for each date, the OLAP system analyzes the dates as being part of a hierarchical structure. The total for any given date, such as 4/17/99, isn't simply linked to that date. Rather, it is linked to a series of grouping related to that date — such as the month, quarter, and year groups — to which that date belonged. See in Figure 14-1.

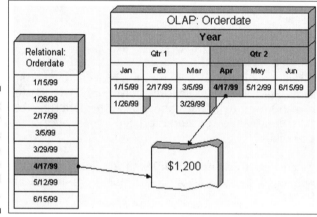

Figure 14-1: OLAP places values into multiple hierarchical groups.

The advantage of the OLAP approach is that if you wanted to look at order totals on any of the date levels (year, quarter, month, or individual), those values already have been calculated. All the application has to do is display the already summarized totals. The ability to quickly display additional levels of detail is called *drilling down*.

OLAP cubes

Of course, there is no magic involved in the ability of the OLAP database to support drilling down through various layers of data. The ability is based on the fact that an OLAP data source is stored in a structure called a *cube*. An OLAP cube is created by executing a series of SQL summary statements that calculate all of the possible values for each of the designated layers using statements to convert relational data into OLAP data. See the following examples.

```
SELECT DatePart(Year,OrderDate) ,sum(OrderTotal)
FROM Orders GROUP BY Orderdate
SELECT DatePart(Year,OrderDate),
DatePart(Quarter,Orderdate),sum(OrderTotal)
FROM Orders GROUP BY Orderdate
```

```
SELECT DatePart(Year,OrderDate),
DatePart(Month,Orderdate),sum(OrderTotal)
FROM Orders GROUP BY Orderdate
```

The values calculated by all of the summary statements are then stored in a special data structure that is optimized to work with interfaces, like the Pivot table displays in Excel 2000. These allow the user to drill down through various layers of data.

OLAP and SQL Server

SQL Server version 7.0 and newer include an OLAP server. Note that while the OLAP server is distributed in SQL Server, it can be used with or without an active SQL Server. The OLAP manager use OLE DB drivers to connect to data sources so that it possible to build OLAP cubes using any valid OLE DB data source such as an Access MDB or an Oracle database.

The primary tool used to create and maintain OLAP data is the Analysis Manager, shown in Figure 14-2.

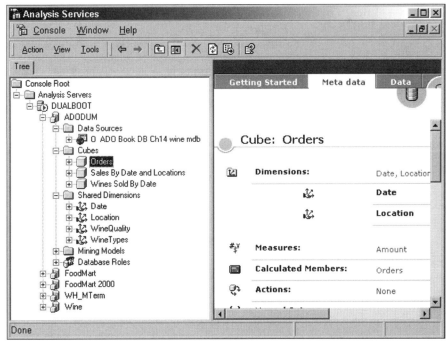

Figure 14-2:
The OLAP
Analysis
Manager
interface.

The Analysis Manager stores OLAP data in four related structures:

- **DataMart:** An OLAP datamart is roughly equivalent to a SQL database. The datamart is the primary container for the structures that actually contain and organize the data. On the disk, each DataMart is given its own folder in which all of the OLAP supporting files are stored.

- **DataSources:** DataSources are OLE DB connections to data providers, which furnish the raw, relational tables from which the OLAP cubes are created. Because the Analysis Manger works with OLE DB, a cube can draw from Access, SQL Server, or any other supported provider. You can create multiple data sources from different types of providers. When the cube is created, it combines the heterogeneous data sources data into a single cube.

- **Dimensions:** Dimensions are specifications that determine what types of groups are created in the multidimensional cube. OLAP allows dimensions to be multiple level structures. One cube can have multiple dimensions. When a cube is processed, summary values are generated for each valid intersection of dimensions and levels.

- **Cubes:** A cube is a special multidimensional data-storage structure that contains all the summarized values for all valid interactions, amounting to the dimensions of the cube.

Defining dimensions

The key to the creation and use of a multidimensional cube is the definition of dimensions. The dimensions control the various levels and sublevels for which the cube stores summary values. In a relational database aggregate, values are calculated for one level at a time based on the groups defined in the GROUP by clause. The statement below calculates a total for each unique combination of ShipState and ShipCity.

```
SELECT ShipState, ShipCity, Sum(OrderTotal)
FROM Orders
GROUP BY ShipState, ShipCity
```

OLAP dimensions can contain multiple levels. Figure 14-3 shows the Dimension Editor in the Analysis Manager. The dimension being defined, called Location, consists of the Ship State, Ship City, and Ship Zip arranged in a hierarchy. Each item in the hierarchy is called a level. In this example, there are three levels.

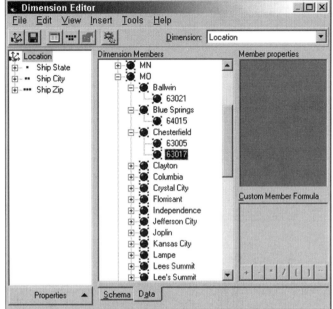

Figure 14-3:
The
Dimension
Editor
shows the
member of a
multi-level
dimension.

The panel in Figure 14-3 shows the *members* of the dimension. The members are the specific data items that are arranged on each level.

You can create as many dimensions as you need to analyze the data in your source database. Figure 14-4 shows a five-level dimension that organizes the wine products into groups based on the color, variety, and vintage. The right panel in the dimension editor shows the members of the dimension.

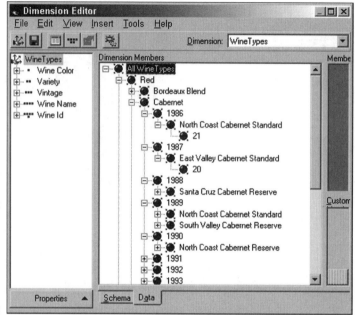

Figure 14-4:
The
WineTypes
dimension is
five levels
deep.

Creating a cube

Creating a cube involves making three selections that define the calculations that are stored in the multidimensional cube.

Figure 14-5 shows the Cube Editor in the Analysis Manager. The left panel shows the Dimensions (Date and Location) and Measures (Amount, OrderCount, and AverageOrder). The fact table, Orders, is shown in the right panel.

- ✔ **Dimensions:** The dimensions represent the categories that are used to summarize the data. The cube shown in Figure 14-5 has two dimensions, Date and Location, which in turn contain multiple levels.

- ✔ **Fact table:** The fact table is the table that contains the data to be analyzed in terms of the selected dimensions. To create a cube, there must be a link between at least one level in the dimension and a field in the fact table. For example, if you have a date dimension (such as year, quarter, or month), then it must link to a date field in the fact table.

- ✔ **Measures:** A measure is a value or expression that is summarized for every valid interaction of the selected dimensions. In the Orders cube shown in Figure 14-5, there are three measures defined:

  - Sum of OrderTotal

  - Count of the number of orders

  - Average order amount

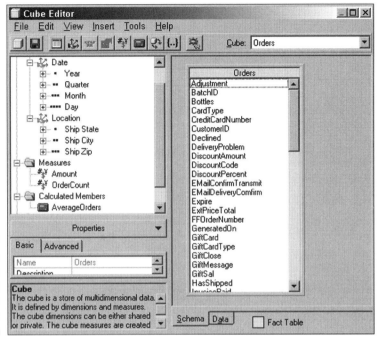

Figure 14-5:
The Cube
Editor in the
Analysis
Manager.

When the cube is processed, it creates a series of files called *aggregations*. In this case, the cube contains 12 aggregations and some 20,000 records in total. These structures are determined by internal algorithms built into the OLAP manager.

When the cube is processed, it generates a value of each measure for each interaction of dimension levels. For example, for May 1999, Martinez, CA, there are three summary values stored in the cube for the OrderTotal, OrderCount, and AverageOrders. This process repeats for every combination of dimension level.

Keep in mind that you are not limited to two dimensions. You might choose to add a third dimension — such as ProductType — to the cube. That means additional intersections (for example, Cabernet sold in Martinez, CA in May 1999) are added to the cube along with all other such combinations.

An OLAP database, called a DataMart, can contain any number of cubes, so it is not necessary that every cube use all of the dimensions. In fact, it is difficult to create displays and user interfaces, which are inherently two-dimensional, that display data with many more dimensions. Also, as you add more dimensions and levels to a cube, you use up more system resources storing the calculated summary values.

Another issues in OLAP management is the storage mode use for the OLAP data.

- ✔ **MOLAP:** M stands for multidimensional. This option stores the cube data in a proprietary file format designed to be accessed by the OLE DB OLAP providers. This file format is optimized for fast data retrieval.

- ✔ **ROLAP:** R stands for relational. This option stores the cube data in database tables on the SQL Server where the Analysis Services are installed. Data in this format is a bit slower to retrieve. However, because it is stored in standard database tables, it is available to non-OLAP applications. It is also easier to backup, copy, and replicate using standard SQL Server administrative functions.

- ✔ **HOLAP:** H stands for hybrid. In this option, data is stored both in relational tables and proprietary files. You get the best of both MOLAP and ROLAP, but you use up more system resources.

The value of OLAP services

As any working professional in the technology field knows, business requirements are likely to change on a daily basis, if not more often. Collecting and processing transaction data, such as orders from a Web site, are always the top priorities in any business. Despite the obvious value in analytical reports, they are often a neglected part of any application because they are the last item to be developed, often long after the transactional parts of the system are already in use.

In addition, tasks such as design reports in Access or Visual Basic are not very efficient uses of programmer hours because a great deal of the work is non-technical layout related to formatting data on a printed page. Further, it is often difficult to pin down the exact number and type of analytical reports required because the users have not had the time or opportunity to think though these requirements in details. They often need to analyze data based on some new business idea that came out of the latest meeting.

One alternative I like to use is to create OLAP resources (cubes) that cover broad areas of concern (such as sales, profitability, product, and inventory) to users, and let users access these cubes with Excel 2000. They can use the drill-down features to shape the display to fit their needs using the familiar Excel interface. In effect, the cubes serve as a source of presummarized data, and the user can make their own reports when they need them.

I find this approach much more efficient than trying to anticipate the exact set of printed reports that satisfy all the users in a business who need to look at some historical data from the OLTP system. It also allows these users to play with historical data as much as they like without putting additional stress on the servers providing the OLTP services.

OLAP and Excel 2000

Excel 2000 supports the use of the OLE DB provider for multidimensional databases directly from Excel 2000 in the PivotTable feature.

1. **In Excel, choose Data⇨PivotTable⇨PivotChart Report.**

2. **Click the External Data Source button and then click Next.**

3. **Click the Get Data button.**

   This runs MSQuery, which may need to be installed the first time you use this feature.

4. **Click the OLAP Cubes tab.**

   You need to create a new data source.

5. **Click <New data Source> and then click OK.**

6. **Type a name.**

   For this example, type **ADODUMOrders**.

7. **In the OLAP Provider box, select Microsoft OLE DB Provider for OLAP Services and then click the Connect button.**

   In this example, you connect to a cube file.

8. **Click Cube File and then enter (or browse to find) the cube file that you want to use.**

   For this example, you can use the following file on the CD: Ch14\Orders.cub.

9. **Click Finish and then click OK twice.**

10. **When you are back in the PivotTable wizard, click Next, and then click Finish.**

You have now attached the cube data to the worksheet, as shown in Figure 14-6. The PivotTable tool bar displays the names of the dimensions and measures onto the PivotTable to define a working model.

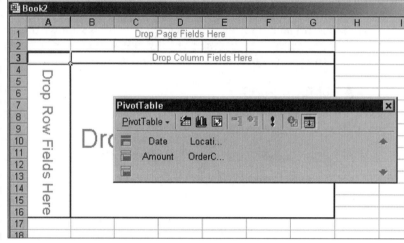

Figure 14-6:
The
PivotTable
toolbar
allows you
to drag and
drop
dimensions
and
measures.

Figure 14-7 shows the PivotTable created by dragging the Date dimension to the column bar, the Location dimension to the row bar, and the OrderTotal measure to the value area.

Figure 14-7:
Cube data
displayed in
a PivotTable
in Excel
2000.

	A	B	C	D
1				
2				
3	Amount	Year		
4	Ship State	1999	Grand Total *	
5	AK	785.7	785.7	
6	ca	638674.6262	638674.6262	
7	CO	49770.91	49770.91	
8	DC	70.41	70.41	
9	IA	12955.74	12955.74	
10	ID	10522.31	10522.31	
11	IL	123883.03	123883.03	
12	LA	4290	4290	
13	MN	44304.345	44304.345	
14	MO	28164.97	28164.97	
15	MT	1272.05	1272.05	
16	ND	0	0	
17	NE	3679.24	3679.24	
18	NM	8562.99	8562.99	
19	NV	6937.5725	6937.5725	
20	OR	24710.02	24710.02	
21	WA	71887.46	71887.46	
22	WI	33835.64	33835.64	
23	WV	14806.45	14806.45	
24	Grand Total *	1079113.464	1079113.464	
25				

Local cubes

The information in a OLAP database is not typically subject to the type of edits, additions, and deletions that are characteristic of relational databases. OLAP databases are snapshot summaries of the transactional database, usually taken at fixed interval such as at the end of a month or other fiscal period.

Because the cube data does not need to be constantly updated, it is possible to make copies of the OLAP data and distribute them to locations and users who do not have constant network access to the OLAP server. For example, users who travel with laptops may want to be able to analyze data on an airplane.

The OLAP server stores its data in a series of files that correspond to the different levels of data needed to support the defined dimensions of the cube. However, you can generate copies of the OLAP data, called *local cubes*. A local cube is a single file, with a CUB extension, that contains some or all of the data from an OLAP server cube. The CUB file can be moved to any drive on any computer. Applications that use the MSOLAP provider, like Excel 2000, can access the CUB and use that data in the same way that they use cube data supplied by an OLAP server on a network.

By far the simpler method is to use Excel 2000 to copy a PivotTable linked to an OLAP cube into a CUB file. From the PivotTable toolbar, select PivotTable⇨Client-Server settings⇨Create local data file. This copies the displayed OLAP data into a CUB file. Note that only the data currently displayed saves in the CUB file. For example, if the table shown in Figure 14-7 is saved to a local cube file and it doesn't contain any city or zip information, that's because you have not drilled down to those levels. Excel loads the data from the OLAP server on an as-needed basis. If you don't expand a dimension to show lower levels, that data is never loaded by Excel; consequently, it is not included the local cube.

If the dimensions have a few members, like the Date dimension, then you can probably just double-click the items to drill-down to the next level of each item until you have the details (quarters and months) that you need.

However, in the case of the Location dimension, expanding each state to show the cities — and then expanding each city to show the zip codes — is quite a tedious and time-consuming task. Fortunately, Microsoft includes VBA in Excel, so you can automate the process. Below is a procedure that expands all of the items in a dimension level. In Excel 2000, this has the effect of forcing Excel to requery the OLAP and load the data for each of the newly expanded levels.

```
Sub ExpandLevel()
Dim W As Worksheet
Dim PT As PivotTable
Dim PTFld As PivotField
Dim PTItem As PivotItem
Set W = ActiveWorkbook.Worksheets(2)
Set PT = W.PivotTables(1)
Set PTFld = PT.PivotFields("[Location].[Ship State]")
For Each PTItem In PTFld.PivotItems
PTItem.DrilledDown = True
Next
End Sub
```

Note that the code references are not OLAP structures but Excel PivotTable structures. They have similar meaning, but the terminology is different. An OLAP dimension is a `PivotField`. An OLAP dimension level is a `PivotItem`.

If you want to expand the next level, simply change `PivotField`.

```
Set PTFld = PT.PivotFields("[Location].[Ship City]")
```

When you have loaded all of the required levels, use the PivotTable/Client-Server settings command to generate a cube file.

Accessing OLAP Data with ADO

If simply allowing users to connect to existing cubes with Excel 2000 is not adequate for all of your users, you can use ADO to create any number of custom interfaces that interact with the data stored in the OLAP cubes.

The examples in this section use the local cube files included on the CD, but they work the same way for connections made directly to the OLAP server.

The MDAC (Microsoft Data Access Components) includes the MSOLAP (Microsoft OLAP) driver, which is the OLE DB provider for OLAP. With this provider, you can access the data in an OLAP cube or cube file using two different language styles:

- ✔ **MDX:** This is MDX (multidimensional data extensions) query language, which is used to define and return data structures that have a multidimensional structure. MDX statements define data sets in terms of column and row dimensions. The result of a MDX query is a an object called a `CellSet`, which is organized in a structure that is similar to an Excel 2000 pivot table.

- ✔ **SQL:** ADO allows you to use standard SQL `SELECT` statements to access data stored in a multidimensional data source. The SQL approach flattens out the hierarchical structure of the cube and returns a table-like list of the specified data.

Connecting to an OLAP source

When connecting to an OLAP data source, you use the MSOLAP OLE DB provider. If the source is an OLAP server available on a local network, you can use the name of the server as the Data Source. The `Initial Catalog` is the name of the DataMart that you want to access.

```
Sub ConnectOLAPServer()
Dim Cnt As New ADODB.Connection
Cnt.Open "Provider=MSOLAP;Data Source=DualBoot;Initial Catalog=ADODUM;"
End Sub
```

To connect to a cube file, simply change the server name to the path of the CUB file. ***Note:*** Because a cube file is inherently only a single cube, there is no DataMart involved and no need for an `Initial Catalog` parameter.

```
Sub ConnectCubeFile()
Const CFolder = "C:\ado book\db\chp14\"
Dim Cnt As New ADODB.Connection
Cnt.Open "Provider=MSOLAP;Data Source=" & CFolder & "OLAPorders.cub"
End Sub
```

Using HTTP to connect

One of the new features added to ADO in Version 2.5 is the ability to use the basic Web services protocol, HTTP, as a means of connecting to services on an IIS Web server (see Chapter 15 for more information).

The following technique uses HTTP to make a connection to a Web server that also has installed the SQL Server 2000 Enterprise Edition version of the OLAP services (which, at the time of this writing, is still in beta testing). However, this looks like an interesting feature, so I thing it is useful to mention it here.

The SQL Server 2000 version is supplied with a file called `MSOLAP.ASP`. After the OLAP Analysis Services have been installed, you can place a copy of the `MSOLAP.ASP` in the home folder of the Web server. This ASP acts as a gateway between the Web server and the OLAP services. The code below uses the URL of a Web server (in this case, the one in my office) as the DataSource.

```
Sub HTTP1()
Dim Cnt As New Connection, R As New ADODB.Recordset
Cnt.Open "Provider=MSOLAP;DataSource=http://208.185.177.211/;initial
            catalog=ADODUM"
End Sub
```

This technique uses the Web server as a substitute or proxy for the OLAP server. The MSOLAP.ASP is then used to pass OLAP commands to the OLAP server and to return response to the client application. This approach eliminates the need to directly expose the OLAP server while making the service available over an Internet network.

ADO recordsets

ADO allows you to access OLAP cube data by using the ADO recordset object. Using recordsets to access OLAP data allows you to work with the OLAP data as if it were a set of relational data. When the OLAP data is retrieved as a recordset, you deal with records and fields in the same way that you do if the source is a traditional relational database.

Further, controls such as the hierarchical hlexGrid can display a recordset extracted from an OLAP cube by assigning the recordset to the grid's data-source property (see Chapter 10).

Keep in mind that when you place OLAP data into a recordset object, the data is flattened from a multidimensional structure to a simply table-style list.

For example, if you want to refer to the Ship State level of the Locations dimension in the Orders cube, put a colon between the dimension name and the level name.

```
SELECT [Locations:Ship State] FROM Orders
```

Note that a recordset object flattens the OLAP structure into a list. This means that the recordset equivalent of an OLAP cube contains one record for every intersection stored in the cube. The procedure below returns the value 9,957, which is the total content of the cube file. This is what happens when you flatten a cube into one long list.

```
Sub SQLMD1()
Dim Cnt As New ADODB.Connection
Dim R As New Recordset
Dim RKount
Cnt.Open "Provider=MSOLAP;Data Source=DualBoot;Initial catalog=ADODUM;"
R.Open "Select [Location:Ship State],[Location:Ship City],[Location:ship
            zip],[Measures:Amount] FROM Orders", _
Cnt, adOpenStatic
Do Until R.EOF
RKount = RKount + 1
R.MoveNext
Loop
Debug.Print RKount
End Sub
```

You can use the SQL DISTINCT clause to drop duplicate items. This helps obtain a more useful list of dimension contents. See Figure 14-8.

```
Private Sub Form_Load()
Dim Cnt As New ADODB.Connection
Dim RS As New ADODB.Recordset
Dim Gr As New MSHFlexGrid
Cnt.Open "Provider=MSOLAP;Location=C:\ado book\db\chp14\OLAPOrders.cub;"
RS.Open "SELECT DISTINCT [Location:Ship State] FROM Orders ", Cnt
Set Gr = Me.Grid1.Object
Set Gr.DataSource = RS
End Sub
```

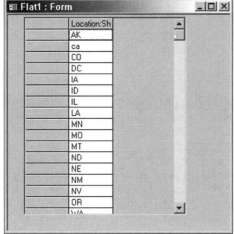

Figure 14-8:
The
contents of
an OLAP
dimension
are
displayed as
a recordset.

MDX queries

The query model used by SQL is designed to retrieve data stored in relational tables. To facilitate retrieval of data from multidimensional sources, the MSOLAP provider supports the use of Multidimensional Extensions (MDX).

The MDX language (yes, another language) allows you to express your data requests in terms of dimensions and levels as defined when you created the OLAP cube. The statement below refers to the Date dimension of the Orders cube. The result of this query is the value associated with the entire Date dimension: that is, the Amount value for all of the orders on all dates.

```
SELECT {[Date]} On Columns From Orders
```

The SQL equivalent is shown below.

```
SELECT Sum(OrderTotal) As Amount
FROM Orders WHERE OrderDate Is Not Null
```

You can place this statement into a programming content by using it to define the contents of a recordset, as shown in MDX1.

```
Sub MDX1()
Dim Cnt As New ADODB.Connection, R As New ADODB.Recordset
Dim F As ADODB.Field
Cnt.Open "Provider=MSOLAP;Data Source=" & CFolder & "orders.cub;"
R.Open "SELECT {[Date]} On Columns From Orders", _
Cnt
For Each F In R.Fields
Debug.Print F.Name, F.Value
Next
End Sub
```

The key difference between retrieving SQL summary information and OLAP summary information is that SQL must gather the underlying data and calculate the summary each time. OLAP merely locates the already calculated value. Using the OLAP cube reduces the stress on the database resources.

An MDX viewer

A full discussion of the MDX language is beyond what can be covered in this chapter. However, you can use some simple ADO code to create a form that helps you experiment with the MDX statements.

The form is bound to a table called Statements that has a field named `Statements`, which is used to store the text of MDX statement. The form displays: a text box for editing the statement field; and an execute button that converts the statement into a recordset, which is displayed in the grid control. See Figure 14-9.

Figure 14-9: The MDX Tool form allows you to execute MDX commands and see the results in the grid below.

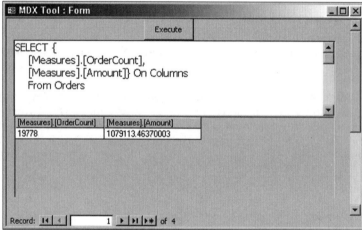

The code shown below uses the `Statement` field to execute an MDX statement and display the results in the grid.

```
Private Sub Command2_Click()
Dim Cnt As New ADODB.Connection
Dim RS As New ADODB.Recordset
Dim Gr As New MSHFlexGrid
Cnt.Open "Provider=MSOLAP;Location=e:\ado book\OLAPOrders.cub;"
RS.Open Me.Statement.Value, Cnt
Set Gr = Me.Grid1.Object
Set Gr.DataSource = RS
End Sub
```

Figure 14-9 shows the results of the MDX statement below. In this case, the referenced items are from the Measures dimension. The results are the totals for `Amount` and `OrderCount` for the entire cube.

```
SELECT {[Measures].[OrderCount],
[Measures].[Amount]} On Columns
From Orders
```

The MDX statements that follow are stored in the Statement table of the `Multidimensional.MDB` file. The statement above is Record #1 in the Statement table.

MDX dimension intersections

Because MDX queries simply return data summary totals that were calculated when the cube was created, you can think of an MDX statement as a description of which dimension intersections you want to view. For example, suppose you want to see the Amount for the state of MO in the second quarter 1999. (See Figure 14-10.)

You can specify a specific element in a dimension by listing the hierarchy of levels. The expression below selects the second quarter of 1999.

```
[Date].[1999].[Quarter 2]
```

The statement below lists the dates along the column axis and the state name along the row axis (Record #3).

```
SELECT { [Date].[1999].[Quarter 2]} ON COLUMNS,
{[Location].[MO]} ON ROWS FROM Orders
```

You can include more than one member of the level by listing the elements you want to display (Record #4).

```
SELECT { [Date].[1999].[Quarter 2],[Quarter 4]} ON COLUMNS,
{[Location].[WA],[OR],[OR]} ON ROWS
FROM Orders
```

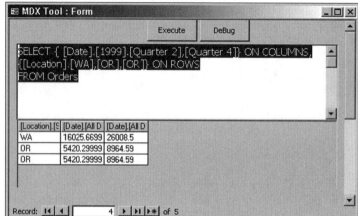

Selecting the measure

You may have noticed that the values returned for any MDX query always reflect the Amount measure. That is because the Amount measure — the first measure defined in the cube — is treated as the default. You can specify an alternative measure by using the WHERE clause. The statement below, Record #6, returns the OrderCount value instead of the Amount.

```
SELECT {[Date].[Quarter 2],[Quarter 4]} ON COLUMNS,
{[Location].[WA],[CA],[OR]} ON ROWS
FROM Orders
Where [Measures].[OrderCount]
```

Calculating a new member

While a cube is meant to provide a broad array of precalculated data, it is likely that there are some values that you have not included in your cube. You can generate these values by creating a new member in an MDX statement. For example, suppose that you want to display a set of values that represent the average order amount rather than the total order amount.

In the Orders cube, you have both the Amount and OrderCount measures. From these values — already stored in the cube — you can calculate an arithmetic average. The WITH MEMBER clause is added to the front of an MDX statement to create a new calculated member which can then be referenced in the SELECT portion of the statement.

```
WITH MEMBER [Dimension].newname AS
'calculation string'
```

The statement below uses the `WITH MEMBER` clause to create a calculated measure AvgSale, which is defined as the `'Measures.[Amount]` divided by the `Measures.[OrderCount]`. Note that the `WHERE` clause must specify the `[AvgSale]` measures to ensure that is the measure that is displayed (Record #7). The result, shown in Figure 14-11, shows the average calculated for each of the dimension intersections included in the query.

```
WITH MEMBER Measures.[AvgSale] AS
'Measures.[Amount]/Measures.[OrderCount]'
SELECT {[Date].[Quarter 2],[Quarter 4]} ON COLUMNS,
{[Location].[WA],[CA],[OR]} ON ROWS
FROM Orders
WHERE measures.[AvgSale]
```

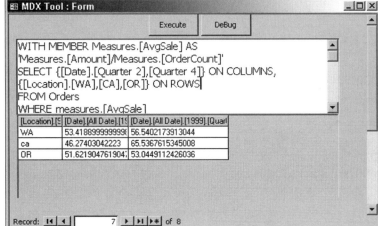

Figure 14-11: A calculated member generates averages for all the selected items.

MDX collections

In many cases, you want to select all of the items that exist within a dimension level. For example, the `[Quarter]` level contains four quarters for each year. Instead of listing the items, you can use the `Members` property to include all of the members with a single reference.

```
[Quarter].Members
```

The same is true of other levels in other dimensions. The expression below refers to all of the states included in the `[Location]` dimension.

```
[Location].[Ship State].Members
```

The statement below (Record #8) includes all of the members of the [Quarter] and the [Ship State] dimension levels. The result is shown in Figure 14-12.

```
SELECT {[Quarter].Members,[Date].[1999]} On Columns,
{[Location].[Ship State].Members,[Location]} On Rows
FROM Orders
```

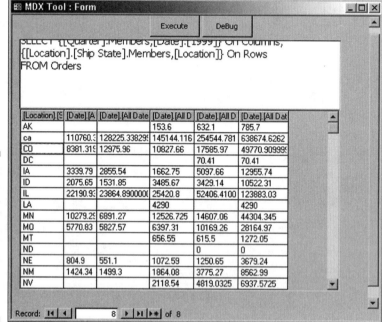

Figure 14-12: The `Members` property includes all the members of the specified level.

One very interesting aspect of the data displayed in Figure 14-12 is that it shows not only the values for the individual members, but it also includes summary totals. The first four columns display the members of the [Quarter] dimension level. The fifth column displays the total for all quarters.

The interesting part is how this total is produced. It is not produced by a calculation that sums the quarters. That is not necessary because the summary total was already calculated when the cube was created.

Instead, all you need to do in an MDX statement is to refer to the level in the dimension hierarchy that has the value you want — in this case, [Date].[1999], which contains the totals for the year 1999. Note that the yearly total appears as the fifth column because the item — [Date].[1999] — is listed after [Quarter]. If you want to start with the year's total, you simply rearrange the order of the item list.

Use a similar approach to create a row at the bottom of the listing that shows the total for each quarter for all states. This is accomplished by adding a reference to the entire [Location] dimension in the On Rows item list. Because the [Location] dimension includes all of the members of the [Ship State] level, that reference creates the column total. In the lower right-hand cell (the intersection of [1999] and [Location], you get the total value of all of the orders in 1999.

The type of display shown in Figure 14-12 may not seem very remarkable. It is exactly the type of grid that most business users like to have in their spreadsheet models. But it is also the type of display that is difficult to create using standard relational database tools based on SQL queries. For example, the SQL statement below is roughly equivalent to the MDX statement used in Record #8.

```
SELECT DatePart(Quarter,OrderDate),ShipState,
Sum(OrderTotal) FROM Orders
GROUP BY DatePart(Quarter,OrderDate),ShipState
ORDER BY DatePart(Quarter,OrderDate),ShipState
```

But when you execute this statement, you do not get the output that you see in Figure 14-12. Rather, the results look like the listing below. Note that the values are the same (such as CA, Qrt1 = 110,760). However, instead of the values being listed in columnar form, the relational output (linearly oriented) lists them horizontally. Additionally, there is no standard way to get the output to include the row and column totals provided by the MDX statement.

```
NULL      NULL      NULL
1         CA        110760.3894
1         CO        8381.3200
1         IA        3339.7900
1         ID        2075.6500
1         IL        22190.9300
1         MN        10279.2900
1        .MO        5770.8300
```

The point I want to stress is that OLAP data formatted through MDX can generate the types of output that most business users want to work with. It bridges the gap between the relational database (which has the data these users need to work with) and the spreadsheet applications (which are typically the applications through which users want to work with the data). That is why creating an OLAP cube can solve a large number of reporting needs. This is a much more efficient approach than typing to build Access or VB report forms.

Calculated aggregations

In addition to numeric calculations, you can use MDX to generate aggregations that are not already part of the cube. For example, the states WA, OR, and CA can be thought of as the West Coast region. The source data for the cube didn't contain any regional designations and no regional dimension was created in the cube.

You can solve this problem by aggregating the specific state elements into a new collection called *West Coast*. You can create an ad hoc grouping with the WITH MEMBER clause and the Sum function, which has the following general form. If you are using the default measure — in this example, Amount — you can omit the measure parameter.

```
Sum({element1, element2,...},measure)
```

The MDX statement below, Record #9, adds a summary level for the three West Coast states. The result appears in Figure 14-13.

```
WITH MEMBER [Location].[West Coast] AS
'Sum({CA, WA,[OR]})'
SELECT {[Date].[Quarter].Members} ON COLUMNS,
{[Location].[CA],[WA],[OR] ,[Location].[West Coast]} ON ROWS
FROM orders
```

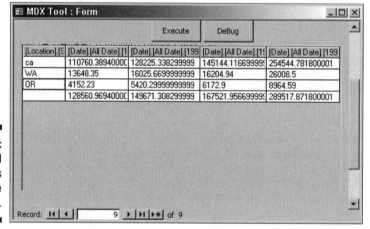

Figure 14-13:
A calculated grouping is added to the cube data.

ADOMD

In addition to placing OLAP data into an ADO recordset object, ADO includes a special object library designed just for use with OLAP data sets. The library is called Active Data Objects Multidimensional (ADOMD).

There are two object supported by ADOMD:

  ✔ **Catalog:** A *catalog* is an object representation of the cube itself and how it is organized.

  ✔ **CellSet:** A *CellSet* is the data object that results form an MDX query.

  Unlike a recordset that organizes MDX data as a two-dimensional list of records and fields, a CellSet is organized into a three-layered structure. These three layers include:

  • **Axes:** An axis is equivalent to one of the ON layers in a MDX query. In the queries used in this book, there are only two axes, ON ROWS and ON COLUMNS. MDX supports three additional layers on top of those dimensions: pages, sections, and chapters.

  • **Positions:** Each axis contains a collection of position that represent points along the axis.

  • **Members:** Each point contains a collection of members.

Taken together, the Axes, Positions, and Members collections describe the structure of the CellSet. The data is contained with Cell objects. The Cell collection contains one cell for every data point included in the cell set. Cells can be directly referenced by number or they can be associated with the elements of the Members collection.

Populating a TreeView

One of the challenges associated with OLAP databases is finding useful and interesting ways to expose the data to the user. Figure 14-14 shows a TreeView control that displays information extracted from the Orders OLAP cube. The TreeView control is one of the sets of ActiveX controls provided with Visual Basic or Office 2000 Developers edition. The tree view provides an alternative way to display a large amount of data by spreading the information onto roots and branches of a tree that can be expanded or collapsed to fit the needs of the user.

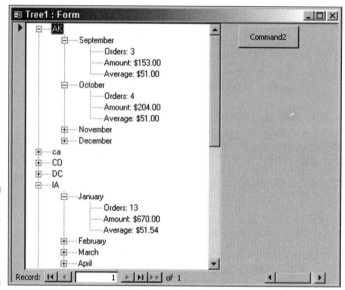

Figure 14-14:
Summary
data orga-
nized in a
tree display.

Using CrossJoin

The example shown in Figure 14-14 creates a tree in which the top level is the Ship States. Under each state are listed the months in 1999. Each month then contains a set of branches that show the total sales, total units, and average sale size for that state in that month.

When you use a tree view, you need to keep in mind that the data sets need to be organized vertically. Unlike a grid, a tree view does not have additional columns. Instead, the branches can be expanded to show lower levels of detail.

Normally, an MDX statement creates a grid-style display with elements being spread both vertically (rows) and horizontally (along the column axis). In this example, the Month dimension usually spreads across the column axis. However, the months dimension could be rolled up along the rows axis as a subset of each Ship State.

Figure 14-15 shows the type of data roll-up that fits the tree view's display characteristics. The vertical axis consists of two levels. The first level lists the Ship States. Within each Ship State is a second level of detail listing each month's sales for that state.

Figure 14-15:
A CrossJoin
rolls up one
dimension
as a subset
of a higher
level
dimension
on the same
axis.

		OrderCount	Amount
AK	September	3	$153.00
	October	4	$204.00
	November	10	$427.00
	December	1	$0.00
ca	January	815	$30,007.00
	February	876	$38,757.00
	March	841	$42,111.00
	April	950	$48,643.00
	May	939	$43,819.00
	June	882	$35,471.00
	July	932	$48,443.00
	August	937	$47,496.00
	September	1,021	$49,199.00
	October	1,537	$95,298.00

MDX allows you to nest levels on the same axis by using a `CrossJoin` function in an MDX statement. The statement below (Record #11 in the Statements table) uses a `CrossJoin` operator to create a multi-level vertical axis. The horizontal axis does not contain dimension information. Instead, it merely lists the data measures to associate with each unique row (state and month combination) on the vertical axis.

```
Select
{measures.[OrderCount],measures.[Amount]} ON COLUMNS,
NON EMPTY
{CrossJoin([Location].[Ship State].members,
[date].[Month].members)} ON ROWS
FROM orders
```

Note the use of the `NON EMPTY` before the `ON ROWS` axis. When you perform `CrossJoin`, it may be the case that many of the combinations do not produce any dates. For example, there were no sales in AK in January 1999. The `NON EMPTY` clause excludes these empty rows from the data set.

Using the Node object

Unlike the ActiveX grid controls, the `TreeView` control does not bind to data sources. Instead, you need to write a procedure that places each item on the tree at the proper level so that it forms the display you have in mind.

Each item displayed on a tree is represented by a Node object. You add items to a `TreeView` by using the `Add` method of the Nodes collection. To add a Node at the top level of the tree, create a statement like the one below. The first two arguments are left blank (indicating a top-level item). The third argument becomes the name of the node.

Note: Node names must be unique. They are used to refer to the node in programming code, but they do not appear on the screen. What *does* appear on the screen is the fourth argument, which is the Text property of the node. The text items, however, are not required to be unique.

```
Tree.Nodes.Add ,,"[Ship State].[CA]","CA"
```

To add a second or lower level node, you would add two more arguments to the statement:

> ✔ The name of the node level to which you want to attach the new node
>
> ✔ Its relationship

The constant tvwChild makes the new node a child of the node specified in the first argument. The statement below adds a node — May — as a child of the [Ship State].[CA] node.

```
Tree.Nodes.Add "[Ship State].[CA]",tvwChild, _
"[Ship State].[CA].[May]","May"
```

Keep in mind that when you populate a tree, you cannot add a child until after you have added the parent node.

Using the CellSet object

The data upon which the nodes in the tree are based is contained in the result set of the MDX statement. Instead of placing that data into a table-like structure — a recordset object — you can use the ADOMD to place the data in a CellSet object. A CellSet is organized by axes, positions, and members that reflect the multidimensional nature of OLAP data sets.

In this example, the nodes of the tree correspond to the Positions and Members that appear along the vertical axis (refer to Figure 14-15).

Each Position represents a collection of items that appear at the same location on the specified axis. In this example, each is a unique combination of state and month. When MSOLAP generates a CellSet based on the MDX statement used in this example, it creates a structure of Position objects organized like the sample below. Each position object is given a unique number (the Ordinal property) that indicates its location on the axis. The Position object contains a collection of Member objects that correspond to the levels of data on the axis. In this example, because the CrossJoin creates a two-level vertical axis, each Position has two members (state and month).

```
Position: #1 {State:AK}{Month:September}
Member 1: [Ship State].[AK]
Member 2: [Month].[September]
```

OLAP and ASP

ADO and ADOMD make it easy — easier than you may think at first — to access OLAP data through a Web interface. On the server side, you can create ASPs that access OLAP data through the MSOLAP provider available on the IIS Web server.

On the client side, users with Office 2000 can take advantage of the PivotControl, which is included with Office 2000. This control can be called on the client side, from which it can access an OLAP server. This approach allows you to use a Web page in place of Excel 2000 as the container for PivotTable operations.

Server-side OLAP

Server-side scripting has the advantage of being the universal method by which data can be accessed through a Web client. As with ADO recordsets, you create a connection object only with the MSOLAP provider instead of the SQLOBEDB provider.

You can create CellSet objects by passing a MDX statement to the OLAP server. In this case, the data set lists the Wine varieties and the total sales for each variety.

```
<%@ Language=VBScript %>
<HTML><BODY>
<%
Set Cnt = Server.CreateObject("ADODB.Connection")
Cnt.Open "Provider=MSOLAP;DataSource=PACKBELL;Initial catalog=ADODUM;"
Set DSet = server.CreateObject("ADOMD.Cellset")
Dset.ActiveConnection = cnt
DSet.Open "SELECT {[Measures].[Ext Price]} ON Columns, NON EMPTY
            {[WineType].[Variety].Members,[WineType]} ON ROWS From winesales"
%>
```

After creating the CellSet object, you can use VBScript to insert the data onto the page. The OLAP model fits the HTML model very well. You can see that the code needed to display the data is relatively simple. This is a result of the simplified structure OLAP provides for accessing sets of summary data. The MDX instructions simply refer to the already calculated and organized value sets within the source cube.

```
<Table Border=1 cellpadding=6>
<TR><TD>Wine</TD><TD>Sales</TD></TR>
<% For Each P in DSet.Axes(1).Positions
For Each M in P.Members
Response.Write "<TR><TD>" & M.Caption & "</TD>"
Response.Write "<TD Align=right>" & Formatnumber(DSet(0,P.Ordinal),2,,,True) &
            "</TD></TR>"
Next
Next
%></Table></BODY></HTML>
```

Client-side OLAP

If you have a locally available OLAP server and Office 2000 desktops, you can provide access to PivotTable by using client-side Web operations in IE.

You can create a client-side object reference to the PivotTable control using the OBJECT tag shown below. Recall from Chapter 13 that the class ID of the controls is the same on all desktops (unless Microsoft decides to change it).

```
<object ID="PCtrl" CLASSID="CLSID:0002E520-0000-0000-C000-000000000046"
style="HEIGHT: 500px; WIDTH: 500px" width="518" height="384">
</object>
```

The control loads into the Web page as a bank. You can use the Window OnLoad event to populate the control with a connection to an OLAP data source.

The ActiveView property of the PivotTable control has the following methods that define the layout of the PivotTable:

- ✔ **DataMember:** Specifies the cube to attach the PivotTable to
- ✔ **FieldSets:** Represents the dimensions in the OLAP cube
- ✔ **ColumnAxis:** Assigns a FieldSet to the column axis
- ✔ **RowAxis:** Assigns a FieldSet to the row axis
- ✔ **DataAxis:** Selects measures to populate table

The scrip below uses the PivotTable methods to define the working table when the page loads into the browser. The result is a fully functional PivotTable, similar to the one contained in Excel, that can be used from a Web page.

```
<SCRIPT LANGUAGE=vbscript>
<!--
Sub window_onload
PCtrl.ConnectionString = _
"Provider=MSOLAP;Data Source=yourserver;Initial catalog=ADODUM;"
PCtrl.DataMember = "WineSales"
PCtrl.ActiveView.ColumnAxis.InsertFieldSet _
PCtrl.ActiveView.FieldSets("Date")
PCtrl.ActiveView.RowAxis.InsertFieldSet _
PCtrl.ActiveView.FieldSets("[WineType]")
PCtrl.ActiveView.DataAxis.InsertTotal _
PCtrl.ActiveView.Totals("Bottles")
End Sub
```

Keep in mind that the connection between the Web browser and the OLAP server or local cube file must be established at the client. This means that the client computer must have network access to the OLAP provider or the Pivot control cannot populate.

Chapter 15

ADO Data in Office 2000

. . . .

In This Chapter

▶ Using the Outlook Object Library

▶ Using the Excel Library

▶ Creating mail messages from ADO data

▶ Creating HTML e-mails

▶ Addressing e-mails with ADO data

▶ Creating Excel worksheets

▶ Linking worksheets to ADO data sources

. . . .

*O*utlook has been one of the most popular components of Office since it was introduced in its early form following the release of Windows 95. While some people use Excel or Word as their main Office application, many use Outlook daily for managing e-mail, appointments, and contacts. Most of the work done with Outlook is done manually by user interactions with the Outlook interface.

ADO and Outlook

All of the structures within Outlook are exposed as ActiveX objects that can be manipulated from VB/VBA application. You can use Outlook in combination with ADO data providers to generate Outlook items such as mail messages, contact records, and appointments. Conversely, you can use Outlook as a source of data and store and organize that data in ADO data sources.

The Outlook library

To manipulate Outlook programmatically, you need to attach the Outlook Object Library to the current project. In VB, use Project⇨References; in VBA, use Tools⇨References and select the Microsoft Outlook Object Library 9.0. Version 9.0 corresponds to Outlook 2000.

All connections to Outlook begin with the `Outlook.Application` object.

```
Dim OL as new Outlook.Application
```

If you want to create a mail message, use the `CreateItem( )` function. The statement below uses the OL (application object) to create a new mail message.

```
Set Mess = OL.CreateItem(olMailItem)
```

The properties of the `MailItem` object allow you to specify the details of the message:

- ✔ **To.** Sets the e-mail address for the recipient of the message by assigning a text string.
- ✔ **Subject.** This property sets the text of the subject line of the message.
- ✔ **Body.** This property sets the contents of the message as text.

When you have set the message's `To`, `Subject`, and `Body` properties, you can send the message with the `Send` method.

```
Mess.Send
```

Creating messages from data sources

Used in its simplest form, you can use ADO to supply information required to fill in the message properties when you create a message.

```
Sub SendMessage1()
    Dim Order As New ADODB.Recordset, Email As New ADODB.Recordset
    Order.Open "SELECT * FROM Orders WHERE WineOrderID = 5151", _
        CurrentProject.Connection
    Email.Open "SELECT emailaddress FROM Customers WHERE CustomerID = " _
        & Order!CustomerID, CurrentProject.Connection

    Dim OL As New Outlook.Application
    Dim Mess As Outlook.MailItem
    Set Mess = OL.CreateItem(olMailItem)
    Mess.To = Email!EmailAddress
    Mess.Subject = "Order #" & Order!WineOrderID
    Mess.Body = "Order #" & Order!WineOrderID & " received on " & _
        Order!OrderDate
    Mess.Send
End Sub
```

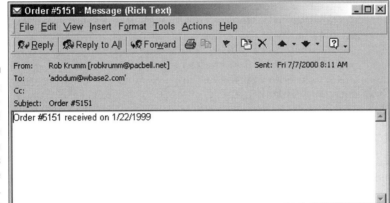

Figure 15-1:
A simple
e-mail
message
based on
the contents
of database
records.

Formatting a message

Using an ADO recordset with Outlook allows you to automate processes such as sending e-mails to customers when they place orders. If you want the message returned to the user to be as generic as possible, you can construct a plain-text message based on the order you want to confirm.

While there are many ways to write the code for such an e-mail, my own preference is to use VB/VBA object technology and create an `Email` object using a Class module. In this case, I created a module called `Email` that has the following properties:

✔ **WineOrderID:** This property is the ID of the order that you want to confirm by e-mail. The code associated with this property contains the ADO operations that provide the `Email` object with data about the specified order. When you set the `WineOrderID`, that value is used to create three recordsets — `vCust`, `voOder`, and `vDetails` — that provide all of the data needed to fill out the message text.

```
Public Property Let WineOrderID(ByVal vNewValue As Variant)
    vWineOrderID = vNewValue
    vOrder.Open "SELECT * FROM Orders WHERE WineOrderid = " & vWineOrderID, _
        Cnt
    vCust.Open "SELECT * FROM Customers WHERE Customerid = " & _
        vOrder!CustomerID, Cnt
    VDetails.Open "SELECT WineProductCatalog.Vintage & ' ' & _
        WineProductCatalog.WineName," & _
        "OrderDetails.Bottles, OrderDetails.Price, OrderDetails.ExtPrice " _
        & "FROM WineProductCatalog INNER JOIN OrderDetails ON Wi" _
        & "neProductCatalog.WineID = OrderDetails.WineID WHERE Orderlink = " & _
        vWineOrderID, Cnt
End Property
```

✔ **BillAddressBlock:** This property returns the billing address block for the designated customer. The code for this property, shown below, uses the data in the `vCust` recordset to compose a block of text that writes out the customer's address block. The constant `vbCrLf` inserts the `CR` and `LF` characters that start a new line so that the `Block` is a multiline text block. Note that the last line has an extra vbCrLf so that each block ends with a blank line.

```
Public Property Get BillAddressBlock() As Variant
    Dim Block
    Block = "Bill To:" & vbCrLf & "========" & vbCrLf
    If Not IsNull(vCust!CompanyName) Then
        Block = Block & vCust!CompanyName & vbCrLf
    End If
    Block = Block & vCust!FirstName & " " & vCust!LastName & _
        vbCrLf & vCust!BillAddress1 & vbCrLf
    If Not IsNull(vCust!BillAddress2) Then
        Block = Block & vCust!BillAddress2 & vbCrLf
    End If
    Block = Block & vCust!BillCity & ", " & vCust!BillState & _
        vCust!BillZip & vbCrLf
    If Not IsNull(vCust!billcountry) Then
        Block = Block & vCust!billcountry
    End If
    BillAddressBlock = Block & vbCrLf & vbCrLf
End Property
```

✔ **CustShipAddressBlock** and **OrderShipAddressBlock:** This property returns the ship-to-address block. In this case, you can draw the shipping address from either the customer record or the order-ship-to fields. The programming for these properties is the same as for `BillAddressBlock`, except that the fields are different.

✔ **OrderDetails:** This property produces a list of the products ordered. The code below creates one or more detail lines showing the products ordered by the customer.

```
Public Property Get OrderDetails() As Variant
    Dim Block
    Block = "Item" & Space(41) & "    Bottles" & "       Price" & "      Amount" & _
        vbCrLf
    Do Until VDetails.EOF
        Block = Block & Padded(VDetails(0), 45, "R") & _
        Padded(Format(VDetails(1), "#,###"), 10, "L") & _
        Padded(Format(VDetails(2), "currency"), 10, "L") & _
        Padded(Format(VDetails(3), "currency"), 10, "L") & vbCrLf
        VDetails.MoveNext
    Loop
    OrderDetails = Block & vbCrLf
End Property
```

The `Padded` function, shown below, adds spaces to the left or right side of a given string so that the total is always the same length. This function allows you to place items into columns. Keep in mind that these columns only align if the e-mail client displays the text in a monospaced font, such as Courier. Proportionally spaced fonts don't show the items in the correct alignment.

```
Private Function Padded(S, PadSize, LeftRight)
    Dim spaces
    If Len(S) - 1 >= PadSize Then
        S = Mid(S, 1, PadSize - 1)
    End If
    spaces = PadSize - Len(S)
    If LeftRight = "L" Then
        Padded = String(spaces, Chr(32)) & S
    Else
        Padded = S & String(spaces, Chr(32))
    End If
End Function
```

✔ **OrderSummary:** Lists the order totals using code similar to that used for `OrderDetails`.

The entire code for the `Email` class module is supplied on the CD (that accompanies this book) in the Office.MDB file. Once the `Email` class is created, you can use that object to generate text in the designed formats anytime you need on a report or in an e-mail message. `SendMessage2` shows how the object is used to generate the e-mail message shown in Figure 15-2. Using the `Email` object greatly simplifies any coding you need to do that involves sending text blocks in any message.

```
Sub SendMessage2()
    Dim OL As New Outlook.Application, _
        Mess As Outlook.MailItem
    Dim Body As New Email
    Body.WineOrderID = 4775
    Set Mess = OL.CreateItem(olMailItem)
    Mess.To = "adodum@wbase2.com" ' use field = Email!EmailAddress
    Mess.Subject = "Order #" & Body.WineOrderID
    Mess.Body = Body.BillAddressBlock & Body.OrderShipAddressBlock & _
        Body.OrderDetails & Body.OrderSummary
    Mess.Send
End Sub
```

You can send batches of e-mails by using an ADO recordset to define a group of records for which e-mails need to be generated. For example, you can use a field, `OrderConfirmEmail`, to indicate if an e-mail has been sent to confirm each order. `SendMessage3` sends an e-mail for any new orders, and marks the order record with a time stamp that indicates when the e-mail was sent.

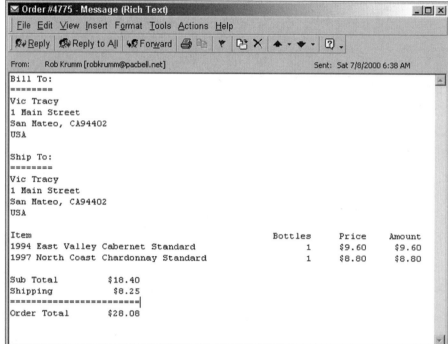

Figure 15-2:
E-mail
composed
from ADO
data
sources.

```
Sub SendMessage3()
    Dim OL As New Outlook.Application, Mess As Outlook.MailItem
    Dim Body As New Email, R As New ADODB.Recordset
    R.Open "SELECT * FROM Orders WHERE OrderConfirmEmail = False", _
    CurrentProject.Connection, adOpenKeyset, adLockOptimistic
    Do Until R.EOF
        Set Mess = OL.CreateItem(olMailItem)
        Body.WineOrderID = R!WineOrderID
        Mess.To = "adodum@wbase2.com" ' use field = Email!EmailAddress
        Mess.Subject = "Order #" & Body.WineOrderID
        Mess.Body = Body.BillAddressBlock & Body.OrderShipAddressBlock & _
            Body.OrderDetails & Body.OrderSummary
        Mess.Send
        R!OrderConfirmEmail = True
        R!OrderConfirmEmailTS = Now()
        Set Body = Nothing
        R.MoveNext
    Loop
End Sub
```

Sending messages to multiple recipients

A variation on e-mail processing to use the ADO data source to create a mail-
ing list of addresses to send the same e-mail, such as an e-mail newsletter or
a special offer. For example, suppose you wanted to let all of you wine club
members know about a special promotion.

There are two ways to create multiple-recipient mail messages. One way is to create a string that contains multiple addresses, such as: john@x.com; mary@y.com; and so on. ClubMembersString uses this method to create the string EmailAdds that contains the list of addresses.

```
Sub ClubMembersString()
    Dim OL As New Outlook.Application, Mess As Outlook.MailItem
    Dim R As New ADODB.Recordset, EMailAdds
    R.Open "SELECT * FROM Customers WHERE WineClubmember = True", _
        CurrentProject.Connection, adOpenKeyset, adLockOptimistic
    Do Until R.EOF
        EMailAdds = EMailAdds & R!EmailAddress & ";"
        R.MoveNext
    Loop
    Set Mess = OL.CreateItem(olMailItem)
    With Mess
        .To = EMailAdds
        .Subject = "Special Offer to Wine Club Members"
        .Body = "Hurry, Hurry, etc."
        .Send
    End With
End Sub
```

However, Outlook has a limit on the size of the string that it accepts as the To property of a message. If you have a large list, you can use an alternative approach, which is to use a Recipient object that can be added to the Recipients collection of the mail message object, as shown in the code fragment below. The type olTo indicates that address type, which can be olCC or olBCC.

```
Dim MailTo As Outlook.Recipient
Set MailTo = Mess.Recipients.Add(R!EmailAddress)
MailTo.Type = olTo
```

The code above shows a slight variation on the way that object programming has been discussed in most of this book. In most cases, you create an object, define its specific properties, and then add it to another object's collection. In Outlook, the object (in this case, a recipient) is created when you add it to the Recipients collection. You can set properties, like Type, after you have added the object to the collection. ClubMembersObject sends a mail message to multiple recipients using the Recipients collection. This method is not limited to any specific number of recipients. You can also determine the number of recipients by using the Count property of the Recipients collection of the MailItem object.

```
Sub ClubMembersObject()
    Dim OL As New Outlook.Application, Mess As Outlook.MailItem
    Dim R As New ADODB.Recordset
    Dim MailTo As Outlook.Recipient
    R.Open "SELECT * FROM Customers WHERE WineClubmember = True", _
        CurrentProject.Connection, adOpenKeyset, adLockOptimistic
    Set Mess = OL.CreateItem(olMailItem)
    With Mess
        .Subject = "Special Offer to Wine Club Members"
        .Body = "Hurry, Hurry, etc."
    End With
```

```
        Do Until R.EOF
            Set MailTo = Mess.Recipients.Add(R!EmailAddress)
            MailTo.Type = olTo
            R.MoveNext
        Loop
        Debug.Print Mess.Recipients.Count
        Mess.Send
    End Sub
```

Checking e-mail addresses

One of the methods supported by the Recipient object is the Resolve method. This is the operation that Outlook performs to attempt to validate an address when you use the Check Names command on the Outlook Tools menu. The CheckAddress procedure shows how you can use this method to check the validity of an e-mail address even when you don't want to send a message.

```
Sub CheckAddress()
    Dim OL As New Outlook.Application
    Dim Mess As Outlook.MailItem
    Dim Re As Outlook.Recipient
    Set Mess = OL.CreateItem(olMailItem)
    With Mess.Recipients.Add("Walter@aol")
        .Type = olTo
        If .Resolve = True Then
            MsgBox "Address Valid"
        Else
            MsgBox "Invalid Address."
        End If
    End With
End Sub
```

It is probably a good idea to scan your database to make sure there aren't any obvious bad e-mail addresses before you use the data table to generate email. CheckAllAddress shows how you can apply the Resolve method to all of the e-mail addresses in the Customers table without actually sending any messages. In this case, a note is added to the Notes field of any customers who do not appear to have a valid e-mail address.

```
Sub CheckAllAddress()
    Dim OL As New Outlook.Application
    Dim Mess As Outlook.MailItem
    Dim Re As Outlook.Recipient
    Dim R As New Recordset
    Set Mess = OL.CreateItem(olMailItem)
    R.Open "select * from Customers where customerid = 3032",
            CurrentProject.Connection
    Do Until R.EOF
        Debug.Print R!EmailAddress
        Set Re = Mess.Recipients.Add(R!EmailAddress)
        If Re.Resolve = True Then
            Re.Delete
        Else
            R!notes = R!notes & vbCrLf & "Invalid Email Address"
        End If
        R.MoveNext
    Loop
End Sub
```

The Outlook e-mail address check may not provide ideal results in weeding out problem e-mail addresses. For example, if an e-mail entry contains a space, `la costa@hotmail.net`, Outlook simply truncates the *la* and resolves that `costa@hotmail.net` as a valid address (when in fact, it has probably been misentered). In Chapter 12, you find a VBScript function that catches this entry as an invalid entry.

Data-enhanced HTML messages

Many of the e-mail client programs currently in use, including Outlook, support sending HTML as the body of the message. For example, you may prefer to send users a fully formatted e-mail message, as shown in Figure 15-3.

Using HTML not only improves the appearance of the message, but it also simplifies coding because HTML table formatting handles details such as column width and alignment. To code in HTML, I created three simple constants for the `EmailHTML` class.

```
Const S = "<TR><TD>"
Const E = "</TD></TR>"
Const M = "</TD><TD>"
```

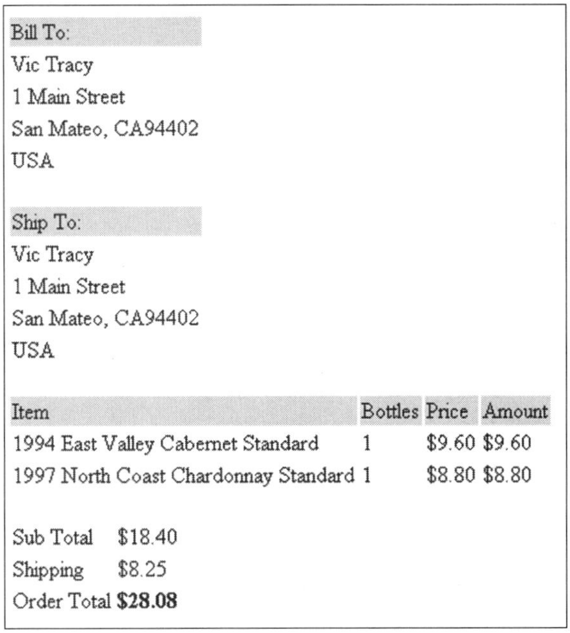

Figure 15-3: HTML-formatted e-mails allow you to mail formatted documents to many users.

Bill To:
Vic Tracy
1 Main Street
San Mateo, CA94402
USA

Ship To:
Vic Tracy
1 Main Street
San Mateo, CA94402
USA

Item	Bottles	Price	Amount
1994 East Valley Cabernet Standard	1	$9.60	$9.60
1997 North Coast Chardonnay Standard	1	$8.80	$8.80

Sub Total $18.40
Shipping $8.25
Order Total **$28.08**

The `BillAddressBlock` procedure shows how the block can be coded for HTML table formatting by inserting the constants where cell or row spacing is needed.

```
Public Property Get BillAddressBlock() As Variant
    Dim Block
    Block = "<TABLE><TR><TD bgcolor=#DDDDDD>Bill To:<TD></TR>"
    If Not IsNull(vCust!CompanyName) Then
        Block = Block & S & vCust!CompanyName & E
    End If
    Block = Block & S & vCust!FirstName & " " & vCust!LastName & _
        E & S & vCust!BillAddress1 & E
    If Not IsNull(vCust!BillAddress2) Then
        Block = Block & S & vCust!BillAddress2 & E
    End If
    Block = Block & S & vCust!BillCity & ", " & vCust!BillState & _
        vCust!BillZip & E
    If Not IsNull(vCust!billcountry) Then
        Block = Block & S & vCust!billcountry & E
    End If
    BillAddressBlock = Block & "</TABLE><BR>"
End Property
```

HTML works even better when you have a series of rows to write, such as in the Details section of the message.

```
Public Property Get OrderDetails() As Variant
    Dim Block
    Block = "<TABLE><TR
            bgcolor=#DDDDDD><TD>Item</TD><TD>Bottles</TD><TD>Price</TD><TD>Am
            ount" & E
    Do Until VDetails.EOF
        Block = Block & S & VDetails(0) & M & _
                Format(VDetails(1), "#,###") & M & _
                Format(VDetails(2), "currency") & M & _
                Format(VDetails(3), "currency") & E
        VDetails.MoveNext
    Loop
    OrderDetails = Block & "</TABLE><BR>"
End Property
```

To use the `EmailHTML` object instead of the text-based `Email` object, you need to change the `MailItem` property used to define the body of the message from `Body` to `HTMLBody`. Using this property automatically sets the message format to HTML so that the HTML text creates a message like the one shown in Figure 15-3.

```
Sub SendMessageHTML()
    Dim OL As New Outlook.Application
    Dim Mess As Outlook.MailItem
    Dim Body As New EmailHTML
    Body.WineOrderID = 4775
    Set Mess = OL.CreateItem(olMailItem)
    Mess.To = "adodum@wbase2.com" ' use field = Email!EmailAddress
    Mess.Subject = "Order #" & Body.WineOrderID
    Mess.HTMLBody = Body.BillAddressBlock & Body.OrderShipAddressBlock & _
        Body.OrderDetails & Body.OrderSummary
    Mess.Send
End Sub
```

There is another approach to composing formatted output for HTML-enabled clients. That approach utilizes XML to create messages that actually carry their own structured data block in the message. This technique is covered in Chapter 16.

Accessing E-Mail with ADO

You can use ADO to directly access the information in Outlook folders as an ADO recordset using the Jet 4.0 OLE DB provider. The recordsets produced by the Exchange/Outlook provider included in Jet 4.0 provides a subset of the full Outlook/Exchange data. You are also limited in ADO record operations such as view, edit, insert, and delete. If you want to manipulate the messages or the folder structure, you need to use the Outlook Object library.

Reading from a mailbox

To read messages from a mailbox, you can use the OLE DB provider to connect to a Microsoft Exchange and Outlook data. The data can be stored remotely on an Exchange server, or locally in a personal folder(.pst) or personal address book (.pab) file.

Using the Jet Exchange/Outlook is useful for reading information stored in message folders, address books, and other items. For most purposes, access is read-only and not all fields are available. However, the access provides the data in a standard ADO recordset structure so it is easy to select, sort, and navigate the recordset. If you need full access to the Outlook model, you have to use the Outlook Object Library used in the previous section to create messages.

You can set the provider for the connection to the Jet engine.

```
Cnt.Provider = "Microsoft.Jet.oledb.4.0"
```

Then you need to complete a connection string that contains the following elements:

- **Exchange 4.0:** The name of the driver.
- **MAPILEVEL:** The exact name of a mailbox you want to accesss.

  This is the name you see, including spaces and dashes, that appears when you open the Outlook user interface. The name is followed by a vertical bar (|) character.
- **TABLETYPE:** Use 0 for folders or 1 for address books.

> ✔ **DATABASE:** A path where a temporary (.MDB) file can be written to
> store system tables used by the driver.
>
> ✔ **PROFILE:** The name of the Exchange profile to use when Outlook is
> using an Exchange mailbox.

The example below uses `Mailbox - Rob Krumm Mail` and the profile MS
Exchange Settings.

```
Cnt.Open "Exchange 4.0;" & _
    "MAPILEVEL=Mailbox - Rob Krumm Mail|;" & _
    "PROFILE=MS Exchange Settings;" & _
    "TABLETYPE=0;DATABASE=C:\WINDOWS\TEMP\;"
```

Once you have the connection established, you can access a folder by writing
a SQL statement in which the table name is the name of the folder you want
to access. `Mail1` opens the `InBox` folder and selects messages sent by
Marnie Purciel. Note that `[From]` refers to the From field of the message.
Further, information like the actual e-mail address used by the sender is not
available with the Jet driver.

```
Sub Mail1()
    Const MailBox = "Mailbox - Rob Krumm Mail"
    Const Profile = "MS Exchange Settings"
    Dim Cnt As New ADODB.Connection
    Dim MBox As New ADODB.Recordset
    Dim Catalog As New ADODB.Recordset
    Dim F As Field
    Cnt.Provider = "Microsoft.Jet.oledb.4.0"
    Cnt.Open "Exchange 4.0;" & _
        "MAPILEVEL=" & MailBox & "|;" & _
        "PROFILE=" & Profile & ";" & _
        "TABLETYPE=0;DATABASE=C:\WINDOWS\TEMP\;"
    MBox.Open "Select * FROM inbox where [From] = 'Marnie Purciel'", Cnt
    Do Until MBox.EOF
        For Each F In MBox.Fields
            Debug.Print F.Name, F.Value
        Next
        MBox.MoveNext
    Loop
End Sub
```

The `CopyMessages` procedure uses the data made available through the Jet
provider and loads the messages from the selected user into a table called
`MailCatalog`.

```
Sub CopyMessages()
    Const MailBox = "Mailbox - Rob Krumm Mail"
    Const Profile = "MS Exchange Settings"
    Dim Cnt As New ADODB.Connection
    Dim MBox As New ADODB.Recordset
    Dim Hist As New ADODB.Recordset
    Hist.Open "mailcatalog", CurrentProject.Connection _
        , adOpenKeyset, adLockOptimistic
    Cnt.Provider = "Microsoft.Jet.oledb.4.0"
```

```
    Cnt.Open "Exchange 4.0;" & _
        "MAPILEVEL=" & MailBox & "|;" & _
        "PROFILE=" & Profile & ";" & _
        "TABLETYPE=0;DATABASE=C:\WINDOWS\TEMP\;"
    MBox.Open "Select * FROM inbox where [From] = 'Marnie Purciel'", Cnt
    Do Until MBox.EOF
        With Hist
            .AddNew
            !MailFrom = MBox("From")
            !Received = MBox("Received")
            !Subject = MBox("Subject")
            !Message = MBox("Body")
            .Update
        End With
        MBox.MoveNext
    Loop
End Sub
```

This technique provides you with a method for storing information in
Exchange/Outlook in a relational data source. One use for this is to place a
copy of the entire message related to a particular person, department, or project into a database table. If you have several users working on the same task,
such as customer service, they can use a routine like CopyMessages to pull
together all of the correspondence from many mailboxes in one location
where it can be attached to other database operations.

Use the Outlook Object Library to manipulate and modify the Outlook folders
while accessing the data. CopyMessagesMAPI performs the same operation
as CopyMessages but it does so by accessing the Outlook folder structure
directly.

Instead of using a SQL statement to select the desired messages, the
Restrict method is applied to filter the Items in the InBox folder for a specific criterion, in this case [From] = 'Marnie Purciel'.

In addition, a second folder, Backup, is used to move each copied message
out of the InBox into the backup folder. This means that you won't have to
worry about copying the same message more than once because the InBox is
cleared of the message after it has been loaded into the database table.

```
Sub CopyMessagesMAPI()
    Dim OL As New Outlook.Application
    Dim NS As Outlook.NameSpace
    Dim MBox As Outlook.MAPIFolder
    Dim Archive As Outlook.MAPIFolder
    Dim Flds As Outlook.Folders
    Dim MsgList As Outlook.Items
    Dim Msg As Outlook.MailItem

    Set NS = OL.GetNamespace("MAPI")
    Set MBox = NS.GetDefaultFolder(olFolderInbox)
    Set Flds = NS.Folders("Mailbox - Rob Krumm Mail").Folders
    Set Archive = Flds("BackUp")
    Set MsgList = MBox.Items.Restrict("[From]='Marnie Purciel'")
```

```
        Dim Hist As New ADODB.Recordset
        Hist.Open "mailcatalog1", CurrentProject.Connection _
            , adOpenKeyset, adLockOptimistic
        For Each Msg In MsgList
            With Hist
                .AddNew
                !MailFrom = Msg.SenderName
                !Received = Msg.ReceivedTime
                !Subject = Msg.Subject
                !Message = Msg.Body
                .Update
            End With
            Msg.Move Archive
        Next
    End Sub
```

Excel and ADO

You can interchange data between an ADO data source and Excel though ADO code. This approach is faster and more powerful than the built-in Access-to-Excel and Excel-to-Access features. I point out in Chapter 14 that you can get around the need to hard-code a lot of reports by building OLAP cubes. The same is true with spreadsheets. In many cases it is faster, easier, and more useful to output data to a worksheet than to a printed page. The users can take the data output from the data source and modify the data to make the report they want. Because many more users are comfortable with Excel than ADO, you can solve a lot of problems by providing the data in a format that users feel confident in manipulating.

To write the code used in this section, you must add a reference to the Microsoft Excel Object Library 9.0 to your VB/VBA environment using either the Project⇨References or the Tools⇨References menu command.

Using an ADO data source in a worksheet

You can create a worksheet and populate it with data from any ADO data source using VB/VBA code. Below is a simple procedure that generates an ADO recordset, R, that needs to be written into an Excel spreadsheet.

```
Sub SummaryXLS()
    Dim R As New ADODB.Recordset
    R.Open _
    "SELECT Customers.EnteredBy As [Sold By], Count(Orders.WineOrderID) AS
            Sales, Sum" _
    & "(IIf([orders.ShipState]=" & Chr$(34) & "CA" & Chr$(34) _
    & ",[OrderTotal],0)) AS InState, Sum(Orders.OrderTotal) AS [All Sales] FROM
            Cus" _
    & "tomers INNER JOIN Orders ON Customers.CustomerID = Orders.CustomerID
            WHERE (((Or"
```

```
      & "ders.OrderDate) Between #10/1/1999# And #10/31/1999#)) GROUP BY
              Customers.Entere" _
      & "dBy", CurrentProject.Connection
      CreateXLS R, "rpt1099"
End Sub
```

The `CreateXLS` procedure begins by defining a series of objects that represents the elements of the Excel interface: that is, workbooks, worksheets, and cell ranges. The procedure then uses two pointers, `Row` and `Col`, to place the fields and records in the ADO recordset into corresponding positions in the worksheet. If the data type of the ADO field is `adCurrency`, a numeric format is applied to the cell.

```
Function CreateXLS(ADOData As ADODB.Recordset, FileName)
    Const Comma = "#,##0.00_);(#,##0.00)"
    Dim Ex As New Excel.Application
    Dim WB As Excel.Workbook
    Dim W As Excel.Worksheet
    Dim X As Excel.Range
    Dim Row, Col
    Set WB = Ex.Workbooks.Add
    Set W = WB.Worksheets("sheet1")
    W.Name = "ADOdata"
    Row = 1
    For Col = 1 To ADOData.Fields.Count
        W.Cells(Row, Col).Value = ADOData.Fields(Col - 1).Name
    Next
    Do Until ADOData.EOF
        Row = Row + 1
        For Col = 1 To ADOData.Fields.Count
            If IsNull(ADOData(Col - 1)) Then
                W.Cells(Row, Col).Value = 0
            Else
                W.Cells(Row, Col).Value = ADOData(Col - 1)
            End If
            If ADOData(Col - 1).Type = adCurrency Then
                W.Cells(Row, Col).NumberFormat = Comma
            End If
        Next
        ADOData.MoveNext
    Loop
    'autofit
    W.UsedRange.Columns.AutoFit
    WB.SaveAs FileName & ".xls"
    Ex.Visible = True
End Function
```

The `AutoFit` method uses the Excel feature to automatically adjust the width of the columns. Note that when run from an object interface, the Excel application runs in a hidden mode. To see the new worksheet, you must set the `Visible` property to `true`.

 When testing a new procedure that uses the Excel application object, you may find that if you stop the code for an error or a change that you are leaving multiple sessions of Excel running invisibly. You can check this by using the Ctrl+Alt+Del command to bring up the Task Manager window. You may find many different Excel sessions on the list even though none are visible on the screen. You can use the Task Manager to kill off these sessions.

Creating a worksheet from an ADO recordset

Keep in mind that because ADO is available to any VB/VBA application, it can be used from Office applications like Excel or PowerPoint to load data from ADO sources directly into the application.

The procedure shown in the previous section runs outside Excel and builds an Excel worksheet. An alternative approach is to place the ADO code into an Excel workbook and have Excel reach out and load the ADO data automatically.

For example, you can add ADO code to the On_Open event of a workbook. Each time the workbook is opened, it accesses the specified ADO provider and loads a recordset into a spreadsheet. This is basically how the Excel⇨Get External data command operates, but ADO is faster and capable of a wider variety of data access operations and features.

To write ADO code in Excel, you need to use the Tools⇨References menu in the VBA editor to add the Microsoft Active Data Objects library to the VBA environment.

Once added, you can proceed to write ADO code that looks almost exactly like the code that was used in the previous section. The primary difference is that the code is running in the workbook that receives the data so it is not necessary to create the workbook and worksheet objects. Instead, you can simply reference those objects in the open workbook.

The Workbook_Open below accesses the Office.mdb database file as the data source and runs the same query as in the previous section. Once the recordset is created, the CreateXLS procedure is used to copy the recordset data into the first worksheet.

```
Private Sub Workbook_Open()
    Dim R As New ADODB.Recordset
    Dim Cnt As New ADODB.Connection
    Cnt.Open "Provider=Microsoft.Jet.OLEDB.4.0;" & _
        "Data Source=O:\ADO Book\DB\Chp15\Office.mdb;"
    R.Open _
    "SELECT Customers.EnteredBy As [Sold By], Count(Orders.WineOrderID) AS
            Sales, Sum" _
        & "(IIf([orders.ShipState]=" & Chr$(34) & "CA" & Chr$(34) _
        & ",[OrderTotal],0)) AS InState, Sum(Orders.OrderTotal) AS [All Sales] FROM
                Cus" _
        & "tomers INNER JOIN Orders ON Customers.CustomerID = Orders.CustomerID
                WHERE (((Or" _
        & "ders.OrderDate) Between #10/1/1999# And #10/31/1999#)) GROUP BY
                Customers.Entere" _
        & "dBy", Cnt
    CreateXLS R
End Sub
```

This function is essentially the same as the one used in the previous section with two changes. First, there is no need to create the Excel workbook. All you need to do is refer to the ActiveWorkbook object that connects your code to the currently open workbook.

Second, to insure that the data is up to date, all the old data is deleted using the Delete method `W.UsedRange.Columns` object. In essence, you delete all of the columns currently in use to return the worksheet to its blank state before filling in the worksheet with the data in the newly created recordset.

```
Function CreateXLS(ADOData As ADODB.Recordset)
    Const Comma = "#,##0.00_);(#,##0.00)"
    Dim WB As Excel.Workbook
    Dim W As Excel.Worksheet
    Dim X As Excel.Range
    Dim Row, Col
    Set WB = ActiveWorkbook

    Set W = WB.Worksheets(1)
    W.UsedRange.Columns.Delete 'clear old data

    Row = 1
    For Col = 1 To ADOData.Fields.Count
        W.Cells(Row, Col).Value = ADOData.Fields(Col - 1).Name
    Next
    Do Until ADOData.EOF
        Row = Row + 1
        For Col = 1 To ADOData.Fields.Count
            If IsNull(ADOData(Col - 1)) Then
                W.Cells(Row, Col).Value = 0
            Else
                W.Cells(Row, Col).Value = ADOData(Col - 1)
            End If
            If ADOData(Col - 1).Type = adCurrency Then
                W.Cells(Row, Col).NumberFormat = Comma
            End If
        Next
        ADOData.MoveNext
    Loop
    'autofit
    W.UsedRange.Columns.AutoFit
End Function
```

You can use this basic approach to connect any worksheet dynamically with any ADO data source.

Chapter 16

ADO Documents

· ·

In This Chapter

▶ Sending formatted reports as e-mail messages

▶ Building your own XML converter

▶ Using the stream object to create files

▶ Converting recordsets to XML/DHTML documents

▶ Creating XML/DHTML documents from recordsets

▶ Accessing documents with the record object

▶ Downloading files from a Web site

· ·

*Y*ou can read HTML formatted messages using many e-mail programs other than Outlook. However, if you're sending e-mail to users who you know have Outlook, such as people within your own organization, you may want to take advantage of Microsoft-specific features to get even greater benefits.

Building an XML Converter

You can build a simple XML converter that takes any ADO recordset and then create a data island for that information in an e-mail message or any other DHTML document.

Take a look at the following outline to see the structure you're going to create in this case. If your goal is to display the contents of a single recordset , use the following XML structure as a general container for a recordset. The `<Recordset>` tag functions as a container for the entire recordset. The `<Record>` tag needs to appear once for each record in the recordset. The actual data is contained in a series of field level tags.

```
<Recordset>
   <Record>
      <Field1>...data...</Field1>
      <Field2>...data...</Field2>
   </Record>
</Recordset>
```

You can write a series of simple functions that format the elements of an ADO recordset into XML data elements:

```
<FirstName>Walter</FirstName>
<LastName>Lafish</LastName>
```

The required information can be obtained using the field Name property and the field Value property. WriteXMLRow generates a series of field tags based on the Fields collection and the Name and Value properties.

```
Function WriteXMLRow(R As Recordset)
    Dim F As ADODB.Field
    Dim XMLstr
    For Each F In R.Fields
        XMLstr = XMLstr & "<" & F.Name & ">" & _
            F.Value & "</" & F.Name & ">" & vbCrLf
    Next
    WriteXMLRow = XMLstr
End Function
```

You can use the WriteXMLRow function to build a complete XML data island. The WriteXMLRs function uses a recordset object to construct a data island. This function starts with an XML tag that names the data island ADOData.

Next, the procedure executes the WriteXMLRow function once for each record in the recordset. The structure is completed when closing tags are added.

```
Function WriteXMLRs(R As Recordset)
    Dim XMLstr
    XMLstr = "<xml id=adodata>" & vbCrLf & _
        "<Recordset>" & vbCrLf
    Do Until R.EOF
        XMLstr = XMLstr & "<Record>" & vbCrLf & WriteXMLRow(R) & "</Record>" &
            vbCrLf
        R.MoveNext
    Loop
    WriteXMLRs = XMLstr & "</Recordset>" & vbCrLf & "</xml>"
End Function
```

To display the data island in a DHTML document, you need to construct a DHTML table, which is bound to the ADOData data island. The WriteHTMLTable function uses the same recordset object as the WriteXMLRs function. WriteHTMLTable uses the Fields collection to write out a DHTML table structure that binds table columns to each of the fields in the recordset.

The first part of the function uses the field Name property to write column headings. The second part uses the Fields collection to bind table cells to each field by Name.

```
Function WriteHTMLTable(R As Recordset)
    Dim HTMLStr, F As ADODB.Field
    HTMLStr = "<TABLE DATASRC=#adodata border = 1>" & vbCrLf & _
        "<THEAD>" & vbCrLf & "<TR>"
    For Each F In R.Fields
        HTMLStr = HTMLStr & "<TD bgcolor=#DDDDDD><B>" & StrConv(F.Name,
            vbProperCase) & "</B></TD>" & vbCrLf
    Next
    HTMLStr = HTMLStr & "</THEAD>" & vbCrLf & "<TBODY>" & vbCrLf
    For Each F In R.Fields
        HTMLStr = HTMLStr & "<TD><SPAN DATAFLD='" & F.Name & "'></SPAN></TD>" &
            vbCrLf
    Next
    WriteHTMLTable = HTMLStr & "</TR></TBODY></TABLE>"
End Function
```

To create the complete DHTML/XML code, you need to combine the output of the `WriteXMLRs` and the `WriteHTMLTable` into one stream of text. The `XMLandHTMLform` function returns the code for the entire DHTML/XML document based on a recordset object. Because all of the functions operate from the same recordset object, the names that are generated in the XML and DHTML sections match exactly. The `XMLandHTMLform` function also provides a `HeadingText` variable that can be used:

```
Function XMLandHTMLform(R As ADODB.Recordset, Optional HeadingText = "Data")
    XMLandHTMLform = "<HTML><BODY>" & _
        "<H1>" & HeadingText & "</H1>" & _
        WriteXMLRs(R) & _
        WriteHTMLTable(R) & _
        "</BODY></HTML>"
End Function
```

You need to create one more function, called `CleanHTML`, before you can generate the code required. `CleanHTML`, shown in the following lines of code, replaces special characters from the text, such as an ampersand (&), with the HTML code equivalent, &amp.

Even though the `CleanHTML` function can clean up other characters, the ampersand is definitely the most troublesome symbol because it gets in the way of the XML parser. Be sure you use `CleanHTML` to remove it.

```
Function CleanHTML(HTMLStr)
    Dim Pstr
    Pstr = HTMLStr
    If InStr(Pstr, "&") Then
        Pstr = Replace(Pstr, "&", "&amp;")
    End If
    CleanHTML = Pstr
End Function
```

Writing an XML message

With the XML and DHTML functions in place, you can generate an e-mail message that display as a formatted report.

The `CleanHTML` function is used to scrub the output of `XMLandHTMLform` function, which has converted the recordset `RS` to an XML island and a corresponding DHTML bound table. The entire block of XML/DHTML code is assigned to the `HTMLBody` property of the message:

```
Sub E-mailXML1()
    Dim OL As New Outlook.Application
    Dim Mess As Outlook.MailItem
    Dim Rs As New ADODB.Recordset
    Dim SHtml
    Set Mess = OL.CreateItem(olMailItem)

    Rs.Open "SELECT * FROM [Monthly Report]", CurrentProject.Connection
    Mess.HTMLBody = CleanHTML(XMLandHTMLform(Rs, "Monthly Sales Report"))
    Mess.To = "Robkrumm@pacbell.net"
    Mess.Subject = "Report"
    Mess.Send
End Sub
```

When the user opens the message in Outlook, the message body uses Internet Explorer features to generate the formatted display shown in Figure 16-1.

Using this approach, you can, in a few lines of code, generate an e-mail message that contains the contents of any ADO recordset as a formatted table.

From: Rob Krumm [robkrumm@pacbell.net]

Monthly Sales Report

Enteredby	Countofwineorderid	Instate	Sumofordertotal
Amber	47	1421.4064	3071.0464
Amy	58	2574.1468	3838.7968
Anne	50	1889.5839	3276.5839
Bambi	38	1358.2184	2412.8684
Bruce	52	2014.666	2991.616
Carl	75	2370.2859	4223.7359
Cathy	53	2013.1112	3180.0112
Eric	58	3081.0188	3993.0688
Frank	47	1367.0176	2346.7176
Fred	51	1427.6868	2698.2868
Gail	58	1682.1076	4144.2176
Hank	49	1639.9783	2820.9283
Harry	50	2122.4568	3302.1968
Heather	48	1852.3152	2702.6152
Henry	46	2239.0244	3577.0244

Figure 16-1: This e-mail message displays the XML data in a table bound to the data island.

Sending a link in an e-mail message

An alternative to sending the full contents of the XML/DHTML document is to send a message that contains a hyperlink to a DHTML document. This approach enables you to create a document, place it on a network share or in a Web folder, and then have users gain access to the document by clicking the hyperlink that you send them in an e-mail message. One advantage of sending a link via e-mail is that you can conserve resources:

- ✔ You only have to create a single copy of the report, which saves you time.

- ✔ All you have to do is send the link in the e-mail message — not the entire XML/DHTML code — which saves your mail server's resources.

```
Dim OL As New Outlook.Application
Dim Mess As Outlook.MailItem
Set Mess = OL.CreateItem(olMailItem)
Mess.Body = "Monthly Report Link File://c:\MonthlyReport.htm"
Mess.To = "Robkrumm@pacbell.net"
Mess.Subject = "Report"
Mess.Send
```

Using a stream object

Of course, the hyperlink doesn't do any good unless you place a document at the specified location with the desired content. To make sure that's what users find, use the text that is generated from the XMLandHTMLform as the content of an HTM file in the desired network share or Web folder.

Version 2.5 of ADO enables you to read data directly from and write data directly to files. Prior to this version, you needed to use some other facility to create and read files. In VB/VBA you have to use a set of statements (which go back to the oldest versions of Microsoft BASIC) called *low-level file commands*.

ADO Version 2.5 adds two new objects that encapsulate a wide range of file-related operations within the ADO model. The file-related objects are important because they allow programmers to deal with files without depending on a specific Visual Basic feature to create persistent objects such as files that are stored on a disk. ADO 2.5 can create and manipulate these file objects in VB, VBA, VBScript, C++ or any other language capable of using ADO.

The ADO Stream object is designed to bridge the gap between data stored in memory, such as recordsets and data stored in persistent objects, such as disk files.

You can load data stored in a file into a stream object. Other memory objects (such as recordsets, which can then transfer the data to the ADO data provider) can access the data in the stream object. In practical terms, this bridge enables you to open a Web document and store the source code in a memo field associated with an ADO recordset.

In this instance, you want to go in the other direction. The data generated by the XMLandHTMLform function needs to be stored in a disk file so that other users can access the information by means of a hyperlink.

You can place any sort of text data into a stream object by using the WriteText method of the stream object. Keep in mind that the WriteText method refers to writing data from some source into the stream.

The following example stores a text phrase to a stream object. The Size property returns the total number of characters stored in the stream.

```
Sub WriteToStream()
    Dim Strm As New ADODB.Stream
    Strm.Open
    Strm.WriteText "Today is " & Date
    MsgBox Strm.Size
End Sub
```

The FileXML1 procedure creates a disk file that contains the XML/DHTML data generated by the XMLandHTMLform function. First, the output of XMLandHTMLform is stored in the stream object S_DHTML. The data is transferred to a disk file using the SaveToFile of the stream object.

```
Sub FileXML1()
    Dim S_DHTML As New ADODB.Stream
    Dim R As New ADODB.Recordset
    R.Open "SELECT * FROM [Monthly Report]", CurrentProject.Connection
    With S_DHTML
        .Open
        .Type = adTypeText
        .WriteText CleanHTML(XMLandHTMLform(R, "Monthly Sales Report"))
        .SaveToFile "o:\MonthlyRepo/rt.htm", adSaveCreateOverWrite
    End With
End Sub
```

LinkXML1 goes one step farther. In this example, the file is created and a hyperlink to the file location is sent in an e-mail message. When users open the e-mail, they can click the hyperlink and view the report stored in the XML/DHTML document.

```
Sub LinkXML1()
    Dim S_DHTML As New ADODB.Stream
    Dim R As New ADODB.Recordset
    R.Open "SELECT * FROM [Monthly Report]", CurrentProject.Connection
```

```
    With S_DHTML
        .Open
        .Type = adTypeText
        .WriteText CleanHTML(XMLandHTMLform(R, "Monthly Sales Report"))
        .SaveToFile "o:\MonthlyReport.htm", adSaveCreateOverWrite
    End With
    Dim OL As New Outlook.Application
    Dim Mess As Outlook.MailItem
    Set Mess = OL.CreateItem(olMailItem)
    Mess.Body = "Monthly Report Link File://o:\MonthlyReport.htm"
    Mess.To = "Robkrumm@pacbell.net"
    Mess.Subject = "Report"
    Mess.Send
End Sub
```

Using new versions of ADO with Access 2000

When you install new updates to MDAC (Microsoft Data Access Components), references to older versions of ADO remain. (The references are there for the purpose of maintaining backward compatibility.) When you start a new project in Visual Basic, you usually choose the most recent version of Visual Basic that's available. However, if the project is a VBA project in an Access 2000 database, the initial ADO library that's automatically chosen for you is ADO Version 2.1, which was the version available when Access 2000 was released.

Version 2.1 doesn't include the Record and Stream objects, so if you find them missing from your ADO object list, select Tools⇨References and check which version of the ADO library is in use in the project. Change from 2.1 to 2.5 or newer to have the record and Stream objects available.

Documents with Records and Streams

In addition to the Stream object, ADO 2.5 includes a new object called a *record*, which adds a tree-structured storage system to ADO.

For easy access to a document or a folder, use a URL as a connection parameter when opening a record. The statement below opens a record object that corresponds to the DEFAULT.ASP file in the root folder of the Web site located at 208.185.177.211, my office Web server.

```
RecObj.Open "default.asp", "URL=http://208.185.177.211/"
```

The record consists of a set of 18 standard fields; the fields return information about the document. The procedure below lists the fields and their values for the DEFAULT.ASP.

```
Sub OpenRecord()
    Dim webfolder As New ADODB.Record
    Dim F As ADODB.Field
    webfolder.Open "default.asp", "URL=http://208.185.177.211/"
    For Each F In webfolder.Fields
        Debug.Print F.Name, F.Value
    Next
End Sub
```

Below are the fields and values returned for the DEFAULT.ASP document.

```
RESOURCE_PARSENAME              default.asp
RESOURCE_PARENTNAME             http://208.185.177.211
RESOURCE_ABSOLUTEPARSENAME      http://208.185.177.211/default.asp
RESOURCE_ISHIDDEN
RESOURCE_ISREADONLY
RESOURCE_CONTENTTYPE
RESOURCE_CONTENTCLASS
RESOURCE_CONTENTLANGUAGE
RESOURCE_CREATIONTIME           5/26/2000 9:11:17 AM
RESOURCE_LASTACCESSTIME
RESOURCE_LASTWRITETIME          7/9/2000 10:55:51 AM
RESOURCE_STREAMSIZE              257
RESOURCE_ISCOLLECTION           False
RESOURCE_ISSTRUCTUREDDOCUMENT
DEFAULT_DOCUMENT
RESOURCE_DISPLAYNAME            default.asp
RESOURCE_ISROOT                 False
RESOURCE_ISMARKEDFOROFFLINE     False
```

Two fields of general interest in dealing with any set of files and folders are

- **RESOURCE_ISCOLLECTION:** Identifies documents that are folders that contain other documents. This field is true for folders and false for documents.

- **RESOURCE_STREAMSIZE:** Returns the number of bytes in the file.

Getting a folder listing

The record object supports the GetChildren method to make navigating through a tree-structure document source easy for you to do. The GetChildren method loads all of the documents (folders and files) contained in the current record into a recordset.

ListFolderContents uses the GetChildren method to create a recordset named Contents. The Contents recordset contains all of the items from the root folder of the Web site.

```
Sub ListFolderContents()
    Dim Contents As ADODB.Recordset
    Dim webfolder As New ADODB.Record
    webfolder.Open "", "URL=http://208.185.177.211/"
    Set Contents = webfolder.GetChildren
```

```
    Do Until Contents.EOF
            Debug.Print Contents("RESOURCE_PARSENAME"), _
                Contents("RESOURCE_ISCOLLECTION")
        Contents.MoveNext
    Loop
End Sub
```

ListFiles uses the RESOURCE_ISCOLLECTION field to determine if a record is a folder or a file. The procedure lists only the records that point to files rather than folders.

```
Sub ListFiles()
    Dim Contents As ADODB.Recordset
    Dim webfolder As New ADODB.Record
    webfolder.Open "", "URL=http://208.185.177.211/"
    Set Contents = webfolder.GetChildren
    Do Until Contents.EOF
        If Contents("RESOURCE_ISCOLLECTION") = False Then
            Debug.Print Contents("RESOURCE_PARSENAME"), _
                Contents("RESOURCE_STREAMSIZE")
        End If
        Contents.MoveNext
    Loop
End Sub
```

Calculating space used

You can use the GetChildren method to calculate the total size of all the files in a folder. The ListFolderFilesSize procedure calculates the total by summing the RESOURCE_STREAMSIZE values of each file.

```
Sub ListFolderFilesSize()
    Dim Contents As ADODB.Recordset
    Dim webfolder As New ADODB.Record
    Dim SpaceUsed
    webfolder.Open "", "URL=http://208.185.177.211/"
    Set Contents = webfolder.GetChildren
    Do Until Contents.EOF
        If Contents("RESOURCE_ISCOLLECTION") = False Then
            SpaceUsed = SpaceUsed + Contents("RESOURCE_STREAMSIZE")
        End If
        Contents.MoveNext
    Loop
    Debug.Print SpaceUsed
End Sub
```

Downloading files

You can combine the operation of the Record object with the Stream object to create ADO operations that can copy documents from one location to another.

Being able to combine these functions becomes immediately useful when the stream object is linked to a record object. For example, say you open a record object that refers to a document file on a Web site. The following statement opens the RSEdit1.Asp in the Chp13 folder:

```
RecObj.Open "rsedit1.asp", "URL=http://208.185.177.211/chp13"
```

You can associate the record object with a stream object by using the record as the source parameter for the Open method of the stream object:

```
StreamObj.Open RecObj
```

In effect, the preceding statement opens a channel between the ADO objects in memory and the contents of the file stored on the Web site. If you apply the ReadText method to the stream, you cause the data stored in the document to flow through to stream object in memory. The ReadText method enables you to specify the exact number of characters from the file that you want to read. The constant asReadAll uses the RESOURCE_STREAMSIZE field to read all of the contents of the file. The following statement invokes the ReadText method on a stream called StreamObj. The asReadAll parameter specifies that all the text from the source should be read.

```
StreamObj.ReadText(asReadAll)
```

The effect of the following statement is to save a copy of the text contained in the rsedit1.asp file to a new file located on the local C drive. This new file is called copyof.Asp.

```
StreamObj.SaveToFile "C:\copyof.Asp"
```

By combining the ADO record and stream objects, you get the equivalent of the CopyFile command included in Visual Basic but not available in VBA or VBScript.

DownLoadFileText1 illustrates the first half of this task. It reads the text from the file and displays it in the debug window.

```
Sub DownLoadFileText1()
    Dim Doc As New ADODB.Record
    Dim DocContents As New ADODB.Stream
    Doc.Open "rsedit1.asp", "URL=http://208.185.177.211/chp13"
    DocContents.Type = adTypeText
    DocContents.Charset = "ascii"
    DocContents.Open Doc, adModeRead, adOpenStreamFromRecord
    Debug.Print DocContents.ReadText(adReadAll)
End Sub
```

`DownLoadFileText1` adds parameters you need to complete the coding. The parameters are

- ✔ **Type:** Sets the document type to either `adTypeText` or `adTypeBinary`.
- ✔ **Charset:** Sets the character coding to the proper system, such as `ascii`.
- ✔ **adModeRead:** Sets the operational mode to read only. If permission is available, you can write data back to the source file using the `adModeReadWrite` setting.
- ✔ **adOpenStreamFromRecord:** Specifies a data flow through a record object.

`DownLoadFileText` adds the final step and saves the stream to a local file. If you stream the data from a source file to a destination, specifying the `ReadText` or `Read` methods isn't necessary. The `SaveToFile` initiates a read-all operation on the source:

```
Sub DownLoadFileText()
    Dim Doc As New ADODB.Record
    Dim DocContents As New ADODB.Stream
    Doc.Open "MakeList1.asp", "URL=http://208.185.177.211/chp13"
    DocContents.Type = adTypeText
    DocContents.Charset = "ascii"
    DocContents.Open Doc, adModeRead, adOpenStreamFromRecord
    DocContents.SaveToFile "C:\MakeList1.Asp"
End Sub
```

Part VI
The Part of Tens

The 5th Wave   By Rich Tennant

"You ever get the feeling this project could just up and die at any moment?"

In this part . . .

What For Dummies tome would be complete without the ubiquitous Part of Tens? Answer: None. This part contains a list of my favorite tools and resources on the Web to keep you warm on blustery nights.

Chapter 17

Ten Useful Web Links

You can find a live set of these links at `www.wbase2.com`. Click ADO For Dummies, and then click Ten Links.

ADO 2.6 Reference

The ADO 2.6 Reference is the online reference section for the ADO Software Developers Kit. The online kit contains the basic documentation about the objects, properties, methods, and events supported by the current version of ADO. You can find the reference by going to

`msdn.microsoft.com/library/psdk/dasdk/ados4piv.htm`

ASPZone

ASPZone is a site with some commercial elements that allows authors of books about active server pages to provide ASP and samples and examples. The idea is that you'll be interested enough to buy the full book. But ASPZone isn't all about the sell, sell, sell mentality. It's a well-maintained site with up-to-date information that can help your programming. Go to

```
www.aspzone.com/
```

Data Access Overview

This resource, available from the Microsoft site, offers articles that give you an overview of data-access topics such as ASDO, OLE DB, and ODBC. Go to

```
msdn.microsoft.com/library/backgrnd/html/bgdataaccessoverview.htm
```

DevX.com

DevX is an independent commercial site that offers development information for programmers. DevX is a gateway to a number of sites that have development information and resources. Go to

```
www.windx.com
```

KAMATH.com

KAMATH is a personal Web site that has information about the latest active server technology from Microsoft including ASP, Java, and SQL Server. Go to

```
www.kamath.com/
```

LearnASP.com

The LearnASP site is a great resource for ASP developers on all levels. The focus of the site is to share examples and ideas, but there is also a commercial aspect to the site, as well. Go to

```
www.learnasp.com/learn/
```

Microsoft ADO Home Page

The Microsoft ADO home page is *the* ADO technology page in the Microsoft site. Visit the page for a good place to start when you seek general information and what's new with ADO.

```
www.microsoft.com/data/ado/default.htm
```

Microsoft Data Access Components Download

Use this link to download the latest version of the MDAC (Microsoft Data Access Components) system. The MDAC system includes the ADO components OLE DB drivers and ADO programming components.

Use this link to download the latest version of the MDAC system. The MDAC system includes several ADO components, including OLE DB drivers and ADO programming components.

```
www.microsoft.COm/data/download.htm
```

Microsoft Office Developers Home Page

The Microsoft Office Developers home page is the place to go when you're looking for information about building applications with Office tools.

```
msdn.microsoft.com/officedev/
```

MSDN Magazine

MSDN provides monthly articles about a variety of Microsoft technologies. Go to

```
msdn.microsoft.com/msdnmag/
```

Chapter 18

Ten Programming Tips

*P*rogramming is a science and a craft. This chapter presents ten tips to enhance your craft.

Access 2000 MDB versus ADP

If you're building a database application in Access 2000 that connects to a SQL Server, you have a choice between creating an Access MDB or an Access ADP. Here is a quick summary of the practical differences between these two types of Access databases:

- ADP files attach directly to the SQL Server database using the ADO provider for SQL Server. ADO is much faster.

- MDB files cannot modify SQL Server source objects such as tables or views.

- ADP files do not support the query object found in Access MDB files.

- ✔ MDB files treat SQL Server views and stored procedures as attached tables.

- ✔ MDB files can have tables from several different SQL Servers, Access MDB files, or other data sources open at the same time.

- ✔ In an MDB file you can use an Access query to perform a JOIN between tables stored in different servers or data formats. Even though performance is slow, you may find it necessary to use this feature.

- ✔ MDB queries can include sorting.

- ✔ In an MDB file, stored procedures are defined as queries using the Pass-Through query option. ADP files list stored procedures on their own tab.

- ✔ MDB files enables you to run queries without saving them.

- ✔ MDB files enable local tables.

Embedding Queries in Programs

Creating embedded SQL or other language statements is one of the most tedious and error-prone parts of writing a database application. Here is how I go about creating the SQL statements that I use in my database applications in VBA, Visual Basic, or ASPs:

- ✔ **Query or view builders:** Enable you to create the SQL statement using drag and drop, plus other features that eliminate a great deal of the manual entry and eliminate mistakes in syntax and field names.

- ✔ **The Access MDB query grid:** Enables you to include sorting. The ADP View builder does not enable ORDER BY clauses.

- ✔ **The SQL button:** Enables you to display the SQL text that corresponds to the query or view you created.

- ✔ **Pasting the SQL from Access into the VB, VBA, or ASP code:** See the next section on the String Editor for a neat tool to help with this process.

After you have the query in your code, you may need to check out what is going on if the query doesn't perform as expected. In the example below, I use the Debug Print statement to send a copy of the SQL text to the debug window. Keep in mind that when an incorrect SQL statement is used to populate a control, you will not see any error messages. The only indication is that the data doesn't show up.

```
Private Sub Text4_Change()
  If Text4.Text <> "" Then
  RS.Open "SELECT " & ColListLocal & " from customers " & _
  " where lastname like '" _
  & Me.Text4.Text & "%'", Cnt, adOpenStatic
  Set Me.NameList.DataSource = RS

  Debug.Print "SELECT " & ColListLocal & " from customers " & _
  " where lastname like '" _
  & Me.Text4.Text & "%'"

    Me.NameList.Requery
    RS.Close
  End If
End Sub
```

I can then copy the SQL text from the debug window into a query or view window and execute it. In this window the SQL is checked for syntax, and appropriate error messages are returned. You can usually see why the SQL statement wasn't working and make the required correction to the code.

String Editor

The Microsoft Office Developer edition contains a number of special features that are designed to help you develop applications in Office applications. Among the tools included in this addition is a particular favorite of mine called the String Editor, which I use when writing code for Access, Visual Basic, or ASPs. The string editor enables you to enter text and variables and have them pasted as fully delimited strings into you code page. You can load existing expressions into the editor, make changes, and then save the new string back to the module. You can select to use either Access or SQL-compatible operators.

See this URL for information about the string editor:

```
msdn.microsoft.com/library/officedev/odecore/derefode_help_stringeditor.htm
```

Using Linked Servers

Using an Access MDB is not the only way to combine data from different sources in a single application. An even more powerful approach is to use the SQL Server 7.0 feature called Linked Servers.

For example, suppose you have to build an application that combines a SQL Server database with data stored on an Oracle server. On the security branch of the SQL Server Enterprise manager, you can use OLE DB to connect the SQL Server to the Oracle Server as a linked server. Linked servers use OLE DB drivers to attach sources like Oracle databases to SQL Servers. For details on how to set up a linked server, see this URL:

```
msdn.microsoft.com/library/psdk/sql/1_server_10.htm
```

After the linked server is attached, you can perform queries and joins that treat the Oracle data as if it were part of the SQL Server. In addition, you can perform operations that JOIN SQL Server tables with Oracle tables.

For a good article on SQL Server integration with other data sources see:

```
http://msdn.microsoft.com/library/techart/sqlinkserv.htm.
```

Late Binding to Avoid References Problems

Many of the common reference libraries used in VB/VBA applications have different version numbers. For example, the current version of Access 2000 automatically references ADO 2.1 each time you start a new MDB or ADP file.

When you are writing an application that will be distributed to various desktops, you may find that not all the desktops have the same versions of various libraries. You may encounter errors when your code attempts to create instances of objects if the reference in your code is for ADO 2.5 or 2.6 and the target desktop has the ADO 2.1 library (supplied with the current version of Office 2000) only. The code below requires that you set a reference to a specific version of the ADO library in your project. This is called early binding because the data types of the objects are determined when you write the code.

```
Dim Cnt as New ADODB.Connection
Dim R as New ADOBD.Recordset
```

One way to avoid this problem is to use a style of programming called *late binding*. Late binding is the method ASPs use to create objects with the CreateObject() function. The code below creates the same two objects without requiring a reference to a specific type library.

```
Dim Ctn as Object, R as Object
Set Cnt = CreateObject("ADODB.Connection")
Set R = CreateObject("ADOBD.Recordset")
```

Using Compiler Instructions

When you are writing the code for an application, you may want to have the final version use late binding for the reasons discussed in the previous section. But using generic Object variables makes it harder to write the code because the auto complete feature won't work unless you assign the variable a specific object type.

One way to get the best of both approaches is to use compiler instructions. Compiler instructions begin with a #. The example below uses the constant #Coding to determine if early or late binding should be used.

```
#Const Coding = False
Sub EarlyandLate()
    #If Coding = True Then
        Dim Cnt As New ADODB.Connection
        Dim R As New ADOBD.Recordset
    #Else
        Dim Ctn As Object, R As Object
        Set Cnt = CreateObject("ADODB.Connection")
        Set R = CreateObject("ADOBD.Recordset")
    #End If
End Sub
```

When you develop the application setting, the constant False enables you to write the code with the benefit of early binding and autocompletion. To deploy the application, set the constant to True to enable late binding to take place on the user's desktop.

Create ASPs with Visual InterDev

The ASPs and other Web-based documents discussed in this book can be edited in any application that edits standard text. In practice you will probably want to use an editor that helps you create and organize the applications.

Visual InterDev is part of the Visual Studio development suite. It is designed to develop complete Web based applications. A full discussion of the benefits of this program won't fit in this book. For more information, check out their home page at

```
msdn.microsoft.com/vinterdev/default.asp.
```

Visual Basic Class Builder

Class modules do tend to be a bit more verbose than standard procedures and functions. Visual Basic 6.0 includes a utility called a Class Builder. The Class Builder can be used to outline the properties, methods, and collections you want to have in your class module.

The Class Builder creates the basic procedure statements and defines module-level variables. The details of the coding are then added in the usual way. The Class Builder enables you to design the basic model of your class without having to get bogged down in inserting individual procedures. This makes it easier to develop an overall idea of how the class will operate before you have to code the details of each property and method.

While the Class Builder is a Visual Basic add-in, the code generated by the utility can be used in a VB/VBA environment.

MDX Sample Application

In order to help you learn the MDX language, OLAP services include an application called the MDX Sample Application that provides you with an environment in which you can drag and drop all of the elements in a cube in order to compose an MDX query.

The MDX Sample Application connects to a data mart. You can then select any of the cubes in that data mart to work with. The sample application loads tree structures that list all of the elements in the cube's dimension collection. It also includes a list of all of the functions, and there are a lot, supported by the MDX language.

SQL Server 2000 Query Analyzer

In the beta copies of SQL Server 2000, the Query Analyzer has been vastly improved to create SQL queries. Unlike previous versions in which the query tool in SQL server was little more than a blank window, the SQL 2000 version includes a complete listing of database items (such as tables, queries, procedures, columns, and indexes.), a list of Transact SQL language elements, and code templates. All of these items can be dragged and dropped into the query window.

The Query Analyzer 2000 does not go as far as the Access or SQL Server 7.0 view designer, which enables you to visually generate joins between tables, but it does offer a lot more support for writing procedures in Transact SQL than is available on current version of SQL Server. This is a real timesaver. Also, because most of the Transact SQL code is compatible with earlier versions, you can use the Query Analyzer 2000 with SQL Server 7.0. It isn't compatible with version 6.5.

Writing Reports as Word Documents

I personally don't like to spend my time designing report forms. One trick I like to do is add a routine that writes a document (either HTML or Word format) based on the content of any ADO recordset. This one routine can be added to any form to provide a generic way to dump data into a printable, and even more importantly, an editable document.

The ability to dump data into a Word document is all users need to create the document they need. Because they can edit the output, they can annotate the dumped data until they have what they need for the meeting and presentation of the report.

Appendix

About the CD

*O*n the CD-ROM:

- ✔ Sample files from this book
- ✔ Commercial verison of Netscape Communicator
- ✔ Commercial verison of Microsoft Internet Explorer
- ✔ Microsoft MDAC

System Requirements

The CD is designed to work with a Windows 95, 98, NT, or 2000 computer that has a 2x CD-ROM drive. The actual hardware requirements depend on the other programs that you run, such as Microsoft Access. Generally, you should have at least a 300 MHz Pentium processor, 1GB of empty hard drive space, and 64MB of RAM to apply the steps demonstrated in this book. You may be able to get by with less resources, but maybe not.

Some of the examples in the book require an Internet connection if you want to follow along. I recommend a fast Internet connection (at least as fast as a 56kbps dialup modem connection), unless you're a very patient person.

If you need more information on the basics, check out *PCs For Dummies,* 7th Edition, by Dan Gookin; *Macs For Dummies,* 6th Edition, by David Pogue; *Windows 95 For Dummies,* 2nd Edition, by Andy Rathbone; or *Windows 98 For Dummies,* (all published by IDG Books Worldwide, Inc.).

How to Use the CD

If you are running Windows 95 or 98, follow these steps to get to the items on the CD:

1. **Insert the CD into your computer's CD-ROM drive.**

   Give your computer a moment to take a look at the CD.

   When the light on your CD-ROM drive goes out, double-click the My Computer icon (it's probably in the top left corner of your desktop.)

   This action opens the My Computer window, which shows you all the drives attached to your computer, the Control Panel, and a couple other handy things.

2. **Double-click the icon for your CD-ROM drive.**

   Another window opens, showing you all the folders and files on the CD.

3. **Double-click the file called License.txt.**

   This file contains the end-user license that you agree to by using the CD. When you are done reading the license, close the program, most likely NotePad, that displayed the file.

4. **Double-click the file called Readme.txt.**

   This file contains instructions about installing the software from this CD. It might be helpful to leave this text file open while you're using the CD.

5. **Double-click the folder for the software you are interested in.**

   Be sure to read the descriptions of the programs in the next section of this appendix (much of this information also shows up in the Readme file). These descriptions will give you more precise information about the programs' folder names, and about finding and running the installer program.

6. **Find the file called Setup.exe, or Install.exe, or something similar, and double click that file.**

   The program's installer walks you through the process of setting up your new software.

To run some of the programs, you may need to keep the CD inside your CD-ROM drive. This is a Good Thing. Otherwise, the installed program would have required you to install a very large chunk of the program to your hard drive space, which would have kept you from installing other software.

What You'll Find

Here's a summary of the software on this CD.

Microsoft Internet Explorer

For Windows 95/98/NT 4.0 or later. Commercial version. As they say in St. Tropez, "You can never be too thin or have too new a Web browser." Spare yourself the agonizing drip, drip, drip of downloading this rascal — just install it from this CD.

Netscape Communicator

For Windows 95/98/NT 4.0 or later. Commercial version. Don't forget to check your work with the next most popular web browser around. Again, you save big minutes by installing from this CD instead of a remote server at the end of a very long, very thin wire.

Microsoft MDAC

For Windows 95/98/ NT 4.0 or later. Commerical version. This is a package of components integrated to provide a complete data access solution. These tools are demonstrated in this book in copious detail.

Sample files from the book, by the authors

For Windows 95/98/NT 4.0 or later. Files on the CD include the specific examples from the book, plus the database files they call. You can browse these files directly from the CD, or you can copy them to your hard drive and use them as the basis for your own projects in space/time manipulation. To find the files on the CD, open the D:\SAMPLE folder.

If You've Got Problems (Of the CD Kind)

I tried my best to compile programs that work on most computers with the minimum system requirements. Alas, your computer may differ, and some programs may not work properly for some reason.

The two likeliest problems are that you don't have enough memory (RAM) for the programs you want to use, or you have other programs running that are affecting installation or running of a program. If you get error messages like *Not enough memory* or *Setup cannot continue*, try one or more of these methods and then try using the software again:

- ✔ **Turn off any anti-virus software that you have on your computer.** Installers sometimes mimic virus activity and may make your computer incorrectly believe that it is being infected by a virus.

- ✔ **Close all running programs.** The more programs you're running, the less memory is available to other programs. Installers also typically update files and programs. So if you keep other programs running, installation may not work properly.

- ✔ **Have your local computer store add more RAM to your computer.** This is, admittedly, a drastic and somewhat expensive step. However, adding more memory can really help the speed of your computer and allow more programs to run at the same time.

If you still have trouble with installing the items from the CD, please call the IDG Books Worldwide Customer Service phone number: 800-762-2974 (outside the U.S.: 317-572-3342).

Index

IDG Books Worldwide, Inc., End-User License Agreement

READ THIS. You should carefully read these terms and conditions before opening the software packet(s) included with this book ("Book"). This is a license agreement ("Agreement") between you and IDG Books Worldwide, Inc. ("IDGB"). By opening the accompanying software packet(s), you acknowledge that you have read and accept the following terms and conditions. If you do not agree and do not want to be bound by such terms and conditions, promptly return the Book and the unopened software packet(s) to the place you obtained them for a full refund.

1. **License Grant.** IDGB grants to you (either an individual or entity) a nonexclusive license to use one copy of the enclosed software program(s) (collectively, the "Software") solely for your own personal or business purposes on a single computer (whether a standard computer or a workstation component of a multiuser network). The Software is in use on a computer when it is loaded into temporary memory (RAM) or installed into permanent memory (hard disk, CD-ROM, or other storage device). IDGB reserves all rights not expressly granted herein.

2. **Ownership.** IDGB is the owner of all right, title, and interest, including copyright, in and to the compilation of the Software recorded on the CD-ROM ("Software Media"). Copyright to the individual programs recorded on the Software Media is owned by the author or other authorized copyright owner of each program. Ownership of the Software and all proprietary rights relating thereto remain with IDGB and its licensers.

3. **Restrictions on Use and Transfer.**

   (a) You may only (i) make one copy of the Software for backup or archival purposes, or (ii) transfer the Software to a single hard disk, provided that you keep the original for backup or archival purposes. You may not (i) rent or lease the Software, (ii) copy or reproduce the Software through a LAN or other network system or through any computer subscriber system or bulletin-board system, or (iii) modify, adapt, or create derivative works based on the Software.

   (b) You may not reverse engineer, decompile, or disassemble the Software. You may transfer the Software and user documentation on a permanent basis, provided that the transferee agrees to accept the terms and conditions of this Agreement and you retain no copies. If the Software is an update or has been updated, any transfer must include the most recent update and all prior versions.

4. **Restrictions on Use of Individual Programs.** You must follow the individual requirements and restrictions detailed for each individual program in Appendix A of this Book. These limitations are also contained in the individual license agreements recorded on the Software Media. These limitations may include a requirement that after using the program for a specified period of time, the user must pay a registration fee or discontinue use. By opening the Software packet(s), you will be agreeing to abide by the licenses and restrictions for these individual programs that are detailed in Appendix A and on the Software Media. None of the material on this Software Media or listed in this Book may ever be redistributed, in original or modified form, for commercial purposes.

Installation Instructions

1. **Insert the CD into your computer's CD-ROM drive.**

   Give your computer a moment to take a look at the CD.

2. **When the light on your CD-ROM drive goes out, double click the My Computer icon (tt's probably in the top left corner of your desktop.)**

   This action opens the My Computer window, which shows you all the drives attached to your computer, the Control Panel, and a couple other handy things.

3. **Double click the icon for your CD-ROM drive.**

   Another window opens, showing you all the folders and files on the CD.

4. **Double click the file called License.txt.**

   This file contains the end-user license that you agree to by using the CD. When you are done reading the license, close the program (most likely NotePad) that displayed the file.

5. **Double click the file called Readme.txt.**

   This file contains instructions about installing the software from this CD. It might be helpful to leave this text file open while you are using the CD.

6. **Double click the folder for the software you are interested in.**

   Be sure to read the descriptions of the programs in the next section of this appendix (much of this information also shows up in the Readme file). These descriptions give you more precise information about the programs' folder names, and about finding and running the installer program.

7. **Find the file called Setup.exe, or Install.exe, or something similar, and double click that file.**

   The program's installer will walk you through the process of setting up your new software.

IDG BOOKS WORLDWIDE
BOOK REGISTRATION

Register
This Book
and Win!

We want to hear from you!

Visit **http://my2cents.dummies.com** to register this book and tell us how you liked it!

- Get entered in our monthly prize giveaway.

- Give us feedback about this book — tell us what you like best, what you like least, or maybe what you'd like to ask the author and us to change!

- Let us know any other *For Dummies*® topics that interest you.

Your feedback helps us determine what books to publish, tells us what coverage to add as we revise our books, and lets us know whether we're meeting your needs as a *For Dummies* reader. You're our most valuable resource, and what you have to say is important to us!

Not on the Web yet? It's easy to get started with *Dummies 101*®: *The Internet For Windows*® *98* or *The Internet For Dummies*® at local retailers everywhere.

Or let us know what you think by sending us a letter at the following address:

For Dummies Book Registration
Dummies Press
10475 Crosspoint Blvd.
Indianapolis, IN 46256

BESTSELLING
BOOK SERIES